PUBLIC-SECTOR BARGAINING

Second Edition

PUBLIC-SECTOR BARGAINING

Second Edition

INDUSTRIAL RELATIONS RESEARCH ASSOCIATION SERIES

Editorial Board

Benjamin Aaron

Joyce M. Najita

James L. Stern

The Bureau of National Affairs, Inc., Washington, D.C.

Library of Congress Cataloging-in-Publication Data

Public sector bargaining/editorial board, Benjamin
    Aaron, Joyce M. Najita, James L. Stern.—2nd ed.
      p. cm.—(Industrial Relations Research Association
    series)
    Includes index.
    ISBN 0-87179-566-3. ISBN 0-913447-37-4 (pbk.)
    1. Collective bargaining—Government employees—
United States. 2. Collective bargaining—Government
employees—Canada. I. Aaron, Benjamin. II. Najita,
Joyce M. III. Stern, James L. IV. Bureau of National
Affairs (Washington, D.C.) V. Series.
    HD8005.6.U5P8 1988
    331.89'041'353—dc19   87-32025
                                       CIP

Printed in the United States of America
International Standard Book Number 0-87179-566-3 (hardcover)
0-913447-37-4 (softcover)

Preface

Ten years have passed since the first edition of this volume was issued. In that time, there have been considerable changes in the public sector bargaining picture, particularly in the legislation governing public-sector labor relations. Scholars have examined various facets of public sector bargaining and interesting new research results have been reported. Some of the material contained in the original volume needed to be revised and updated, and in other areas new developments needed to be examined and reviewed. Public-sector bargaining, in contrast to its counterpart in the private sector, has solidified its hold among state and local governments, though it suffered a setback in the federal sector and only recently has shown signs of recovery.

This revised edition was undertaken to update the materials contained in the first edition. Accordingly, the original subject chapters have been retained and rewritten by the original authors, who in some cases have been joined by a partner. In the one case where the original author was unable to participate in the revision, the new author has rewritten the chapter completely. As in the previous work, the several authors have focused on organizing and interpreting the available data rather than undertaking new research, in attempts to delineate basic trends in the field.

Mary Green Miner of BNA Books suggested the revision of this work, and the IRRA Executive Board decided to designate it as a volume in its IRRA Research Series. We are pleased that this joint production of the book will make it more available than otherwise possible to students, practitioners, and others interested in the subject matter. We wish to express our appreciation of the efforts of our fellow authors who prepared comprehensive revisions or new chapters in record time. Also, we want to thank IRRA Editor, Barbara D. Dennis, for her customary valuable assistance.

The Editors

Contents

CHAPTER 1

The Extent of Collective Bargaining in the Public Sector

JOHN F. BURTON, JR., AND TERRY THOMASON*

The history of collective bargaining and membership in bargaining organizations by public-sector workers can be divided into three parts.[1] Prior to 1960 the public sector was largely unorganized and most of the literature provided reasons why government employees were impervious to organizers. Then, from the early 1960s to the mid-1970s, membership and bargaining increased rapidly in the public sector. Burton concluded that this period was largely unanticipated and could not adequately be explained, even in retrospect.[2] Partial explanations were (1) changes in workers' attitudes about the propriety of bargaining, (2) a more aggressive stance by many organizations representing public-sector workers, and (3) public-policy changes that facilitated bargaining. Burton asserted, however, that the favorable legislation was as much a result as a cause of the increased strength of public-sector bargaining organizations. This downgrading of the role of legislation has been challenged in several recent articles, and the controversy over the role of public policy is one of the main themes of this chapter.

The third phase of membership and bargaining in the public sector began in the mid-1970s. Depending on the particular measure used, the recent period is characterized by slow growth, stagnation, or

---

*Both of Cornell University. *Note:* The authors wish to thank Donald Cullen, Ronald Ehrenberg, Michael Goldfield, Cynthia Gramm, Casey Ichniowski, Harry Katz, Thomas Kochan, Jonathan Plotkin, Gregory Saltzman, Leo Troy, and Robert Valletta for their comments on an earlier draft. Helpful comments were also received from Larry T. Adams and Silvana Pozzebon. We also appreciate the invaluable assistance provided by Carla Weiss, reference librarian at the Martin P. Catherwood Library of the New York State School of Industrial and Labor Relations. All are hereby absolved for remaining errors.

[1] The boundaries between the historical periods are not sharply defined. The start of the rapid-growth phase could be assigned to 1959, when the first state law facilitating public-sector bargaining was enacted by Wisconsin. Also, certain measures of bargaining activity, such as the number of workers covered by written contracts, continued to increase after the mid-1970s, which we consider the end of the rapid-growth phase.

[2] John F. Burton, Jr., *The Extent of Collective Bargaining in the Public Sector*, in Public-Sector Bargaining, eds. Benjamin Aaron, Joseph R. Grodin, and James L. Stern (Madison, Wis.: Industrial Relations Research Association, 1979), 1–43.

even a decline in public-sector bargaining. As with the beginning of the second phase of rapid growth, the stagnation phase was largely unanticipated. Moreover, given the normal lag in scholarly research, few studies have yet appeared to offer reasons for the stagnation, although there are several possible explanations. This chapter reviews these three phases of public-sector bargaining and concludes that, in light of the demonstrated inability of scholars to anticipate the emergence of the second and third phases, any prediction of the future of public-sector bargaining is of questionable value.

An Overview of Developments

This section first discusses the variety of concepts that can be used to measure the extent of collective bargaining and membership in bargaining organizations and reviews the several sources for data pertaining to the public sector. Changes since 1956 in the extent of membership in bargaining organizations in the private and public sectors are then reviewed. Subsequent sections examine the reasons for the developments in each sector.

Concepts and Sources of Data

Measuring the number of workers in organizations that engage in bargaining is particularly difficult in the public sector because of the historical importance of three types of organizations. As discussed in more detail in Burton,[3] the classification system is a spectrum along which organizations can be roughly placed, rather than a taxonomic system with three well-defined categories. *Unions* stand at one end of the spectrum and are characterized by primary reliance on collective bargaining to establish rules for working conditions, by assistance to individual employees when disputes arise concerning applications of the rules, and by endorsement of the strike. Most unions also are affiliated with the AFL-CIO, although there are important exceptions. At the other end of the spectrum are *nonbargaining organizations*, which include professional associations such as the American Bar Association. These organizations do not collectively negotiate with individual employers to establish rules for working conditions. Non-bargaining organizations also (1) typically formulate and apply work rules to individual members rather than protect individual members from employers' applications of the rules and (2) include members of the profession who are supervisors.

Somewhere on the spectrum between unions and nonbargaining organizations are *bargaining associations* which, like unions, rely on collective bargaining to achieve an agreement with an employer con-

---

[3] *Id.*

cerning working conditions. Bargaining associations are more likely than unions, however, to emphasize political action to gain influence over working conditions and to include supervisors as members. Also, bargaining associations are less likely to endorse strikes, are generally unwilling to be called unions, and are not affiliated with the AFL-CIO. The National Education Association (NEA) is an example of a bargaining association.

This chapter is concerned with unions and bargaining associations, which collectively will be termed *bargaining organizations*. In general, the distinction between unions and bargaining associations has narrowed over time, and for much of our analysis the difference can be ignored. A complicating factor is that the public-sector data originally included only membership in unions, whereas the current data are more inclusive and pertain to membership in bargaining organizations.[4]

Another distinction must be made among the various types of activities or achievements of a bargaining organization. The organization can be measured in terms of the number of workers who are members. Alternatively, the organization can be measured by the number of workers who are represented by the organization in bargaining. In some instances, nonmembers are included in bargaining units and so representation exceeds membership. In other instances, membership exceeds the number of workers represented in bargaining, as when the organization is in the midst of an organizing campaign and has not yet achieved majority status. Still another type of achievement is the negotiation of a written contract. Membership can exceed the number of workers covered by a written contract because the bargaining organization has been unable to obtain or is uninterested in obtaining a written contract. The distinctions among *membership*, *representation*, and *coverage by a written contract* are significant both for the data and for the analysis of the public sector.

We rely on several sources of data (which are discussed further in the Appendix at page 50). The Bureau of Labor Statistics (BLS) published biennially a directory of membership in bargaining organizations based on mail surveys of the organizations. That series began publishing separate data for the private and public sectors in 1956; the series was confined to union membership until 1968, and then separate data series for union membership and membership in bargaining organizations began. The BLS series was discontinued after 1978. Troy and Sheflin (T-S) have recently published data based on union financial

---

[4] The data series that distinguishes between membership in unions and bargaining associations in the public sector has been discontinued.

reports.[5] The data series includes private and government membership for each year since 1897; the government series was confined to unions prior to 1962, when many bargaining associations were added. A third source of data is the Current Population Survey (CPS), an annual survey of the population by the Bureau of the Census. From 1973 until 1977, the series measured membership in unions, thereafter in unions and employee associations.

There is no single data source for the entire public sector that measures the number of workers (including nonmembers) represented by bargaining organizations or the number of workers covered by written contracts. Subsequent sections provide such data for federal employees and for state and local employees, together with additional membership data for these sectors.

Membership Developments in the Private and Public Sectors

The data series on membership for the entire nonagricultural economy as well as for the private and public components are presented in Table 1 for 1956 to 1986. This is not an appealing display because some of the series have been discontinued, some have discontinuities in definitions, and all are dissimilar. Nor do they provide an entirely consistent picture.

Each data series in Panel A shows a decline in membership in bargaining organizations for the entire nonagricultural sector. The T-S data on membership in bargaining organizations show a drop from 31.4 percent of employment in 1956 to 19.4 percent in 1984. The BLS data for overlapping years show slightly higher percentages organized, while the CPS data for overlapping years show slightly lower percentages organized. Still, the general picture of a persistent trend toward a smaller percentage of workers organized is reinforced by the similar patterns in the different series.

There also is a congruence of trends for the private-sector data shown in Panel B. Over the 1956–1984 period, the T-S data show a decline in membership in bargaining organizations from 34.5 to 16.6 percent of employment. Again the downward trend is evident in the available data from the BLS and CPS series, with the values for corresponding years slightly higher for the BLS data than the T-S data, and slightly lower for the CPS data.

The close correspondence among the trends in the three series does not exist for the public sector (Panel C), although the comparisons are severely complicated by the short time spans of the BLS and CPS series. The data show a considerable increase in membership

---

[5] Leo Troy and Neil Sheflin, *Union Sourcebook: Membership, Structure, Finance, Directory* (West Orange, N.J.: Industrial Relations Data and Information Services, 1985).

TABLE 1

Membership Density for Total Economy, by Private and Public Sectors and by Data Source, 1956–1986

Year	Panel A: All Nonagricultural						Panel B: Private Sector						Panel C: Public Sector					
	All Bargaining Organizations			Unions Only			All Bargaining Organizations			Unions Only			All Bargaining Organizations			Unions Only		
	T-S	BLS	CPS	T-S	BLS	CPS	T-S	BLS	CPS	T-S	BLS	CPS	T-S	BLS	CPS	T-S	BLS	CPS
1956	31.4	—	—	28.9	—	33.4	34.5	—	—	—	38.1	—	—	—	—	11.1	—	12.6
1960	28.6	—	—	26.5	—	31.4	31.9	—	—	—	37.0	—	—	—	—	10.8	—	12.8
1964	30.2	—	—	26.1	—	28.9	31.0	—	—	—	33.8	—	26.0	—	—	—	—	15.1
1968	29.5	—	30.5	25.3	—	27.8	29.9	32.4	—	—	32.2	—	27.3	32.6	—	—	—	18.2
1972	28.8	—	29.4	23.7	—	26.4	27.3	30.7	—	—	30.4	—	35.4	33.9	—	—	—	18.4
1974	28.3	—	29.1	22.7	—	25.8	26.2	29.3	—	—	29.1	—	38.0	37.7	—	—	—	20.5
1976	27.9	—	28.3	22.1	—	24.5	25.1	28.2	—	—	27.9	—	40.2	39.4	—	—	—	20.3
1978	25.1	—	27.1	20.1	—	24.0	22.5	24.7	—	—	24.4	—	36.7	38.9	—	—	—	23.1
1980	23.2	—	23.3	18.6	—	—	20.6	—	20.4	—	—	—	35.1	—	35.3	—	—	—
1982	21.9	—	—	17.8	—	—	19.0	—	—	—	—	—	35.1	—	—	—	—	—
1983	20.7	—	20.3	16.7	—	—	17.8	—	16.8	—	—	—	34.1	—	36.7	—	—	—
1984	19.4*	—	19.1	—	—	—	16.6*	—	15.5	—	—	—	33.0*	—	35.8	—	—	—
1985	—	—	18.2	—	—	—	—	—	14.6	—	—	—	—	—	35.8	—	—	—
1986	—	—	17.7	—	—	—	—	—	14.0	—	—	—	—	—	36.0	—	—	—

Sources: Densities for T-S and BLS series were computed by the authors using membership data from Leo Troy and Neil Sheflin, Union Sourcebook: Membership, Structure, Finance, Directory (West Orange, N.J.: Industrial Relations Data and Information Service, 1985), Table 3.62 and Appendix A, and U.S. Bureau of Labor Statistics, Directory of National and International Labor Unions in the United States, 1979, Bull. No. 2079 (Washington: U.S. Government Printing Office, 1980), Table 6; and employment data from Council of Economic Advisers, Economic Report of the President (Washington: U.S. Government Printing Office, 1987), Table B-40. CPS densities for 1983–1986 are from Bureau of Labor Statistics, Employment and Earnings, January 1985 (Table 53), January 1986 (Table 58), and January 1987 (Table 60). The CPS densities for 1980 were computed by the authors using data from Larry T. Adams, Changing Employment Patterns of Organized Workers, 108 Monthly Lab. Rev. 25 (February 1985), Table 1.

Notes: Membership data used to compute densities exclude Canadian membership. Private-sector figures exclude agricultural employees. The CPS densities are based on estimates of nonagricultural employment derived from the CPS survey of households. T-S and BLS densities are based on estimates of employment derived from CPS survey of establishments data. All bargaining organizations include unions and bargaining associations, as defined in the text.

*Preliminary.

between 1956 and 1976. In the former year, about 11–13 percent of public-sector employees were in unions and in reality there were few bargaining associations. In the ensuing 20 years, unions increased their membership and a number of bargaining associations emerged (many resulted from the conversion of nonbargaining organizations). Also, Troy and Sheflin (as of 1962) and the BLS (as of 1968) began to include membership in bargaining associations in their public-sector data. As a result of these changes in both the reality of public-sector bargaining and in the score-keepers' rules, the T-S and BLS data show about 40 percent of all public-sector employees organized by 1976. Thereafter the data series diverge. Troy and Sheflin show a peak in public-sector employees in bargaining organizations of 40.2 percent in 1976, and then a sharp decline to 36.7 percent by 1978 and a continuing decline to 33.0 percent by 1984. The BLS series on membership in bargaining organizations also peaks in 1976 at 39.4 percent, but there is only a slight drop to 38.9 percent in 1978, when the series ends. The CPS series shows a slight increase between 1980 (35.3 percent) and 1986 (36.0 percent).[6] Thus the record of public-sector bargaining organizations in the last decade is unclear. At best, they have held their own in terms of the proportion of employees organized (CPS data). At worst, they have experienced a decline in percentage of workers organized that is comparable to the decline in the private sector (T-S data). In either case, the spectacular growth in membership that began in the early 1960s was halted by the mid-1970s. The possible explanations for these private- and public-sector developments are reviewed in the balance of this chapter.

Explanations of the Private-Sector Developments

There has been a recent proliferation of studies of unionization in the private sector, including the publication of four literature reviews since 1980.[7] This renewed interest in unionization is, in part, due to the continuing decline of union density in the private sector, a decline

---

[6] From 1973 to 1976, the CPS defined labor organization to mean "labor union." From 1977 to 1978, the CPS defined labor organization as "labor union or employee association." From 1979 on, labor organization was defined as "labor union or employee association similar to a union." See Edward C. Kokkelenberg and Donna R. Sockell, *Union Membership in the United States, 1973–1981*, 38 Indus. & Lab. Rel. Rev. 497 (July 1985).
[7] These are Jack Fiorito and Charles R. Greer, *Determinants of U.S. Unionism: Past Research and Future Needs*, 21 Indus. Rel. 1 (Winter 1982); Richard N. Block and Stephen L. Premack, *The Unionization Process: A Review of the Literature*, in Advances in Industrial and Labor Relations, Vol. 1, eds. David B. Lipsky and Joel M. Douglas (Greenwich, Conn.: JAI Press, 1983); Herbert B. Heneman, III and Marcus H. Sandver, *Predicting the Outcome of Union Certification Elections: A Review of the Literature*, 36 Indus. & Lab. Rel. Rev. 537 (July 1983); and Jack Fiorito, Daniel G. Gallagher, and Charles R. Greer, *Determinants of Unionism: A Review of the Literature*, in Research in Personnel and Human Resources Management, Vol. 4, eds. Kendrith M. Rowland and Gerald R. Ferris (Greenwich, Conn.: JAI Press, 1986).

that has shown no sign of slowing in recent years (Table 1). One aspect of this research that distinguishes it from past work is a reconceptualization of the unionization phenomenon. Most earlier research treated unionization as a single event: the decision by an individual worker to join a labor organization.[8] Recent studies have recognized that unionization (and "deunionization") is a process that has multiple paths (e.g., an employee may become a union member by voting with the majority in an election, or by becoming employed at a company with a union shop; or an employee may cease being a member by losing his union job after the factory is closed). It is also recognized that unionization has a time dimension with multiple steps (e.g., the organizing campaign, the certification election, negotiation of a first contract, the decertification election), and that it is influenced by the behavior of a number of actors (labor unions, individual workers, management representatives, and government agencies).

Freeman has offered four general reasons to explain the recent decline in private-sector union membership: (1) changing economic structure, (2) union organizing efforts, (3) managerial opposition, and (4) public policy.[9]

Changing Economic Structure

This first explanation attributes the 30-year decline in private-sector union density to shrinking employment in sectors of the economy that are heavily organized, such as manufacturing, and a concomitant increase in sectors that have traditionally been hostile to unionism, such as the service sector. Similar trends that help account for the decline of union density are increasing employment in white-collar as opposed to blue-collar occupations, increasing employment in the South as opposed to the Northeast and Midwest, and increasing employment of women as a proportion of the work force.

Dickens and Leonard examined the impact of these structural changes by dividing the decline in private-sector union density from 1973 to 1981 into three parts: (1) the decline in unionization within each sector, (2) the decline due to a shift in employment between sectors, and (3) an interaction between the first two effects.[10] They controlled for sectoral employment changes by industry, region, occupation, education, gender, race, and age, and determined that

---

[8] See, for example, Orley Ashenfelter and John H. Pencavel, *American Trade Union Growth, 1900–1960*, 83 Q.J. Econ. 434 (1968).

[9] Richard B. Freeman, *Why Are Unions Faring Poorly in NLRB Representation Elections?*, in Challenges and Choices Facing American Labor, ed. Thomas A. Kochan (Cambridge, Mass.: MIT Press, 1985), 45–64.

[10] William T. Dickens and Jonathan S. Leonard, Structural Changes in Unionization: 1973–1981, Working Paper 1882 (Cambridge, Mass.: National Bureau of Economic Research, 1986).

anywhere from 58 to 68 percent of the 2.4 percent decline in private-sector unionization from 1973 to 1981 is due to these sectoral changes. This corresponds with Freeman and Medoff's finding that 72 percent of the decline in private-sector unionization between 1954 and 1979 was due to structural changes.[11] Farber, however, found that only 41 percent of the decline between the mid-1950s and 1977 was due to sectoral shifts.[12] Differences among methods, data sets, and sectors controlled for could account for the differences between these various estimates, but all suggest that the changing economic structure has been a major source of the decline in private-sector unionization.

In many ways, however, the structural-change hypothesis is an unsatisfactory explanation of union growth. By postulating that declining unionization results from the relative expansion of heavily nonunion sectors, the hypothesis begs the question why those sectors have lower union densities initially. In order to fully understand the phenomenon of union decline, we must first understand the underlying reasons for varying rates of unionization among economic sectors. Second, the structural-change argument assumes that each sector's propensity to organize remains constant over time. This assumption is difficult to reconcile with the growth of unionization in the formerly nonunion public sector. Additionally, it has been argued that other western democracies and, in particular, Canada have experienced similar economic shifts but have not undergone the same reduction in union density.[13] Finally, while one must recognize that some of the causes of structural change are exogenous to unionization, i.e., technological change, others are certainly endogenous, i.e., union-induced wage increases that cause companies to move from the highly organized Northeast to the less unionized South. While, for didactic purposes, we treat structural change, management resistance, union organizing efforts, and public policy as distinct sources of growth or decline in unionization, it is clear that these are interrelated. Kochan, Katz, and McKersie have forcefully argued that the recent decline of American unionism is due to the *interaction* of the external environment with the strategic choices made by the principal actors in the industrial relations system.[14]

---

[11] Richard B. Freeman and James L. Medoff, What Do Unions Do? (New York: Basic Books, 1984).

[12] Henry S. Farber, *The Extent of Unionization in the United States*, in Challenges and Choices Facing American Labor, ed. Thomas A. Kochan (Cambridge, Mass.: MIT Press, 1985), 15–43.

[13] Freeman and Medoff, *supra* note 11.

[14] Thomas A. Kochan, Harry C. Katz, and Robert B. McKersie, The Transformation of American Industrial Relations (New York: Basic Books, 1986). Kochan, in *How American Workers View Labor Unions*, 102 Monthly Lab. Rev. 23 (April 1979), presented attitude survey data demonstrating that workers in traditionally nonunion demographic groups, such as female and southern workers, are as favorably disposed to unions as their more heavily unionized counter-

Union Organizing Efforts

Dickens and Leonard attribute 63 percent of the drop in union density to the decline in the union organizing rate (defined as the percentage of the work force participating in an NLRB certification election) and success rate (defined as the percentage of the work force voting for the union in the election).[15] Part of this decline is due to the aforementioned structural changes; unions do not attempt to organize workers outside their "natural territory."[16] In addition, Freeman and Medoff, analyzing data collected by Voos, estimated that organizing expenditures of unions (deflated by a measure of the average hourly earnings of manufacturing production workers) per nonunion worker declined by about 30 percent from 1953 to 1974.[17] Voos, however, has argued that Freeman and Medoff's wage deflator is inappropriate.[18] Employing a CPI deflator instead, Voos found that while the proportion of union budgets spent in organizing activities has declined from 1953 to 1974, real organizing expenditures per organizable, nonunion worker remained stable during this period. Thus, the extent to which union losses have in part been self-inflicted is not clear.

Managerial Resistance

Two managerial approaches to union avoidance, "soft" and "hard," may be distinguished.[19] With respect to the "soft" approach, Kochan, Katz, and McKersie have argued that in the late 1950s and early 1960s management in nonunion plants began introducing "innovative, new systems of human resource management" into their workplaces.[20] These new systems emphasize such practices as direct communication channels between worker and management, employee participation in problem-solving, contingent compensation (such as profit-sharing and pay-for-knowledge schemes), flexible work sched-

---

parts, i.e., males and nonsoutherners. These data do not necessarily imply that the structural argument is invalid. The underlying reasons for the differences in union density between these groups may be due to their capacity to organize rather than to their taste for organization. Similarly, while attitude surveys indicate preferences, it is less clear that they accurately measure the intensity of those preferences. The degree of commitment necessary to join a union or to participate in an organizing drive is obviously greater than the commitment needed to provide a favorable response on a questionnaire.

[15] William T. Dickens and Jonathan S. Leonard, *Accounting for the Decline in Union Membership, 1950–1980*, 38 Indus. & Lab. Rel. Rev. 323 (April 1985).

[16] Dickens and Leonard, *supra* note 10, at 18–19.

[17] Freeman and Medoff, *supra* note 11.

[18] Paula B. Voos, *Trends in Union Organizing Expenditures: 1953–1977*, 38 Indus. & Lab. Rel. Rev. 52 (October 1984).

[19] Donald E. Cullen, *The Decline of Union Membership in the United States: Deindustrialization is Only Part of the Story* (Ithaca, N.Y.: Cornell University, 1987), mimeo.

[20] Kochan, Katz, and McKersie, *supra* note 14.

ules, and autonomous work teams.[21] The Kochan team argues that these systems were not introduced primarily to combat unionism but for their productivity advantages. However, the traditions of adversarial, "job-control" labor relations extant in the unionized sector makes the introduction of the new human resources management into unionized firms difficult. These new nonunion systems were diffused widely throughout the economy in the 1970s, in part because of their cost advantages, the persistent and "deep-seated" hostility of management toward unions, and the increased cost of union labor.

While there is relatively little research concerning the impact of these systems on union organizing, Kochan, McKersie, and Chalykoff present evidence indicating that these workplace innovations are negatively related to two different measures of unionization.[22] Using data from 1975 and 1983 Conference Board surveys of industrial practices, they found that workplace innovations reduced the number of unionized workers in the sampled firms during this period. Depending upon model specification, they estimated that each workplace innovation reduced the number of union workers by 169 to 217 workers.[23] They also found that every workplace innovation reduced the probability that a new plant would become unionized by 2.5 percentage points.

A number of studies have concluded that "hard" managerial opposition to unionism has increased dramatically in recent years and that this increased opposition is, at least in part, responsible for the decline in union density. Flanagan, for example, found that the number of unfair labor practice (ULP) charges brought against employers increased from 10,000 in 1963 to 31,000 in 1980.[24] During this same period, union activity, as measured by the number of representation elections, did not substantially increase. Furthermore, Weiler reports that the percentage of ULP charges against employers that were considered meritorious by the NLRB increased over this same period, indicating that the increase in the number of ULPs was due to increased management opposition rather than a greater tendency of

---

[21] Cullen, *supra* note 19, notes that many aspects of the "soft" approach resemble anti-union tactics that have been used by management since the 1920s—high wages and benefits, job security, and "enlightened personnel procedures." Cullen does acknowledge the unique contribution made by the new human resources management, its emphasis on employee participation.

[22] Thomas A. Kochan, Robert B. McKersie, and John Chalykoff, *The Effects of Corporate Strategy and Workplace Innovations on Union Representation*, 39 Indus. & Lab. Rel. Rev. 487 (July 1986).

[23] In 1983, their sample firms averaged 12,734 employees, with a mean union density of 37 percent.

[24] Robert J. Flanagan, *NLRA Litigation and Union Representation*, 38 Stan. L. Rev. 957 (1986).

workers to file charges.[25] Prosten indicates that the number of consent elections as a proportion of the total number of elections declined throughout the period from 1963 to 1977.[26] He also reports increasing delays between a union's petition for the NLRB to conduct a certification election and the occurrence of the election. Numerous studies show that these management tactics lead to attenuated union success in NLRB elections. Union election success has been shown to be negatively related to management's use of consultants,[27] election delays,[28] nonconsent elections,[29] and employer unfair labor practices.[30] Flanagan concluded that the increasing rate of employer unfair labor practices during the 1960s and 1970s was primarily due to the increasing union relative wage differential.[31] As unions increased their attractiveness to workers, they became increasingly distasteful to employers and many employers decided that the costs associated with illegal union avoidance were justified.

Furthermore, Prosten reports that a 1975 survey of 2,656 unions certified by the NLRB in 1970 revealed that 22 percent of those unions never successfully negotiated a contract.[32] Of those that had negotiated a contract, 13 percent were no longer under contract at the time of the survey. Cooke reports that the failure to negotiate a first contract is positively related to NLRB delays in resolving employer objections to certification election results, discriminatory unfair labor practices (Section 8(a)(3) violations) subsequent to the election, and the employer's refusal to bargain (Section 8(a)(5) violations).[33]

Public Policy

Finally, a number of investigators suggest that public policy plays an important role in either encouraging or discouraging the growth of unions. For example, Sheflin, Troy, and Koeller note a structural shift in two of the leading econometric models of union density around

[25] Paul Weiler, *Promises to Keep: Securing Workers' Right to Self-Organization under the NLRA*, 96 Harv. L. Rev. 1769 (1983).

[26] Richard Prosten, *The Longest Season: Union Organizing in the Last Decade*, Proceedings of the 31st Annual Meeting, Industrial Relations Research Association (Madison, Wis.: IRRA, 1979), 240–249.

[27] John J. Lawler and Robin West, *Impact of Union-Avoidance Strategy in Representation Elections*, 24 Indus. Rel. 406 (Fall 1985).

[28] Myron Roomkin and Richard N. Block, *Case Processing Time and the Outcome of Representation Elections: Some Empirical Evidence*, 1981 U. Ill. L. Rev. 75 (1981).

[29] Ronald L. Seeber and William N. Cooke, *The Decline in Union Success in NLRB Representation Elections*, 22 Indus. Rel. 34 (Winter 1983).

[30] William N. Cooke, *The Rising Toll of Discrimination Against Union Activists*, 24 Indus. Rel. 421 (Fall 1985).

[31] Flanagan, *supra* note 24.

[32] Prosten, *supra* note 26.

[33] William N. Cooke, *The Failure to Negotiate First Contracts: Determinants and Policy Implications*, 38 Indus. & Lab. Rel. Rev. 163 (January 1985).

1937–1938.[34] They attribute this shift to the passage of the Wagner Act. While enactment of the National Labor Relations Act (NLRA) may help explain the surge in union membership in the 1930s, it is also evident that public policy changes were only one of a number of major events in that decade that could have affected unionization. These events include the rise in rank-and-file militancy as typified by the sit-down strike, the emergence of the CIO, and the persistence of high unemployment that produced public disillusionment with laissez-faire capitalism.

A historical analysis of this period does not unambiguously testify to the primacy of the Wagner Act as the cause of increased union density. A resurgence in union militancy occurred in 1933 and 1934, predating the passage of the NLRA, as the number of workers involved in work stoppages increased from 324,000 in 1932 to over 1 million in 1933.[35] The auto industry sit-downs began in late 1936, prior to the Supreme Court's decision in *NLRB v. Jones & Laughlin Steel*,[36] upholding the constitutionality of the NLRA, and, as is widely noted, employers virtually ignored the law prior to that decision. Further developments in labor law do not demonstrate a clear relationship between public policy and union membership. The Taft-Hartley Act of 1947 was largely unfavorable to unions, and yet union density increased in the private sector until 1956. The Landrum-Griffin Act of 1959 was the last significant change in statutory law, and while it also can be characterized as anti-union, it hardly can explain the halving of the private-sector density rate from 1960 to 1986.

Most econometric work concerning the effect of public policy on private-sector union strength has examined the impact of the right-to-work (RTW) statutes that some states have enacted to prohibit union shop agreements. Freeman argues that unionization has declined in those states that have enacted RTW legislation relative to states that have not.[37] A recent review of the literature concluded, however, that many studies finding a negative relationship between the existence of a

---

[34] Neil Sheflin, Leo Troy, and C. Timothy Koeller, *Structural Stability in Models of American Trade Union Growth*, 96 Q.J. Econ. 77 (1981), using the models of Ashenfelter and Pencavel (*supra* note 8) and George Sayers Bain and Farouk Elesheikh, Union Growth and the Business Cycle, and Econometric Analysis (Oxford: Basil Blackwell, 1976). Additionally, Freeman (*supra* note 9) and Weiler (*supra* note 25) argue that the higher union density found in Canada is principally due to more favorable public policy there and, in particular, rules that do not permit the long election campaigns typical in the United States.

[35] This resurgency of militancy has been attributed to Section 7(a) of the National Industrial Recovery Act (NIRA) which gave workers the right to organize and bargain collectively. The significance of the NIRA for unions is uncertain, however. Administration of Section 7(a) was weak. Employers interpreted the act to permit company unions. There was no effective protection for workers who were discriminated against for their union activity; see James R. Green, The World of the Worker: Labor in Twentieth-Century America (New York: Hill and Wang, 1980).

[36] 301 U.S. 1, 1 LRRM 703 (1937).

[37] *Supra* note 9.

RTW statute and unionization have not properly controlled for the causal relationship between the enactment of RTW legislation and low union density (the "simultaneity" issue).[38] In other words, RTW laws are more likely to be passed in states where substantial anti-union sentiment exists, but that anti-union sentiment also determines the proportion of the work force that is unionized. The relevant question is whether RTW statutes have an independent impact on union density after controlling for the effect of public sentiment. After reviewing research that has attempted to control for the endogeneity between RTW legislation and unionization, Moore and Newman conclude that "the effects of RTW laws are more symbolic than real."[39]

Analysis of the influence of public policy on union growth should not be confined to examining the consequences of statutory changes. Another important aspect of public policy involves the administration of the law. Klein and Wanger argue that the Taft-Hartley Act did not begin to have an impact on union membership until the administration of an Eisenhower-appointed NLRB.[40] Tyler has complained that "malevolent administration" in recent years has turned the NLRA into a National Anti-Labor Act.[41] Moreover, court decisions can affect union organizing opportunities, as the history of the American labor movement attests.

Several "lessons" from this brief review of private-sector developments seem most relevant for the public sector. First, the factor that is consistently shown to explain a large proportion of the decline in the private-sector union density is the changing economic structure. Part of that explanation may be applicable to the public sector, such as shifts in jobs from the unionized North to the South, but other parts do not help explain public-sector developments, such as the increases in white-collar jobs and employment of females. Despite the dominance of workers with these characteristics in the public sector, unionization rapidly expanded in the 1960s.

Another lesson from the private-sector studies is that an important determinant of union success is management opposition, which appears to have become increasingly virulent as the union relative

---

[38] See William J. Moore and Robert J. Newman, *The Effects of Right-to-Work Laws: A Review of the Literature*, 38 Indus. & Lab. Rel. Rev. 571 (July 1985).

[39] *Id.* at 583. These authors qualify this conclusion, acknowledging the results of Elwood and Fine's stock-flow analysis which indicates that RTW laws do have an independent impact on union membership by reducing the number of certification elections held as well as the average number of workers in newly created bargaining units; see David T. Ellwood and Glenn A. Fine, The Impact of Right-to-Work Laws on Union Organizing, Working Paper 1116 (Cambridge, Mass.: National Bureau of Economic Research, 1983). This impact remains after controlling for any simultaneity that may exist between union density and RTW laws.

[40] Janice A. Klein and E. David Wanger, *The Legal Setting for the Emergence of the Union Avoidance Strategy*, in Challenges and Choices Facing American Labor, ed. Thomas A. Kochan (Cambridge, Mass.: MIT Press, 1985), 75–88.

[41] Gus Tyler, *Labor at the Crossroads*, in Unions in Transition: Entering the Second Century, ed. Seymour M. Lipset (San Francisco: Institute for Contemporary Studies, 1986).

wage effect increased in recent decades. Less clear as an explanatory factor is union organizing efforts, which may or may not have declined in the recent era.

A final lesson is that examination of the literature leaves unclear the influence of public policy on union growth. Fundamental changes in the legal environment, such as enactment and effective implementation of the NLRA, undoubtedly have some impact on union strength, but more modest variations, such as a state's enacting a right-to-work law, have problematical influences. With these lessons as background, we now examine the factors offered by various authors to explain the developments in the public sector.

Public-Sector Developments

This section reviews the possible explanations for the first two periods of public-sector collective bargaining: the quiescent period that lasted until 1960 and the growth period that ran from the early 1960s until the mid-1970s. The explanations for these periods were reviewed at length in Burton,[42] and (except for an extended discussion of the role of public policy in the growth period) will only be summarized here with most references omitted. The explanations for the stagnation period that began in the mid-1970s are provided in the next two sections.

The Quiescent Period

A number of writers offered explanations for the lack of organization of government workers before the 1960s. Labor market conditions were considered a detriment to organization because the stability of public-sector employment gave workers a sense of security. Labor force developments were also considered detrimental because the public sector had increasing proportions of women, blacks, and white-collar workers, all traditionally difficult to organize. Analysts also stressed that the unfavorable legal environment was a major obstacle to organization. There were prohibitions on strikes, which provide unions with much of their bargaining power, and there were virtually no statutory requirements that public-sector employers recognize or bargain with unions. In addition, civil service laws provided a method of determining working conditions that was a rival to collective bargaining. Some aspects of unions' strategy also limited their success. As late as 1959, the AFL-CIO executive council stated that "in terms of

---

[42] *Supra* note 2.

accepted collective bargaining procedures, government workers have no right beyond the authority to petition Congress—a right available to every citizen."[43]

This catalog of factors that inhibited organization of the public sector prior to the 1960s is reasonably persuasive. Indeed, the explanations seem so reasonable that it is easy to understand why analysts in 1960 would have dismissed the prospect of an impending surge in public-sector bargaining as a delusion.

The Growth Period

Three kinds of factors have been offered to explain the rapid growth of membership in bargaining organizations after 1960: those inherent or well-entrenched in government employment that make organization feasible; those that changed in the pre-1960 period, thus increasing the potential for organization; and those post-1960 factors that triggered or accelerated the growth of bargaining organizations.

Inherent Factors. Bakke argued that several inherent characteristics of public employment encourage collective bargaining, including the use of common standards for working conditions rather than individual employment agreements.[44] In addition, in professions such as teaching there is a community of interest because of common skills and training, and a dependence of individual status on group status. This community of interest increases the interest in collective representation.

Other factors of long standing that facilitated organization of government workers were the interest of professionals in participating in policy making and the tradition in many jurisdictions of low wages for public-sector workers. Still another facilitating factor was that many employees in the public sector were already in organizations that could be co-opted by the unions or transformed into bargaining associations.

Pre-1960 Developments. Several factors changed between the 1930s and the postwar period that increased the potential for organization. The generally low unemployment rates made government workers less willing to overlook undesirable aspects of the job in exchange for job security. As inflation became more of a problem, workers became concerned about the sluggish procedures used to provide wage increases.

---

[43] Jack Stieber, Public Employee Unionism: Structure, Growth, Policy (Washington: Brookings Institution, 1973), at 117.
[44] E. Wight Bakke, *Reflections on the Future of Bargaining in the Public Sector*, 93 Monthly Lab. Rev. 21 (July 1970).

The rapid increase in public-sector employment in the 1940s and 1950s expanded the potential for subsequent organization. Also, as public workers became an increasingly important group of voters, they attracted the attention of politicians. Barrett noted that the growing public-sector labor force included more young workers, who generally distrusted employers, and minority workers, who did not trust the white-dominated management structure, and he argued that these workers were more inclined to support unions.[45] However, this view is at least partially inconsistent with the previous explanation about why unions did *not* emerge before 1960.

Post-1960 Developments. There are, finally, a number of developments after 1960 that arguably triggered or accelerated the growth of public-sector bargaining organizations. The economy's performance during the 1960s does not appear to provide an adequate explanation. Although the economy began a long period of sustained growth in 1961, this macroeconomic development cannot explain the disparate organizing records of unions in the public and private sectors.

A more likely explanation of the growth in bargaining organizations is that public employees' attitudes toward them changed significantly after 1960. It is unclear exactly what initiated the change; part of the explanation might be that the public sector continued to attract younger workers and members of minority groups who were supporters of more militant action. In many cities the civil rights and public-sector unionization movements became intertwined. The changing attitude of public-sector workers toward bargaining received impetus from widely publicized bargaining triumphs and dramatic stoppages; an outstanding example was the 1961 breakthrough of New York City teachers. Although the initiating or sustaining causes of the changing attitudes are not entirely evident, the result is as follows: during the 1960s many public-sector workers began to "think the unthinkable."[46]

As workers changed their attitudes, so also did employee organizations change their policies in order to attract or retain members. The labor movement in general began to pay more attention to the public sector. Several predominantly private-sector unions provided direct assistance to public-sector organizations, including the United Auto Workers' support of the American Federation of Teachers. Within the public sector, unions became more militant and willing to use tactics such as strikes. Public-sector bargaining organizations appeared to

---

[45] Jerome T. Barrett, *Prospects for Growth and Bargaining in the Public Sector*, 534 GERR F-1 (December 17, 1973).
[46] Tim Bornstein, *Public Sector Explosion to Continue*, 426 GERR B-8 (November 8, 1971).

improve working conditions, which in turn attracted more members. Professional associations often either lost members to unions or transformed themselves into bargaining associations.

Public-sector employers also made changes after 1960 that at least accommodated collective bargaining. The civil service model broke down or was abandoned in many jurisdictions, and management structure was adapted to collective bargaining, which in turn facilitated further unionization. One factor that encouraged the spread of bargaining was the lack of resistance to union demands by many public-sector employers, many of whom were relatively unsophisticated on industrial relations matters, as well as the general lack of resistance to settlements among government employers and the public.[47]

The Role of Public Policy. The most controversial portion of Burton's 1979 review of the factors that help explain the rapid growth of public-sector bargaining organizations after 1960 concerns the role of public policy. Burton noted that several authors had stressed the importance of changes in public policy as a source of the growth. These changes included Executive Order 10988 issued by President Kennedy in 1962, which established rudimentary bargaining rights for federal employees, and favorable state legislation for collective bargaining, which began with the 1959 enactment in Wisconsin and was followed by most industrialized states by the end of the 1960s. Although these laws generally did not go as far as the NLRA in encouraging unions and collective bargaining, in some instances— such as those statutes that mandate the agency shop—there is an assist to organization greater than that provided in the public sector.

Burton expressed skepticism about the assertion that changes in public policy were an important cause of the growth of public-sector bargaining. He indicated that drawing conclusions on the topic was particularly difficult because of the dearth of statistical analysis of the role of public policy in fostering growth in public-sector bargaining organizations. But based on his review of private-sector studies, which suggested that modest variations in public policy had problematical influence on union strength, and a review of the studies and data encompassed in the 1979 chapter, Burton offered several conclusions about the influence of public policy.

> Massive changes in public policy undoubtedly can have an impact on the prevalence of bargaining and the extent of membership in bargaining organizations. . . . However . . . at the federal level and in most states, the policy toward public-sector bargaining has evolved since 1960 from supine neglect to encouragement less avid than the national policy

---

[47] Arnold R. Weber, *Prospects for the Future*, in Labor Relations Law in the Public Sector, ed. Andria S. Knapp (Chicago: American Bar Association, 1977), at 5.

toward private-sector bargaining. This relatively limited shift in public policy seems incapable of explaining the magnitude of the growth in public-sector bargaining. Moreover, the lack of congruity between policy changes and membership growth in bargaining organizations is affirmed by the experience in several states—notably Ohio and Illinois— where the lack of major changes in policy has not precluded organization of a significant proportion of public-sector workers. Furthermore, in some instances the enactment of favorable legislation was as much a result of membership growth as a cause of it. To be sure, there are undoubtedly some workers—those with inherently limited bargaining power (such as librarians and social workers) and those with marginal interest in bargaining (such as college professors)—for whom a favorable public policy is virtually a necessary precondition for organization; but, for the bulk of public-sector workers, the public-policy changes of the past 20 years have been no more important in explaining their organization than several other factors, including the changed attitude of these workers toward the propriety and usefulness of bargaining.[48]

The passage warrants some explication. We have "constructed" a five-point Public Policy Influence Index (PPII), which ranges from 5 (public policy is the only factor that makes a difference) to 3 (public policy is one of several factors that make a difference) to 1 (public policy makes no difference). Our view is that for the bulk of public-sector workers, the PPII value is 3 in explaining the extent of membership in bargaining organizations; for some workers (those with limited bargaining power, for example), the PPII value is closer to 5. In the first section, we drew conceptual distinctions among the various types of accomplishments of a bargaining organization that are relevant in discussing the influence of public policy. Public policy probably has more impact on the extent of representation of a bargaining organization (does the organization represent nonmembers?) and on the outcome of the bargaining (is the result a written contract?) than on the number of workers who are members. Thus, while the PPII is 3 for extent of organization for most workers, the PPII is 4 for determining the outcome of bargaining and the extent of representation.

Freeman has provided a contrasting view of the importance of public policy in explaining the growth of public-sector bargaining organizations:

> What caused the spurt of public sector unionism in the late 1960s through the early 1970s? . . . First and foremost were changes in the laws regulating public sector unions. In the federal sector, Executive Order 10988, which President Kennedy announced in 1962 and which was later strengthened by ensuing presidents, was the principal cause of the rapid organization of federal employees. . . . Before 1962 unionization of federal employees was going nowhere; then suddenly, it shot upward. At the state and local level there were a variety of changes in the

---

[48] Burton, *supra* note 2, at 14–15.

law occurring mostly in the 1960s and 1970s . . . which were followed by a rapid growth of unionization. . . . Studies of the spurt in public sector unionism (see Table 4) uniformly show that these laws were a major factor in the growth of public sector unionization. States that enacted laws had rapid increases in unionization in ensuing years. States that did not had no such growth. . . . This is not to say that public sector bargaining does not exist in the absence of a law. Indeed, Ohio is a good counter example. But one counter example does not discredit a social science generalization. For the most part, the spurt in public sector unionism was associated with changes in state laws regulating collective bargaining.[49]

No social science generalization that has exceptions involving a double negative is not totally unambiguous, but we believe the Freeman position can fairly be summarized as: changes in laws regulating collective bargaining are the primary cause of the spurt in public-sector unionism that began in the 1960s.[50] We assign the Freeman view a 4.0–4.5 on the PPII.

How compelling is the evidence in Freeman's Table 4 that "uniformly shows these laws were a major factor in the growth of public sector unionization"? We have examined all four of the published studies and two of the three unpublished studies cited by Freeman,[51] and we consider the evidence unpersuasive. Before we discuss these studies, several general problems are worth noting. First, there is the direction-of-causation problem. Most studies rely on regressions with cross-section data: the units of observation are states and the data are from approximately the same period. The dependent variable measures the extent of unionization (or extent of bargaining) and one (or more) of the independent variables measures some aspect of public policy; a significant coefficient on the policy variable is interpreted as evidence that policy changes influence the extent of unionization. The

---

[49] Richard B. Freeman, *Unionism Comes to the Public Sector*, 24 J. Econ. Lit. 41, 45–48 (1986).

[50] This interpretation of Freeman's position is supported by this passage from Freeman (*supra* note 9, at 62, with emphasis in the original): "The great growth of public-sector unionism was *preceded* by new public-sector labor laws that often required municipalities to bargain with workers who had chosen to unionize. . . . Analyses of the relationship between the presence of law favorable to bargaining and unionization across states and the relationship between the timing of union growth and passage of laws within states show that public-sector unionization was greatly enhanced by changes in the law."

[51] There are seven entries in Freeman's Table 4 under Union Growth. There are two citations to Joseph D. Reid and Michael M. Kurth, *The Importance of Union Security to the Growth of Unionism* (Fairfax, Va.: George Mason University, 1983), mimeo, but one of these appears to refer to Reid and Kurth, *The Organization of State and Local Government Employees: Comment*, 5 J. Lab. Res. 191 (Spring 1984). Portions of Reid and Kurth's 1983 paper have been published as Reid and Kurth, *The Contribution of Exclusive Representation to Union Strength*, 5 J. Lab. Res. 391 (Fall 1984). The only entry we have not examined is Harrison S. Lauer, *The Effect of Collective Bargaining in Municipal Police Forces on Wages, Salaries, and Fringe Benefits*, Undergraduate Thesis for Department of Economics, Harvard College, 1979.

problem is that even if the direction of causation is from changes in extent of unionization to changes in public policy, the coefficient on the policy variable in a cross-section regression can be statistically significant.

A second, though related, causation problem is found in studies that utilize cross-section regressions and a "time-dependent" policy variable to establish that favorable legislation causes union growth. The "time-dependent" policy variable is coded to indicate the length of time that the policy has been in effect, e.g., for a state that has had legislation permitting public-sector collective bargaining in effect for two years, the policy variable is valued 2, the policy variable for a state that has had legislation for three years is valued 3, etc. The rationale for this type of policy variable is the conjecture that the impact of policy on union growth is cumulative: the longer the law has been in effect, the greater the impact on unionization. A significant coefficient on this "time-dependent" variable does not, however, resolve the causality issue. Suppose, for example, that public-sector employees in different states begin to organize, initially, at different times (for reasons unrelated to the enactment of public policy). Further assume that these public-sector unions grow at similar rates in each state, and that after reaching a "critical mass" of membership, they use their strength to enact favorable legislation.[52] A cross-section regression in which the dependent variable is the extent of unionization in each state 10 (or 15) years after the growth process began in the first state will have a statistically significant coefficient in the policy variable—that measures time since enactment—even though the direction of causation was entirely from union growth to favorable laws.

The third general problem with several of the studies is that the dependent variable is not extent of unionization but the extent of coverage by a written collective-bargaining agreement. Especially during the surge of unionization during the 1960s and early 1970s, organization often preceded negotiation of a written contract. Indeed, Burton noted that as late as 1976 the "data indicate that about half of all full-time state and local employees are organized, while . . . only about one-third of all state and local employees (full- and part-time) are in recognized bargaining units, and only about one-quarter are covered by written contracts."[53] Thus the difference between organization and coverage by a written contract is not trivial, and deciding whether favorable laws preceded organization cannot be determined from evidence that such laws preceded formal bargaining. With these general problems as background, we now examine each of the studies cited by Freeman.

---

[52] We are not suggesting that the example presents an accurate description of the patterns of union growth and legislative enactments.

[53] *Supra* note 2, at 23.

Moore found that the percentage of each state's government employees unionized was higher in 1968 if the state had a comprehensive collective bargaining law (after controlling for other factors such as urbanization).[54] As noted by Burton, the study can be challenged since the dependent variable measured *federal*, state, and local government employment and membership by state (with over 60 percent of the union membership among federal employees), while the independent variables are primarily relevant for state and local government employees, especially the variable measuring the status of the state collective-bargaining laws.[55] Another problem with the study is that a cross-section regression with observations from one year (1968) showing that favorable laws are associated with greater unionization makes it difficult to determine the direction of causation (the first general problem discussed above).

Moore[56] is cited by Freeman as showing that "mandatory bargaining laws help AFT, not NEA." Moore presented several types of evidence. Separate time-series regressions were run to determine the annual percentage change in membership in the AFT and in the NEA from 1919 to 1970. In each regression, two measures of government policy were included: the percentage of teachers residing in states having mandatory collective-bargaining laws covering teachers in each year, and a dummy variable with a value of one for each year after 1962 to test the impact of President Kennedy's Executive Order 10988. Neither variable was statistically significant in either time-series regression. Moore also ran four cross-section regressions across states with the dependent variables being 1970 AFT membership as a percentage of the state's teachers, 1970 NEA membership as a percentage of the state's teachers, the percentage of the teachers covered by written negotiation procedures in 1970, and the percentage of instructional staff covered by comprehensive agreements in 1969. For the cross-section regressions, the actual bargaining law status was replaced by the predicted value of the bargaining law "in order to eliminate the possibility of simultaneous equation bias" resulting from the possibility that union strength may cause favorable laws. Interestingly enough, although Moore indicated that "numerous variations of the models were estimated" and that "only the most satisfactory results (in terms of R^2 and significant coefficients) are reported," in the two cross-section regressions with membership as the dependent variables, the two coefficients on permissive laws and the coefficient on the mandatory law in the NEA membership regression were negative and insignifi-

---

[54] William J. Moore, *Factors Affecting Growth in Public and Private Sector Unions*, 6 J. Coll. Neg. Pub. Sector 37 (1977).

[55] *Supra* note 2, at n. 12.

[56] William J. Moore, *An Analysis of Teacher Union Growth*, 17 Indus. Rel. 204 (May 1978).

cant, and the positive coefficient on the mandatory law in the AFT regression "had a t-statistic value slightly below the acceptable 0.10 level" but "is reported as statistically significant anyway" because Moore concluded the results suggested multicollinearity. Apparently the only regression in which a policy variable (the presence of a mandatory bargaining law) reached a significance level of 0.10 on its own was the cross-section using the percent of teachers covered by a written contract in 1980 as the dependent variable.

Dalton presented a series of cross-section regressions testing a two-equation simultaneous model where one dependent variable was the percentage of full-time employees organized in 1977 and the other dependent variable was average monthly earnings.[57] Among the independent variables were two measures of public policy as of 1976: the existence of a mandatory bargaining statute or the existence of a permissive bargaining statute. The regressions were run for six government functions plus total state and local employment. The mandatory bargaining variable had a positive and statistically significant coefficient for workers in all functions except public welfare; the permissive bargaining variable was never significant.

Although Dalton interpreted the results as strongly supporting the hypothesis that the existence of a state labor law will increase the level of organization, the results from a cross-section regression where the extent of organization in 1977 is predicted from 1976 laws does not provide a test of the direction of causation. This point was made in a comment on the Dalton article by Reid and Kurth,[58] which is one of the other studies relied on by Freeman. They provide a single cross-section regression in which the dependent variable is each state's percentage growth of unionism among local employees from 1972 to 1980. One independent variable is a "zero-ten dummy variable measuring the number of years since state law first permitted local governments to engage in collective bargaining. A law passed prior to 1971 was given a value of ten." The coefficient on the variable was positive, which Freeman cites as evidence that "progressive state labor law raises unionism." We have several reservations. First, the results only show that the longer the permissive law had been in effect during the 1970s, the faster unionism had grown during the decade; whether fast growth caused laws or vice versa is not evident (the second general problem we discussed). Second, two other independent variables were the percent of public employees covered by a collective bargaining contract in 1976 (which had a positive and significant coefficient)

[57] Amy H. Dalton, *A Theory of the Organization of State and Local Government Employees*, 3 J. Lab. Res. 163 (Spring 1982).
[58] *Supra* note 51.

and the extent of public-sector organization in the state as of 1972 (or 1976, according to the appendix), which had a negative and significant coefficient. With these as control variables, the meaning of a positive coefficient for the permissive bargaining variable is obscure.

We also are uncertain about the meaning of the results from the unpublished study by Reid and Kurth cited by Freeman.[59] They present a series of cross-section regressions in which the dependent variable is the percentage change between 1972 and 1980 in the percent of the state's education employees belonging to a union or bargaining association and the independent variables include five policy variables.[60] In the three regressions in which all five policy variables are included, all but the agency shop variable are consistently statistically significant with the expected sign. As with the published Reid and Kurth study, the results do not provide clear evidence that the direction of causation runs from laws to unionization, rather than the other direction, especially since one of the control variables in this study of teachers is the extent of teachers organized in 1972, a variable that has significant negative coefficients in all regressions with the policy variables.

The final study cited by Freeman is Ichniowski,[61] which has been superseded by another unpublished paper.[62] Both papers examine the same data set—a 1979 survey of municipal police departments that indicated whether the police were covered by a written contract and, if so, how long that contract had been in effect. Several aspects of public policy were examined, such as statutory requirements that employers engage in good faith bargaining with organized employees and the availability of interest arbitration to resolve bargaining disputes. The length of time these statutory provisions had been in effect was also coded. By comparing the length of time that contracts had been in effect with the length of time that favorable statutory provisions had

---

[59] Portions of Reid and Kurth's 1983 paper have been published in Reid and Kurth's 1984 article, both cited *supra* note 51.

[60] The policy variables are: (1) exclusive representation, a dummy variable with values from 1 to 10 measuring the number of years before 1980 that legislation was enacted authorizing exclusive recognition; (2) dues checkoff permitted, a dummy variable with a value of 1 where legislation permits such arrangements; (3) dues checkoff mandatory, a dummy variable with a value of 1 where legislation requires the employer to deduct union dues once a union has been recognized; (4) agency shop, a dummy variable with a value of 1 where legislation permits or requires an agency shop; and (5) right-to-work laws, a dummy variable with a value of 1 when a public-sector right-to-work law exists or the agency shop is illegal.

[61] Casey Ichniowski, *The Impact of Bargaining Legislation on Police Union Growth: Estimation with Variable-Knot Logistic Splines* (New York: Columbia University, 1984), mimeo.

[62] Casey Ichniowski, *Public Sector Union Growth and Bargaining Laws: A Proportional Hazards Approach with Time-Varying Treatments* (New York: Columbia University, 1986), mimeo. Ichniowski describes the latest paper as a study that uses "a Cox proportional hazards model to estimate the relationship between state-level collective bargaining policies and union growth in the public sector." The paper cited by Freeman relied on estimation with variable-knot logistic splines.

existed, Ichniowski found that, in general, favorable statutory provisions preceded written contracts rather than vice versa; indeed, "where bargaining laws have not been enacted, formal collective bargaining between municipalities is virtually nonexistent."

Of all the studies cited by Freeman, Ichniowski does the best job of testing the direction of causation between favorable laws and public-sector bargaining. The study does not, however, as Freeman states in his Table 4 establish that "[c]ollective bargaining laws are a key factor in police organization." More precisely, the study indicates that such laws precede the negotiation of a written contract, not that such laws precede organization (which is the third general problem we discussed).

There are several studies, in addition to those cited by Freeman, concerning the impact of the legal environment on public-sector union growth. Vanderporten and Hall examined 135 municipalities to determine whether a written contract existed with their police unions in 1973.[63] Most of the data for the independent variables, such as the form of government and the existence of pay parity between police and firefighters, was from 1959–1960, prior to the enactment of any favorable laws. Use of these variables in logit and discriminant analysis correctly predicted about 70 to 80 percent of which cities had written contracts as of 1973. When a dummy variable was added to indicate the presence or absence of a public-sector collective-bargaining law, there was a slight decline in the overall explanatory power of the model. The authors concluded that the "results are consistent with the hypothesis that the conditions which led to unionization existed prior to the dramatic changes in the 1960s in the legal status of public sector collective negotiations."

The question of whether unionization leads to favorable laws or vice versa has usually been examined in studies in which only one of these possible outcomes is the dependent variable.[64] A rare exception is Saltzman,[65] who analyzed state-level data for 1959–1978 to determine whether the growth of teacher unionism during those years was primarily a result or a cause of the public-sector bargaining laws adopted during the period. His analysis is particularly impressive because his data set included separate observations for each state at two-year intervals. Several dependent variables were used, including (1) the annual change in the percentage of teachers in each state covered by collective-bargaining contracts, and (2) the probability in a

---

[63] Bruce Vanderporten and W. Clayton Hall, *Conditions Leading to Collective Negotiations Among Police*, 4 J. Lab. Res. 137 (Spring 1983).

[64] The studies that determine the enactment of favorable laws are outside the scope of this chapter. Freeman (*supra* note 49, at Table 4) provides a partial listing of such studies.

[65] Gregory M. Saltzman, *Bargaining Laws as a Cause and Consequence of the Growth of Teacher Unionism*, 38 Indus. & Lab. Rel. Rev. 335 (April 1985).

year of a change to a law more favorable to collective bargaining. For regressions involving the coverage dependent variable, he found that changes in bargaining laws had a stronger association with the subsequent spread of bargaining than did any of the other explanatory variables. For regressions involving the type of bargaining law as the dependent variable, he found that previous increases in unionization were statistically associated with favorable law changes, but not to the extent that laws induced bargaining coverage. This finding was interpreted by Saltzman as establishing that "bargaining laws appear to have a much greater impact on the extent of bargaining than the extent of bargaining has on bargaining laws" and that "bargaining laws were the key factor leading to the growth of bargaining."

We do not find the Saltzman study conclusive on the issue of the significance of laws in promoting unionization. First, the dependent variable is the existence of a written contract, not the organization of the work force, and organization often preceded negotiation of a written contract among teachers during the 1960s when organization, laws, and written contracts were rapidly spreading.[66] Second, carrying the argument one step further, Goldfield and Plotkin argue that the whole debate on laws versus organization as the originator has been too confined.[67] They contend that the surge of public-sector bargaining activity during the 1960s can best be understood as a broad social phenomenon in which worker discontent first builds, is released by some event such as the 1961 teachers' strike in New York City, and then spreads to organizing activity, with lags to successful organization, to laws, and to formal bargaining arrangements. In this view, neither favorable laws nor successful organization are the ultimate cause of the phenomenon but are only partial manifestations of an ongoing process. These qualifications to Saltzman's work suggest that the precise role played by favorable legislation in promoting unionization among teachers in the 1960s is still unknown.[68]

---

[66] Perry and Wildman make clear that in the absence of statutory authorization, most states held that written agreements between public agencies and employee organizations were illegal, thus forcing the parties to engage in informal bargaining; see Charles R. Perry and Wesley A. Wildman, The Impact of Negotiations in Public Education: The Evidence from the Schools (Worthington, Ohio: Charles A. Jones Publishing Co., 1970), at 38.

[67] Michael Goldfield and Jonathan Plotkin, Public Sector Unionism in the United States: The Reasons for its Take-off in the Early 1960s (Ithaca, N.Y.: Cornell University, 1987), mimeo.

[68] Lewin has also criticized Saltzman "since he explicitly rejected a simultaneous equation model of teacher unionism and bargaining"; see David Lewin, The Effects of Regulation on Public Sector Labor Relations: Theory and Evidence, 6 J. Lab. Res. 77 (Winter 1985). Although Saltzman rejected the approach because all the explanatory variables can be considered exogenous or predetermined, Lewin felt this position may not be justified. Also, Goldfield and Plotkin (supra note 67) have reworked the Saltzman data using a proportional hazards model, which they argue is superior to the model used by Saltzman since the relationships among laws, extent of organization, and collective bargaining are nonlinear. They conclude that their results "suggest that teacher unionism is more likely the cause of the passage of teacher collective bargaining legislation rather than the reverse." They have not, however, replicated Saltzman's procedure of comparing regression results with, first, laws, and then organization as the dependent variables. Thus their conclusion is not compelling.

Saltzman has also examined the impact of the comprehensive bargaining laws enacted in Ohio and Illinois in 1983.[69] These were the two jurisdictions mentioned by Burton as states where the lack of major changes in policy had not precluded organization of a significant proportion of public-sector workers.[70] Indeed, as of 1982, 44.5 percent of all full-time state and local employees were organized in Illinois and 40.6 percent in Ohio. Nonetheless, 54 of 782 Ohio employers (or 7 percent) who responded to a questionnaire indicated that the passage of the law led to the recognition of the union. The law was particularly crucial for the organization of state employees: prior to the law, they were largely unorganized; after, all state employees covered by the law were organized. Significantly, the law also led 80 of the Ohio employers (10 percent of the survey respondents) to adopt solicitation rules, presumably to thwart union organizing attempts, and a number of local government employers hired consulting firms to help them fend off unions. Saltzman considered this aggressive resistance to unionization in the aftermath of favorable legislation a "radical breach" with the patterns of the 1960s and 1970s, a time when public employers did not oppose organizing efforts once the legislatures enacted legislation supporting collective bargaining. In Illinois, one measure of the impact of the 1983 legislation involved school districts with 500 students: before the law, 19 percent had contracts; after, 56 percent. In contrast, the law had little potential impact in school districts with enrollment of 3,000 or more because prior to the law, contracts were already found in over 90 percent of these districts. The Saltzman evidence from Ohio and Illinois demonstrates that favorable legislation can still have an impact on both the extent of organization and of formal bargaining after 20 years of bargaining. However, the evidence is consistent with the views that such legislation is only one of several important determinants of the extent of organization, that the legislation helps certain workers (those with limited bargaining power) more than others, and that unlike the laws enacted prior to the 1980s, new laws may result in increased resistance to unionization by some employers.

Based on our review of both the studies that were available to Freeman at the time he wrote his survey article and the studies that have since become available, we are not persuaded by Freeman's assertion that the spurt in public-sector unionism in the 1960s and 1970s was caused "first and foremost [by] changes in the laws regulating public sector unions."[71] We are not claiming that the laws are

---

[69] Gregory M. Saltzman, *Public-Sector Bargaining Laws Really Matter: Evidence from Ohio and Illinois* (Albion, Mich.: Albion College, 1987), mimeo.

[70] *Supra* note 2.

[71] *Supra* note 49, at 45.

inconsequential, but the evidence does not clearly support the view that the main direction of causation is from laws to union growth. Our views on the role of public policy are explicated earlier in this section. In summary, we consider changes in public policy no more important in explaining the present extent of organization than several other factors, including the changed attitude of workers toward the propriety and usefulness of bargaining. If forced to identify the dominant direction of causation between union strength and favorable laws at the very beginning of the growth phase of public-sector bargaining, we would choose organization over legislation. We would thus align ourself with the author of a recent study of the origins of the Wisconsin laws that, beginning in 1959, provided the first statutory protection for public-sector bargaining. Several factors were considered significant, including the resurrection of the Wisconsin Democratic Party. But perhaps more important, according to the author, was the "long tradition of public sector unions. . . . By the 1950s, public sector unions had members in every county of the state, and they thus had the strength to press for bargaining legislation."[72] It is thus Saltzman the social historian rather than Saltzman the econometrician whom we find most persuasive.

Federal Employees

Table 2 contains membership data from the BLS and the Troy-Sheflin (T-S) series disaggregated by level of government. The T-S data indicate that bargaining organization membership in the federal sector peaked at 1.163 million members, or 43.3 percent of the federal work force, in 1972. Membership density declined during the 1970s, reaching a trough in 1980 at 36.6 percent and since then seems to have stabilized at around 37–38 percent. In contrast, the BLS data show no significant change in density in the federal sector between 1968 and 1978. Throughout this period the membership estimates of the BLS are consistently higher than those of T-S.

Table 3 displays membership density from the T-S series in which the federal sector is disaggregated into postal service employees and executive branch employees. Most, if not all, of this decline would appear to be a loss of membership in the executive branch unions, which shrank from a peak density of 26.4 percent in 1972 to 20.9 in 1983. Table 3 also includes information from the Office of Personnel Management (OPM) indicating the proportion of postal and other federal employees in bargaining units as well as the proportion of

---

[72] Gregory M. Saltzman, *A Progressive Experiment: The Evolution of Wisconsin's Collective Bargaining Legislation for Local Government Employees*, 15 J. Coll. Neg. Pub. Sector 1 (1986), at 13.

TABLE 2

Percentage of Government Employees Organized
(Employment and Members in Thousands)

Year	Total Government			Federal Government			State and Local Government		
	Employment	Members	Percent Organized	Employment	Members	Percent Organized	Employment	Members	Percent Organized
Panel A: Troy-Sheflin Data									
1958	7838	835	10.6	2191	509	23.2	5647	—	—
1960	8353	903	10.8	2270	541	23.8	6083	—	—
1962	8889	2162	24.3	2340	628	26.9	6549	1592	24.3
1964	9596	2496	26.0	2348	727	31.0	7248	1809	25.0
1966	10785	2812	26.1	2564	818	31.9	8221	2035	24.8
1968	11839	3070	25.9	2737	1015	37.1	9102	2270	24.9
1970	12553	3235	25.8	2731	1082	39.6	9822	2958	30.1
1972	13333	4012	30.1	2684	1163	43.3	10649	3589	33.7
1974	14170	4721	33.3	2724	1099	40.3	11446	4244	37.1
1976	14871	5385	36.2	2733	1133	41.5	12138	4837	39.9
1978	15673	5980	38.2	2753	1060	38.5	12920	4610	35.7
1980	16241	5752	35.4	2866	1049	36.6	13375	4567	34.1
1981	16031	5695	35.5	2772	1031	37.2	13259	4442	33.5
1982	15837	5673	35.8	2739	1040	38.0	13098	4382	33.5
1983	15869	5565	35.1	2774	1020	36.8	13096	4251	32.5
Panel B: BLS Data									
1968	11839	3857	32.6	2737	1391	50.8	9102	2466	27.1
1970	12553	4080	32.5	2731	1412	51.7	9822	2668	27.2
1972	13333	4520	33.9	2684	1383	51.5	10649	3137	29.5
1974	14170	5345	37.7	2724	1433	52.6	11446	3911	34.2
1976	14871	5852	39.4	2733	1332	48.7	12138	4521	37.2
1978	15673	6094	38.9	2753	1420	51.6	12920	4674	36.2

Sources: T-S membership data are from Troy and Sheflin, Appendix A. BLS membership data are from Bureau of Labor Statistics, Table 6. Employment data are from Council of Economic Advisers, Table B-40. (See Table 1 notes for complete citations of these sources.) Densities were computed by the authors.
Notes: Membership data exclude Canadian members.

TABLE 3

Federal Employees Organized, in Exclusive Units and Covered by Agreement, 1958–1985
(Numbers of Union Members and Employees in Thousands)

| | Executive Branch | | | | | | | Post Office | | | | |
| Year | Total Employment | Union Membership[a] | | Employees in Exclusive Units[b] | | Employees Under Agreement[c] | | Total Employment | Union Membership[a] | | Employees in Exclusive Units[b] | |
		Number	Percent of Total Employment	Number	Percent of Total Employment	Number	Percent of Total Employment		Number	Percent of Total Employment	Number	Percent of Total Employment
1958	1817	115	6.3	—	—	—	—	538	393	73.1	—	—
1960	1808	113	6.2	—	—	—	—	563	428	76.0	—	—
1962	1896	181	9.6	231	12.2	—	—	588	447	76.0	499	85.3
1964	1884	230	12.2	435	21.2	111	5.9	585	497	84.8	619	91.6
1966	2051	286	14.0	798	34.9	292	14.2	675	532	78.8	619	84.7
1968	2289	386	16.8	916	42.4	557	24.3	731	630	86.1	626	86.2
1970	2158	483	22.4	1083	52.2	602	27.9	726	600	82.5	605	86.8
1972	2073	547	26.4	1142	53.4	753	36.3	697	616	88.4	607	85.8
1974	2140	553	25.9	1190	56.0	985	46.0	707	593	83.9	579	85.7
1976	2126	440	20.7	1190	56.0	1060	49.9	676	641	94.9	576	87.8
1978	2117	475	22.4	1228	58.0	1120	52.9	656	579	88.3	586	88.8
1980	2109	447	21.2	1250	59.3	1167	55.3	660*	583	88.4	606	91.4
1981	2093	456	21.8	1234	59.0	1153	55.1	663	584	88.0	611	92.2
1983	2120	442	20.9	1235	58.2	1140	53.8	663	577	87.1	644	89.9
1985	2148	—	—	1244	57.9	1180	54.9	717	—	—	—	—

Sources: Employment data from 1958 to 1983 are from U.S. Bureau of the Census, Statistical Abstract of the United States, 1960 (Washington: U.S. Government Printing Office, 1960), Table 502; (1966), Table 564; (1969), Table 570; (1973), Table 409; (1976), Table 458; (1978), Table 459; (1983), Table 542; and (1984), Table 528. Employment data are from U.S. Office of Personnel Management, Union Recognition in the Federal Government (Washington: U.S. Government Printing Office, 1985), Table 2. Membership data are from Troy and Sheflin, Appendix A (see Table 1 note for complete citation of this source). Executive branch bargaining unit and contract coverage data are from U.S. Office of Personnel Management, Federal Civilian Workforce Statistics (Washington: U.S. Government Printing Office, February 1985), Table H. Postal Service bargaining unit and contract coverage data are from U.S. Office of Personnel Management, Union Recognition in the Federal Government (1963–1985), Part III—Other Jurisdictions (complete citation supra).

Note: Executive branch employment and organization data for 1976 to 1985 exclude the Tennessee Valley Authority. All Postal Service employees in exclusive units were under agreement.

[a] Employees belonging to a bargaining organization as defined in the text.
[b] Employees in units where exclusive representation rights have been granted to a bargaining organization.
[c] Employees in units under a collective-bargaining agreement with a bargaining organization.

executive branch employees covered by a contractual agreement. These data indicate that many executive branch employees in bargaining units and/or covered by agreements are not members.[73] While membership in the executive branch appears to have declined substantially in recent years, the numbers and proportions of executive branch employees in bargaining units or covered by collective agreements have changed only slightly.

In contrast to the executive branch, membership in postal unions appears to be about the same as the number of employees in exclusive units as well as the number of employees covered by a collective agreement. It appears that the membership density has remained at a consistently high 85–90 percent of the work force since the early 1970s.

Explanatory Factors

Burton characterized the allegiance of federal workers to unions as "broad but shallow,"[74] and attributed these characteristics to a public policy (embodied in a series of executive orders beginning with the promulgation of Executive Order 10988 in 1962 by President Kennedy) that minimized both the benefits and the costs of unionizing. The benefits of collective bargaining were hypothesized to be small because policy prohibited negotiations over wages and other economic subjects. Costs were said to be similarly negligible since federal departments and agencies were required to adopt a position of neutrality during union organizing drives. Also, union security agreements, including the agency shop, are illegal, and so employees do not have to support the union that represents them.

Shortly before that chapter was published, the federal labor relations policy context changed. This transformation was significant in form but slight in substance. The executive orders were replaced by the Civil Service Reform Act (CSRA) enacted in 1978. The CSRA continued the policies of the executive orders that prohibited (1) bargaining over pay practices, other benefits, and governmentwide regulations, (2) all forms of union security, and (3) strikes. Nor did the CSRA include binding arbitration provisions to replace the strike weapon as had been advocated by the major federal employee unions. Thus the CSRA did little to enhance the benefits of unionization.

---

[73] An important example is the American Federation of Government Employees (AFGE). In 1983 AFGE was the exclusive representative of some 724,886 employees and had negotiated contracts for 673,774 employees. However, T-S estimate the AFGE's 1983 membership as only 218,540.

[74] *Supra* note 2, at 22.

On the other hand the perceived costs of unionism have been enhanced by the aggressiveness of federal management toward unions during the Reagan administration.[75] At the same time, the perceived benefits of unionism were further diminished by the continuing inability of federal unions to protect wages under the Federal Pay Comparability Act (FPCA) of 1970.[76]

The provisions of the FPCA require that the pay of federal general service (GS) employees be comparable to that of equivalent private-sector workers. Recommendations based on this standard are made to the President by a presidentially appointed pay agent who considers the views of two advisory groups, the Federal Employees Pay Council and the Advisory Committee on Federal Pay. The President may refuse to accept these recommendations for reasons of "national emergency or economic conditions affecting the general welfare" and substitute an alternative pay plan. Since 1978, both Presidents Reagan and Carter have consistently refused to pass on the recommended comparability increases made by their pay agent. While Congress may override the President's recommendations, it has done so only once, in 1984. This record of failure stands in sharp contrast to the federal unions' record before 1978, when comparability increases had been denied on only one occasion.

Described as a "watershed event in governmental labor relations,"[77] the decertification of the Professional Air Traffic Controllers Organization (PATCO) in 1981 marked a significant departure in federal labor relations policy. While strikes by federal-sector employees had been prohibited since Executive Order 10988 had been issued in 1962, PATCO had successfully conducted job actions in 1968, 1969, 1970, 1976, 1978, and 1980. Although federal authorities had invoked sanctions against the union following a number of these actions, each time the government eventually backed down. On no occasion had federal management employed the full range of punitive measures (discharge of striking workers and decertification of the union) available under existing law. Not surprisingly, PATCO ignored the warnings of the Federal Aviation Administration (FAA) concerning the consequences of a strike in 1981. Unlike FAA behavior in previous strikes, however, this time the FAA followed through on its threats, fired 11,500 workers, and decertified the union.

---

[75] George T. Sulzner, *Federal Labor-Management Relations: The Reagan Impact*, 15 J. Coll. Neg. Pub. Sector 201 (1986).

[76] *Id.* See also Marick F. Masters, *Federal-Employee Unions and Political Action*, 38 Indus. & Lab. Rel. Rev. 612 (July 1985).

[77] Herbert R. Northrup, *The Rise and Demise of PATCO*, 37 Indus. & Lab. Rel. Rev. 167 (January 1984).

Other indications of the federal government's more aggressive labor relations policy may be found. In 1983 the Office of Management and Budget revised the policy first promulgated in the Eisenhower administration that established guidelines for contracting out services to the private sector. These revisions make it substantially easier for private firms to contract for government work.[78] While employee groups have resisted these efforts, the Reagan administration continues to support "privatization," including the establishment of FED CO-OPs, which are cooperatives owned by (former) federal employees that provide service to the government.[79] The implications for unions are not lost on those who advocate "privatization." The January 1986 issue of *Management*, the organ of the Office of Personnel Management, points out:

> Large scale reductions in the number of employes in existing collective bargaining units caused by moves to the private sector would substantially change the composition of bargaining units representing federal employes.
> In future years, this would reduce the unions' power bases in terms of potential membership and might lessen union demands on agency management for bargaining and representational activities.[80]

Elements of the new human resource management systems have been introduced into the federal sector in recent years. Quality of work life (QWL) programs are found in the Postal Service[81] and the Social Security Administration.[82] A Reagan executive order (E.O. 12552) prompted the OPM to promote the establishment of a type of employee "profit-sharing," termed gainsharing, in executive branch agencies.[83] As defined by the OPM, gainsharing is

> any of several programs designed to involve employees in improving the productivity of their work group through better use of labor, capital, materials, and energy. Gains resulting from "working smarter" are shared between the [employer] and the employees according to a predetermined formula that reflects progress toward productivity and profitability.

Gainsharing experiments have been conducted in the Internal Revenue Service, the Navy, the Army, and the Federal Home Loan Bank Board.

---

[78] 21 GERR 1685 (August 22, 1983).
[79] Constance Horner (Director of the Office of Personnel Management), *FED CO-OP: Privatization Package No. 1*, 6 Management 5 (1986).
[80] *Status of Unions During Privatization*, 6 Management 39 (1986).
[81] 23 GERR 1568 (November 4, 1985).
[82] 23 GERR 1137 (August 12, 1985).
[83] 24 GERR 651 (May 12, 1986).

Special Cases—Postal Service

Postal workers have a long history of organization. As can be seen from Table 3, postal employees were highly organized prior to Executive Order 10988 and continue to have a much higher union density than executive branch employees. The employees also enjoy special legislative treatment (under the 1970 Postal Reorganization Act) that gives the National Labor Relations Board authority to determine bargaining units, conduct elections, and consider unfair labor practice charges. The act also establishes mediation, fact finding, and arbitration procedures to resolve collective-bargaining disputes. Burton argued that postal workers received favorable consideration from Congress because, unlike most federal employees, their wide geographic dispersion gives them effective political leverage.[84] The 1970 strike by postal workers also helped their quest for special treatment.

State and Local Employees

The T-S data presented in Table 2 indicate that state and local bargaining organization membership reached a peak of 4.837 million members, or 39.9 percent of the state and local work force, in 1976. Membership and density, according to the T-S series, had declined by 586,000 members, or 7.4 percentage points, by 1983. Most of the decline (according to T-S) occurred between 1976 and 1980, a drop of 5.0 percentage points. Membership reported by the BLS is slightly higher than that reported by T-S for the years 1968 and 1978, while T-S's numbers are higher for 1970 through 1976.

Tables 4 and 5 present data collected by the Bureau of the Census–Department of Labor (BCDL). The data for the years 1976 to 1980 were obtained from a mail questionnaire sent to a sample of approximately 20,000 local governments as well as each state government. The data for 1972 and 1982 were collected from over 80,000 state and local governments in the Census of Governments. The data in Table 4 differ from those presented in Tables 1 and 2 because they pertain only to full-time employment. These data, like the T-S and BLS data in Table 2, indicate that state and local membership density has declined in recent years. In contrast to the T-S and BLS data, the BCDL data, however, show a continuing decline in state and local density after 1972. Another discrepancy between these data and the T-S and BLS data is that the BCDL reports consistently higher levels of both density

---

[84] John F. Burton, Jr., *Federal or State Responsbility for Workers' Compensation?*, Proceedings of the 29th Annual Meeting, Industrial Relations Research Association (Madison, Wis.: IRRA, 1977), 219–227.

TABLE 4

State and Local Government Employees in 1972–1982
(Employees in Thousands)

Level of Government and Function	Total Full-Time Employment				Number of Full-Time Employees Organized				Percent of Full-Time Employees Organized			
	1972	1976	1980	1982	1972	1976	1980	1982	1972	1976	1980	1982
State and local	8,578	9,514	10,314	10,161	4,293	4,737	5,031	4,645	50.0	49.8	48.8	45.7
State Total	2,312	2,596	2,868	2,847	942	992	1,163	1,066	40.7	38.2	40.6	37.4
Education—teachers	266	282	296	290	82	97	107	88	30.8	34.4	36.1	30.3
Education—others	473	548	594	510	115	140	157	151	24.3	25.5	26.4	29.6
Highways	283	257	253	240	163	138	134	127	57.6	53.7	53.0	52.9
Public welfare	112	156	169	167	52	61	69	77	46.4	39.1	40.8	46.1
Hospitals	437	482	523	513	228	230	261	222	52.2	47.7	49.9	43.3
Police protection	62	68	72	75	34	35	37	35	54.8	51.5	51.4	46.7
All other	679	803	961	1,052	268	290	398	366	39.5	36.1	41.4	34.8
Local Total	6,266	6,919	7,446	7,314	3,351	3,745	3,868	3,579	53.5	54.1	51.9	48.9
Education—teachers	2,454	2,721	2,833	2,743	1,807	1,963	1,924	1,765	73.6	72.1	67.9	64.3
Education—others	921	976	1,121	1,123	323	437	497	450	35.1	44.8	44.3	40.1
Highways	268	285	273	265	90	103	103	95	33.6	36.1	37.7	35.8
Public welfare	171	178	193	199	78	77	82	83	45.6	43.3	42.5	41.7
Hospitals	419	428	484	495	129	130	142	80	30.8	30.4	29.3	16.2
Police protection	411	463	499	513	229	253	264	266	55.7	54.6	52.9	51.9
Fire protection	194	210	221	228	149	151	156	152	76.8	71.9	70.6	66.7
Sanitation	117	119	119	108	59	59	48	47	50.4	49.6	40.3	43.5
All other	1,310	1,539	1,704	1,639	488	574	652	641	37.3	37.3	38.3	39.1

Sources: U.S. Bureau of the Census and U.S. Dep't of Labor, Labor-Management Services Administration, Labor-Management Relations in State and Local Governments, Special Studies nos. 75, 88, 102 (Washington: U.S. Government Printing Office, 1976, 1978, 1981), Table 3; and U.S. Bureau of the Census, 1982 Census of Governments, Labor-Management Relations in State and Local Governments, GC82(3)-3 (Washington: U.S. Government Printing Office, 1985), Table 1.

TABLE 5

Proportion of State and Local Government Employees Organized,
in Bargaining Units and Covered by Agreement

Year	Employees Organized		Employees in Bargaining Units	Employees Covered by Contractual Agreements
	Full and Part-Time	Full-Time Only		
Panel A: State and Local				
1972	—	50.0	—	—
1974	—	51.5	31.4	—
1976	—	49.8	35.8	27.7
1978	—	48.1	37.9	31.1
1980	—	48.8	38.4	32.1
1982	37.5	45.7	39.5	30.6
Panel B: State Government				
1972	—	40.7	—	—
1974	—	39.3	19.4	—
1976	—	38.2	22.5	16.0
1978	—	38.1	24.8	21.5
1980	—	40.5	26.7	22.1
1982	29.3	37.4	31.0	28.1
Panel C: Local Government				
1972	—	53.5	—	—
1974	—	56.0	35.8	—
1976	—	54.1	40.8	32.0
1978	—	51.9	42.9	34.9
1980	—	51.9	43.0	38.3
1982	40.8	48.9	43.0	37.5

Sources: U.S. Bureau of the Census and U.S. Dep't of Labor, Labor-Management Services Administration, Labor-Management Relations in State and Local Governments (1976, 1978, 1981), Table 1; and 1982 Census of Governments (1985), Table 1. See Table 4 source note for complete citations.

and membership. Part of this difference in density is explained by the BCDL's failure to include part-time employment in its membership statistics. As can be seen from the 1982 data in the first column of Table 5, membership density is more similar to the T-S density when part-time workers are included, although the BCDL data are still higher than indicated by the T-S data.

The disaggregated data in Table 4 indicate that the decline in unionization throughout the period was not uniform across all functions. The biggest decline was experienced by bargaining organizations representing local hospital employees, which went from a density of 30.8 to 16.2 percent.[85] Other functions showing a substantial decrease (over five percentage points) in union density were state hospital employees, local instructional personnel in education, fire protection, sanitation, and state police. Certain functions increased in density, including state and local educational personnel other than teachers, and local highway employees.

Finally, data in Panel A of Table 5 show that while membership in state and local bargaining organizations was declining, the proportion of employees in bargaining units and covered by contractual agreements increased. Disaggregating by level of government in Panels B and C, we see that most of the increases in both bargaining unit and contractual coverage are in the state sector. While local employees increased coverage, particularly with respect to contractual agreements, both measures seem to have stabilized in recent years. Overall, these data seem to indicate that state and local public-sector unions in the late 1970s and early 1980s were consolidating their membership gains from earlier years.

Explanatory Factors

Structural Changes. One possible explanation for the overall decline or stagnation in unionization of state and local employees relates to structural changes in the distribution of employment in the public sector. Employment in some heavily unionized functions has declined, while employment in relatively nonunionized functions has increased. For example, education instructional staff, the second most highly organized function in state and local government in 1972, decreased as a proportion of total state and local employment from approximately 29 to 27 percent between 1972 and 1982. Similarly, regional shifts in public employment that may affect overall union density are detectable. The share of nationwide state and local government employment located in the 11 states of the old confederacy, a low union density region, increased from about 25 percent in 1972 to approximately 29 percent in 1982.

We conducted a limited test of the hypothesis that structural changes explain the declining extent of organization in the state and local sector. Specifically, two types of structural change were examined: the change in the regional pattern of employment by state and

---

[85] The sharp decline in local hospital union density is puzzling in light of the fact that, overall, union density in the hospital sector (including public, private, and nonprofit) appears to have increased over this period. Kokkelenberg and Sockell, *supra* note 6, estimate that hospital unionization rose from 13.4 percent in 1974 to 17.6 percent in 1980. Surveys by the American Hospital Association show that the percentage of hospitals owned by state or local government with at least one collective bargaining contract increased from 14.9 percent in 1970 to 28.8 percent in 1980; see Edmund R. Becker, Frank A. Sloan, and Bruce Steinwald, *Union Activity in Hospitals: Past, Present, and Future,* 3 Health Care Financing Rev. 1 (1982).

the change in the relative importance of different government functions. Using the methodology employed by Dickens and Leonard[86]
and published BCDL data, we determined the change in union density that would have occurred between 1972 and 1982 if shares of
employment (1) by function, (2) by state, and (3) by function and state,
were held constant at their 1972 levels. Similarly, we allowed shares of
employment to change over this period, while holding unionization
(1) by function, (2) by state, and (3) by function and state, constant at
1972 levels.

Our results reveal that when changes in union density due to
changes in share of employment by function are examined alone,
15.5 percent of the 4.4 percent decline in density for this period is
accounted for by structural change. Our analysis also reveals that
density declined fastest in those functions that experienced the greatest decline in employment share. We find that 27.3 percent of the
1972 to 1982 decline in public-sector unionization is the result of
increasing employment in low density states. In addition we find that
union density declined more rapidly in states that experienced
increased employment. Overall, we find that these two structural
changes account for nearly 50 percent of the decline in union density
in state and local government.

Aside from shifts in employment between functional categories
and states, it is possible that other structural changes have resulted in
the general stagnation of unionization in state and local government. It
is possible that changes in the occupational, age, and gender composition of the public-sector work force have also contributed to the recent
decline in public-sector unionization. Dickens and Leonard were able
to explain nearly 70 percent of the total decline in private-sector
unionization by looking at all these facets of structural change, and if
our simple examination of shifts in employment share by governmental
function and by state were extended to these other factors, it might be
possible to explain a larger proportion of the decline in public-sector
organization of state and local government employees.

Increasing Resistance to Collective Bargaining. One of the principal developments in public-sector labor relations since the
mid-1970s is the increasing pressures on city and state officials to
reduce governmental expenditures. One author has termed this
period "the era of fiscal restraint."[87] The growing public sentiment for
"financial responsibility" in government was crystallized by a number
of events, beginning with the near bankruptcy of New York City in

[86] *Supra* note 10.
[87] Astrid E. Merget, *The Era of Fiscal Restraint*, in The Municipal Year Book (Washington:
International City Management Association, 1980).

1975 and including the passage of Proposition 13 in California in 1978 and Proposition 2½ in Massachusetts in 1980. Since that time, tax-limitation initiatives have been passed in a number of states (including Arkansas, Louisiana, and Missouri), although this movement seems to have abated in recent years.[88]

This hostile public reaction has its roots in the rise in the relative importance of government in the economy. Table 6 documents the rise in total government expenditures. Most relevant in explaining the change in public attitude toward state and local government employees was that between 1950 and 1976, the sector's expenditures grew more than tenfold (and in constant dollars more than fourfold) and its share of GNP nearly doubled. This rapid increase of expenditures put state and local government under considerable financial pressure by the mid-1970s, a problem aggravated by the shortfalls in revenue resulting from the recessions of 1975 and 1982. Table 6 also shows that in the same year that Proposition 13 was passed (1978), federal transfers as a proportion of total state and local revenues began to decline, putting even more pressures on state and local governments. This decline accelerated following the Reagan administration's 1981 budget cuts, which eliminated several federal revenue-sharing programs.

The financial difficulties of state and local governments and the public reaction to the fiscal problems provided public-sector management with the motivation to resist unionization. The capacity to resist resulted from the restructuring of management structure and personnel practices in response to the emergence of collective bargaining. As previously discussed, the initial consequences of bargaining included the breakdown or abandonment of the civil service system in many jurisdictions,[89] and the modification of management structure, such as the centralization of authority for labor relations issues.[90] These trends have continued into the 1980s.[91]

While these management adaptations may have initially encouraged collective bargaining, this restructuring also provided public-sector managers with greater capacity to deal effectively with unions, similar to the ability of employers in the private sector. The trend in the public sector is toward centralization of authority over personnel operations and separation of that authority from operational management.[92] As Foulkes argued for private-sector employers, it is sine qua

---

[88] For example, in 1984 tax limitation initiatives were defeated in Michigan, Nevada, and California; see 22 GERR 2133 (November 12, 1984).
    [89] Joseph P. Goldberg, *Public Employee Developments in 1971*, 95 Monthly Lab. Rev. 56 (January 1972).
    [90] John F. Burton, Jr., *Local Government Bargaining and Management Structure*, 11 Indus. Rel. 123 (May 1972).
    [91] Chester A. Newland, *Public Personnel: Retrenchment, Restructuring, Reorganization*, in The Municipal Year Book (Washington: International City Management Association, 1982).
    [92] *Id.*

TABLE 6

Federal, State, and Local Government Expenditures
(Expenditures in Millions)

Year	Government Expenditures			Expenditures as a Percentage of GNP			Proportion of Total State and Local Revenues	
	1	2	3	4	5	6	7	8
	Total	Federal	State and Local	Total	Federal	State and Local	Federal Revenues	Surplus or Deficit
1950	61	41	23	21.3	14.3	7.8	11.9	−9.0
1960	137	94	50	26.6	18.2	9.7	13.8	−2.7
1970	317	208	134	31.3	20.5	13.2	16.7	−0.4
1974	467	306	206	31.7	20.7	14.0	20.1	4.2
1976	588	394	255	33.0	22.1	14.3	21.7	−0.2
1978	695	471	301	30.9	20.9	13.4	22.0	6.0
1980	890	615	363	32.6	22.5	13.3	21.7	3.5
1981	1007	703	391	33.0	23.0	12.8	21.3	3.8
1982	1112	781	414	35.1	24.7	13.1	19.1	4.5
1983	1190	836	440	34.9	24.5	12.9	18.5	4.2
1984	1275	897	472	33.9	23.8	12.5	17.9	7.0
1985	1402	985	516	35.1	24.6	12.9	17.8	7.3
1986*	1484	1030	558	35.3	24.5	13.3	———	———

Source: Council of Economic Advisers, Economic Report of the President (Washington: U.S. Government Printing Office, 1987). Expenditure data in cols. 1–6 from Table B-76. GNP data used to compute proportions in cols. 4–6 from Table B-1. Data used to compute proportions in cols. 7-8 from Table B-80.
    Note: Total expenditures in col. 1 do not equal the sum of federal plus state and local expenditures in cols. 2 and 3 due to double-counting of federal grants-in-aid to state and local governments.
    *Preliminary.

non that to remain (or become) nonunion or to minimize the role of a union, an organization's personnel function must "have and exercise great power."[93] Furthermore, Stillman reports rising professionalism and erudition among public managers with an increased emphasis on managerial as opposed to engineering qualifications.[94]

There are extensive signs of rising management aggressiveness in personnel practices. Management has increased use of alternative delivery systems such as subcontracting to private-sector firms or

[93] Fred K. Foulkes, Personnel Policies in Large Nonunion Companies (Englewood Cliffs, N.J.: Prentice-Hall, 1980), at 95.
    [94] Richard J. Stillman, Local Public Management in Transition: A Report on the Current State of the Profession, in The Municipal Year Book (Washington: International City Management Association, 1982).

"privatization,"[95] merit pay,[96] part-time employment,[97] and tech-nological change.[98] As is true in the federal sector, state and local governments have begun to adopt the practices of the new human resource management, including QWL programs,[99] quality circles,[100] and contingent compensation.[101] Furthermore, Northrup argues that the federal government's crushing of PATCO provided an inspiration for state and local management.[102] In an instructive example of how far public-sector management has evolved, Saltzman reports that enact-ment of Ohio legislation permitting public-sector bargaining statutes prompted at least one municipal government to hire a consulting firm to combat unionization.[103]

The reactions by the voter and public-sector managers to the expanded size of state and local government in the growth phase of public-sector bargaining (until the mid-1970s) are reflected in several measures. Table 7 shows that state and local employment declined in relative terms (as a percentage of total employment) after 1976. Additionally, Hoertner reports that municipal employment (measured as the number of employees per 1,000 population) declined in all uniformed services from 1975 to 1984.[104] Police went from 2.61 employees per thousand to 2.38, fire from 1.75 to 1.65 employees per thousand, and sanitation from 1.41 to 0.71 employees per thou-sand. These declines in employment rolls, which reflect the increasing fiscal constraints binding state and local governments, offer public-sector managers an opportunity as well as a motive to increase their opposition to unions.

Union Organizing Efforts. Interunion competition results in greater union expenditures in organizing campaigns and, conse-quently, greater success in unionization.[105] In recent years several state employee associations (e.g., those in California, Ohio, Michigan, Arizona, and Oregon) have affiliated with AFL-CIO unions in order to

---

[95] Harry P. Hatry and Carl F. Valente, *Alternative Service Delivery Approaches Involving Increased Use of the Private Sector*, in The Municipal Year Book (Washington: International City Management Association, 1983).

[96] Annie Millar, *Residential Solid Waste Collection*, in The Municipal Year Book (Wash-ington: International City Management Association, 1983).

[97] Newland, *supra* note 91.

[98] David Lewin, *Public Employee Unionism in the 1980s: An Analysis of Transformation*, in Unions in Transition: Entering the Second Century, ed. Seymour M. Lipset (San Francisco: Institute for Contemporary Studies, 1986).

[99] 24 GERR 786 (June 2, 1986).

[100] 22 GERR 1157 (June 11, 1984) and 22 GERR 1475 (July 30, 1984).

[101] 22 GERR 857 (April 30, 1984) and 22 GERR 2146 (November 12, 1984).

[102] *Supra* note 77.

[103] *Supra* note 69.

[104] Gerard J. Hoertner, *Police, Fire, and Refuse Collection and Disposal Departments: Personnel, Compensation, and Expenditures*, in The Municipal Year Book (Washington: Interna-tional City Management Association, 1985).

[105] Freeman, *supra* note 9.

TABLE 7

Employment in Federal, State and Local Government
(Employees in Thousands)

Year	Total Government		Federal Government		State and Local Government	
	Employment	Percent of Total Employment	Employment	Percent of Total Employment	Employment	Percent of Total Employment
1958	7838	15.6	2191	4.4	5647	11.2
1960	8353	15.4	2270	4.2	6083	11.2
1962	8889	16.0	2340	4.2	6549	11.8
1964	9596	16.5	2348	4.0	7248	12.4
1966	10785	16.9	2564	4.0	8221	12.9
1968	11839	17.4	2737	4.0	9102	13.4
1970	12553	17.7	2731	3.9	9822	13.9
1972	13333	18.1	2684	3.6	10649	14.5
1974	14170	18.1	2724	3.5	11446	14.6
1976	14871	18.7	2733	3.4	12138	15.3
1978	15673	18.1	2753	3.2	12920	14.9
1980	16241	18.0	2866	3.2	13375	14.8
1981	16031	17.6	2772	3.0	13259	14.5
1982	15837	17.7	2739	3.1	13098	14.6
1983	15869	17.6	2774	3.1	13096	14.5
1984	16024	16.9	2807	3.0	13216	14.0
1985	16415	16.8	2875	2.9	13540	13.9
1986*	16738	16.7	2899	2.9	13839	13.8

Source: Employment data from Council of Economic Advisers, Economic Report of the
President (Washington: U.S. Government Printing Office, 1987), Table B-40. Proportions com-
puted by the authors.
*Preliminary.

take advantage of the federation's anti-raiding agreements. The resul-
tant diminishing competition may provide part of the answer for the
recent stagnation in public-sector union growth.

Special Cases—Education

In addition to the fiscal constraints experienced by all state and
local functions, education has faced additional pressures from a declining school-age population. Table 8 shows that total elementary and
secondary enrollment declined after 1970. At the same time, teacher
employment increased until 1978. The result was a sharp decline in the
student-teacher ratio until 1984. This ratio increased in 1985, but is
still far below the level of the early 1970s.

Despite the improvement in the student-teacher ratio in the
public schools, which presumably would make these schools more
attractive, since the early 1970s private school enrollment has
expanded. This is a partial explanation of why public school enrollment

TABLE 8

Enrollment and Employment in Elementary and Secondary Education
(In Thousands)

Year	Enrollment			Public School Teachers	Public School Student-Teacher Ratio
	Total	Public	Private		
1959	40,857	35,182	5,675	1,371	29.81
1970	51,272	45,909	5,363	2,055	24.95
1972	50,744	45,744	5,000‡	2,133	23.79
1974	50,053	45,053	5,000‡	2,175	23.01
1976	49,484	44,317	5,167	2,210	22.39
1978	47,636	42,550	5,086	2,214	21.52
1980	46,318	40,987	5,331	2,162	21.42
1981	45,599	40,099	5,500‡	2,117	21.54
1982	45,252	39,652	5,600‡	2,120	21.35
1983	45,043	39,328	5,715	2,125	21.20
1984*	45,005	39,305	5,700	2,150	20.93
1985*	45,050	39,350	5,700	2,150	20.95

Sources: W. Vance Grant and C. George Lind, Digest of Education Statistics (Washington: U.S. Government Printing Office, 1973), Tables 10 and 11; (1975), Table 8; (1978), Table 8; and (1979), Table 8. W. Vance Grant and Thomas D. Snyder, Digest of Education Statistics (Washington: U.S. Government Printing Office, 1986), Tables 4 and 7. Student-teacher ratios calculated by the authors.
*Preliminary.
‡Estimates.

fell and why leaders of the NEA and AFT have opposed Reagan administration proposals for tuition tax credits and vouchers that could be used in public or private schools.[106]

Higher Education. Data showing faculty unionization in higher education are presented in Table 9. These data are estimates of the number and proportion of institutions where faculty are represented by collective bargaining rather than the proportion of faculty who are union members. Additionally, it is important to note that these data include private as well as public institutions, although the private sector accounts for a relatively small proportion of organized faculty. Garbarino estimates that only 7 percent of the organized faculty of four-year institutions and 5 percent of total organized faculty are in privately controlled institutions.[107]

---

[106] 23 GERR 807 (June 3, 1985).
[107] Joseph W. Garbarino, *Faculty Collective Bargaining: A Status Report,* in Unions in Transition: Entering the Second Century, ed. Seymour M. Lipset (San Francisco: Institute for Contemporary Studies, 1986), at 268.

TABLE 9

Enrollment, Employment, and Faculty Representation in Higher Education
(Enrollment and Employees in Thousands)

Year	Total					Two Year		Four Year	
	Enrollment	Employment	Institutions	Employees Represented	Percent of Total Employment	Institutions	Employees Represented	Institutions	Employees Represented
1966	6,390	362	23	5.2	1.4	22	5.0	1	0.2
1967	6,912	390	37	7.0	1.8	35	6.7	2	0.3
1968	7,513	428	70	14.3	3.3	60	11.0	10	3.3
1969	8,005	450	138	36.1	8.0	112	20.0	26	16.1
1970	8,581	473	177	47.3	10.0	137	23.9	40	23.4
1971	8,949	492	245	72.4	14.7	161	27.0	84	45.4
1972	9,215	500	285	84.3	16.9	183	29.7	102	54.6
1973	9,602	527	310	87.7	16.6	189	30.3	121	57.4
1974	10,224	567	337	92.8	16.4	206	32.1	131	60.7
1975	11,185	628	398	102.3	16.3	236	35.0	162	67.3
1976	11,012	633	450	117.0	18.5	261	38.0	189	79.0
1977	11,286	656	480	133.0	20.3	284	51.4	196	81.6
1978	11,260	656	506	140.6	21.4	295	55.5	211	85.1
1979	11,570	675	526	146.8	21.7	306	60.6	220	86.2
1980	12,097	686	534	148.9	21.7	312	62.0	222	86.9
1981	12,372	697	533	149.4	21.4	312	62.2	221	87.3
1982	12,426	701	550	169.1	24.1	316	64.1	234	105.0
1983	12,465	702	546	168.6	24.0	317	64.3	229	104.3
1984*	12,242	700	547	168.2	24.0	320	64.9	227	103.2

Source: Enrollment data are from W. Vance Grant and Thomas D. Snyder, *Digest of Education Statistics* (Washington: U. S. Government Printing Office, 1986), Tables 4 and 87. Other data are from Joseph W. Garbarino, *Faculty Collective Bargaining: A Status Report*, in *Unions in Transition: Entering the Second Century*, ed. Seymour M. Lipset (San Francisco: Institute for Contemporary Studies, 1986).
*Preliminary.

As can be seen, the proportion of faculty represented by unions increased throughout the period (until 1983), although the rise after 1977 was slight.[108] In contrast to elementary and secondary education, the period from 1966 to 1983 was also one of continuing growth in enrollment and employment.[109] Higher education has not been under the same pressures for retrenchment as have the public schools.

Other estimates of the extent of faculty unionism may be obtained from Kokkelenberg and Sockell's analysis of CPS data. They estimate that as of 1974, 8.8 percent of the college and university work force were union members and that by 1980 this figure had risen to 16.3 percent.[110] Unfortunately, they do not provide separate estimates for public and private institutions. In addition these statistics include noninstructional personnel as well as faculty members.[111]

One of the recent principal developments in faculty collective bargaining was the Supreme Court's 1980 *Yeshiva* decision.[112] The Court held that the participation of college faculty in the decision-making process at private colleges was extensive enough to make faculty "managers" as defined by the National Labor Relations Act (NLRA). Since managers are not protected for the purposes of collective bargaining by the NLRA, the *Yeshiva* decision dampened enthusiasm for unionism in private colleges. Garbarino reports that units in 18 privately controlled institutions decertified by 1984.[113] It is difficult to assess the impact of this decision on faculty collective bargaining in the public sector. Some predict that *Yeshiva* may have a "ripple" effect on the public sector, fearing that the same arguments will be used to oppose faculty unionism at public colleges.[114] Indeed, a recent decision by the Pennsylvania Labor Relations Board, citing the *Yeshiva* decision, held that the faculty of the University of Pittsburgh are managers and are thus not permitted to unionize.[115]

---

[108] The growth spurt in 1982 was almost entirely due to the organization of the 18,000 faculty in the California state university and college system.

[109] Both enrollment and employment declined slightly in 1984.

[110] See Kokkelenberg and Sockell, *supra* note 6. As noted in Appendix A, in 1977 the CPS began to reflect membership in employee associations in addition to membership in unions.

[111] However, Kokkelenberg and Sockell, *supra* note 6, do provide separate estimates for faculty by discipline. These data indicate that, in 1980, psychology teachers were the most highly organized discipline with a density of 47.7 percent. Theology teachers were the least organized with a density of zero. This last estimate must be treated cautiously due to the small number of respondents in the sample.

[112] *NLRB v. Yeshiva Univ.*, 444 U.S. 672, 103 LRRM 2526 (1980).

[113] *Supra* note 107, at 270.

[114] 22 GERR 2082 (November 5, 1984).

[115] *United Faculty and University of Pittsburgh*, PLRB No. PERA-R-84-53-W (March 11, 1987).

Conclusions and Prognostications

Gossamer Conclusions

There are three periods in the history of public-sector bargaining: the quiescent period that lasted until 1960, the growth period that ended in the mid-1970s, and the stagnation period that began after that. The reasons for the emergence of the second and third periods are unclear. A plethora of explanations have been offered, but they are generally contradictory with one another or unpersuasive.

Private-sector studies provide little guidance for the public-sector developments. One obvious difficulty is that private-sector unionization has continuously declined for 30 years while the public sector has moved from quiescence to growth to stagnation. Nor do many of the valid hypotheses for the private-sector developments, such as the shift to white-collar jobs, assist our understanding of the public sector, where, for example, many white-collar workers have been organized.

Explanations tailored to the public sector are also relatively useless in explaining the emergence of the second and third periods of bargaining. Burton, in discussing the growth period of public-sector bargaining, concluded, "Nor is the literature that attempts to explain the public-sector developments satisfactory; the recurrent themes are that the recent growth was unexpectedly large and the causes were unusually complex and inscrutable."[116]

We are not yet blessed with many studies analyzing the reasons for the emergence of the stagnation phase of public-sector bargaining. In any case, the emergence of the period was largely unanticipated. The prognostications surveyed by Burton that were made roughly as the third phase began were all off the mark—ranging from Weber's ebullient prediction that unionization would "become predominant, if not nearly universal"[117] to Burton's conservative prediction of a modest deceleration in the growth rate of organized government employees so that "the increase will probably average less than 1 percent a year."[118] How quickly verities become verisimilitudes.

Burton did have the prescience to identify the role played by public policy as the "most tantalizing question about the growth of public-sector bargaining."[119] It still is. With a few exceptions, the studies that have appeared since then have not been well designed to answer the question. If anything, we would assign somewhat less importance to the role of public policy in explaining the major turning points in public-sector unionism than did Burton in 1979, if for no other reason than the entry into the stagnation period of bargaining was accompanied by no obvious explanatory change in public policy.

---

[116] *Supra* note 2, at 36.
[117] *Supra* note 47, at 7–8.
[118] *Supra* note 2, at 40.
[119] *Id.* at 36.

Deficient Research and Disappearing Data

The problems with the data on public-sector unionization and bargaining are severe. The BLS data that were the primary basis of Burton's 1979 chapter have been discontinued. The CPS began collecting membership data in 1973, but has made several changes in the definition of covered organization that reduce the series' utility. The T-S data also have problems, including the present unavailability of data after 1984. We have entered the age of unenlightenment.

The quantity of research on public-sector bargaining has increased, but, as our survey of the studies concerning the role of favorable laws in promoting organization of workers indicates, many have methodological problems. Also, many aspects of private-sector research (e.g., studies of the election process focusing on the decisions of individual workers or on the ability of recognized unions to obtain meaningful first contracts) have not been replicated in the public sector. Studies of this kind may require the construction of new data sets, but given the importance of public-sector bargaining, the effort is justified.

Burton asserted there was "a need to move beyond analysis by egregious example and casual empiricism" if the research on public-sector bargaining is to be improved. He indicated that a necessary first step "is the development of a theoretical model of the determinants of the extent of bargaining and of membership in bargaining organizations," and he cautioned that "the model must be specifically adapted to the public sector, where the bargaining outcome often is reflected in ordinances, laws, or documents other than written contracts, and where the bargaining process uses influence methods such as lobbying as a partial or total substitute for strikes."[120]

The literature of the last decade has done little to satisfy the need for such a theory. Indeed, the continuing dialogue over the role of legislation in promoting unionization and bargaining has underscored the potential value of a comprehensive theory that would consider, inter alia, the various inputs of public policy (including statutes, agency and court decisions, and administration of the law) on the various activities of a bargaining organization (including attracting members, winning bargaining rights, and negotiating written contracts). A change in a particular type of public policy (e.g., a statutory enactment) is likely to have a different impact on these different activities. We have, for example, argued in this chapter that laws have a greater influence on the use of written contracts than on the initial organization of workers, but this essentially ad hoc assertion needs to be incorporated into a comprehensive theory of public-sector bargaining.

Qualified Prognostications

Although the past record of misguided prognostications suggests that being totally noncommittal about the future is the best strategy, we nonetheless cannot resist making some predictions.

---

[120] *Id.* at 37–38.

The financial constraints on the federal government will continue for the foreseeable future because of the deficit problem. This means that management is likely to continue to resist union demands and that most federal-sector unions will be pressed to provide valuable assistance to their members in response to intensified government efforts to test for drug use and AIDS; otherwise, most federal unions are unlikely to reverse the trend toward fewer members.

The bleak financial picture at the federal level will also affect state and local governments because of the demise of revenue-sharing. Lewin, Feuille, Kochan, and Delaney predict that a fiscal crisis may be coming for state and local governments.[121] If so, this will put additional pressure on public managers to resist union demands, which is likely to reduce the attractiveness of unions. It is possible, but unlikely, that management personnel practices will become so hostile that workers will organize for defensive reasons.

The ability to increase the wages of their members relative to nonunion workers may pose a Hobson's choice for unions. Unless unions can demonstrate that bargaining produces higher wages, potential members are hard to capture. If unions do increase the relative wages of their members, however, management is likely to become more virulent in resisting unionization. Flanagan[122] argues that the increasing union relative-wage effect during the 1960s and 1970s helps explain the increasing management resistance to unions in the private sector. In the private sector, the record of the past several decades suggests that higher wages for members have hurt unions more by increasing management resistance than they have helped them by enhancing their ability to attract members.

The private-sector experience concerning the relationship between higher wages and union organizing success is hard to translate to the public sector. Most early studies of the union relative-wage effect in the public sector indicate a smaller impact than in the private sector.[123] Freeman, however, in his 1986 survey article found that more recent studies showed a larger relative-wage effect of unions than the earlier studies.[124] Evidence also indicates that union wage increases in the 1980s have been higher in the public sector than in the private sector. It is unclear whether public-sector unions will, in the future, have a large impact on wages of their members relative to wages of unorganized workers. To the extent the unions do have a substantial relative wage effect, public-sector managers may become increasingly resistant to union demands. If the apparent effect of higher relative wages in the private sector—more management dis-

---

[121] David Lewin, Peter Feuille, Thomas A. Kochan, and John T. Delaney, Public Sector Labor Relations: Analysis and Readings, 3d ed. (Lexington, Mass.: Heath, 1987).

[122] Supra note 24.

[123] Ronald G. Ehrenberg and Joshua L. Schwarz, Public-Sector Labor Markets, in Handbook of Labor Economics, Vol. II, eds. Orley Ashenfelter and Richard Layard (New York: Elsevier Science Publishers, 1986).

[124] Supra note 49.

dain than worker euphoria—is applicable to the public sector, then unions in the public sector may experience membership losses due to their success in negotiating higher wages.

As for the structural factors largely beyond the control of unions, there appears to be a loose relationship between changes in the share of employment by function and changes in the overall proportion of workers who are organized. The prospects for massive changes in public-sector employment are low, but the number of teachers may increase with resulting increases in unionization.

To the extent that public policy has an impact on the extent of organization, there are unlikely to be any major stimuli to organization because of changes in policy in the next decade. With the Ohio and Illinois enactments, all the major industrial states have legislation favorable to public-sector bargaining. A federal law supporting bargaining rights by state and local employees is more likely to withstand constitutional challenges in light of *Garcia*,[125] but the political prospects for such a law are not promising. In any case, the impact of such a law on the extent of organization is debatable. Saltzman suggests that "the enactment of federal legislation giving state and local employees the right to bargain would greatly facilitate the spread of bargaining by teachers and other public employees in states where bargaining activity is now sparse."[126] We are skeptical that, even if such a law were enacted in the next decade, much change in union strength will result.

Our overall prediction for the public sector is that unless there are major shocks, such as a financial crisis for the state and local sector that leads to massive layoffs, the percentage of workers organized in the public sector will not change markedly in the next five to ten years. Essentially this means the continuation of the third phase rather than the emergence of a new phase. If a dramatic change does occur, it is more likely to be a significant weakening of the public-sector union movement than a substantial increase in strength. The continuing rapid decline of private-sector unionization means that public-sector unions are increasingly vulnerable politically. If a fiscal crisis occurs in state and local government, the anti-union pressures (whether justified or not) are likely to overwhelm unions. The collapse of the Knights of Labor in the 19th century may become a disturbing analogy.

Appendix

There are four principal sources of data on union membership and collective bargaining coverage. Unfortunately, as noted in the text, the sources yield widely varying figures. This Appendix attempts to determine the reasons for the variation in these estimates and to reconcile the differences among them.

---

[125] *Garcia v. San Antonio Metropolitan Transit Authority*, 105 S. Ct. 479, 27 WH 65 (1985).
[126] *Supra* note 65, at 351.

Bureau of Labor Statistics (BLS)

These data were obtained through a biennial mail survey of labor organizations. Organizations surveyed include "all AFL-CIO affiliates and unaffiliated unions known to be interstate in scope . . . [and] those professional and State public employee associations believed to be engaged in collective bargaining or representational activities." Significantly, municipal employee associations were not included, which results in an underestimation of public-sector membership.

It has also been suggested that the BLS's reliance on union self-reports led to an overestimation of membership since unions often exaggerate these figures. Studies conducted by the BLS found that many individuals who do not pay dues are reported as members by unions asked to indicate the "average number of dues-paying members."[127] In a survey of 203 national unions and employee associations, Chaison found that over half of the 49 responding organizations included retirees in their membership statistics.[128] These retirees represented 7.9 percent of the total membership reported by the 49 respondents. Similarly, unemployed persons were included by nearly a third of the respondents and represented 6.1 percent of total membership.

Troy-Sheflin (T-S)

These membership data are derived primarily from the financial records of unions and employee associations. For organizations that do not report financial information (including unions of state, county, and municipal public employees), Troy and Sheflin use "a variety of sources . . . including the organizations' own published membership figures."[129] To the extent that financial records are used, the T-S data do not suffer from the BLS's weakness of reporting nondues-paying persons as members. The T-S data set also appears to be much more inclusive than the BLS, including information on independent municipal and local organization membership.

The most troubling aspect of the T-S data is their treatment of organizations that have both public and private membership. Troy and Sheflin allocate membership in these "mixed" organizations between the public and the private sectors on the basis of a 1978 BLS survey in which each "mixed" organization reported the proportion of its membership that consisted of public employees. To determine the size of

---

[127] U.S. Department of Labor, Bureau of Labor Statistics, *Directory of National and International Labor Unions in the United States*, Bull. Nos. 1185, 1395, 1493 (Washington: U.S. Government Printing Office, 1955, 1964, 1966).

[128] Gary N. Chaison, *A Note on the Limitations of Union Membership Data*, 23 Indus. Rel. 113 (Winter 1984).

[129] *Supra* note 5.

public-sector membership for each "mixed" organization for the period 1962–1983, T-S applied this 1978 proportion to the organization's total dues-paying membership for each year. For example, if the organization reported in 1978 that 25 percent of its membership were government employees and if T-S estimated the organization's average annual dues-paying membership to be 100,000 in 1984, then T-S would estimate the organization's 1984 public-sector membership at 25,000.

This method assumes that the proportion of each organization's membership that consisted of public-sector employees did not substantially change from 1962 to 1983. Given the decline of private-sector density and the concomitant public-sector density increase, this assumption is questionable. The proportion of public-sector membership in these organizations probably increased throughout this period. This means that the T-S data underestimate public-sector membership from 1979 to 1983 and overestimate it from 1962 to 1977.

A comparison of the T-S private and public membership data with analogous figures from the CPS supports this hypothesis. In Table 1, the 1980 T-S private density is only one-half of a percentage point greater than the 1980 CPS density, while in 1984 the T-S private density is 1.1 percentage points higher than the CPS estimate. On the other hand, the T-S public-sector densities are consistently lower than the CPS densities, the difference increasing from 0.7 percentage points in 1980 to 2.8 percentage points in 1984.

Current Population Survey (CPS)

The CPS data are obtained by an annual survey of over 100,000 households conducted by the Bureau of the Census. Respondents provide information on the labor force status of each member of their household. Although information concerning membership in labor organizations was first solicited in 1973, published membership data that distinguish between private- and public-sector employees were not available until 1980. These data have three principal weaknesses: (1) as noted in the text, the CPS definition of a labor organization has not been consistent from 1973 to 1986,[130] (2) respondents may not be aware of the union status of each household member, and (3) the CPS data exclude self-employed persons. Of these three problems only the second should result in a lack of comparability between the CPS and the T-S public-sector data for the 1980–1984 period; no other definitional changes occurred during this time and few public employees are self-employed.

---

[130] *Supra* note 6.

Bureau of the Census-Bureau of Labor Statistics (BCDL)

Data from this source come from the 1972, 1977, and 1982 Census of Governments as well as an annual sample survey of governments conducted every year between these censuses except for 1973 and 1981. Information was provided by city and state officials who responded to a mail questionnaire. Membership data for every year (except 1982) pertain only to full-time employees (who are more likely to be organized than part-time employees), which accounts for the consistently higher density of the BCDL data compared to the T-S, BLS, and CPS data, as noted in the text.

CHAPTER 2

Unionism in the Public Sector

JAMES L. STERN*

The dramatic increase in public-sector union membership associated with the spread of collective bargaining from the private to the public sector has been cited frequently as one of the most significant developments on the labor front in the past 25 years.[1] In this chapter, the characteristics of the major public-sector unions are examined.

At the outset it should be noted that with the exception of the federal sector, public-sector union decision making is decentralized. Bargaining leaders are usually representatives of municipal or state councils rather than national union representatives. This is contrary to the pattern found in the bargaining of major manufacturing units, for example, and gives rise to a situation in which the role of the national union president of the public-sector union is relatively less important than that of his private-sector counterpart. Analysis of unions that are active at the municipal and state levels is complicated, therefore, by this decentralized decision-making structure and the various patterns of public-sector unionism that have emerged in many cities and states.

Just the fact that labor relations legislation may be unique to one group of employees provides sufficient grounds for differences in the way the union conducts itself in a particular locality. Clearly, in jurisdictions where unions have not secured legal bargaining rights, their priorities will differ somewhat from union activities emphasized in localities where this goal has been achieved. And the union structure, even its finances, and the role of the union leader will be affected.

Another problem complicating the analysis of public-sector unions is the entrance into this field of what Jack Stieber identified as the "mixed unions"[2]—those primarily private-sector unions which are now organizing public-sector employees. Several of the latter unions, such as the Teamsters, the Laborers, and the Service Employees

---

*University of Wisconsin.
[1] A review of the Proceedings of the Industrial Relations Research Association shows that many sessions have been devoted to various aspects of public-sector bargaining.
[2] Jack Stieber, Public Employee Unionism (Washington: The Brookings Institution, 1973), 19–20.

52

(SEIU), have become important public-sector unions in some localities but represent no public-sector employees in others. The reader is warned, therefore, that generalizations about public-sector unions are advanced with more than the usual reservations about exceptions to general practices.

The format adopted in this chapter is to examine unions by level of government and governmental structure and function. In the first of the subsequent sections, the postal unions are discussed. This is followed by examinations of the unions covered by the Civil Service Reform Act;[3] then the unions active in the education field, including higher education; and finally the unions at the local and state levels. The term *union* is used throughout this chapter to mean employee organization and includes groups which are popularly identified as associations (California State Employees Association), professional societies (American Association of University Professors), and fraternal orders (Fraternal Order of Police). The concluding section of the chapter is addressed to membership trends of public-sector unions and speculation about their future.

Table 1 shows the estimated public-sector membership of major unions representing public employees. As can be seen by inspection of the table notes, some of these estimates are informed guesses. For the sake of consistency, the basic data are the 1983 figures assembled by Troy and Sheflin from the Labor Management Reporting and Disclosure Act financial reports.[4] In subsequent sections of this chapter dealing with specific unions, more up-to-date figures compiled by Gifford[5] and Freeman[6] are used.

The Postal Unions

The major postal unions—the National Association of Letter Carriers (NALC) and the American Postal Workers Union (APWU)—date back to the turn of the century and are among the older American trade unions. The APWU is a 1971 amalgamation of the postal clerks union, three smaller craft unions, and one breakaway industrial union of clerks and carriers. The structure, policies, and problems of these and several smaller unions of postal employees are easier to explain and understand if one first examines the institutional framework within which they pursued their goals. Also, the examination of the institu-

---

[3] Title VII, Civil Service Reform Act, 92 Stat. 1191–1216 (1978).
[4] Leo Troy and Neil Sheflin, U.S. Union Sourcebook: Membership, Finances, Structure, Directory, 1st ed. (West Orange, N.J.: Industrial Relations Data and Information Services, 1985).
[5] Courtney D. Gifford, Directory of U.S. Labor Organizations, 1986–87 Ed. (Washington: BNA Books, 1986).
[6] Richard B. Freeman, *Unionism Comes to the Public Sector*, 24 J. Econ. Lit. 41, 46 (March 1986).

TABLE 1

Public-Sector Union Membership, 1983

Teachers[a]	
Education Association; National (Ind.)	1,444,000
Teachers; American Federation of (AFL-CIO)	457,000
University Professors; American Association of (Ind.)	58,000
State and Local Government	
State, County & Municipal Employees; American Federation of (AFL-CIO)	955,000
Service Employees' International Union (AFL-CIO) (1985)	560,000[c]
Governmental Employees; Assembly of (Ind.)	340,000
Fire Fighters; International Association of (AFL-CIO)	157,000
Police; Fraternal Order of (Ind.)	150,000
Teamsters, Chauffeurs, Warehousemen & Helpers of America; International Brotherhood of (Ind.) (1985)	150,000[c]
Laborers' International Union of North America (AFL-CIO) (1985)	85,000[c]
Communications Workers of America (AFL-CIO) (1987)	85,000[d]
Nurses' Association; American (Ind.) (1987)	25,000[e]
Automobile, Aerospace & Agricultural Implement Workers of America; International Union, United (AFL-CIO) (1987)	25,000[d]
Postal Service	
Postal Workers Union; American (AFL-CIO)	226,000
Letter Carriers; National Association of (AFL-CIO)	203,000
Letter Carriers' Association; National Rural (Ind.)	40,000
Post Office Mail Handlers (Laborers' International Union of North America, AFL-CIO)	40,000
Federal Government[b]	
Government Employees; American Federation of (AFL-CIO)	218,000
Treasury Employees Union; National (Ind.)	47,000
Federal Employees; National Federation of (Ind.)	34,000
Metal Trades Council (AFL-CIO) (1985)	24,000[f]
Government Employees; National Association of (Service Employees' International Union, AFL-CIO) (1985)	23,000[f]
Machinists & Aerospace Workers; International Association of (AFL-CIO) (1985)	12,000[f]

Source: Leo Troy and Neil Sheflin, U.S. Union Sourcebook: Membership, Finances, Structure, Directory, 1st ed. (West Orange, N.J.: Industrial Relations Data and Information Services, 1985), 6-1-6-39, unless otherwise noted.

Note: The table was prepared by Mark Nakamura.

[a]Includes support personnel in schools and faculty and support personnel in higher education.

[b]Includes employees covered by the Civil Service Reform Act. Independent agencies such as the Tennessee Valley Authority are not included.

[c]From Richard B. Freeman, Unionism Comes to the Public Sector, 24 J. Econ. Lit. 41, 46 (March 1986); based on discussions with union officials.

[d]Based on discussions with union officials.

[e]Calculated from data in U.S. Bureau of the Census, 1980 Census of Population: Vol. 1, Characteristics of the Population; Ch. D, Detailed Population Characteristics; Part 1, United States Summary, PC80-1-D1-A (Washington: U.S. Government Printing Office, 1984); U.S. Bureau of the Census, 1982 Census of Governments: Vol. 3, Government Employment; No. 3, Labor-Management Relations in State and Local Government, GC82(3)-3 (Washington: U.S. Government Printing Office, 1985); and discussions with ANA officials. A small but indeterminate number of ANA members are represented by other organizations for collective bargaining purposes.

[f]Based on discussions with the U.S. Office of Personnel Management.

tional framework provides essential background information for understanding the subsequent review of activities of federal-sector unions outside the Postal Service.

The Legal Framework for Lobbying and Bargaining

Postal unions are among the most experienced and effective congressional lobbyists. President Theodore Roosevelt attempted to restrict their lobbying efforts by announcing his 1906 "gag" rule forbidding such efforts. It was to no avail, however, as the postal unions obtained passage of the 1912 Lloyd-La Follette bill protecting the rights of federal employees to petition Congress for improvements in their wages and working conditions. It is interesting to note that the 1912 act was the only congressional legislation protecting the right of nonpostal federal employees to engage in efforts to improve their wages and working conditions until the passage of the Civil Service Reform Act of 1978.

From 1912 to 1961, postal unions, aided in later years by unions representing federal employees in other government departments, lobbied individual congressmen, pressed for favorable appropriations, and supported relevant legislation. Their power under both Democratic and Republican administrations was considerable. For example, one of the few Eisenhower vetoes which was overridden was a postal bill—an action which is generally attributed to the lobbying skill and power of the postal unions.

Despite their success through lobbying, postal union leaders mounted campaigns to replace what they characterized as "collective begging" with collective bargaining. During the 1960 presidential campaign, they were successful in extracting a pledge from John Kennedy that, if elected, he would support bargaining by postal and other federal employees. Lack of congressional support for fulfillment of this commitment led Kennedy to issue Executive Order 10988 in January 1962, establishing a labor-management relations program for federal executive-branch employees.

The initial executive order provided for only a limited scope of bargaining and did not create a central administrative agency, thereby leaving the final determination of such sensitive questions as unit determination and unfair labor practices to each cabinet-level department head. As a first step, however, Executive Order 10988 was regarded by postal unions and other federal employee unions as their "magna carta."

By the end of the decade, dissatisfaction with the framework for bargaining led to the issuance of Executive Order 11491.[7] The new

---

[7] Executive Order 11491 was issued in October 1969. It has been clarified and revised slightly

order did not broaden the scope of bargaining, but it did establish a centralized administrative structure. Although the political clout of the postal unions was primarily responsible for the creation of the revised bargaining system, and although the new system was seen as a substantial improvement by nonpostal federal unions, it was a case of too little, too late, so far as postal unions were concerned. Led by the industrial union which represented postal workers in New York City, but which had not gained exclusive recognition at the national level under the bargaining structure created under Executive Orders 10988 and 11491, postal employees struck successfully for improved economic benefits and a new bargaining structure similar to that in the private sector.

The 1970 Postal Reorganization Act established the Postal Corporation and placed its labor relations activities under the private-sector Labor Management Relations Act. For purposes of representation, unfair labor practices, and other such matters, postal unions, as private-sector unions, could turn to the National Labor Relations Board (NLRB). Scope of bargaining was broadened greatly to include the wages, hours, and the conditions-of-employment concept found in the private sector with specific exemptions for pensions, which were still set by Congress, and for some personnel actions maintained within the Civil Service jurisdiction. Also, compulsory union membership was prohibited and, in place of the right to strike, unions were given the right to take "interest" disputes to arbitration.

Postal Unions and the Old and New Bargaining Structures

Under Executive Order 10988, national agreements had been negotiated by the Post Office Department with the seven craft unions holding national exclusive representation rights. These unions were (1) the National Association of Letter Carriers (NALC), the AFL-CIO union representing most city letter carriers; (2) the National Association of Post Office and General Services Maintenance Employees, a union of maintenance employees which at that time was an independent union; (3) the National Association of Special Delivery Messengers, AFL-CIO; (4) the National Federation of Post Office Motor Vehicle Employees, AFL-CIO; (5) the National Rural Letter Carriers' Association, a union which was then and is still (in 1987) an independent union; (6) the United Federation of Postal Clerks, AFL-CIO; and (7) the National Association of Post Office Mail Handlers, Watchmen,

---

by subsequent amendments that are not relevant to this discussion of federal-employee unions. For example, employees of TVA and the State Department have been excluded from the scope of 11491 as amended. Since space limitations preclude discussions of these unions, there is no need to explore the frameworks governing their labor relations activities.

Messengers and Group Leaders, AFL-CIO, a craft union which has become the Mail Handlers Division of the Laborers' International Union, AFL-CIO. The two large unions represented the letter carriers and the postal clerks, while the other five unions represented the five smaller occupational groups.

Two important postal unions had not gained exclusive national bargaining rights under Executive Order 10988, although they had formal recognition at the national level (in effect, consultation rights at that level) and exclusive bargaining rights in many localities. One of these unions was the National Postal Union (NPU), an industrial union with exclusive bargaining rights in New York City, Philadelphia, and St. Paul and a membership of over 80,000 in 1970, making it the third largest postal union. It was composed primarily of workers who had broken away from the major AFL-CIO postal clerks union in 1958. The other outside union in much the same position was the National Alliance of Postal and Federal Employees, a union claiming to have about 45,000 members, most of whom were black. The Alliance was the fourth largest postal union, holding exclusive bargaining rights in Washington, D.C., and other cities in the South and formal recognition at the national level.

When Congress passed the 1970 Postal Reorganization Act and restructured the labor relations framework, it gave the NLRB the authority to do away with the concept of minority-union representation, formal recognition, and dual recognition at two levels, i.e., recognition of one union at one level and of a different union at another level. This situation stimulated the amalgamation of the three small craft unions with the United Federation of Postal Clerks and the breakaway NPU group; in 1971, these unions joined together to form the American Postal Workers Union (APWU), the largest postal union.

The Alliance of Postal and Federal Employees lost its local exclusive bargaining rights under the new bargaining structure and its membership declined. It continues to exist primarily as a civil rights, labor, and fraternal organization for black postal workers and was reported to have about 20,000 members in 1985.[8] The Alliance does not have bargaining rights for any postal employees and has been unable to challenge incumbent unions because of its failure to gain the necessary showing of interest to force a representation election. It maintains a health plan with about 100,000 participants and claims that its members and other postal employees can obtain greater satisfaction by filing unfair labor practice charges with the NLRB, by filing com-

---

[8] Gifford, *supra* note 5, at 53.

plaints with the Equal Employment Opportunity Commission, or by
making use of veterans' complaint procedures than they can by using
the postal grievance procedure.

Both the APWU and NALC are AFL-CIO unions with memberships of approximately one-quarter million.[9] Since they are the
major unions representing postal employees, each is discussed separately below. The only non-AFL-CIO union holding national exclusive
bargaining rights in 1986 for a significant number of employees is the
National Rural Letter Carriers' Association (NRLCA), with about
40,000 members. Although it cooperates with the AFL-CIO in
national negotiations about basic economic matters, it negotiates its
own national craft agreement. The Mail Handlers Division of the
Laborers Union also negotiates its own national agreement. The major
and key bargaining process, however, is the joint negotiations of the
APWU and NALC with the Postal Service.

The major concerns of postal unions today are similar to those of
private-sector unions, but in addition these unions are faced with some
problems unique to their industry as well as some that are faced by
other unions representing federal employees. An example of a unique
situation is the impasse-resolution procedure mandated under the
Postal Reorganization Act. It calls for fact-finding and substitutes
interest arbitration for the right to strike. An example of a concern
shared by postal and other unions of federal employees is the attempt
to interpret the Hatch Act liberally to permit greater freedom of
political action by both postal and other federal employees. The Merit
Systems Protection Board found the presidents of the two major postal
unions and the largest federal nonpostal employees union guilty of
violating the Hatch Act and gave them 60-day suspensions. This was a
symbolic penalty because these three leaders are long-term union
officials in leave-without-pay status.[10]

Attempts to improve the grievance arbitration process and to cope
with Employee Involvement and Quality of Work Life programs (EI/
QWL) while resisting management attempts to create a dual wage
structure are illustrative of postal union efforts to resolve problems
similar to those faced in the private sector. For example, the APWU
and NALC have had more than a decade's experience with an expedited arbitration program and in 1985 initiated a new experimental
progressive discipline program under which warning letters are

---

[9] The APWU and NALC reported memberships of 255,000 and 275,000, respectively, in the
BNA survey (Gifford, *supra* note 5), but made average per capita payments to the AFL-CIO from
1983 to 1985 for 232,000 and 182,000 members, respectively. Troy and Sheflin (*supra* note 4)
report membership figures of 226,000 and 203,000 for these two unions in 1983.

[10] 32 Daily Lab. Rep. A-5 (February 19, 1987).

issued, rather than 7-, 10-, and 14-day suspensions.[11] The NLRB is considering the APWU claim that the unilateral establishment of the EI/QWL program is an unfair labor practice.[12] The arbitration award resolving the 1984 impasse over a new agreement denied the Postal Service request for a dual wage structure but did agree to lower starting salaries for new employees.[13]

Another familiar problem facing postal unions is that of maintaining their respective jurisdictions in the face of little of no employment growth because of the introduction of new technology and competition from private mail and package-delivery services. These developments underlie the continuing reports of attempted raids and mergers of the various unions. Urbanization of the countryside brings the NALC-represented city carriers into competition with the rural carriers represented by the independent NRLCA. Technological changes blur the boundaries between the jobs performed by the bulk mail handlers represented by the Mail Handlers Division of the Laborers Union and some of the postal clerks represented by the APWU.

Although the two larger unions, the APWU and NALC, have indicated their desire to absorb the two smaller unions, their efforts have not as yet proceeded to the point of an NLRB election. The Postal Service apparently would prefer to bargain with one big union and in 1981 petitioned the NLRB for a 600,000-person unit consisting of the employees represented by the four unions.[14] However, the NLRB rejected this possibility. The dispute between the APWU and the Mail Handlers was the subject of awards in 1980 and 1983 under the AFL-CIO Internal Disputes Plan.[15] The 1983 award held that the APWU convention resolution stating the long-term objective of absorbing the mail handlers' jobs was not deemed to be a violation of the Internal Disputes Plan. The Internal Disputes Plan does not prohibit the NALC, an AFL-CIO union, from raiding the independent NRLCA, but the announced drive of the NALC in the early 1980s fell short of gathering the 30 percent showing of interest, according to the NRLCA.[16]

In 1979, the APWU and NALC created committees to explore the possibility of merging their organizations.[17] The effort did not succeed, but the two unions signed a formal agreement in 1981 providing that

[11] The expedited arbitration program is described in 17 Coll. Bargaining Neg. & Cont. 37 (1983). The experimental program is described in the APWU monthly publication, 15 Am. Postal Worker 5 (November 1985).
[12] Am. Postal Worker, *supra*, at 6.
[13] 249 Daily Lab. Rep. D1–D14 (December 27, 1984).
[14] 917 GERR 59 (June 15, 1981).
[15] 854 GERR 6 (March 24, 1980) and 21 GERR 1951 (October 3, 1983).
[16] 917 GERR 15 (June 15, 1981).
[17] 839 GERR 5 (December 3, 1979).

the two unions would bargain jointly with the U.S. Postal Service.[18] They have continued to do so and acted jointly in the arbitration proceedings resolving the 1984 national contract dispute.[19] The likelihood of conflict between the NRLCA and the three AFL-CIO unions has been reduced by the portion of the 1984 arbitration award which set the NLRCA contract termination date six months behind that of the other three unions.[20] Conflict with the Mail Handlers did arise in 1987, however, when that union settled independently before the major unions.

These developments reflect the continuing pressure to consolidate negotiations further and to integrate activities of the various unions, and this pressure increases internal political friction within each union. Some notion of the political stability and problems of postal unions can be gleaned from a brief review of APWU and NALC leadership changes and internal political developments.

The APWU in 1978

When the United Federation of Postal Clerks, the National Postal Union, and the three smaller craft unions amalgamated in 1971 to form the American Postal Workers Union, each union preserved its craft rights by perpetuating the two-tier bargaining system and maintained its bureaucratic structure by keeping the union positions that existed prior to the amalgamation. Although it was generally recognized that such a condition was necessary at the outset to achieve agreement on the amalgamation, it had been assumed that a smaller and more efficient top-leadership structure could be created as incumbents retired and the new union acquired a sense of identity.

Six years after merger, however, the structure was even more top heavy than it had been originally. The president of the APWU from its formation in 1971 until his death in 1977, Francis S. Filbey (who had been president of the United Federation of Postal Clerks prior to the merger), described the 54-member governing body of the union in 1977 as unwieldy and overloaded, and said,

> [while it] was understandable, as the price of bringing five unions together in 1971, that you would need to retain a cast of characters bigger . . . than you would find in *War and Peace*, . . . it went without saying that such topheavy totals were a temporary aberration. Everyone supposed that the profile would be slimmed down by attrition. . . . [A]t least 20 national office holders have retired or died since merger [but] not a single office has been abolished. So much for attrition.[21]

---

[18] 898 GERR 13 (February 2, 1981).
[19] 22 GERR 2078 (November 5, 1984) and 22 GERR 2180 (November 26, 1984).
[20] 5 Daily Lab. Rep. A-11 (January 8, 1985).
[21] 691 GERR 5 (January 17, 1977).

These remarks were made about six months after the 1976 APWU convention delegates had refused to increase the per capita tax until five elected regional coordinators were added to the 49-member national executive board, which had been created at the time of the merger. Although Filbey argued that regional coordinators should be appointed by and should be responsible to nationally elected officers, his views did not prevail. Perhaps direct election is popular because it gives the rank-and-file leader a greater say in the running of the union, or because it creates positions to which secondary union leaders can aspire.

Upon Filbey's death, the national executive board selected Emmet Andrews, its director of industrial relations, to complete the unexpired term of office. Andrews was reelected in 1978 by more than 10,000 votes; however, the results of this election were protested in over a dozen offices and were subsequently reviewed by the U.S. Department of Labor and a U.S. district court.[22] Moe Biller, the president of the large New York City APWU local, who had led a demonstration against the 1978 contract that Andrews had negotiated, ran against Andrews and two other contenders for the APWU presidency in 1980. Biller won this election with approximately 45,000 votes. Andrews and the two other candidates, Ted Valliere and David Johnson, who were also national officers of the APWU, received approximately 26,000, 22,000, and 15,000 votes, respectively. Biller probably would not have won if the incumbents had not opposed each other.[23] He was joined in office by other members of his slate who were primarily leaders of large local unions.[24]

Along with the election of a new set of top leaders in 1980, the APWU also made some progress in streamlining its bureaucracy and making the union more efficient. It reduced its national executive board from 52 to 14 members and increased the terms of its top officers from two to three years. Biller and most members of his slate were successful in the 1983 and 1986 elections and have continued the task outlined by Filbey of restructuring the union.

Contrary to Filbey's plan of reducing the number of elected officials and increasing the number of appointed representatives, the Biller-led union has done away with part-time and full-time appointments and now elects all national officials—89 of them as of the 1986 elections. Most of them are national business agents handling contract administration problems.[25] The craft structure that Filbey hoped to integrate into a more homogeneous union has been preserved. How-

[22] 814 GERR 9 (June 11, 1979) and 825 GERR 9 (August 27, 1979).
[23] 883 GERR 10 (October 13, 1980).
[24] 875 GERR 8 (August 18, 1980).
[25] 16 APWU News Serv., No. 23 (October 28, 1986).

ever, it seems to be operating satisfactorily, much like a multicraft council. Each of the craft groups has a representative on the 14-person executive board while at the same time the power of the board and the president between conventions has been increased, thereby increasing the efficiency of the union.

Although incumbent officials seem relatively secure and no widespread opposition has surfaced, less than half of the 250,000 APWU members bother to vote in the national referendums and the winners, with about 50,000 votes, usually have only about 10,000 more votes than the one or more candidates running against them. Probably, the nonvoters are content with matters as they stand at present but conceivably could be mobilized against the incumbents if there is as much dissatisfaction about the 1987 agreement as there was about the 1978 agreement.[26]

The membership of the APWU is now nearly 50 percent female and, although there is no woman on the executive board, there are four female national business agents. One woman ran for the third top office, secretary-treasurer, in 1986 and was defeated by the male incumbent by only 7,000 votes. The APWU women's group, called POWER (Post Office Women for Equal Rights), is established under the APWU constitution and encourages women to be active in the union.

A growing number of Hispanics have been hired by the U.S. Postal Service and are expected to gain greater representation in the APWU structure in the future. In 1986, a Hispanic candidate from Texas for the national office of organization director defeated a long-term incumbent from New York, and a New York Hispanic was elected to the post of Northeast Regional Coordinator in a four-way contest.[27] As of 1986, there were no Hispanics or women on the executive board, but five of the 14 board members, including the executive vice president, were black. In broad terms, APWU political developments seem to parallel those that are observed on the national scene, i.e., increased influence of minority groups and women, particularly in geographic areas where population is expanding faster than the average.

The Letter Carriers

The National Association of Letter Carriers (NALC) is similar in many respects to the old clerks' union which now forms the core of the APWU. Leadership in the NALC flowed from Edward Gainor (1915–1941), to William Doherty (1941–1962), to Jerome Keating (1962–1968), to James Rademacher (1968–1976), and to J. Joseph

---

[26] *Id.*
[27] *Id.*

Vacca (1977–1978). The usual road to the presidency was from local-union office to national office and eventually to the top spot. Until the 1976 election of Vacca, most elections had not been close, and an heir-apparent assumed office without strong opposition. The 1976 election illustrated, however, the increasing importance of collective bargaining and the spread of a militant caucus from a New York-based group to one with support across the country.

Vincent Sombrotto, president of the large New York City local, had run against Rademacher in 1974 but had been defeated by a large margin. In 1976, however, Sombrotto, running against Vacca, the executive vice president of the NALC and candidate of the outgoing administration, was defeated by only about 5,000 votes out of approximately 120,000 votes cast by 55 percent of the members in a national referendum.[28] The Vacca slate took most of the 27 offices by margins in excess of the margin at the top of the slate, although the Sombrotto slate won two national offices and three national business-agent positions. Sombrotto's campaign relied in part on membership dissatisfaction with the results of the 1975 negotiations and his claim that Vacca had not pressed strongly for improvements.

Dissatisfaction with the 1978 national agreement led both APWU and NALC members to refuse to ratify it,[29] and it was criticized publicly by George Meany, then head of the AFL-CIO. Sombrotto focused on this dissatisfaction and opposed the agreement in his campaign to defeat Vacca in the union's 1978 election (as did Moe Biller in his campaign against Emmet Andrews in the APWU election).[30] Subsequently the agreement was modified through an arbitration process and was ratified by the memberships of both unions.[31] Sombrotto did not run a slate in 1978 as he had in 1976; rather, he concentrated on his attempt to replace Vacca as president while permitting most of the other national officers to run unopposed. His strategy was successful; he defeated Vacca resoundingly, receiving approximately 75,000 votes compared to Vacca's 43,000.[32]

Sombrotto solidified his hold on the presidency in the 1980 elections, winning with over 80 percent of the vote along with other members of his slate which now included most of the national officers who had supported Vacca in 1976.[33] In 1982, Sombrotto was reelected without opposition and, by a narrow margin, gained an increase in the per capita tax and the lengthening of the term of office of national

[28] 687 GERR A6–A7 (December 13, 1976).
[29] 774 GERR 8 (August 28, 1978).
[30] 772 GERR 3–6, 7 (August 14, 1978).
[31] 781 GERR 6 (October 16, 1978).
[32] Id.
[33] 884 GERR 5–6 (October 20, 1980).

officials from two to four years.[34] Since that time, there has been less internal dissension and the union has focused mainly on problems with the Postal Service and a national administration which it regarded as unfriendly.

Unlike the APWU, the NALC has not opposed employee-involvement programs and signed an agreement with the Postal Service in March 1982 to introduce these programs on a trial basis. At a conference in August 1983, representatives of management and union gave favorable reports on the progress of the program.[35] The NALC, a single craft union, is more homogeneous than the multicrafted APWU and appears to have the greater sense of solidarity needed to participate in the "trust me" style of labor relations that is a feature of the program. Also, minority groups seem content with the current union leaders and, although the percent of female letter carriers doubled between 1974 and 1982, only about 10 percent of the letter carriers are women.[36]

The Federal Executive-Branch Unions

Without the postal unions, it is doubtful whether Presidents Kennedy and Nixon would have issued the famous executive orders creating and revising a labor-management framework for federal executive-branch employees. The slowness of the unions in this sector to take advantage of their opportunities after the first executive order was issued reflects primarily the poor position from which these unions started. In 1962, unions of federal employees—with the exceptions of the long-established International Association of Machinists (IAM) and AFL-CIO Metal Trades Council (MTC) units in shipyards and other industrial-type establishments—were underfinanced, understaffed, and relatively inactive. For the most part they were loosely affiliated locals in various federal agencies which supported a small national office in Washington to pursue their goals through the traditional political paths.

The major unions in the federal service and their approximate estimated membership as of 1983 are: American Federation of Government Employees (AFGE), AFL-CIO, 218,000 members; National Federation of Federal Employees (NFFE), independent, 34,000 members; and National Treasury Employees Union (NTEU), independent, 47,000 members.[37] Each of the unions is discussed separately in this section of the chapter. Analysis of the annual report of the

---

[34] 977 GERR 11 (August 30, 1982).
[35] 21 GERR 1732–33 (August 29, 1983).
[36] 977 GERR 13 (August 30, 1982).
[37] Troy and Sheflin, *supra* note 4, at 6–7, 6–21, 6–31.

Civil Service Commission shows that these three unions represent approximately 75 percent of the federal employees covered by labor agreements. On the assumption that the ratio of the number of members to number of employees covered by agreements held by the three is a reasonable proxy for the relationship of membership to agreement-coverage among all federal unions, the 300,000 estimated membership of the three unions generates an estimate of 400,000 union members covered by the executive order.

This 400,000 estimate is somewhat higher than the Office of Personnel Management's estimate of 331,000 employees for whom union dues were being deducted.[38] It should be emphasized, as is explained subsequently, that membership statistics and representation data in the federal sector differ significantly from those found in the private sector. Unions in the federal sector have won elections entitling them to represent 1.24 million employees, about 60 percent of those covered by the Civil Service Reform Act.[39] The estimates suggest, however, that no more than one third of these employees are union members.

In addition to the three unions representing the largest number of federal employees, another 80 unions hold recognition rights, including the formerly independent National Association of Government Employees (NAGE) which is strong in New England and which in recent years has organized workers in local government and in private firms doing government business. In 1982, NAGE (which in 1985 represented about 67,000 employees) merged with the Service Employees International Union (SEIU), a union with which it had been competing in elections involving state and local government employees in New England. The merger put NAGE under the umbrella of the AFL-CIO "no raid" agreement and thereby reduced the efforts of AFGE to take over NAGE's federal employees as well as those of SEIU and American Federation of State, County and Municipal Employees to take over its local government employees.[40]

Two other AFL-CIO groups representing a substantial number of federal employees are the IAM and MTC, representing approximately 34,000 and 67,000 federal employees, respectively—primarily wage-board employees in shipyards and other industrial-type situations. Of the 373,000 wage-board employees, 88 percent were represented by unions in 1985, compared to 53 percent of the general-schedule employees. Organization of the general-schedule employees (white-

---

[38] Estimate calculated by the Office of Employee, Labor and Agency Relations of OPM. It believes that dues are checked off for between 25 and 30 percent of the employees represented.
[39] 71 GERR Reference File 211, Union Recognition in the Federal Government, 1985.
[40] 993 GERR 8 (December 27, 1982).

collar workers) followed the organization of the wage-board employees (blue-collar workers) and in recent years has plateaued at slightly over the 50 percent mark.

In addition to the employees covered by the Civil Service Reform Act (CSRA), there are several groups of federal employees which have organized under separate legislative arrangements. Employees of the Tennessee Valley Authority are well organized by a variety of unions. State Department employees are represented by an independent union.

The American Federation of Government Employees (AFGE), AFL-CIO

The American Federation of Government Employees was founded in 1932 by the AFL after the existing union, the National Federation of Federal Employees (NFFE), withdrew from the AFL because of jurisdictional disputes and policy differences with AFL unions representing blue-collar craft workers. AFGE is the major union representing federal employees and in 1985 represented about 690,000 of the 1.25 million employees in bargaining units. The union started with a membership of less than a thousand members in 34 locals, mainly located in the Washington, D.C., area.[41] By 1961, its membership (based on AFL-CIO average per capita payments) had increased to 68,000 and, in the following decade under the impetus of the executive order, experienced its most rapid growth to almost 290,000 members.[42] Since that date, although the number of employees it represents has continued to increase, its membership has declined significantly and was reported to be about 200,000 in 1983.[43]

The "free rider" problem of AFGE and other federal unions seems to be much greater than the problem faced by private-sector unions and unions of state and municipal employees. To some extent, of course, the federal prohibition on compulsory payment of union dues could be cited as the obvious cause of the problem. Employees may vote for union representation and then be unwilling to pay dues voluntarily. But this explanation is not sufficient to account for the variations in the gap between membership and representation among the different unions which operate under a legal framework prohibiting compulsory payment of dues or service fees. Membership in the postal unions is probably as close to the number of employees represented as is found in private-sector union-shop situations, despite the legal prohibition against compulsory union membership.

---

[41] Jack and Lorna Nevin, The Story of the American Federation of Government Employees (Washington: AFGE, 1976), 13.

[42] Per capita payments reported in Gifford, supra note 5, at App. A, 62.

[43] Id.

A second factor that may shed further light on this question is the relatively low number of employees who bother to vote in union representation elections. From 1971 to 1975, 57 percent of eligible voters participated in elections under the executive order as compared to 88 percent of the eligibles in NLRB private-sector elections and a similar figure for postal-system elections.[44] It seems quite possible that the membership figures of many federal unions reflect the number of employees who voted for the union in the representation election, and the gap between membership and representation consists of those employees who did not vote and those who voted against the union.

Although the elimination of the prohibition against agency shops may be a necessary step if membership figures are to approach representation figures, it should be kept in mind that the possibility of compulsory payment of union dues or a service fee may tend to bring out many voters who will vote against the union in order to avoid the possibility of being obliged to pay dues in the future. AFGE might find it more difficult to win representation elections in such a situation. In any event, this large gap between membership and representation figures is an unusual aspect of industrial relations in the federal sector.

Until the mid-1970s, AFGE's internal political struggles were relatively mild. John Griner was president of AFGE from 1962 until 1972, when he resigned because of poor health. His successor, Clyde Webber, who had been the executive vice president since 1966, died in 1976. The current president, Kenneth Blaylock, is much younger than his predecessors and, at the time of his election, was expected to lead AFGE into a more militant posture than it had traditionally maintained.

Blaylock, who was 41 years old when he became president in 1976, is from Alabama and rose through various offices to that of national vice president from the Southeast region of AFGE in 1972. Contrary to the geographical dispersion pattern of members in traditional private-sector unions, AFGE's five-state Southeast region contains more members than any other district—reflecting the concentration in the domain of powerful southern legislators of defense agency units employing large numbers of civilian workers. Although the changing of top leadership in 1976 brought to power individuals who had announced that the prevailing business-as-usual policies of AFGE would now be terminated, the changes made in the following decade have not been dramatic.

Blaylock gained the presidency in 1976 by a very narrow margin over Royal Sims, a long-time leader of the AFGE Veterans Administration Center in Philadelphia who had become the first black national

[44] Anthony F. Ingrassia, *Status Report on Federal Labor-Management Relations*, Civil Serv. J. 40 (July–September 1977).

vice president in 1968. In 1978 and 1980, he was reelected in close election contests, but in 1982, his presidency seemed more secure when he received almost 60 percent of the votes cast in the first ballot against three challengers and thereby avoided a runoff election. In 1984, Blaylock received 75 percent of the votes at a smooth-running convention, but in 1986, although he won on the first ballot, he received only about 52 percent of the 170,000 votes cast.[45]

Blaylock worked hard to gain passage of the Civil Service Reform Act in the late 1970s and supported Jimmy Carter for the presidency in 1980. Neither position was popular, however, and neither received the support of delegates to the 1978 convention. Also, the 1980 convention delegates did not endorse Carter's reelection and criticized aspects of the CSRA, and some of the delegates were unsympathetic with Blaylock's rhetoric favoring the conversion of AFGE to a more militant union on the private-sector-union model. Another factor, possibly the most important one splitting the union, is the ongoing fight between Blaylock and his supporters who favor greater centralization of power and the opponents led by the 15 elected national vice presidents. As bargaining units have been consolidated and national agency agreements negotiated, the workload has shifted from the local to the national scene. The vice presidents, however, have successfully opposed the efforts to reduce the number of regions and to restructure the union.

It is possible that restructuring will be approved at a future convention. The issue is a continuing one because of the cost of maintaining the full-time salaried vice presidents. If AFGE were a fast-growing organization, operating costs might not be crucial, but when membership is declining, as it has been in the past 15 years, the need to economize becomes paramount. Despite efforts to increase the membership, the union has only about two-thirds as many members as it had at its peak in the early 1970s.[46] Women and minority group members play an increasing role in AFGE and the first woman was elected to its 18-person national executive council in 1980.

The key question faced by AFGE is whether it can persuade the 400,000 nonmembers which it presently represents to join the union. Presumably, AFGE will pursue this goal politically in order to remove the prohibition against union-security provisions and also will intensify its organizational efforts. Neither of these goals is easily attainable in the short run. Federal employee unions seem to be enjoying less

[45] Election results are taken from 677 GERR A4–A8 (October 4, 1976); 722 GERR 8–9 (August 14, 1978); 878 GERR 6–8 (September 8, 1980); 977 GERR 7–8 (August 30, 1982); 22 GERR 1683 (September 3, 1984); and 24 GERR 1127 (August 18, 1986).
[46] Troy and Sheflin, *supra* note 4, and Gifford, *supra* note 5.

public support in 1987 than they did 20 years ago, and it is quite possible that during this decade neither Congress nor the nonmembers will respond favorably to AFGE efforts.

The National Federation of Federal Employees (NFFE), Independent

The National Federation of Federal Employees started out in 1917 as the AFL union of federal-government employees and has since gone through several significant changes in character. As noted previously, NFFE left the AFL in 1931 because of jurisdictional and policy differences with the craft unions; NFFE supported the adoption of the general-service schedule and a civil-service-type compensation plan, while the crafts adhered to the wage-board approach and the tying of individual craft rates to the prevailing private-sector union rate for that craft.[47] At the time of the withdrawal, NFFE reportedly had almost 50,000 members, but membership declined over the next 30 years as a result of AFGE inroads.

When Executive Order 10988 was issued in 1962, NFFE condemned it and brought an unsuccessful court suit challenging the constitutionality of the President's action. Only after a two-year losing battle accompanied by a further decline in membership did the union reverse its position. The reversal was brought about by the newly elected president, Nathan T. Wolkomir, who defeated the incumbent who had opposed the executive order.[48] Under Wolkomir's leadership, NFFE rebuilt its membership and increased the number of employees it represents from about 32,000 in 1967 to 150,000 in 1985. It should be kept in mind, however, that only about 34,000 of these employees pay dues to the organization. After 12 years in office, Wolkomir retired in 1976 and was succeeded by James M. Pierce, Jr., who had been the union's education and training director. Pierce was reelected by acclamation in 1986 to his sixth two-year term.[49]

In view of the fact that NFFE is a small independent union that represents employees scattered across the nation, one wonders about its continued viability as a separate organization. Furthermore, it has been able to persuade only 25 percent of the employees it represents to pay dues. However, it has held its own against other unions representing federal employees and proudly stated at its 1984 convention

---

[47] Murray B. Nesbitt, Labor Relations in the Federal Government Service (Washington: BNA Books, 1976).
[48] 54 GERR A-7 (September 21, 1964).
[49] 24 GERR 1245 (September 15, 1986).

that it was fiscally sound.[50] In an interview in 1985 its long-term president made it clear that his members had no desire to reaffiliate with the AFL-CIO.[51]

NFFE shares common problems with other unions representing federal employees regardless of whether they are AFL-CIO affiliates, but tends to join with the other nonaffiliated unions rather than AFGE in carrying out specific programs. For example, NFFE joined with NTEU and the Senior Executive Association (SEA) in establishing a new self-help charity to aid federal employees who lost their jobs because of reductions in force or furloughs.[52] In the long run, with its tradition of local autonomy, NFFE will face continuing pressures to join with other organizations in bargaining as bargaining units are consolidated and national agency agreements are negotiated. But, by 1986, these pressures had not yet reached the point at which NFFE was seriously considering merger with one of the other organizations representing federal employees.

The National Treasury Employees Union (NTEU), Independent

The National Treasury Employees Union is an unusual union. Originally organized by the professionals in the Internal Revenue Service, it has extended its occupational jurisdiction to cover clerical employees, and its agency jurisdiction to cover all of the Treasury Department and also employees of other agencies.

The predecessor organization to NTEU, the National Association of Collectors of Internal Revenue, was formed in 1938 by field employees in that agency who were seeking civil service status.[53] In the 1950s, as the Internal Revenue Service was restructured, the organization expanded its jurisdiction to cover all IRS employees and changed its name to the National Association of Internal Revenue Employees (NAIRE). The organization changed its name again in 1973 to NTEU, in recognition of its further expansion within the Treasury Department. As of 1985 NTEU represented slightly more than 100,000 employees, of whom about 50 percent are dues-paying members.

Vincent Connery, the president of NTEU from 1966 to 1983, was a strong leader who formulated and developed the program carried on by his successor, Robert Tobias. Tobias, who had been the general counsel of the union, was elected to a four-year term as president in 1983 with Connery's blessing.[54] Connery believed in central control of the union and reliance on a paid professional staff to service local

---

[50] 22 GERR 1760 (September 17, 1984).
[51] 23 GERR 1020–22 (July 15, 1985).
[52] 24 GERR 1077 (August 11, 1986).
[53] The NTEU Story (Washington: National Treasury Employees Union, undated).
[54] 21 GERR 1642 (August 15, 1983).

unions, in contrast to the other federal unions that featured many elected officers, decentralized administration, and shared power. The union undertook important legal actions to preserve its rights and aggressive organizing efforts to gain representation rights outside the Treasury Department.[55] Also, the centralized NTEU benefited from the system of labor relations that permitted unions which won unit consolidation elections to negotiate with the government agency on a national level, thereby expanding the scope of bargaining beyond that available to individual units.

NTEU opposed the Civil Service Reform Act unsuccessfully and condemned the AFGE president for going along with President Carter. It favored legislation broadening the scope of bargaining to include salaries. Connery pointed out that salaries could be bargained at the agency level and disputes resolved by arbitration.[56] Although Tobias had some problems in 1983 in asserting the same degree of control that Connery had demonstrated, it appears that he has guided the union along the same path and shares the philosophy that Connery enunciated. Tobias also favors salary bargaining at the national departmental level with disputes subject to arbitration.[57] In 1983, NTEU signed an agreement with the Internal Revenue Service to establish quality circles. This was seen by Tobias as providing a means for greater employee input into areas formerly reserved to management.[58] At its convention in 1985, NTEU passed the dues increase sought by Tobias as well as resolutions endorsing union efforts to increase compensation.[59]

Federal unions have faced difficult times in the eighties and, as noted earlier, total federal union membership has declined significantly. However, NTEU has done better than the other unions in retaining the allegiance of general-schedule employees and has maintained its membership at the peak achieved in 1981.[60] Factors such as its relatively militant membership, centralized authority, aggressive leadership, and successful efforts to move bargaining from the local level to the agency-head level suggest that NTEU will continue to be an important federal union in the future.

Professional Air Traffic Controllers Organization (PATCO), AFL-CIO

It would be inappropriate to conclude this section about federal unions without reference to the demise of the Professional Air Traffic Controllers Organization (PATCO) in 1981. PATCO had represented a

---

[55] A GERR special report about Connery, written shortly before he resigned, provides the reader with an interesting story about his career and the history of the NTEU (21 GERR 1550 [July 25, 1983]).

[56] *Id.*

[57] 21 GERR 2027 (October 10, 1983).

[58] *Id.* at 2004.

[59] 23 GERR 1208 (August 26, 1985).

[60] Troy and Sheflin, *supra* note 4, at 6–31.

17,000-person national unit of air traffic controllers from 1972 until 1981 when it engaged in an illegal and unsuccessful strike. Most of the strikers ignored a presidential back-to-work order and were fired, and the organization was decertified.[61] Less than six years later, however, a replacement organization, the National Air Traffic Controllers Association (NATCA), an autonomous affiliate of the Marine Engineers Beneficial Association (MEBA), held its founding convention and subsequently won a new national unit of 12,800 employees.[62]

Just prior to the 1981 PATCO strike the administration had engaged in bargaining with the union about matters excluded from the scope of the Civil Service Reform Act. In effect, the government had bowed to pressure from PATCO to bargain about wages and hours. Although the administration had rejected the demand for a 32-hour week, it had agreed to pay overtime after 36 hours, thereby giving controllers 42-hours pay for 40-hours work. Also, it had agreed to give controllers a 6 percent wage increase in addition to the 4.8 percent increase proposed for all federal employees later that year.[63]

If this package had been ratified by PATCO and by congressional legislation, it would have represented the breakthrough that federal unions are still seeking in 1987. From the point of view of those who advocate broad-scope bargaining by federal employees on an agency basis, the decision of PATCO to reject the government offer and to engage in a losing strike was a significant setback. If there had not been a strike and Congress had ratified the administration's settlement with PATCO, a new bargaining procedure would have been established for at least one group of federal employees and might very well have spread to others.

The prospects of achieving this union goal in 1987 seem dim. However, a new Congress and new administration in 1988 may be more willing to consider broadening the scope of bargaining. Without such a broadening, or passage of mandatory agency-shop legislation, it is unlikely that federal unions will make great strides in organizing the remaining federal employees.

Unions in Education

The dramatic shift in image from the milquetoast-like teacher to the militant unionist which has accompanied the adoption of collective bargaining procedures by teachers at all levels of instruction is one of the well-publicized developments in public-sector labor relations. The three major unions in the field and their estimated membership in

---

[61] 24 GERR 5 (January 6, 1986).
[62] 24 GERR 1312 (September 29, 1986), 25 GERR 848 (June 15, 1987).
[63] 919 GERR 5 (June 29, 1981).

1985 are as follows: National Education Association (NEA), independent, membership about 1.7 million; American Federation of Teachers (AFT), AFL-CIO, membership about 610,000; and American Association of University Professors (AAUP), independent, membership about 55,000 active nonstudent members.[64]

In contrast to union experience in the federal sector, union and association membership in the education field exceeds the extent of collective-bargaining coverage. Some AAUP members belong to chapters that do not engage in collective bargaining. Many NEA members are in locals in southern states where there is no bargaining. And, because of the rivalry between the NEA and AFT, some teachers may be paying a service fee to one organization while maintaining membership in the other.

In education, as in other parts of local and state government, the national union usually is not involved in the collective bargaining process. The key decision-makers are either local union officers or officials of district councils, UniServ districts (discussed later in this chapter), or state councils. For this reason, national office-holders and national policy are less important in these organizations than in industrial unions in the private sector.

The National Education Association (NEA), Independent

The predecessor organization to the present-day National Education Association was founded in Philadelphia in 1875 by educational administrators and college professors. For most of its long existence, it has functioned as a professional organization promoting the cause of public education and the improvement of teaching. In the 25 years since 1962 when the NEA was defeated by the American Federation of Teachers (AFT) in the battle to represent New York City school teachers, the organization has undergone a sharp metamorphosis. Today in many sections of the country it is indistinguishable from the AFT insofar as its bargaining stance is concerned. In several respects, however, it still differs from the AFT.

First, as a matter of ideology the NEA has maintained that affiliation with the AFL-CIO is not desirable. Second, in states where bargaining is not well rooted, school administrators have been influential in the affairs of the organization. Third, in part because of membership losses to the AFT in major cities in the Northeastern, Middle Atlantic, and North Central states, more conservative positions on policies have been adopted than otherwise would be the case.

---

[64] Gifford, *supra* note 5, at 43, 56, 58.

The difference between the AFT and NEA in the late 1970s was illustrated by the eagerness with which the AFT sought bargaining rights for educational-support personnel and the reluctance of the NEA to do so. At the 1977 convention the NEA assembly defeated the recommendation to give support personnel full membership rights,[65] although it reversed its position two years later and agreed to full membership for support personnel by 1982.[66] Also, in the late 1970s, the delegation from Texas was the largest state group at the conventions and in 1977 helped to defeat a constitutional amendment which would have disqualified supervisors and administrators from active membership.[67]

In the decade preceding 1987, there was a gradual increase in the role played by the three national officers—the president, vice president, and secretary-treasurer. The constitutional ban on reelection was amended to permit two two-year terms starting in 1974, and in 1977 the national officers were reelected for the first time.[68] After defeating subsequent attempts to further amend the constitution by permitting a third two-year term, the delegates agreed to this change in 1986. Mary Hatwood Futrell, a popular black female leader who had been a classroom teacher in Alexandria, Virginia, served as the secretary-treasurer for two two-year terms starting in 1980 and then as president for two more two-year terms. In 1987, she became the first person elected to a third term as president.[69]

The increased length of service of the top officers and the resignation in 1983 of the veteran executive director, Terry Herndon, suggest that the officers will play a relatively more active role compared to their predecessors. Herndon was succeeded by his assistant, Don Cameron, who, as executive director, is responsible for the day-to-day operations of the 550-person staff and $83 million budget.[70] Approximately 38 percent of the budget is spent on services for local affiliates, primarily the UniServ program described below.

In 1976, the NEA endorsed a candidate for the presidency of the United States for the first time. It supported Jimmy Carter in both 1976 and 1980 and Walter Mondale in 1984. The 1980 convention was considered the most politically oriented of its many conventions.[71] However, the Reagan victory and subsequent endorsement of tuition tax credits by his administration put the NEA on the defensive. The

---

[65] 716 GERR 15 (July 11, 1977).
[66] 819 GERR 15 (July 16, 1979).
[67] 716 GERR 17 (July 11, 1977).
[68] *Id.* at 15.
[69] 25 GERR 961 (July 13, 1987).
[70] 21 GERR 1444 (July 11, 1983).
[71] 870 GERR 13 (July 14, 1980).

organization concentrated its political efforts on its successful attempt to defeat the tuition tax credit plan and its less successful attempts to gain greater federal support for education.[72]

In the area of bargaining legislation, the NEA supported the idea of federal legislation that would "guarantee meaningful collective bargaining rights to the employees of public schools, colleges, and universities." The NEA-backed statute would "allow for the continued operation of state statutes that meet federally established minimum standards."[73]

Another development of the last decade worthy of note is the attempt by the NEA, along with the AAUP and AFT, to organize institutions of higher education, a development that is discussed subsequently in the section of this chapter about the AAUP.[74]

Key officials of the NEA are appointed rather than elected directly by the rank and file or convention delegates. At the national level, the key position is that of executive director. It is filled by someone hired by the nine-person executive committee that consists of the three full-time national officers and six board members at large—all of whom are elected at the representative assembly and who serve also on the board of directors, a group of about 125 people elected by the state affiliates.

Similarly, at the state level, state executive directors are appointed by state officers and boards of directors, who, in turn, have been elected by delegates to state conventions. National staff members and state staff members in states without bargaining laws are concerned with the usual broad range of activities, other than bargaining, carried on by most unions—political and legislative activity, organizing, legal actions, education, research, affirmative action, and special-projects and crisis-related functions. In states where bargaining has statutory protection and is widespread, the state office may help local unions and UniServ districts, particularly in strike situations.

The UniServ district is a structural unit of the organization created to administer bargaining activities. Typically, there is a local union for each school district and each local union has a contract which it has negotiated with the school board. But most districts, except the largest ones with a thousand or more teachers, cannot pay the salaries of full-time negotiators—nor is there a need for a full-time staff representative for each small unit. By persuading independent local unions in the same general geographic area to combine forces in maintaining a UniServ office and staff, the NEA has created the mechanism for providing staff help in contract negotiation and administration.

---

[72] 971 GERR 14 (July 19, 1982).
[73] Today's Education, A Special Issue, 5 NEA Today 68 (1986).
[74] 971 GERR 15 (July 19, 1982).

The NEA is attempting to provide one UniServ staff representative for each 1,200 teachers. The staff-representative subsidy provided by the national and state organizations is sufficient to induce
most small locals to join their UniServ district. Although the negotiators and state directors are appointed by elected officials of the
organization, the usual path to these key offices is through the elected
hierarchy.

The American Federation of Teachers (AFT), AFL-CIO

The American Federation of Teachers was formed in 1916 by
about two dozen teachers' groups across the country with a total
membership of approximately 3,000 members. The Chicago Federation of Teachers, which had existed since the turn of the century and
which had joined the AFL in 1913, was the key group in early AFT
activities. Its long-time leader, Carl Megel, was president of the AFT
from 1952 to 1964. In the 1960s when the New York City local of the
AFT, the United Federation of Teachers (UFT), gained bargaining
rights for New York City teachers after defeating the NEA affiliate in an
election, the balance of power shifted from Chicago to New York, and
Charles Cogen, past president of the New York group, was elected
AFT president. In 1974, Albert Shanker, who was then the president
of the UFT and an AFL-CIO vice president, became president of the
AFT. His decision to retain the presidency of the New York City local
until 1987 while serving as the national president reflects the fact that
the important bargaining decisions vitally affecting the life of the union
are made at the local level.

The 610,000-member AFT is primarily the union of teachers in
major cities and holds bargaining rights in New York, Chicago, Philadelphia, Detroit, Boston, Pittsburgh, Cleveland, Minneapolis, Den-
ver, and Baltimore. Leaders of these locals serve as unpaid national
officers and guide AFT activities between conventions. The only full-
time national officer paid by national funds is the secretary-treasurer
who directs the daily activities of the AFT. The president, Albert
Shanker, and the 34 vice presidents who comprise the AFT executive
board receive expenses but no salaries from the national organization.
As local officials, however, these national AFT officers receive salaries
from their locals and devote most of their time to local union activities.
The AFT structure, like the NEA structure, reflects the importance of
bargaining decisions made at the local level.

The AFT has approximately 2,200 local unions. The national office
supplies the same wide range of nonbargaining services to its units as
does the NEA. The national office also supplies the organizers and
conducts the campaigns to persuade teachers to join the AFT rather
than the NEA. In states where there are local unions, the AFT main-

tains a state organization that handles legislative matters, participates in organizational drives, and helps the locals handle bargaining problems. In some areas, locals have banded together to form area councils. Since AFT strength is in its big-city locals, however, the elected officials and staff of these locals provide the essential services to most AFT members.

At its 1977 convention, the AFT, like the NEA, faced the question of organizing groups other than teachers. But unlike the NEA, which declined to give paraprofessionals full rights at that time, the AFT passed a constitutional amendment permitting it to organize workers outside of schools and educational institutions. In the 10-year period since that decision was made, the AFT has organized a substantial number of employees in the health-care field and in state civil-service positions as well as paraprofessionals and school-related personnel (referred to as PSRP units) and faculty and PSRPs at community colleges and other institutions.[75]

At its 1986 convention, the AFT reported that it had increased its membership by nearly 154,000, to 624,000, in the past 10 years.[76] This increase of approximately 33 percent during a period when most unions were shrinking is quite unusual. Some of these new members were formerly members of independent groups, such as state civil-service associations, but many are new members in units that have gained bargaining rights during this period. Although there are periodic discussions of the desirability of an NEA/AFT merger,[77] the rivalry between the two organizations continues unabated. The AFT reported that between November 1984 and June 1986, the AFT was successful in fending off raids on units in Detroit, Baltimore, Washington, D.C., St. Louis, and Broward County, Florida, involving a total of almost 58,000 school employees.[78] The NEA and AFT also continue their competition to gain representation rights of higher education units throughout the country.

Although some of the dramatic percentage gains in membership reported by the AFT are in southern states where there are no laws mandating bargaining, a large number of new members are in states where bargaining is well established. One factor that may contribute to the expansion of membership is the passage of legislation in Illinois and Ohio. In particular, the existence of mechanisms for resolving contract disputes by third party determination of issues on which the parties are unable to reach agreement may encourage teachers in rural

---

[75] 24 GERR 960 (July 14, 1986).

[76] 71 Am. Teacher 6, 17 (September 1986).

[77] At its 1983 convention, for example, the AFT passed a resolution calling for merger talks and teacher unity because of the threat of tuition tax credits. 21 GERR 1466 (July 18, 1983).

[78] 71 Am. Teacher 16 (September 1986).

areas and small districts where they have not been strong enough to organize and bargain. Binding arbitration has had a similar effect among rural teachers in Wisconsin.

In 1982, the AFT went from annual to biennial conventions, effective in 1984.[79] Given the lack of rivalry for the presidency of the AFT and the fact that bargaining decisions are made locally, there was no strong opposition to this money-saving modification. It is possible that AFT leadership at the local level may change considerably in response to changes in the ethnic, racial, and sexual demographics of teachers in major cities. An indication of a possible trend is the 1984 election of Jacqueline Vaughn, a black woman and a long-time active union leader, as president of the Chicago Teachers Union, which is the largest AFL-CIO local union of the Chicago Federation of Labor.

In 1986, in keeping with the AFL-CIO drive to promote membership, the AFT launched its associate member program. This program is designed to attract retired teachers, teachers who have left the profession who may possibly return, and active teachers in areas where there is no AFT local. Dues are relatively low for associate members, and in return they receive the union publications and have access to the various group-insurance plans and discount programs.[80]

The American Association of University Professors (AAUP), Independent

From the 1960s to the present (1987), the AAUP has struggled with the question of identifying its role in higher education when collective bargaining comes to the campus. Essentially, it has been forced by the organizing efforts of the NEA and AFT to establish arrangements under which it could become the bargaining agent, singly or jointly with the NEA or AFT, while at the same time attempting to continue its traditional role in the areas of academic freedom, protection of individual rights, and promotion of higher education. The effort to reconcile its function "as a broad based professional association concerned with protecting academic freedom and tenure" with its role as the "collective bargaining agent for university faculty" seems to be a perennial question engendering debate at almost every annual conference.[81]

In 1966 the AAUP adopted a policy stating that it "should oppose the extension of the principle of exclusive representation to faculty members in institutions of higher education. . . ."[82] It reaffirmed its

---

[79] 970 GERR 17 (July 12, 1982).
[80] 71 Am. Teacher 4 (November 1986).
[81] 22 GERR 1318 (July 2, 1984).
[82] 52 AAUP Bull. 229 (Summer 1966).

support of faculty governance in 1969, but "recognize[d] the significant role which collective bargaining may play in bringing agreement between faculty and administration on economic and academic issues."[83] In 1972 the AAUP abandoned its opposition to exclusive representation and stated: "The AAUP will pursue collective bargaining, as a major additional way of realizing the Association's goals in higher education, and will allocate such resources and staff as are necessary for a vigorous selective development of this activity beyond present levels."[84] It is clear that the AAUP changed its policy because of the pressure from local chapters on campuses where NEA or AFT affiliates were likely to become sole representatives of the faculty if the AAUP did not attempt to become the bargaining agent.

At its annual meeting in 1984, the AAUP approved without debate a revision of its collective-bargaining policy that expresses a more positive endorsement of collective bargaining than did the 1972 statement.[85] The stronger endorsement of bargaining did not mean, however, that the conflict between the AAUP role as a professional association and as a bargaining agent had been resolved. What it did mean was that the two groups—the "traditionalists" and the leaders of the Collective Bargaining Congress of the AAUP—believed that neither group was strong enough to flourish separately and, therefore, that it was necessary to continue the search for the best structural arrangements for continuing both the traditional and the bargaining activities of the AAUP.[86]

This conflict within the AAUP was reflected in the changes in both the number and types of members. At the beginning of the 1970s, the AAUP had approximately 90,000 members, most of whom were individual members not covered by bargaining. By 1984, the membership had dropped to 52,000 active members, two-thirds of whom were in chapters engaged in collective bargaining.[87] The rise of collective bargaining also created financial problems for the organization by increasing the need of local chapters for funds to carry on bargaining and diminishing their willingness to contribute full dues to the national AAUP office to finance traditional activities.

AAUP leaders have been hard pressed to work out satisfactory financial and voting arrangements. In 1986, individual annual dues were $72. Special arrangements were devised for members in large

---

[83] 55 AAUP Bull. 490 (Winter 1969).
[84] 58 AAUP Bull. 46–61 (Spring 1972) contains a summary of the development of the positions on bargaining taken by the AAUP leadership and the reasons for and against the change.
[85] 22 GERR 1318 (July 2, 1984).
[86] 22 GERR 2307–2308 (December 17, 1984).
[87] Joseph W. Garbarino, Faculty Collective Bargaining, in Unions in Transition, ed. Seymour Martin Lipset (San Francisco: ICS Press, 1986), 278. This estimate may overstate the decline. The Chronicle of Higher Education states that AAUP peak membership was only 78,000 (32 Chron. Higher Educ. 19 [July 16, 1986]).

bargaining chapters such as the California Faculty Association (CFA) and the University of Hawaii Professional Assembly (UHPA). CFA members paid full dues, but two-thirds of the money was rebated to the CFA for its activities.[88] UHPA became an affiliated organization paying a fixed sum per member ($10.50 annually in 1986) and received full membership benefits but did not have voting rights except for the UHPA board members for whom full dues were paid.[89]

The competition for bargaining rights for faculty among the NEA, AFT, and AAUP led to the formation of coalitions, thus creating further complications. In 1984, according to Joseph Garbarino, there were 547 institutions bargaining with faculty units composed of a total of 168,000 persons. The AFT claimed a membership of 75,000 persons in higher education, some not in bargaining units, while the NEA claimed that 62,000 of its members were in colleges or universities and the AAUP claimed about 52,000 members.[90] Although the AAUP seems to have fewer members than the other two organizations, it is more prestigious in the eyes of faculty and therefore has been sought as a coalition partner by both of the other organizations. And, because of financial considerations and the greater political strength that was thought to accompany coalitions, the AAUP has been willing to form coalitions with the AFT and NEA.

An analysis of the bargaining units in higher education shows that in 1984, 28 percent of the 170,320 individuals in bargaining units were in coalitions, 13 percent were represented by the AAUP, 30 percent by the AFT, 28 percent by the NEA, and 2 percent by independent organizations.[91] The major coalitions in 1984 were on the campuses of City University of New York (AFT/AAUP), California State University Colleges (NEA/AAUP and California State Employees Association), the Pennsylvania State College System (AFT/AAUP), and the University of Hawaii (NEA/AAUP). In 1986, however, the CUNY unit disaffiliated, thereby reducing AAUP membership by 9,500.[92] In August 1986, the Penn State unit also voted to disaffiliate, leaving the AAUP as a partner in only two coalitions.[93]

Current trends suggest that AAUP will have less of a role in collective bargaining in higher education than NEA or AFT. Although the AAUP prestige is still valued at major institutions where bargaining has not yet penetrated, it does not seem to be of primary importance on most of those campuses that have opted for bargaining. One

[88] 71 Academe 6a (November–December 1985).
[89] Id.
[90] Garbarino, supra note 87 at 272–273.
[91] Id. at 274.
[92] 72 Academe 12a (November–December 1986).
[93] Id.

mechanism suggested by the former general secretary of the AAUP in order to preserve its traditional functions outside of bargaining was the creation of an AAUP Foundation insulated from the organization's collective bargaining activities.[94] As of 1987, however, this approach had not been adopted and the AAUP continues to struggle financially to maintain both its traditional role and its collective-bargaining role.

Unionism in Municipal and State Governments

Although the American Federation of State, County and Municipal Employees (AFSCME), AFL-CIO, is the dominant union of local and state government employees outside of education, many other organizations represent sizable numbers of public employees. In many states there are heated organizational battles among various AFL-CIO unions, as well as between AFSCME and independent unions such as the Teamsters and the National Education Association. In Illinois and Ohio the passage of bargaining legislation effective in 1984 was followed by contested elections for representation rights.

In the Cook County, Illinois, election in 1984, for example, AFSCME won bargaining rights in five units, the International Brotherhood of Electrical Workers won rights in two, a coalition of Service Employees International Union and the Teamsters won rights in one, and the Combined Counties Police Association won in one.[95] In Ohio, the state's 51,494-member work force was divided into 14 bargaining units and elections were held in 13 of these units in 1985. AFSCME faced competition from the Communications Workers of America (CWA), the United Food and Commercial Workers Union (UFCW), District Council 1199 (the National Union of Hospital and Health Care Employees), and a coalition of building trades unions, all of which are AFL-CIO unions, as well as from the following independent unions: Ohio Education Association, Fraternal Order of Police, Ohio Nurses Association, and the Teamsters.[96] AFSCME won representation rights in the seven larger units, 1199 and the Fraternal Order of Police won rights in two units, and the UFCW and Ohio Education Association each won rights in one unit. The CWA and the Teamsters which initially had challenged AFSCME in the larger units were not successful in gaining rights in any unit.

The organizing competition among AFL-CIO unions has supposedly been brought under control, according to the president of AFSCME who told a meeting of the National Public Employer Labor

[94] 70 Academe 19a (September-October 1984).
[95] 22 GERR 1437 (July 23, 1984).
[96] 23 GERR 567–569 (April 15, 1985); 23 GERR 1396–1398 (September 30, 1985); 23 GERR 1617–1618 (November 11, 1985); 24 GERR 11–12 (January 6, 1986).

Relations Association in March 1986 that, before an organizing campaign even begins, an AFL-CIO arbitrator will weigh competing unions' claims and will determine which union should be given the right to be on the ballot.[97] Although this will not eliminate the competition with the NEA, Teamsters, and other organizations not affiliated with the AFL-CIO, it should reduce interunion rivalry, if it is widely observed by the various organizations.

The organizing conflict has been extensive within two groups: the state civil-service employees who have been represented by independent organizations and the clerical and other nonteacher units in school systems. AFSCME's victories in Ohio are in part attributable to the fact that the formerly independent Ohio State Classified Employees Association had affiliated with AFSCME prior to the representation elections. In the 1981–1983 period, 943,000 state employees were in bargaining units. AFSCME represented 44 percent of these employees and independent associations represented 8 percent of them. Also, state employees in various parts of the country are represented by the CWA, Teamsters, UFCW, and other unions.[98]

Most of the contests for nonteacher units in school systems have been between AFSCME and the local NEA affiliate that represents the teachers. In some instances, however, it is reported that the Service Employees International Union (SEIU), Teamsters, Laborers' International Union of North America (LIUNA), and United Automobile Workers Union (UAW) have sought to represent these employees.

In the health-care field, the American Nurses Association (ANA), similar to professional associations in education, has been drawn into the collective-bargaining arena in order to maintain its representation function. The ANA bargains for private-sector nurses covered by the National Labor Relations Act as well as for nurses employed by city, county, and state governments. In recent years, some groups of salaried doctors in both the private and public sectors have sought to bargain with their employers. Competition to represent the nonprofessional employees of hospitals and nursing homes in both the private and public sectors reflects the continuing fight of 1199, AFSCME, SEIU, and LIUNA for bargaining rights.

In the protective-services field, the International Association of Fire Fighters (IAFF), AFL-CIO, has little competition for the right to represent firefighters, in contrast to the situation among police where several organizations are active. It is estimated that slightly over half of

---

[97] 24 GERR 455 (March 31, 1986).
[98] Helene S. Tanimoto and Gail F. Inaba, *State Employee Bargaining: Policy and Organization*, 108 Monthly Lab. Rev. 51–55 (April 1985).

the 600,000 full-time police officers are members of unions,[99] and about half are members of the Fraternal Order of Police.[100] For the most part, police officers are organized into independent organizations at the local level which combine loosely at the state level. The SEIU has organized some police on the West Coast and also, by virtue of its absorption of the National Association of Government Employees (NAGE), acquired the New England-based police groups that had belonged to NAGE.

National membership figures can be misleading in specific situations because some unions tend to be strong in one region and weak in others. For example, SEIU has considerable strength in the California public sector and almost none in Wisconsin. The UAW is a factor in public-sector unionization in Michigan and the Teamsters have organized public employees in various locations. Another factor making it more difficult to analyze public-sector unions is the degree to which bargaining is local in character. Local unions and district councils are relatively autonomous groups where bargaining strategy is concerned. One unit may be militant, favoring the strike, while another may prefer arbitration.

The role of the Assembly of Governmental Employees (AGE) is an interesting one. It has been the umbrella organization for the independent state civil-service employee associations (CSEAs) that traditionally lobbied on behalf of state employees prior to the advent of collective bargaining. As bargaining has spread, however, more and more of the state affiliates have left AGE and affiliated with other unions. The New York State organization, which formerly was the largest CSEA in AGE, affiliated with AFSCME in 1978 and the second largest, the California CSEA, affiliated with the SEIU in 1983. Despite these and other losses of state affiliates, AGE continues to function as a central clearinghouse for independent associations with a substantial number of members. In 1984, it reported that it had 22 affiliates representing almost a half-million members, many of whom presumably are not covered by bargaining.[101] Further erosion of AGE membership will probably occur if bargaining laws are passed in states that currently have none and if public-sector collective bargaining continues to spread.

This review of public-sector unions is made more complicated by the shift of the local transit industry in the past 35 years from the private sector to the public sector. Practically all major city transit

[99] U.S. Bureau of the Census, 1982 Census of Governments: Vol. 3, Government Employment; No. 3, Labor-Management Relations in State and Local Governments, GC82(3)-3 (Washington: U.S. Government Printing Office, 1985), Table 1.

[100] Gifford, *supra* note 5 at 53.

[101] 22 GERR 1666 (August 27, 1984).

systems have gone public during this period and, strictly speaking, the unions in this industry which traditionally have not been thought of as public-sector unions should be included in that category.

The three major unions representing bus drivers and other local transit employees are the Amalgamated Transit Union (ATU) and the Transport Workers Union (TWU), each with approximately 140,000 members, and the local transit division of the United Transportation Union (UTU), which represents a smaller number of local transit workers than the other two unions. Although the ATU is the dominant union in the field nationally, the TWU represents bus drivers in New York City, Philadelphia, San Francisco, and Miami, and the UTU represents drivers in several other cities including Los Angeles and surrounding communities.[102] Bargaining procedures and union policies in the local transit industry frequently were quite different from those covering other public employees of the same city or county; however, as public-transit labor relations is integrated into the public-sector labor relations policies of the employer, bargaining policies and procedures in transit unions are becoming more like those of other public-sector unions.

Space limitations and the impossibility of analyzing in any depth the many unions active in the public sector have made it necessary to limit the following portion of the chapter to a relatively brief summary of AFSCME and to omit discussions of other unions.

The American Federation of State, County and Municipal Employees (AFSCME), AFL-CIO

The American Federation of State, County and Municipal Employees was founded in the early 1930s by scattered groups of public employees who had affiliated individually with the AFL. The pioneering organization to affiliate in 1932 was the Wisconsin State Employees Association under the leadership of Arnold Zander, who subsequently became the first president of AFSCME. Originally, the individual units of local-government employees were included within AFGE, but in 1936 AFSCME was chartered separately by the AFL.[103] At the time it had about 10,000 members, and by 1950 its membership had increased to over 80,000. When the AFL and CIO merged in 1955, the 30,000-member, public-employee CIO affiliate, the Government and

---

[102] James L. Stern et al., Labor Relations in Urban Mass Transit (Madison: Industrial Relations Research Institute, University of Wisconsin, 1977).

[103] Information about the early history of AFSCME and its development may be found in Leo Kramer, Labor's Paradox (New York: John Wiley & Sons, 1962); Richard Billings and John Greenya, Power to the Public Worker (Washington: E.B. Luce, 1974); Stieber, *supra* note 2; and an article about AFSCME by Jerry Wurf and Mary Hennessy in Collective Bargaining in Government, eds. J. Joseph Loewenberg and Michael H. Moskow (Englewood Cliffs, N.J.: Prentice-Hall, 1972).

Civil Employees Organizing Committee, merged with AFSCME. By 1960, the union had about 180,000 members and was entering a period of internal strife.

Jerry Wurf, the executive director of the large New York City AFSCME District 37, defeated Arnold Zander for the AFSCME presidency in 1964. In his campaign, he argued that the union must devote more of its efforts to collective bargaining. Over the following 17 years, the union, under Wurf's leadership, increased its membership from a little more than 200,000 members to almost one million members, and became the third largest AFL-CIO union. [104] After Wurf died of a heart attack late in 1981, Gerald W. McEntee, a long-time AFSCME vice president and executive director of the large Pennsylvania AFSCME council, was elected by AFSCME's executive board to fill out the presidential term expiring in 1984. Although McEntee was opposed by William Lucy, the black secretary-treasurer in 1981, and won only narrowly, he was not opposed when he ran for a full four-year term in 1984. Lucy was reelected secretary-treasurer. [105]

In the 1984–1986 period, AFSCME became the largest union in the AFL-CIO, reporting more than one million members in a 1984 tally of its membership. It had 400,000 members in the health-care field, 190,000 clericals, 110,000 technicals and professionals, and 100,000 in law enforcement. It had members in 47 states under almost 3,500 contracts. More than 400,000 of its members are women and about 30 percent of its membership is black or Hispanic. [106]

In the mid-seventies, Wurf stopped payment of AFSCME dues to the AFL-CIO Public Employee Department (PED). Along with the NEA, NTEU, and IAFF, AFSCME participated in the Coalition of American Public Employees (CAPE). This organization was designed to give public-employee unions an independent voice, in competition with PED. Nearly a decade had passed before AFSCME rejoined a restructured PED in which separate divisions had been created for state and local government employees and for federal and postal employees. [107] McEntee apparently established good personal relationships with the presidents of the AFT (Shanker) and SEIU (Sweeney) despite their jurisdictional conflicts, [108] and was elected by acclamation to a two-year term as the president of the PED in September 1985. Under the PED's new structure, the president will be a state/local government representative and the secretary-treasurer, a federal/postal representative, with the representatives alternating

[104] 942 GERR 33 (December 14, 1981) and 943 GERR 14–15 (December 28, 1981).
[105] 22 GERR 1253 (June 25, 1984).
[106] *Id.* at 1254.
[107] 23 GERR 246 (February 25, 1985).
[108] 21 GERR 2095 (October 24, 1983).

these positions for ensuing terms.[109] In 1986, it was too soon to determine whether the PED, as the united voice of public-sector unions, will be more effective than it had been previously.

Despite the spotlight on the national leaders, it should be kept in mind that bargaining is essentially decentralized and that the most important bargaining decisions are being made at the municipal- and state-government bargaining-unit levels. The key decision maker in AFSCME bargaining in the smaller municipalities is the full-time district-council representative helping the local negotiate the contract. In the larger cities, key decisions are usually made by the full-time executive director of the AFSCME district council in the area, with the approval of the bargaining team. Victor Gotbaum, executive director of the New York City AFSCME council, and his counterparts throughout the nation have considerable power and autonomy. However, in contrast to major steel and auto bargaining, national AFSCME leadership usually does not participate in these contract negotiations.

Analyses of the councils, however, reveal varying patterns of operation. In some councils, staff members are elected (Philadelphia, for example). In others, staff members are appointed by the executive director. Some directors favor the appointment of college-trained or private-sector, union-trained full-time staff, while others pick local activists who have demonstrated ability. The traditions of the district council and the composition of the membership provide partial explanations for these differences. The less-educated, less-skilled female and minority-group members may not aggressively seek union leadership roles and may prefer to rely upon staff professionals chosen from outside their ranks.

The most important factor explaining the various postures of the councils is the absence or presence of bargaining legislation and the degree to which legislation, where it exists, facilitates employee organization. In most instances, it is only after success on the legislative front that the union can turn its attention to serious bargaining.

Conclusions and Speculation About the Future

Many of the conclusions and speculations voiced nearly 10 years ago in the first edition of this volume have come to pass. As predicted, public-sector unions have grown at a lower rate in the past decade than they did in the previous decade. However, predictions reflecting an overall average are much like estimates of comfort with one foot in boiling water and the other in the freezer—on the average it's comfortable! In the federal sector, unions have not grown, as was predicted,

---

[109] 23 GERR 1409 (September 30, 1985).

but have shrunk. AFSCME and the AFT, on the other hand, have made substantial progress in expanding their membership in the local- and state-government sector.

The decline in the federal sector reflects the adverse political climate in which federal unions have been operating in recent years. And, contrary to the prognostications of AFGE leaders, employees have not rebelled against the adverse climate and joined the union in record numbers. Instead, many of them seem to have decided that it is not worthwhile maintaining their membership in or joining a union which is unable to deliver the goods. In order to reverse this situation, the federal unions need to have a sympathetic administration and Congress.

Passage of legislation providing for a broader scope of bargaining and an agency shop would provide the basis for a renewal of federal-union strength. If these developments occur, federal-union membership can be expected to expand rapidly. If the legislation is not changed or at least if the general public attitude toward unions does not improve, it is anticipated that federal-union membership will remain at its current level. Possibly, AFGE losses will be offset by NTEU gains, but in the present environment it is doubtful whether there will be overall gains.

The postal unions illustrate how a different legislative framework permits a union to maintain itself at a high unionization level. Even without any agency-shop arrangements, but with broad-scope bargaining including wages, the postal unions have increased their absolute numbers although even they may not be maintaining the high percentage of organized workers that they have had in the past. Postal unions continue to condemn arbitration and to maintain that true bargaining requires the right to strike, but one suspects that much of this is rhetoric. Postal unions continue to have influence in Congress and to use the threat and use of arbitration to improve their situation relative to federal employees. Given their ability to do so in an adverse climate with a hostile administration, it seems likely that postal unions will continue to flourish.

Probably, the major threat faced by the postal unions is that of competition for business from the private sector. To the degree that private express-mail and package services divert customers from the post office, employment in the Postal Service will be decreased, or at least prevented from growing. Combined with the job-elimination effects of new technology, the competition may mean that the postal unions will be operating on a stagnant base. This in turn will mean that the opportunity and ability to organize further will be lessened.

Unionism in the field of education probably will continue to grow at a slow rate unless Congress enacts a national local-government bargaining bill. The constitutional barrier posed by the *National*

League of Cities[110] decision no longer exists and the possibility of legislation will depend upon the political climate in 1988 and subsequently. If minimum bargaining standards are provided by federal legislation, it is likely that there will be a substantial increase in teachers' unions in those states in which there currently is no state law. Competition between the NEA and AFT will continue, but it is doubtful that rivalry will dampen organizing efforts and may very well have a stimulating effect.

Union membership in higher education is likely to grow at a slow rate in the next decade under the prevailing legal climate. If a national bargaining law is passed, it seems probable that the growth will be faster. Also, if the antipathy toward unionism changes on the "flagship" campuses in states where there is bargaining legislation, growth will increase substantially. Currently, however, neither of these changes seems likely in the near future.

The growth of union membership at the state and local level has been slow and is not likely to change. Much of AFSCME's recent growth is attributable to the passage of legislation in California, Illinois, and Ohio and the decisions of formerly independent state civil-service associations to affiliate with AFSCME. Further increases from those sources will be small and, as in education, substantial increases will depend upon passage of national legislation.

Although the political clout of public-sector unions does not seem great at the moment (1986), the revised PED and the more politically active NEA provide the unions with a stronger base for future efforts. Mergers of independent groups such as the NEA and NTEU with AFL-CIO unions are possible, but what seems more probable is that there will be an increase only in the number of joint efforts, such as the NEA- and AFT-mounted drive to defeat tuition tax credits.

Two final questions come to mind: will differences between public- and private-sector unionism be seen as more or less important than they have in the past and will unions based on occupation prevail over general unions? As public-sector unionism matures and as public-sector management and the public become more accustomed to it and the occasional conflicts that arise, it is likely that the perceived differences between public- and private-sector unionism will diminish. Given the traditions and heritage of this country, however, it is unlikely that these differences will decrease to the level that exists in other western industrialized nations.

Occupationally-based unions are dominant in education and the public-safety sectors of society and are likely to maintain that dominance. General unions, however, are dominant among unskilled and

---

[110] *National League of Cities v. Usery,* 426 U.S. 833 (1976).

semiskilled blue- and white-collar workers. The borderline area where the pattern is not clear is among professionals, technical workers, and skilled workers. In some states these workers have preferred the narrow craft union or professional association over the general union, while in other situations the opposite has been true. It seems likely that this mixed pattern will prevail and that in the future public-sector unions will continue to exhibit a great variety of structural patterns.

CHAPTER 3

Management Organization for Collective Bargaining in the Public Sector

MILTON DERBER*

The subject of this chapter is so wide-ranging in scope that detailed, comprehensive treatment is not possible. I have therefore made two arbitrary decisions on coverage. First, I have placed the primary focus on state and local government, with which I have been mainly concerned as a researcher and practitioner, devoting only a few pages at the end to the federal sector. Second, I have confined the discussion to five topics which have been of greatest interest and relevance to me and have disregarded others that might be judged of equal significance.

I start with an analysis of what may seem a peculiar question: Who is public management? I hope to demonstrate that this is indeed a question of considerable practical as well as theoretical importance. In the next major section, I examine the apparent trend toward centralization of management authority for bargaining, and in the third, I explore the complicated problem of management internal organization and procedures for effective bargaining, including the utilization of bargaining specialists and their relations with the top policy makers, line officials, the personnel staff, budget makers, and the pertinent legislative body. Following this, I turn to the organizational problems confronting management in the contract-administration stage. Finally, I discuss the problems of managing under fiscal stress which prevailed during much of the decade after 1973.

Who Is Public Management?

From a collective bargaining perspective, the concept of public management poses problems not normally found in the private sector. The private employer is readily identified as an entity, and the line of

*University of Illinois at Urbana-Champaign. *Note:* I am indebted to my colleague, Peter Feuille, and to R. Theodore Clark, Jr., for a number of valuable comments. For their assistance in the revision of this chapter, I am most appreciative to the Board of Editors and to Helene S. Tanimoto, Mark E. Nakamura, and Eva L. Goo of the Industrial Relations Center of the University of Hawaii.

management responsibility for bargaining is usually clear and direct. But in the public sector the formal responsibility often differs from the actual.

Constitutional, Political, and Bureaucratic Considerations

The reasons for such confusion and ambiguity are many.[1] One major factor is the constitutional system of checks and balances that distributes authority for policy making and implementation among the legislative, executive, and judicial branches. Even the executive or legislative responsibilities may be legally shared among separately elected executive officers (e.g., the governor and the secretary of state) or among legislative bodies (e.g., the state legislature and home-rule municipal councils). Legislative bodies in turn often delegate rule-making authority to other agencies, such as a civil service commission, a school board, or a municipality. Arvid Anderson has pointed out that

> the education law, civil service law, welfare laws, statutes affecting police and fire [sic], prevailing wage statutes, pension statutes, statutes affecting the fiscal authority of the municipal employer and the timetable for budgetmaking, all affect and may operate as constraints on the authority of the public employer.[2]

Another significant factor is that apart from the federal Congress and the state legislatures, few public agencies have either the authority or the means to raise all or most of the money they need to perform their functions. Furthermore, to an increasing extent, public bodies obtain their funds from a multiplicity of sources rather than a single source. When a lower level of government receives grants from a higher level, the transfer is often accompanied by constraints on the use of the funds or conditions are specified about the qualifications or methods of the personnel involved.[3]

Finally, but not least in importance, political forces may shape the allocation of responsibility for collective bargaining. A strong mayor or governor typically prefers a centralized bargaining system under his direct control; a weak chief executive may be obliged to share responsibilities with other elected officials in executive or legislative or even administrative positions, resulting in a highly fragmented management approach. In some cases (e.g., where a union is linked to a party

---

[1] See, for example, my article, *Who Negotiates for the Public Employer*, in Perspective in Public Employee Negotiation, ed. Keith Ocheltree (Chicago: Public Personnel Association, 1969), 52–53.

[2] *The Structure of Public Sector Bargaining*, in Public Workers and Public Unions, ed. Sam Zagoria (Englewood Cliffs, N.J.: Prentice-Hall, 1972), 43.

[3] An example is the Urban Mass Transportation Act which specifies that before any federal funds are provided to a state or local government for the operation of a transit system, the U.S. Secretary of Labor must certify that arrangements have been made to protect the interests of affected employees, including the continuation of collective bargaining rights.

machine), the ultimate authority for bargaining may lie with a political leader or group that holds no formal governmental position but operates behind the scene.

The appointed bureaucracy or professional staff may also exercise widely varying degrees of responsibility in collective bargaining in relation to the elected officials who are formally their superiors. A city manager, a school superintendent, or the head of a municipal or state department, possessing a strong personality as well as labor relations expertise and long experience, may assume a dominant role in collective bargaining, whereas less well-endowed counterparts may have little or no role.

A number of these ambiguous strands were reflected in a March 1977 decision of the State of Washington Supreme Court.[4] The issue was whether, under the state public employee relations law, the state budget director was obliged to negotiate with an employee union over the state salary plan. The court held that the budget director was "the public employer" for wage bargaining because he had the power to review and approve the plan prepared in the first instance by the personnel board. On the other hand, the negotiations conducted by the budget director were only of a "meet and confer" nature and could not lead to an agreement binding the governor at whose pleasure the budget director served. Furthermore, the governor had to submit the salary plan for final action by the legislature.

Citizen Interest Groups

Public management's bargaining structure may also be strongly influenced by the activities of interest groups that believe they (as members of the sovereign public) are entitled to a voice in the collective bargaining process. In some instances the group may desire representation on management's bargaining team, in others the right to attend the bargaining sessions, in still others the opportunity to present their views to the bargaining team or to the legislative body prior to the approval of a collective agreement. Illustrations of such interest-group desires are found in laws in Montana, Oregon, and Florida requiring student representation in university negotiations and in the court petition of a Parents' Union to obtain the right to participate in negotiations during the 1972–1973 Philadelphia teachers' strike.[5]

---

[4] *John Ortblad v. State of Washington*, Case No. 44331, March 12, 1977, 712 GERR 8 (June 13, 1977).
[5] Richard P. Schick and Jean J. Couturier, The Public Interest in Government Labor Relations (Cambridge, Mass.: Ballinger Publishing Co., 1977), 45–67.

Because general government services must be paid for by the public through the tax system, public management has a relationship to its public that is very different from that of private management to its firm's customers. In the latter case, typically, a concerned customer can exercise the choice of buying or not buying, but lacks the power to influence the private management's collective bargaining policies or procedures. In the former case, a concerned public may seek to replace the responsible managers or force a change in bargaining policies.

Thought about the public's role in negotiations led Sam Zagoria, then director of the Labor-Management Relations Service, a public-employer organization, to advocate

> giving either party by law the right to take [a] contested issue to public referendum, hitching the factfinders' recommendation on the next regular or special election ballot. In effect, the issue would be taken to the citizens of the community, the ultimate public employer, for them to decide whether they want to supersede the instructions implicit in their earlier election of municipal officials by giving them newer directives based on the issue before them.[6]

Although the idea has not won wide support, at least three cities in Colorado adopted the use of the public referendum as the terminal point for an impasse procedure. The public referendum mechanism was also used in San Francisco in November 1975 when Proposition B was passed by a two-to-one margin abolishing a formula that tied pay for city craft workers to the prevailing wage rate for similar occupations in private industry.[7]

Frank P. Zeidler, former mayor of Milwaukee and a specialist in public-sector labor relations, has noted that taxpayers often believe that they are not represented at the bargaining table because they are not sure that the public-employer representatives represent them. "The taxpayer recognizes that the negotiator or negotiators for his side have several pressures at work on them other than taxpayer interests."[8]

A Theory of Diffused Management Responsibility

The diffused character of public management has been stressed by a number of students. Thomas Kochan, for example, in a study of fire-service bargaining in 228 cities, observed that "a number of semi-autonomous management officials (both administrative and elected)

---

[6] *Resolving Impasses by Public Referendum*, 96 Monthly Lab. Rev. 37–38 (May 1973).
[7] 651 GERR B22 (April 5, 1976).
[8] *The Public Interest in Collective Bargaining*, in Perspective in Public Employee Negotiation, *supra* note 1, at 9.

often share decision-making power over issues traditionally raised by
unions in collective bargaining."[9] Community interest groups were
also found by Kochan (and others)[10] to become involved in the bargaining process. Kochan concluded that multilateral bargaining was a
function of several variables, most notably the extent of internal conflict among management officials and the degree to which employee
organizations use political pressure tactics. In short, the political context of municipal collective bargaining may lead to a fragmented management authority structure in contrast to the more unified management approach in private-sector bargaining.

One possible consequence of such fragmentation in management
bargaining responsibility is the use by unions of the "end run." It is a
rare public-employee organization that does not have friends and
supporters among elected public officials. At every level of government the unions and associations devote often considerable resources
(personnel, communication channels, financial contributions) in support of the election of particular candidates as well as in general
lobbying. Sometimes these officials may "leak" information to employee representatives during or prior to bargaining. In other cases, if
the employees cannot achieve their demands from the management
negotiators, they may appeal informally to their elected friends to try
to influence management positions or to secure more favorable consideration at a higher decision-making level. Numerous examples come to
mind: the schoolboard member who urges the finance committee to
approve the police association's wage demands, the party professional
who advises a county board to make bargaining concessions as a trade-
off for union support in a forthcoming election.[11]

Need for Legal Specification of Management Responsibility

Because of these potentially negative results of fragmentation,
there seems to be widespread agreement among practitioners and
students that management responsibility for collective bargaining
should be clearly specified in law or administrative guidelines,
although no specific uniform rule may be feasible. Where the constitutional structure requires a sharing of responsibility, agreements

---

[9] A Theory of Multilateral Bargaining in City Governments, 27 Indus. & Lab. Rel. Rev. 525,
526 (July 1974). See also Thomas A. Kochan, George P. Huber, and L.L. Cummings, Determinants of Intraorganizational Conflict in Collective Bargaining in the Public Sector, 20 Ad. Sci. Q.
10–23 (March 1975).

[10] Kenneth McLennan and Michael H. Moskow, Multilateral Bargaining in the Public
Sector, in Proceedings of the 21st Annual Meeting, Industrial Relations Research Association
(Madison, Wis.: IRRA, 1968), 34–41; Hervey A. Juris and Peter Feuille, Police Unionism: Power
and Impact in Public Sector Bargaining (Lexington, Mass.: D.C. Heath & Co., 1973), 45–52.

[11] For the observations of one experienced management negotiator, see R. Theodore Clark,
Jr., Politics and Public Employee Unionism: Some Recommendations for an Emerging Problem, 44
U. Cin. L. Rev. 680–689 (1975).

entered into in one forum should be clearly contingent on action in another, with an obligation on the part of both sides to the initial agreement to support it fully and wholeheartedly in its progress through any other requisite decision-making forum.

Some states have attempted to provide a degree of specification in their public-employment collective-bargaining laws. For example, New York's Taylor Law defines the various political units (state, county, municipality, special district, etc.) which fall within the meaning of the term "government" or "public employer" and gives the Public Employment Relations Board the power to determine a "joint public employer" for bargaining purposes.

In addition, the New York law contains definitions of the terms "chief executive officer" and "legislative body of the government" in the case of school districts, and it defines collective bargaining "agreements" as "the result of the exchange of mutual promises between the chief executive officer of a public employer and an employee organization . . . except as to any provisions which require approval by an appropriate legislative body."

The Connecticut Municipal Employee Relations Act goes a step further. It specifies (Sec. 7-474(a)) that "the chief executive officer, whether elected or appointed, or his designated representative or representatives shall represent the municipal employer in collective bargaining. . . ." The act also mandates that where an agreement contains provisions conflicting with any charter, special act, ordinance, or regulation or certain hours and retirement statutes, the agreement must be referred to the appropriate legislative body within a set period and the latter must approve or reject the agreement within a given time. The Connecticut act defines as employer for collective bargaining "a district, school board, housing authority or other authority established by law, which by statute, charter, special act or ordinance has sole and exclusive control over the appointment of and the wages, hours and conditions of employment of its employees . . ." (Sec. 7-474(d)).

The Hawaii public employee bargaining act not only defines 13 appropriate bargaining units within the state, but specifies in the case of multiemployer units who shall negotiate on behalf of the employers, how many representatives each employer may have, and how many votes each employer shall be entitled to (Sec. 89-6(b)).

Multiemployer Arrangements

Although cities and states have sought to avoid fragmentation of bargaining units by consolidating occupations, departments, and agencies under a single bargaining authority, there has been surprisingly little interest among local management groups in establishing multiemployer bargaining units with corresponding management coordinating organizations.[12] A notable exception is the use of regional bargaining by some school boards in Michigan. Peter Feuille et al. report a variety of interemployer arrangements to exchange bargaining information (partly to counter union whipsawing tactics), but the benefits of such arrangements have not persuaded these public agencies to give up their bargaining autonomy. Nor, despite some union pressures, especially in education, to widen bargaining units, does the prospect for a change in management attitude on this subject appear strong. An interesting nonbargaining development in the summer of 1986 was the creation of a joint state and local government labor-management committee to review cooperatively a variety of issues and problems in the public sector. The committee was set up with the assistance of the U.S. Department of Labor's Bureau of Labor-Management Relations and Cooperative Programs and the Federal Mediation and Conciliation Service.[13]

Supervisors as Part of Management

The problem of defining management for purposes of collective bargaining has one other aspect that merits note. This pertains to the drawing of management boundaries, i.e., which supervisory or managerial staff members are to be treated as "management" and therefore to be excluded from appropriate bargaining units or to be confined to special units separate from the employees they supervise. For the private sector, the federal Labor Management Relations Act defines management boundaries broadly, encompassing first-line supervisors who are excluded from the protective definition of "employee" under the act. In the public sector, however, employee organizations *historically* counted even middle and upper supervisory and managerial officials not only as members but often as leaders. This was particularly true in the specialized services of education, health care, firefighting, and police protection, but it also applied to the general civil service. As a result there was strenuous resistance among some employee organizations, as well as some managers, against proposals to adopt private-sector policies on management boundaries.

One of the strongest attacks on the effort to maintain a distinction between the public and the private sector in this (and other) respects was made by former NLRB chairman, Edward B. Miller. In a speech to the National Public Employer Labor Relations Association, he assailed those public employers who

---

[12] See Richard Pegnetter, Multiemployer Bargaining in the Public Sector: Purposes and Experiences (Chicago: International Personnel Management Association, PERL 52, 1975); Peter Feuille, Hervey A. Juris, Ralph Jones, and Michael Jay Jedel, *Multiemployer Bargaining Among Local Governments*, in Proceedings of the 29th Annual Meeting, Industrial Relations Research Association (Madison, Wis.: IRRA, 1977), 123–131.

[13] 17 Labor-Management Relations Service Newsletter Nos. 7 and 8, 1, 4 (July/August 1986).

seemed bent on proving they were different. Some public employers, for example, insisted on ignoring all the experience about bargaining units which had been developed in the private sector under the National Labor Relations Act. . . .

We also saw units which included supervisors and managers. You probably read some of the same scholarly articles that I did wherein lines were "blurred" in the public sector. We were told that in schools and in police departments and in fire departments, existing associations of employees ignored these kinds of lines, and thus we would have to accept that when bargaining took place in this public institutional framework we would have to have units quite different from those in the private sector.[14]

Tim L. Bornstein of the University of Massachusetts similarly concluded, in discussing the fire department problem, that

in the long run, it is all but inevitable that your deputies and your captains, and perhaps even your lieutenants, will systematically be excluded from collective bargaining. The reason is that collective bargaining, which can be a very helpful, useful, constructive institution in the conduct of public affairs, has to operate according to rules which assure that both sides have a reasonable measure of leverage. And if, in a community, only the fire chief or one or two deputies are excluded from the bargaining unit, then who is left to assure that policy is carried out faithfully and effectively?[15]

Most states with public-employee relations legislation have, indeed, incorporated a Taft-Hartley-type definition of supervisor as part of management into their laws, as has the federal government in its executive orders. In some branches of government, most notably education, top and middle managers, like superintendents and principals, have been obliged to abandon their dual role of management and employee.

Nonetheless, as Stephen Hayford and Anthony Sinicropi have concluded, after a comprehensive national survey, "The bargaining rights status of public sector supervisors is far from being settled. While it is clear that . . . federal employment experience has paralleled that of the private sector, several state legislatures and/or administrative agencies have chosen a more expansive approach. . . ."[16] This approach has taken two principal forms: (1) many individuals with supervisory titles are not held to be supervisors for statutory purposes because they "are not really managers"; (2) "bona fide supervisors" are granted bargaining rights but are usually placed in bargaining units separate from the employees whom they supervise.

---

[14] 702 GERR 39–40 (April 4, 1977).
[15] 718 GERR 12 (July 25, 1977).
[16] Stephen L. Hayford and Anthony V. Sinicropi, *Bargaining Rights Status of Public Sector Supervisors*, 15 Indus. Rel. 44, 59 (February 1976).

A few cases may be illustrative. The Minnesota law provides that supervisory and confidential employees, principals, and assistant principals may form their own organizations and the latter may receive exclusive representation rights for the purpose of negotiating terms and conditions of employment as though they were essential employees, i.e., with the right to invoke binding arbitration (Sec. 179.65(6)). Wisconsin's *municipal* employment relations act generally does not consider a supervisor to be a covered employee, but it distinguishes firefighters from other municipal employees and explicitly defines supervisors as the chief and the officer directly below him in single-station communities and all offices above the rank of the highest ranking officer at each single station in municipalities with more than one station. Firefighting and law-enforcement supervisors may organize separate units for the purpose of negotiating with their municipal employers, although the statute's other provisions do not apply to them. Moreover, the Wisconsin Employment Relations Commission (WERC) may require a supervisory unit of firefighters or police to be organized separately from the local employee unit, but it may not prevent affiliation by a supervisory representative with the same parent state or national organization as the employee representative (Secs. 111.70(1)(b), (1)(o)(2), and (3)(d)).

Wisconsin's *state* employment relations act authorizes the WERC to establish two statewide units of professional and nonprofessional supervisory employees, but the certified representatives may not be affiliated with labor organizations representing other categories of nonsupervisory employees. Moreover, the supervisory representatives may not bargain on any matter other than wages and specified fringe benefits (Sec. 111.81(3)(d)). Hawaii's public-employee bargaining law, like Wisconsin's, specifies appropriate bargaining units, but it distinguishes between supervisory employees in blue-collar positions and those in white-collar positions. In New Jersey, the schools receive a bit of special attention in this area with the provision that the term "managerial executive" shall mean the superintendent of schools or his equivalent, and the law further provides that no supervisor shall have the right to be represented in collective negotiations by an employee organization that admits nonsupervisory personnel to membership "except where established practice, prior agreement or special circumstances, dictate the contrary" (Sec. 34:13A-5.3).

Practice often indicates even wider divergence. A 1977 survey in New York City noted that, among others, deputy chiefs in the fire and police departments, supervisors below the level of borough superintendents in the sanitation department, and housing-project managers in the housing authority belong to a union. The conclusion reached was that "many managers identify not with the City but with the union they belong to."[17] In Boston in 1986 some 410 middle-level managers were reportedly affiliated with a salaried employees' division of the United Steelworkers of America.[18]

The foregoing provisions and practices, and others like them, reflect the tensions and the ambiguities of public-sector management. On the one hand, many top executives (particularly those in elective positions) have failed to appreciate the importance of adequately motivating, training, and rewarding middle and lower managerial and supervisory personnel so as to bind them to the management side. On the other hand, many supervisory personnel have been impressed by the organizational achievements of the people whom they supervise and are determined to keep pace.

Most of the foregoing discussion on the definition of management is based on experience in the period before 1980. In the ensuing decade the central tendency appears to have been a further sharpening and broadening of boundary lines between management and other employees. Although considerable diversity among states and localities continued, this tendency was promoted by the Reagan administration and reinforced by the courts. The tough managerial stand of the federal government in the Air Traffic Controllers strike (1981), the U.S. Supreme Court's decision in the private-sector *Yeshiva University*[19] case, the defensive posture of public- as well as private-sector unions during the deep recession of the early eighties, the growing concerns over public-sector budgets and expenditures, and the increased knowledge and sophistication in managerial circles—all contributed to the trend.

Centralization of Management Authority for Bargaining

The distribution of management responsibility for bargaining appears to be at least partly related to the structure of the bargaining unit. The wider and more comprehensive the bargaining unit, the greater the likelihood that management responsibility for bargaining will be centralized. When bargaining units are smaller, narrower, and more numerous, centralized authority is more difficult to maintain, and there is a tendency for responsibility to be dispersed (formally or informally) among a variety of agencies, departments, and institutions. Several empirical surveys support this thesis.

After an extensive study in 1968–1969 of local government in some 40 cities and towns (part of The Brookings Institution's Studies of Unionism in Government), John Burton concluded that "bargaining

---

[17] *Reporter at Large*, The New Yorker (August 1, 1977), 38.
[18] 24 GERR 627–628 (May 5, 1986).
[19] 444 U.S. 672, 103 LRRM 2526 (1980).

forces a centralization of authority within management which over-
comes the fragmentation of control over various [personnel] issues
typical in a nonunionized unit of local government."[20] As bargaining
develops, "[c]ollective bargaining will shift authority for personnel
issues to the executive branch at the expense of the legislative branch
and the civil service system," and within the executive branch,
"[a]uthority for bargaining will be centralized and primary responsibility assigned to an individual or officer directly responsible to the chief
executive."[21]

The relationship between management authority and bargaining
structure suggested by the foregoing is by no means an iron law. In the
cases of New York State and New York City, we find centralized
managerial responsibility for bargaining with widely divergent bargaining-unit systems. The state has five broad horizontal units and
three vertical units covering about 180,000 employees; the city has
about 100 units (reduced from 400) covering some 250,000 employees.
Bargaining for the state is conducted by the governor's Office of
Employee Relations; bargaining for the city is the responsibility of the
mayor's Office of Labor Relations. The history of management labor
relations policy in both state and city is one of increasing centralization
under the chief executive.[22] In the city, this centralization has occurred not only within the executive branch, but also as between the
executive and legislative branches. In the state, the legislature has retained its traditional power over appropriations, but has invariably
assented to the collective-bargaining agreements.

Raymond Horton, David Lewin, and James Kuhn, however, have
cautioned against overgeneralizing the centralization thesis. They
offer three reasons for a "diversity" hypothesis:

> First, the formal dispersion of political power, particularly at the
> local government level in American cities, is so well-advanced that
> political "end-runs" around newly designated labor relations agencies
> and actors remain possible. Second, and closely related to the above
> point, one must distinguish between formal and informal power struc-
> tures. The mere act of creating new labor relations institutions and

---

[20] John F. Burton, Jr., *Local Government Bargaining and Management Structure*, 11 Indus.
Rel. 123, 124 (May 1972).

[21] *Id.* at 138.

[22] For a history of the city's labor relations, see Raymond D. Horton, Municipal Labor
Relations in New York City (New York: Praeger Publishers, 1972); Horton, *Report to State Charter
Revision Commission on Reforming New York City's Labor Relations Process*, 594 GERR E1-E8
(February 24, 1975); and Jack Bigel, *Municipal Finance and Its Implications for Negotiations, A
Case History*, in The Evolving Process—Collective Negotiations in Public Employment, Association of Labor Relations Agencies publication (Fort Washington, Pa.: Labor Relations Press, 1985),
530–546. The state's structure is described in Donald H. Wollett, *State Government: Strategies
for Negotiations in an Austere Environment—A Management Perspective*, in Proceedings of the
1976 Annual Spring Meeting, Industrial Relations Research Association (Madison, Wis.: IRRA,
1976), 504–511.

delegating to them responsibilities to make decisions previously reached elsewhere in government does not mean, in fact, that the locus of control over decision-making also changes. Third, in certain cities where public employees are well-organized and politically strong, formal bargaining programs may result in a redistribution of power from public officials to municipal unions. This may represent a form of centralization, but not of the kind customarily anticipated by academics or public officials.[23]

A Lewin study of the evolution of management structure in the City and County of Los Angeles lends some support to the diversity thesis.[24] Despite an apparent formal centralization of public-management authority in these two major governmental units, multiple sources of authority remain. In the city, the Personnel Department, departmental commissioners, the city council, and the council's personnel committee, as well as the city administrative officer (the chief negotiator) and the mayor have all been participants to one degree or another in municipal labor relations. In the county, where decision making is more highly centralized than in the city, a five-member board of supervisors controls virtually all of the departments. Nevertheless, the county administrative officer (the chief negotiator), the personnel department, and the board of supervisors share negotiating responsibility.

Bargaining by state employees reflects the same tendency to centralize, as two separate 1974–1975 surveys of state government collective bargaining, by Ralph T. Jones and this author indicate. Jones (after a study of eight widely spread states) perceived the appearance of a "life cycle" pattern wherein "management structure evolves into and through distinctive growth and maturity patterns characterized by an almost instinctive thrust toward increasing centralization."[25] His study found that state bargaining was initiated under a variety of environmental circumstances which greatly affected the first management structures. Vertical units involving department-level contracts resulted in decentralized administration within state management. Horizontal units resulted in centralized administration. "Whatever the initial structure, however, subsequent events lead to further centralization. Decentralized administration becomes inappropriate as statewide units are established. These in turn begin to fade as pressures for coalition bargaining surface."[26]

[23] Raymond D. Horton, David Lewin, and James W. Kuhn, *Some Impacts of Collective Bargaining on Local Government*, 7 Ad. & Soc'y 509 (February 1976).
[24] David Lewin, *Local Government Labor Relations in Transition: The Case of Los Angeles*, 17 Lab. Hist. 191 (Spring 1976).
[25] Ralph T. Jones, *Public Management's Internal Organizational Response to the Demands of Collective Bargaining*, draft final report prepared by Contract Research Corp., Belmont, Mass., for Labor-Management Services Administration, U.S. Department of Labor, Contract No. L-74-207, undated, mimeo, 27.
[26] *Id.* at 32. This trend toward centralized state government bargaining must be distinguished from multiemployer local government bargaining as discussed earlier.

My own research in the 12 midwestern states discovered three main bargaining patterns in which the allocation of management bargaining authority, the nature of the bargaining unit, and the scope of bargaining issues were interrelated.[27] Where bargaining coverage was widespread and the scope of bargaining was comprehensive (including pay, hours, and fringe benefits), government responsibility for bargaining tended to be centralized at the level of the governor or a civil service commission. Wisconsin, one of the pioneers in state government bargaining, illustrated the evolutionary process from widely dispersed, limited-scope management bargaining to a highly centralized system including the formal intermeshing of the executive and legislative roles. Iowa, influenced by its neighbor's experience, adopted a centralized bargaining system controlled by the governor's office from the outset. Other states with limited bargaining coverage and, typically, limited scope of issues reflected two different patterns. In some of these states (e.g., Missouri and North Dakota), responsibility was left to the heads of the agencies involved, and the chief executive followed a hands-off policy. In others of this group (e.g., Ohio, Nebraska), there was a centralized unit acting on behalf of the governor to maintain a measure of statewide uniformity. However, in such states, a tradition of departmental autonomy often resisted the centralization effort. As bargaining units evolved to a statewide scale, the centralization process tended to be strengthened.

Management's Internal Organization for Bargaining

Centralization of management responsibility in collective bargaining was fostered by a mounting recognition that the bargaining process demands professional skills, specialized knowledge, quick access to relevant data, and quantities of time and energy. After a few exposures to the process, many executives and legislators were happy to relinquish the function to others on their staff. Most recruited bargaining specialists, on a part-time or full-time basis, to represent them in bargaining and to advise them on policy.

In his 1969 Brookings survey of municipal and county management, David Stanley found that the

> largest group of cities and counties [in a sample of 15] are relying on their personnel or civil service staffs to assume labor relations responsibilities. Only large cities with a multiplicity of bargaining units have set up full-

---

[27] Milton Derber, Charles Maxey, and Kurt Wetzel, Public Management's Internal Organizational Response to the Demand of Collective Bargaining in the Twelve Midwestern States (Washington: U.S. Department of Labor, Labor-Management Services Administration, 1977). See also Milton Derber, Peter Pashler, and Mary Beth Ryan, Collective Bargaining by State Governments in Twelve Midwestern States (Champaign: Institute of Labor and Industrial Relations, University of Illinois, 1974).

time labor specialists or units. More cities can be expected to follow their lead. . . . The larger more thoroughly unionized governments can be expected to move toward the industrial pattern—a department of labor relations headed by a vice mayor or an assistant manager for labor relations, who will supervise not only bargaining and employee relations but also selection and training activities.[28]

An Iowa study of the city manager's role in collective bargaining in 1975, shortly after the state enacted a comprehensive public-employee bargaining law, revealed a similar tendency.[29] Nine of sixteen managers had initially assumed the role of chief negotiator, either because they had been explicitly hired with the function in mind (two cases) or were required to assume the responsibility by city charter or by an ordinance adopted by the city council. However, most of the group indicated that the excessive time demanded by negotiations and the difficulty of maintaining consistency across multiple bargaining units had led them to consider seriously the appointment of a full-time labor relations specialist. The other seven managers had decided, for lack of experience in bargaining, to delegate the function to a committee (typically the city's chief finance officer, a personnel officer, and several department heads) or had hired an outside consultant, usually a lawyer with labor relations expertise. A 1986 report by the International City Managers Association revealed that 91 percent of the cities surveyed give responsibility for collective bargaining to the personnel department.[30]

Functional specialization in bargaining has raised a number of interesting questions and problems for management generally. Where in the management structure should the bargaining specialists be located? What role should department administrators play in the bargaining process, and how should their department interests be protected? How should communication lines be maintained with legislators who must approve any agreed items or vote appropriations to finance the agreements? Once negotiations have been completed, who should be responsible for contract administration and the settlement of grievances?

The answers to these and related questions have varied widely, not only at different levels of government but also within the same level. Contributory factors are numerous—the size and complexity of the bargaining unit, the legal framework, the distribution of political power, and the attitudes of management leaders, among others.

---

[28] David T. Stanley, Managing Local Government Under Union Pressure (Washington: The Brookings Institution, 1972), 27–28.
[29] Peter A. Veglahn and Stephen L. Hayford, An Investigation into the City Manager's Role in the Collective Bargaining Process, 5 J. Coll. Neg. Pub. Sector 289 (1976).
[30] 18 Labor-Management Relations Service Newsletter No. 4 and 5, 7 (April/May 1986).

The Location of the Bargaining Specialist

Small governmental units (municipality, school board, or state institution) often hire a lawyer or industrial relations specialist on an ad hoc basis to represent management at the bargaining table. The consultant confers mainly with the chief executive (city manager or mayor) or a governing board, performs his function of negotiating an agreement with the union, and then withdraws from the scene. No systematic information is available on the characteristics or the role of these part-time representatives. General observation indicates that they are numerous, that they satisfy an essential need, and that a corps of such specialists have acquired multiple clients in various regions of the country.

Larger government units often appoint a full-time specialist as employee-relations director in the manner of a private corporation. Sometimes the labor-relations director handles all personnel matters; sometimes personnel and labor relations are treated as separate functions. As a staff specialist, the labor-relations director is usually responsible to a top administrative officer—the mayor or city manager, the civil service head, the superintendent of schools, the administrator of a hospital, the state director of administration or director of personnel, or the governor, as the case may be. Numerous variations may be cited.

In a national study of police unionism, Hervey A. Juris and Peter Feuille found that bargaining responsibility rested with the executive branch (mayor or city manager) or the city council. In "strong mayor" cities (Buffalo, Boston, New York, New Haven, Seattle), the executive branch prepared the budget, the city negotiators received instructions from the mayor, and at critical times the latter would enter the negotiations himself. In "weak mayor" cities (Milwaukee, Omaha, Los Angeles), the council was the dominant management factor. In council-manager cities, although the labor-relations specialists were attached to the city manager's office, the council typically provided negotiating directions or guidelines to them either directly (Oakland, Rochester, Vallejo) or through the manager (Cincinnati, Hartford, Dayton). In one instance, however, Juris/Feuille reported that the manager was able to persuade the council that "it was less costly politically to let him handle labor relations than to become involved themselves."[31]

In state government, as collective bargaining expanded, professional negotiators were employed increasingly to represent management at the bargaining table. In New York,[32] for example, Governor

---

[31] Juris and Feuille, *supra* note 10, esp. 62–63.
[32] Derived mainly from Jones, *supra* note 25, at App. A, State Report.

Rockefeller initiated the bargaining process shortly after the passage of the Taylor Law in 1967 by appointing a management negotiating team composed of his secretary, the president of the Civil Service Commission, and the director of the budget. It became clear in the following two years that these three top officials were far too involved in other functions to carry the collective bargaining responsibility. As a consequence, the governor requested the legislature to establish by law an Office of Employee Relations (OER) to bargain and administer contracts for the state. The director of the OER reported directly to the governor and became part of the governor's informal cabinet. The director's subordinates included a deputy director, who also served as director of the division of contract negotiation and administration, a research director who also served as director of the grievance division, and a legal counsel who served as the director of the legal division. Five assistant directors were responsible for preparing for negotiations and contract administration.

In Wisconsin, as in New York, comprehensive centralized bargaining followed the passage of a new bargaining law in 1971.[33] Bargaining responsibility for the state was conferred upon an Employment Relations Section established within the Department of Administration (DOA), with easy access through the DOA secretary, a cabinet member, to the governor. The Director of Employment Relations was designated the chief state negotiator. Together with a staff of five professionals, he developed management positions prior to bargaining, conducted bargaining, monitored all third-step (department) grievances, and represented management in all grievance cases submitted to arbitration. Whereas under an earlier law the Bureau of Personnel (which administered the merit system) acted as adviser to department negotiators, the post-1971 system separated responsibility for the labor relations function from that of the personnel function. In late 1977, following a comprehensive review of the state's personnel system, a bill was enacted that removed personnel functions from the Department of Administration and created a new Department of Employment Relations (headed by a secretary) with responsibility for the administration of the state civil service system, the affirmative action program, and collective bargaining (Sec. 230).

Minnesota provides an example of a shift in labor relations responsibility from an independent Civil Service Board to the governor, with a team of top management officials as the governor's surrogates.[34] Under an initial "meet and confer" law (1965), state employee relations were controlled by the Civil Service Department, whose head was ap-

---

[33] Derber, Maxey, and Wetzel, *supra* note 27, at 6–7.
[34] *Id.* at 10–12.

pointed by a part-time Civil Service Board. When a bargaining law was enacted in 1971, negotiating responsibility was given jointly to the Director of Civil Service and the Commissioner of Administration, a key member of the governor's cabinet. In 1972 two state negotiators were hired within the Civil Service Department. The following year (1973) statutory revisions changed the title of Director of Civil Service to Commissioner of Personnel, made him a gubernatorial appointee instead of an appointee of the Civil Service Board, and limited the power of the board mainly to merit-employment procedures and merit appeals.

In Oregon[35] more than a decade of experimentation and change produced a comparatively weak central Employee-Relations Section (ERS) located in the Executive Department, but not strongly supported by the governor or the legislature. The supervisor of the Employee-Relations Section reports to the director of the Personnel Division who in turn reports to the director of the Executive Department. The ERS negotiators obtain their guidelines from the director of the Executive Department who consults with the governor. On occasion unions have made "end runs" to the governor to obtain concessions that the state negotiator has rejected. Agreements reached at the bargaining table may be altered at different levels—by either the Personnel Division (after a public hearing) or the Public Employment Relations Board if a merit-system rule is involved, by the governor, or (as has frequently happened) by the legislature. In addition, some 45 agencies or departments have the power to bargain on local issues such as work schedules, travel pay, supervisory appraisals, and maternity leave. All agency appointments must be reviewed and approved by the Personnel Division and the Executive Department director.

While the more highly developed collective-bargaining systems have led to the employment of centrally located professional negotiators, as illustrated above, numerous municipal, county, and state agencies continue to rely on line or staff officers with little or no expertise or experience.

Relations with Line Officials

When responsibility for negotiations is assigned to a central labor relations office, or is retained by the chief executive, a major problem arises as to the involvement of the heads of the operating departments and agencies. At least two reasons support some degree of such involvement. One is the specialized knowledge possessed by the administrator. The other is the concern of the administrator with the

---

[35] Jones, *supra* note 25, at App. A, State Report.

impact of the labor agreement on the functioning of his agency. If an agreement is to be meaningfully applied, it must be understood and, for best results, accepted by the people who must live with its provisions. Not the least of the negotiator's problems in some jurisdictions is the hostility of managers at various levels to the idea of collective bargaining and their reluctance to help make it work. In some cases elaborate steps may be taken to frustrate bargaining.

The chief executive (mayor, city manager, school superintendent) who handles negotiations directly usually communicates informally with his main subordinates, asking for information or ideas as needed. Sometimes one or more line administrators may sit in on the negotiations. On the other hand, it is not uncommon for such officials to remain wholly in the dark about the negotiations and even to learn about them later than some of their unionized employees. The negative consequences for administrative morale and efficiency are obvious.

Professional management negotiators, whether at the central or agency level, are usually sensitive to the internal communication problem. However, they have not always been successful in coping with it, either because of limitations of staff and time or because bargaining strategy impels them to hesitate to reveal their plans to others for fear of leaks. Moreover, in large and complex organizations (a major city, a large school district, or a state), size creates serious communications barriers. In addition, organizational politics, competition for power, interpersonal relations, differences in age and experience in office, geographical spread of offices, and a host of other internal factors may encourage close involvement with some officials and total neglect of others.

Juris and Feuille found that in the early days of collective bargaining, police managers in several cities (e.g., Dayton, Omaha) were excluded entirely from the bargaining process by the mayor's or city manager's office. This approach led to a lack of sufficient information to evaluate union proposals properly and had to be changed. In three other cities (Detroit, Los Angeles, Rochester) the police chief was granted total authority over nonwage issues, while the city labor relations bureau, the city administrative officer and city council, and the city manager's labor officer, respectively, bargained on cost items. This arrangement prevented tradeoffs between economic and noneconomic issues in bargaining and was also altered.[36]

Stanley cites the case of a police negotiation where the city representatives agreed to a time-off provision without the prior knowledge of the police chief.[37] The result was the loss of the equivalent of 11 men

[36] Juris and Feuille, *supra* note 10, at 64–65.
[37] Stanley, *supra* note 28, at 28.

for a provision that, in the opinion of the chief, was thrown in by the union for bargaining purposes. Such an example can be attributed to inexperience or carelessness. But what is to be done when the negotiator is representing an organization that has a multiplicity of departments and agencies? Is it possible to develop a system that will avoid such misjudgments?

In Wisconsin, to cite one answer, the state negotiator set up an Employment Relations Council consisting of 36 members, one from each of the state's principal operating and staff units. This council meets with the negotiating staff to review existing agreements and rules, to help evaluate union demands and develop management positions, and to keep all departments informed of the progress in negotiations. Several of the departments most directly concerned with the particular negotiations have representatives on the bargaining team. Despite the general approval by department officials of this system, the fear was expressed by several that the needs of a particular department might be compromised during negotiations. Some smaller and less influential departments believed that their needs would be given less weight than those of larger departments.[38]

Relations with the Personnel Staff

If the labor relations and personnel functions are handled by the same individuals or housed in the same office, communications involving the possible overlap between the collective bargaining agreement and personnel rules and regulations are not likely to be a problem. If, however, as often happens the functions are separated, then the state or local government negotiator and the personnel specialist must exercise considerable care to consult with each other, draw upon their respective expertise, and avoid conflict between rules and collective agreements.

Donald Wollett, New York state negotiator, tells of a situation that occurred in 1976 when a blizzard prevented many employees from getting to work and the Director of State Operations (DSO) decided that state offices should be shut down for the day.[39] The question arose as to whether employees who got to work were entitled to compensatory time off. According to past practice, they were not, but the DSO was persuaded to reverse the policy. Since Wollett had a proposal on the bargaining table to reduce personal-leave time and the DSO decision had the effect of adding a day, his position at the bargaining table was "fatally undermined."

---

[38] See Derber, Maxey, and Wetzel, *supra* note 27, at 45.
[39] Wollett, *supra* note 22, at 506.

The possibility of policy conflict becomes even more serious when civil service rules and regulations may be affected. The State of Michigan offers an atypical but instructive illustration of how to cope with this dilemma.[40] Initially (in the 1970s) departmental managers of the state classified service were permitted to "confer with" employee-association or union representatives over local working conditions; however, they were prohibited from altering the rules of the very strong Department of Civil Service (DCS). The DCS officers also held conferences directly with employee representatives, but generally played what they perceived as a traditional civil service role by arbitrating the interests of both employees and management. Communications between the DCS and the line departments took the form of either a general policy memorandum or informal, individual department, civil service correspondence. Line officials reportedly felt that the "neutral" role of the DCS was not functioning on behalf of management and reduced the ability of the line to deal effectively with employees. In 1980 the Civil Service Commission decided to revise its rules by establishing a system of collective bargaining. Representing management in the bargaining process were a state employer appointed by the governor and departmental employers designated by state departments. The DCS itself appointed a three-member neutral employment-relations board to resolve disputes over grievances, representation issues, and interests.[41]

Relations with the Budget Makers

In smaller bargaining situations, the management bargainers typically are also responsible for fund raising, i.e., voting tax levies. Bargaining and budgeting are closely integrated. This is illustrated by most school districts where the board and the superintendent fulfill the dual functions for management. In a large city or a state, however, the relationship becomes more complex.

The City of New York offers an example.[42] Initially (1960) collective bargaining was handled under the mayor's close surveillance by the chief examiner of the Bureau of the Budget, with the director of the Personnel Department playing a secondary role. However, as bargaining spread, a new mayor (in 1966) found it desirable to establish for bargaining purposes an independent specialized Office of Labor Relations which had no responsibility for the budget or finance. The Bureau of

---

[40] Derber, Maxey, and Wetzel, *supra* note 27, at 48.
[41] 863 GERR 17–19 (May 26, 1980).
[42] See Frederick O'R. Hayes, *Collective Bargaining and the Budget Director*, in Public Workers and Public Unions, ed. Sam Zagoria (Englewood Cliffs, N.J.: Prentice-Hall, 1972), 89–100; Horton, *Report, supra* note 22.

the Budget and the Personnel Department were "virtually eliminated from the labor relations process." It became their responsibility simply to implement bargaining decisions that affected the budget and the civil service system. The result, as one budget director put it, was to turn budgeting "into a kind of roulette game." There was a total lack of synchronization between collective bargaining and the budgeting process. The operating budget was usually formulated and approved with only a rough (usually inadequate) estimate of bargaining costs.

As the Charter Revision Commissioner noted,

> Much of the general looseness historically associated with preparation, adoption, and administration of the City's expense budget results from participants in the budgetary process, executive as well as legislative, having inadequate information about what is by far the single largest component of the expense budget—labor costs.

One of the commission's major recommendations was to synchronize bargaining and budgeting by requiring all collective bargaining agreements to expire on June 30, settling all negotiations through agreement or binding arbitration by a specified date that would enable incorporation of the new costs flowing from the contracts into the expense-budget process, and prohibiting the comptroller from paying wage increases after the beginning of a fiscal year unless specified in a collective bargaining agreement signed prior to the cutoff date.

New York's early experience was temporarily altered by the city's fiscal crisis of the mid-seventies. However, as Jack Bigel noted, since the end of the fiscal crisis, contract negotiations have returned to "normal." A 1971–1972 survey of some 30 state and local government units in Illinois found many similar problems emanating from the separate dynamics of the bargaining and budget-making processes.[43] The authors also recommended that bargaining and budget-making schedules have a common target date, but noted the need for flexibility to cope with inevitable deviations.

Stanley's study of local governments likewise revealed a variety of management efforts to synchronize bargaining and budgeting as well as to assure that bargaining decisions reflect budgeting realities.[44] Often, however, those responsible for the budget did not appear to have direct relations with the bargainers or to participate in the bargaining process. Instead the mayor or city manager or council finance committee set guidelines for the bargainers on the basis of information provided by the budget department and political judgment of the elected officials.

---

[43] Milton Derber, Ken Jennings, Ian McAndrew, and Martin Wagner, *Bargaining and Budget Making in Illinois Public Institutions*, 27 Indus. & Lab. Rel. Rev. 49 (October 1973).
[44] Stanley, *supra* note 28, at ch. 6.

Management efforts to integrate bargaining and budgeting have taken a number of different paths at the state government level. One pattern illustrated by Pennsylvania provides for close but informal contact between the Bureau of Labor Relations in the Office of Administration and the Bureau of the Budget in the Budget Department. No one from the budget bureau is appointed to the bargaining team, but that bureau is consulted at the top level in decision making on state economic issues. In Wisconsin there is a similar relationship except that for a time both the employment-relations section and the budget officer were located in the Department of Administration. Subsequently the employment-relations unit was removed from the DOA. In Minnesota the Commissioner of Finance, who is responsible for central budget functions, sits with the Commissioner of Personnel, the Commissioner of Administration, and the governor's executive secretary on a top-level committee that prepares the bargaining guidelines for the state negotiator. In Hawaii, to cite another variant, a representative of the Department of Budget and Finance serves as one of the governor's official representatives in all negotiations pertaining to the state classified service, together with the state's chief negotiator and the Director of Personnel Services. The New York structure is similar to Hawaii's but more complex. Representatives of the Employee Compensation and Relations Unit (ECRU) within the Budget Division serve on the negotiating teams for each of the state's bargaining units. The ECRU estimates and analyzes the cost of union demands. It also serves as a training resource for departmental and agency budget examiners who assist the agencies in contract administration just as the ECRU staff assists the state negotiators in collective bargaining.[45]

It seems clear from the foregoing discussion that for management to neglect the interrelationships between bargaining and budget making is to incur serious risks respecting the effectiveness of collective bargaining and the fiscal stability of government. Structure must be adapted to function. The negotiators and the budget makers can contribute to each other's area of responsibility. Whether this communication is done formally or informally matters less than that it be recognized by public management as a necessary activity for both.

Relations With the Legislative Body

One of the distinctive features of public collective bargaining is that agreements about money (pay, fringe benefits) usually require legislative approval, and those concerning certain nonfinancial matters

---

[45] The data on Pennsylvania, Hawaii, and New York came from Jones, *supra* note 25. The data on Wisconsin and Minnesota came from Derber, Maxey, and Wetzel, *supra* note 27. Not all subsequent organizational changes have been reported.

(civil service rules and regulations) often do. As noted earlier, some legislative bodies have, for this reason, retained responsibility for collective bargaining rather than leaving it to top-management officers. Most legislative bodies, however, have found the technical intricacies and time requirements of collective bargaining too demanding and have adopted a more limited role. Questions about the legislative role include a number of different aspects: whether the legislature should be involved in the preparation of the bargaining guidelines, whether it should be represented at the bargaining table, whether legislative leaders should approve the agreement before it is formally signed, whether the legislature should have the authority to revise the terms of an agreement or merely approve or disapprove, and whether it should remain wholly aloof from the collective-bargaining process and simply act on relevant appropriations and legal rules.

In most school districts and many municipalities, the legislative body (school board or city council) is totally involved from preparation for bargaining to approval of the agreement and voting of necessary funds. Members of the legislative body may even participate in the bargaining team, although as the specialized character of collective bargaining becomes increasingly appreciated, the legislators tend to withdraw to the background except in crises. At the other extreme are the cases in which the legislature (typically state legislatures and large city councils) try to disassociate themselves from the bargaining process and act on appropriations and other bills as in the days before bargaining. In between are the legislative bodies that accept a limited responsibility for collective bargaining by requiring the submission to them of negotiated agreements for approval or disapproval.

The argument for a shared responsibility for the legislative body and the executive branch is that both represent the community or public interest and therefore should coordinate their actions in relation to the employee organizations. A division between the two branches of government, it is found, will encourage "end runs" and undermine the effectiveness of the negotiators. An opposing view is that public managers (including the chief executive) have a different role in government than legislators and that the latter must take into account the interests of both management and nonmanagement employees as well as the interests of other public groups that are not ordinarily represented at the bargaining table.

Such philosophic differences are usually overridden by pragmatic political considerations and the distribution of power. In New York City the virtual exclusion of the city council and the Board of Estimate from collective bargaining and the supremacy of the mayor have been attributed to the former's inability to develop strong public or official confidence.[46] In Chicago, the mayor's dominant role (until the Democratic Party split in the 1980s) can be explained by his party's monopoly of power and the integration of most of the unions into the party machinery. At the state level, however, in both New York and Illinois, a vigorous two-party system has given the governor responsibility for bargaining, while the legislature retains the final voice on appropriations.

One of the most ingenious and atypical systems of linking the state negotiators from the executive branch with a closely divided two-party legislature is found in Wisconsin. There the collective bargaining law provides for the establishment of a Joint Legislative Committee on Employment Relations (JOCER) on which the leaders of both parties in both houses are represented. The state negotiator must consult prior to bargaining with this committee in order to secure tacit approval of his bargaining position. After negotiations with the union, he must return to the committee for its approval or disapproval of the tentative bargaining agreement. If the agreement is disapproved, he must return for further negotiations. The agreement finally approved can then expect quick appropriations support in the legislature without the likelihood of an "end run" by either party from the bargaining table. The JOCER system worked well until 1977 when a strike of state employees occurred and communications between the negotiators and the legislators broke down. A settlement was rejected by JOCER, and it became necessary for the bargainers and the union to renegotiate the agreement. To avoid a recurrence, the legislature subsequently tightened up the consultation procedure between the state negotiators and JOCER in the 1977 statute (Sec. 230).

Michigan, in contrast, has virtually insulated state employee relations from legislative impact by virtue of a constitutional provision that grants the state Civil Service Commission plenary power over all conditions of employment and authority to set wage rates and fringe benefits subject only to a veto of two-thirds vote in both houses of the legislature. There has not been such a veto since the rule was adopted in the mid-1930s.

Administering the Agreement

The ultimate success of collective bargaining lies in the manner in which the terms of a negotiated agreement are applied. Hence management must be as concerned with its organization for administrative

---

[46] Horton, *Report, supra* note 22, at E5. See Paul F. Gerhart, Political Activity by Public Employee Organizations at the Local Level: Threat or Promise (Chicago: International Personnel Management Association, 1974) for a broader discussion.

purposes as it is for negotiation of the agreement. In small units, no serious problems need arise. The chief executive negotiator can readily communicate with line officers on the meaning of the agreement, and if issues emerge at the workplace, the supervisors can quickly turn to the negotiator or his superior.

In the typical small school district, for example, the superintendent or one of his assistants provides the integrating role between the negotiating and the administrative process. Usually only a single level of supervision (the principal) lies between the superintendent's office and the teachers. Somewhat larger schools with a departmental structure may have a second level of supervision, but the principal ordinarily is responsible for day-to-day personnel problems. Matters can be readily referred to the superintendent's office or, if need be, to the school board.

The situation of the small municipality is much the same. The mayor or city manager is normally well versed in the agreement. If an aide, legal counsel, or personnel director conducts negotiations on their behalf, the tie is close. The operating heads of the municipal departments have quick access to the central office and should be able to obtain authoritative answers to questions about the meaning of the agreement. If a conflict situation arises through misapplication of the agreement, the reason usually lies in interpersonal failings.

In larger governmental units (a complex school district, a major city, or an entire state), size and complexity do demand close attention to management's organization for administering the agreement. This cannot be left simply to informal interpersonal relations. The state of Illinois offers one type of integrative structure. Each department or agency (subject to the Civil Service Code) has assigned to it a personnel officer who is a member of the state Department of Central Management Services (formerly the Department of Personnel). This officer is also responsible to the operating head of the particular agency, or one of his chief assistants, so that he has dual lines of communication—one within the agency for the conduct of the agency's personnel business, the other to the state's central personnel office so as to implement state rules and regulations, including the terms of the applicable state collective bargaining agreement. It is the responsibility of the personnel officer to assist the agency's line officials in the day-to-day effectuation of the agreement through advice and information, including the settlement of employee grievances. These personnel officers are usually subordinate to the senior line officials; they are not power centers and can often be frustrated by line officials who are hostile to collective bargaining or reluctant to deal cooperatively with union representatives. The state's personnel network then is largely dependent upon the quality of its field representatives, particularly their ability to persuade operating officials that they can be valuable sources of information about personnel rules and regulations and useful aides in dealing with the union organization.

In other states the departmental or agency personnel or labor relations staffs are responsible exclusively to the operating units. The central labor relations office then has the difficult task of developing communications with a variety of individuals in whose selection it had no voice and over whose conduct it has no control. These field personnel people attach primary importance and loyalty to their employers. Even when the governor issues a memorandum mandating close cooperation with central personnel and strict adherence to the terms of applicable agreements, there may be considerable variation in practice. Some department heads are much more influential than others at the cabinet level and may be able to achieve more autonomy. The situation may be even more difficult when the governor, for one reason or another, fails to give the state labor negotiators the authority to control departmental action.

Managing Under Conditions of Fiscal Stress

The first decade of extensive public-sector collective bargaining occurred under conditions of general economic affluence. The decade from the mid-1970s to the mid-1980s, in contrast, was a period of severe fiscal stress for many states and local governments. Two factors shaped the new environment. First, two serious recessions occurred during the 1970s followed by an even more drastic national economic decline in the early 1980s. Second, national public policy shifted sharply from Carter's welfare society to Reagan's program of curtailment and devolution of many domestic functions from the federal government to the state and localities. Devolution meant not only increased fiscal and administrative responsibility for the states and local governments, but also severe reductions in federal grants-in-aid and revenue sharing.

One of the earliest and most dramatic cases of fiscal stress was the near-bankruptcy in the mid-1970s of the nation's largest city, New York. The situation was salvaged only through large financial loans from local employee pension funds, the state and federal governments, and private business combined with a program of employee concessions in bargaining and cost-cutting retrenchment in the number of employees, benefits, and work rules. From 1974 to 1983 the balance of power shifted markedly from labor to municipal management,[47] although union membership in the public sector continued to rise.

---

[47] For an incisive analysis and interpretation, see Raymond D. Horton, *Fiscal Stress and Labor Power*, in Proceedings of the Thirty-Eighth Annual Meeting, Industrial Relations Research Association (Madison, Wis.: IRRA, 1986), 304–315.

Most local government was not as seriously threatened as New York City but the widespread pressure to cut costs and to improve productivity was evidenced by the passage of such tax-constraining measures as Proposition 13 in a California referendum (1978) and Proposition 2½ in Massachusetts (1980), performance or merit pay, contracting-out, health-care cost containment, and a variety of forms of pay freezes and givebacks.[48] The initiative for responding to the fiscal situation rested mainly in the hands of management while employees and their unions became preoccupied with job security and the protection of as much of their hard-gained benefits as possible.

Although economic forces largely dictated the changing power balance, the philosophy and programs of the Reagan administration were a major factor in the early 1980s. The Reagan administration approach to public-sector labor relations will be discussed in more detail at a later point. Here it is necessary to note only that it helped set the tone for many state and local governments and strongly precipitated many of the economic problems encountered by local government. On the positive side, management responded with improved training programs; tighter controls over costs and inefficiencies in recruitment, job classification, and health and welfare plans; incentives to enhance performance and productivity; and joint labor-management cooperation. On the other hand, many employees suffered losses or freezes in pay and benefit levels, reductions in employment, and a tightening of discipline and work rules. Collective bargaining tended to be dominated by managements who pursued a tougher line and were disposed to "take a strike" rather than to compromise or agree to third-party arbitration. Even after the economic environment began to recover in 1983 and unions became more aggressive, many managements persisted in asserting an adversarial posture.

There were, of course, some moderating forces. In states like New York and Massachusetts, the unions maintained close political ties with Democratic Party governors. Likewise, in Illinois Republican Governor James R. Thompson, and in Ohio Democratic Governor Richard Celeste, gave their support to the enactment of long-contested public-sector bargaining bills in 1983. In a number of states and local governments, joint labor-management committees were established on management initiative or with management cooperation to cope with problems like increasing productivity, alcoholism and drugs, health-care cost containment, and affirmative action. In numerous areas, led

---

[48] Daniel J.B. Mitchell concluded, however, that such pay concessions were less widespread than in the private sector. See his *Concession Bargaining in the Public Sector: A Lesser Force*, 15 Pub. Pers. Mgmt. 23–40 (Spring 1986).

by the states of Washington and Minnesota, agreements to establish comparable-worth compensation structures were negotiated despite discouraging case decisions by the federal judiciary.

In Higher Education

Collective bargaining for academicians came to higher education more than a decade after it was firmly established in the public schools and junior or community colleges. Most of the early unionized four-year institutions were state colleges and small private colleges, but the negotiation of contracts at the City University of New York (1969) and at Rutgers and the State University of New York (1971) heralded the extension of collective bargaining to the ranks of major institutions as well. In 1980 the U.S. Supreme Court decided in the *Yeshiva University* case that the full-time faculty of that institution were managerial employees and therefore excluded from the protections of the National Labor Relations Act. This decision effectively "chilled" private-sector organizing and served to widen the gap between private and public sector organizing. By 1986, an estimated 83 percent of all certified bargaining agents were to be found at public colleges.[49]

The rapid growth period occurred mainly in the 1970s. However, the coverage of multicampus systems gradually increased in the 1980s as well, including the notable addition of the California State University System in 1983. Among these large and complex systems, those in Maine, Vermont, Massachusetts, New York, Connecticut, New Jersey, Pennsylvania, Florida, and Hawaii are fully unionized. With the important exception of their main campuses, the systems in several of the midwestern "Big Ten" universities and in the state of California are substantially unionized.

The advent of collective bargaining has had significant implications for university and college administration. In a perceptive look into the future, Harold H. Haak, president of California State University at Fresno, after only two years of collective bargaining experience in his system, foresaw the following tendencies affecting the role of top administrators, especially university presidents:[50]

1. The emergence of an employer/employee model as contrasted with a collegial relationship, with the president part of a distinct management group.

---

[49] Directory of Faculty Contracts and Bargaining Agents in Institutions of Higher Education (New York: National Center for the Study of Collective Bargaining in Higher Education, Baruch College, City University of New York, 1986), 7.
[50] Harold H. Haak, *Collective Bargaining in the Year 2000: A President's Perspective*, 36 J. College & Univ. Pers. Ass'n 24 (Summer/Fall 1985).

2. Closer ties between the presidents and their governing boards and less close ties with faculty.

3. Conflicting interests among faculty mediated through the collective bargaining agent rather than directly by the president and higher administration.

4. The legitimation of conflicts between the president and faculty on an "institutional" rather than a "personal" basis.

5. The gradual clarification but not complete elimination of ɔoundary lines between "employment conditions" and "professional matters."

Haak was less inclined to predict the often anticipated loss of influence of university presidents in multicampus systems or their conversion to "middle manager" status because of the use of bargaining specialists. Nor did his experience reflect diminished rule-making flexibility and greater uniformity in the areas of faculty salaries or other employment conditions. He was particularly surprised that traditional governance procedures, such as the academic senate, continued to coexist with collective bargaining on an amicable basis.[51]

A very different conception of the impact of collective bargaining upon university governance was presented by Robert Nielsen, assistant to the president for higher education of the American Federation of Teachers (AFT) and Irwin H. Polishook, president of the faculty union at CUNY and a vice president of the AFT.[52] These union leaders contended that the industrial-union model has been erroneously applied to faculty unionism and collective bargaining and that stereotypes have developed which have exaggerated the "adversarial and confrontational aspects" of the bargaining process and handicapped the development of a more appropriate concept inherent in the term "bargaining guild."

Nielsen and Polishook asserted that faculty unionism was not an effort to create a bilateral adversarial system of governance, but rather a *response* to the historical transition from "college" to "corporation" in which the administration became "management" and professors were reduced to "employees." Collective bargaining, they argued, "did not alter the character of the university but rather adapted itself to the objective conditions of employment found in a particular work environment."[53] Most contracts represented an effort to "maintain and strengthen existing governance structures and to prevent further encroachments by management into areas of traditional faculty authority."[54]

---

[51] *Id.* at 25.
[52] *Higher Education and Collective Bargaining: Past, Present, and Future*, 36 J. College & Univ. Pers. Ass'n 52–57 (Summer/Fall 1985).
[53] *Id.* at 54.
[54] *Id.*

Whatever the validity of these opposing views, and examples can be found of both, it is clear that the policies and structures of university administrators relating to collective bargaining have evolved in varied ways depending upon such contextual factors as enabling legislation, the history of unionization, the degree of centralization of policy making, the nature of governance practice prior to collective bargaining, and the attitudes of top-level administrators and trustees. No two developmental patterns as among states have been identical and even within states different approaches can be found. In 1984, James P. Begin, a leading student of relations in higher education, stated:

> At this point the diversity of collective bargaining-governance relationship is the most prevalent characteristic of collective bargaining . . . despite the current instability and diversity, the expectation that traditional governance and bargaining would be competitive at the cost of traditional procedures has not been fulfilled.[55]

Available evidence seems to indicate a high degree of willingness on the part of the administrative (as well as the faculty) side to experiment with and adapt new or modified procedures. Illustrative is the experience at the University of California where, under a state piecemeal approach, preparations for collective bargaining by the administration had extended over several years.[56] A 1984 addendum to a detailed article on the pre-1983 history revealed a sweeping series of structural changes. For example, the Vice President-Academic and Staff Personnel Relations position was eliminated and bargaining responsibility given to a Senior Vice President for Administration. A Management Advisory Council was replaced by a University Labor Relations Council. A Collective Bargaining Operations Group was replaced by a broader Labor Relations Group. These were functional, not simply semantic, changes.

This brief discussion has concentrated on the top level of administration vis-à-vis the faculty.[57] Collective bargaining has also affected the roles of lower levels from deans to department heads. These middle and first-line administrators are often vital figures in the imple-

---

[55] James P. Begin, *Higher Education*, in The Evolving Process—Collective Negotiations in Public Employment, Association of Labor Relations Agencies publication (Fort Washington, Pa.: Labor Relations Press, 1985), 455.

[56] See Thomas M. Mannix, *The California Experience: An Unusual Law, Institution and Approach*, in Collective Bargaining in Higher Education: The State of the Art, ed. Daniel J. Julius (Washington: College and University Personnel Association, 1984), 149–161. For a study of the early years of the CUNY system, see Bernard Mintz, Living with Collective Bargaining: A Case Study of the City University of New York (New York: National Center for the Study of Collective Bargaining in Higher Education, Baruch College, City University of New York, 1979).

[57] For a detailed study of the relationship between the top administration and the state government, especially in terms of budgetary items, *see* E.D. Duryea and Robert S. Fisk, Collective Bargaining: The State University and the State Government in New York (Buffalo: Department of Higher Education, SUNY, 1975).

mentation of top-level policy, including the interpretation and application of collective-bargaining agreements. They stand between the faculty and top-level administration and are subject to pulls and tugs from both directions.[58] In that process communications are extremely important and ambiguities often emerge. Especially in the early years before a new set of attitudes and procedures crystallizes, the lower level administrators are frequently uncertain of higher administration intentions and of their own relationships with faculty spokespersons and representatives. Over time procedures become institutionalized, policies are clarified, and their attitudinal climate adapts to the collective bargaining system.

At the Federal-Government Level

The preceding discussion has been concerned mainly with management in state and local government. Many of the concepts, propositions, and issues also apply to management in the federal government. The latter, however, has some distinctive features which merit comment although space limitations preclude a detailed examination.

From a collective bargaining perspective, the executive branch of the federal government, the nation's largest single employer, should be subdivided into three principal segments: (1) the quasi-autonomous Postal Service whose 600,000 employees are covered by the 1970 Postal Reorganization Act and the (mainly private sector) Labor Management Relations Act of 1947; (2) the classified civil service, with over 1.6 million employees, who (with some minor exceptions) were subject to a series of presidential executive orders starting on January 17, 1962, with Executive Order 10988 of President John Kennedy and who finally were covered by the Civil Service Reform Act of 1978 on the initiative of President Jimmy Carter; and (3) the wage-board system, with over 400,000 blue-collar employees, who were also subject to the executive orders and the Reform Act but who have a history of collective bargaining focused on area prevailing-wage rates. Because both the postal and wage-board systems share many characteristics of private-sector collective bargaining, the discussion in this section will be devoted to the classified civil service.

---

[58] For some of the problems faced by middle and lower management, see 36 J. College & Univ. Pers. Ass'n No. 2 (Summer/Fall 1985), especially the article by Joyce M. Gattas, *A Dean's Perspective*, 28–31; and Daniel J. Julius, ed., Collective Bargaining in Higher Education: The State of the Art (Washington: College and University Personnel Association, 1984), especially Pt. 4, *The Administration of the Contract*. For a broad study on academic authority, see Kenneth P. Mortimer and T.R. McConnell, Sharing Authority Effectively (San Francisco: Jossey-Bass, 1978).

It should be noted at the outset that President Carter's principal objective in enacting the Reform Act was to control and improve the efficiency of the federal bureaucracy and that the collective-bargaining section (Title VII) was incorporated mainly to win the support of the federal unions and to facilitate the passage of the elaborate personnel reforms proposed. The main reforms included the restructuring of the bipartisan Civil Service Commission into the Office of Personnel Management (OPM) and the Merit Systems Protection Board (MSPB), the creation of a British-style Senior Executive Service (SES),[59] and the development of performance-evaluation and merit-pay systems.[60]

Title VII evolved from the preceding executive orders. Like them, it provided for a very narrow scope of bargaining (excluding, for example, general pay changes and fringe benefits), reinforced exclusive managerial rights and functions, and held strikes and slow-downs to be unfair labor practices. However, it also reconstituted the Federal Labor Relations (Council) Authority along Taft-Hartley lines, clarified exclusive bargaining and national consultation rights, and expanded grievance procedures, including grievance arbitration.

Although the federal unions were generally unhappy with the limitations placed on collective bargaining, they viewed the statutory enactment a step in the right direction. Their relations with Carter's Director of Personnel Management, Alan Campbell, who had been chairman of the Civil Service Commission and who espoused a bipartisan, gradualist approach, were generally moderate and mutually respectful, despite disappointments with respect to the early implementation of segments of the highly complex law.

The election of Ronald Reagan in 1980 and his appointment in 1981 of Donald Devine as OPM Director, however, brought on more than four years of controversy and bitterness unprecedented in federal personnel annals. First, President Reagan and his OPM director were basically hostile to the Reform Act, because they viewed it as a Carter product. Second, militant government unionism and collective bargaining were anathema to the Reagan administration and the severity of its response to the illegal Air Traffic Controllers' strike of August 1981 cast a shadow over the entire bureaucracy. Third, President Reagan's determination to cut the costs of nondefense government

---

[59] California, Minnesota, Wisconsin, and Oregon set up senior executive programs prior to the federal Civil Service Reform Act and five other states followed between 1979 and 1981. *See* H.O. Waldby and Annie Mary Hartsfield, *The Senior Management Service in the States*, 4 Rev. Pub. Pers. Ad. 28–39 (Spring 1984).

[60] See Patricia W. Ingraham and Carolyn Ban, eds. Legislating Bureaucratic Change: The Civil Service Reform Act of 1978 (Albany: State University of New York Press, 1984), esp. 20 and ch. 8. See also Charles H. Levine, ed., The Unfinished Agenda for Civil Service Reform: Implications of the Grace Commission Report (Washington: The Brookings Institution, 1985).

combined with the deep national recession that took hold in 1981 and 1982 added a further component of employee disaffection—fear of reduction in force and pay and benefit freezes and cuts.

Devine was not only an ardent follower of Reagan's ideology, but attempted to implement it with intensity, speed, and disregard for the views of the federal unions. Many of the regulations that he proposed to increase efficiency or to reduce costs raised serious morale problems among employees at large, including the newly created Senior Executive Service. Some of the subject areas on which Devine's views and proposals encountered strong resistance included staff and cost reductions and freezes, contracting-out and privatization, drug- and polygraph-testing, the coverage of agencies supported by the Combined Federal (charities) Campaign, performance pay, health insurance and retirement revisions, and degree of protection for whistle blowers.

His stands on collective bargaining issues repeatedly antagonized the union leadership. Among such issues were the refusal to rehire all but a few of the discharged air traffic controllers, opposition to negotiating pay for travel and per diem expenses for employee representatives, challenging arbitration awards in the courts, accusing three top union leaders of unlawful political activity under the Hatch Act, supporting contracting-out of governmental functions, advocating the idea of privatization or the substitution of private for public enterprise, and limiting pay increases. His campaigning in 1984 for the most conservative Republican candidates like Senator Jesse Helms aroused the ire of Democrat politicians. He was accused of being an ideologue and of politicizing the civil service.

When President Reagan nominated Devine for a second four-year term as OPM Director, his opponents urged the Senate to reject him and the ensuing turmoil led Devine to withdraw his name from consideration. His successor, Constance Horner, although an equally staunch Reaganite, was more moderate in tone and style and gradually restored a calming, if not harmonious, atmosphere in the federal service. In an interview in October 1985 with a Bureau of National Affairs, Inc., staff member shortly after her appointment, Horner stated: "I think that one of the chief goals of my tenure will be to try to manifest a reconciliation, that I think is beginning to occur, just a little bit, between the civil service and the current Administration on the one hand and the civil service and the public on the other hand."[61]

While controversy characterized relationships at the top of the federal service, the attitudinal climate at agency levels was often much more positive. For example, in September 1983 the Internal Revenue Service and the National Treasury Employees Union (NTEU) negoti-

---

[61] 23 GERR 1558 (October 18, 1985).

ated a set of guidelines on the use of quality circles. At the end of 1984 the NTEU expressed a new emphasis on cooperation with federal agencies. In August 1985 the Social Security Administration launched a quality of work life program to deal with systems modernization. The following month Secretary of Labor William Brock directed a study of the Department's management and of employee morale following a critical report by the General Accounting Office of the approach of his predecessor, Raymond Donovan. While these were promising developments, they did not offset the continuing differences over pay increases, some benefit programs, and privatization ideology.

Conclusion

As the preceding discussion indicates, public management has been confronted with a variety of structural and procedural problems emanating from the rapid growth of public unionism and collective bargaining since the middle 1960s. Experimentation, consciously contrived or unplanned, has been rife throughout the country and at all levels of government. A large number of outside labor relations specialists have been attracted by the challenges and rewards. Both personnel staff and line administrators from within have sought to develop new, needed skills by formal training and trial-and-error experience. Old management structures and practices have been discarded or revised; new ones have been introduced. But the time period has been short (few systems go back more than a decade or two), and the problems are complex. Hence, most of the basic issues remain at least partially unresolved despite a noticeable advance in knowledge and understanding and a substantial development in bargaining expertise.

CHAPTER 4

Collective Bargaining and Compensation in the Public Sector

DANIEL J.B. MITCHELL*

In the late 1970s, when the chapter on this topic was being prepared for the previous edition, the world of collective bargaining was dominated by the private sector. Within the private sector, union wage settlements generally outpaced nonunion wage adjustments. True, the proportion of private union-represented workers slipped slightly each year, but the pace of slippage was sufficiently slow that the now commonplace phenomenon of "concession bargaining" was virtually unknown.

Meanwhile, bargaining in the public sector was something of a backwater. Although some academics had begun to pay attention to the subject, collective bargaining for government employees was still viewed as an offshoot of private-sector industrial relations. Thus, state legislatures would typically turn to the framework of the amended Wagner Act when they regulated bargaining with public employees, and government managers hired private-sector industrial relations experts to handle their new bargaining obligations.

The view from the 1980s is profoundly different. Unions in the private sector lost substantial membership in the first half of the 1980s, but public-sector unions basically held their own.[1] By 1985 the proportion of private-sector wage and salary earners represented by unions was only 16 percent, while in the public sector the ratio was 43 percent.[2] These discrepancies were reflected in shifts in bargaining power as well as in the public/private mix of union-represented workers.

It is not surprising that academic research into public-sector wage setting, bargaining, and related topics has expanded substantially, and

---

*University of California, Los Angeles
[1] Throughout the text, no distinction is made between unions and employee associations. Although the distinction was relevant at one time, it carries little meaning in the 1980s.
[2] Courtney D. Gifford, ed., Directory of U.S. Labor Organizations, 1986–87 ed. (Washington: BNA Books, 1986).

an increasing number of reviews of this literature are now available.[3] Rather than simply describe what has already been done in earlier periods, this chapter will begin with an empirical overview of public-sector bargaining and wage setting *during the 1980s*. References to the analytical and empirical literature in subsequent review sections will also be confined almost exclusively to research in the 1980s. It will be suggested that public-sector industrial relations now has lessons for the private sector.

Pay Trends in the 1980s

Table 1 compares public and private pay trends on a total compensation basis for the years 1980-1986. As price disinflation occurred, wage inflation also moderated in the private sector. Various forces, including dollar appreciation (and the resulting import competition), severe recession, and deregulation sparked a dramatic union wage concession movement. This movement did not remain confined to distressed industries; it spilled out of its initial confines and lowered wage norms throughout the private sector.[4] As preexisting private contracts expired, nonunion pay increases pulled ahead of wage settlements determined under collective bargaining.

By the mid-1980s, pay adjustments in the public sector generally outpaced private levels. Especially in the education sector, where

TABLE 1
Public and Private Pay Trends in the 1980s as
Indicated by the Employment Cost Index

Sector	1980	1981	1982	1983	1984	1985	1986
Private sector							
Union	11.1%	10.7%	7.2%	5.8%	4.3%	2.6%	2.1%
Nonunion	8.9	9.4	6.0	5.7	5.2	4.6	3.6
All	9.8	9.8	6.4	5.7	4.9	3.9	3.2
State & local government							
Elementary & secondary schools	n.a.	n.a.	7.3	5.9	7.7	6.3	5.8
All	n.a.	n.a.	7.2	6.0	6.6	5.7	5.2

Source: Current Wage Developments, various issues.
Note: Figures refer to changes in total compensation (wages, benefits, and payroll taxes).

---

[3] See, for example, Richard B. Freeman, *Unionism Comes to the Public Sector*, 24 J. Econ. Lit. 41 (March 1986); Werner Z. Hirsch and Anthony M. Rufolo, *Shirking, Monitoring Costs, and Municipal Labor Productivity*, in The Economics of Municipal Labor Markets, eds. Werner Z. Hirsch and Anthony M. Rufolo (Los Angeles: UCLA Institute of Industrial Relations, 1983), 277.
[4] Daniel J.B. Mitchell, *Shifting Norms in Wage Determination*, 2 Brookings Papers on Econ. Act. 575 (1985).

studies such as the Gardner Report pointed to low pay for teachers as a source of student deficiencies, deliberate attempts were made to raise compensation levels.[5] In addition, pay adjustments that had been repressed by taxpayer revolts in the late 1970s, such as the one surrounding California's Proposition 13, showed evidence of subsequent wage "catch-up" pressures.[6]

Union Versus Nonunion Pay Adjustments

Unfortunately, there are no indexes that directly compare union and nonunion pay trends in government. However, information that is available suggests that union pay adjustments at the state and local level were not disproportionate sources of wage pressure during the 1980s. For example, Table 2 divides states, localities, and school districts (a subdivision of localities) by unionization rate. The "low union" ("high union") designation on the table refers to jurisdictions in states where the overall unionization rate for public workers *in that jurisdictional level* was below (above) the average for all states.[7] A presentation in this form is necessitated by the paucity of data; because the unit of observation is the state rather than the individual jurisdiction, only interstate—as opposed to intrastate—variation can be reflected in the table.

During the period of economic slump (1979-1982), government wages in areas with relatively low unionization rose at or above the rates in more highly unionized areas. Except at the state government level, this pattern continued from 1982 to 1985. In the earlier period, slower growth of per capita income, area wages, and government employment in more highly unionized public jurisdictions might have accounted for the seeming lack of union-related wage pressure, but these factors generally reversed in the later period without leading to

---

[5] National Commission on Excellence in Education, A Nation at Risk: The Imperative for Educational Reform (Washington: U.S. Dept of Education, 1983).

[6] Daniel J.B. Mitchell, *The New Climate: Implications for Research on Public Sector Wage Determination and Labor Relations*, 34 Lab. L.J. 473 (August 1983). Proposition 13 drastically cut local government revenue obtained from property taxes. For information on the employment impact of this proposition, see Frank Levy, Dale Shimasaki, and Bonnie Berk, *Sources of Growth in Local Government Employment: California, 1964–78*, 72 Am. Econ. Rev. 278 (May 1982).

[7] As discussed in the text, the unit of observation is the state. "State" is defined to include the District of Columbia. Not all states have school districts; hence, there are fewer than 51 school district observations shown in Table 2. Data on per capita incomes were drawn from the Survey of Current Business, various issues. Per capita income figures for 1979–1982 are based on a somewhat different definition than those for 1982–1985. Figures on government employment and government wages are from the annual publication, Public Employment, released by the U.S. Bureau of the Census as part of its Government Employment Series. Unionization rates were drawn from the 1982 Census of Governments and appear in U.S. Bureau of the Census, Labor-Management Relations in State and Local Governments, GC82(3)-3 (Washington: U.S. Government Printing Office, 1985), Table 2. Area wages refer to the entire state and are taken from the series appearing in Employment and Wages and related press releases.

TABLE 2

Changes in Per Capita Income, Area Wage Levels, and
Government Employment, by Degree of Unionization

		State Government		Local Government		School Districts	
		Low Union	High Union	Low Union	High Union	Low Union	High Union
Average annualized change in:							
Per capita income:	1979–82	8.5%	8.5%	8.6%	8.4%	8.7%	8.4%
	1982–85	5.8	6.4	5.7	6.6	5.5	6.1
Area wage levels:	1979–82	8.5	8.4	8.5	8.4	8.6	8.2
	1982–85	3.8	4.4	3.9	4.5	3.8	4.4
Government employment:							
	1979–82	.4	.4	.4	− 1.3	1.3	− .1
	1982–85	2.2	2.1	1.4	1.5	2.6	2.1
Government wage:	1979–82	9.0	8.4	9.3	9.3	9.0	8.4
	1982–85	4.8	6.1	5.8	5.6	5.8	5.5
Average ratio of government wage to area wage, 1982		1.18	1.21	1.06	1.20	1.07	1.18
Number of observations		27	23	30	21	21	24

Source: See text and footnotes.
Note: High union refers to areas in states with unionization rates at the jurisdiction level indicated which are above the 1982 average. Averages for state government, local government, and school districts were 36.0, 47.0, and 51.6 percent, respectively. Low union refers to areas with below-average unionization. Unionization rates are the proportion of full-time employees represented by unions. Government wage refers to average monthly earnings in October of year shown of full-time government employees. Government employment refers to both full- and part-time workers. Area wage level refers to annual wages per employee in state covered by unemployment insurance. For Maryland, area wages for all employees were projected from 1984 to 1985 using figures for private employees only. The ratio of government wages to area wages is on an annual basis, i.e., government monthly wages have been multiplied by 12.

relative upward pressure on union wages. Thus, just as unions were not linked to relative wage pressures in government in the latter half of the 1970s,[8] neither were they associated with a wage push in the first half of the 1980s.

_____

[8] Daniel J.B. Mitchell, *Unions and Wages in the Public Sector: A Review of Recent Evidence*, 12 J. Coll. Neg. Pub. Sector 337 (1983).

The results of the regression analysis reported in Table 3 more precisely confirm the lack of a union association with upward wage pressure. Again using states as units of observation, trends in government pay during 1982–1985 were regressed against the unionization rate, changes in area wages, and earlier government wage trends (1979–1982).[9] Unionization appears in the equations as either an insignificant or a slightly negative influence on pay adjustments during this period. State and local pay trends were influenced primarily by area wage movements (positively) and by past government pay trends (negatively). The latter finding strongly suggests catch-up influences. Relatively low government pay increases—perhaps due to fiscal strains—in the early period tend to be "made up" subsequently as budget outlooks improve.

The Wage Concession Movement in Government

It is paradoxical, but perhaps symptomatic of the growing importance of the public sector in industrial relations, that President Reagan's firing of striking air traffic controllers in 1981 is often seen as a

TABLE 3

Regressions Relating to Wage Catch-Up and
Unionization: Cross-Sections, 1982–1985

	State Government	Local Government	School Districts
Constant	4.98**	6.95**	6.32**
Unionization rate, 1982	.02	−.02**	−.01
Change in government wage, 1979–82	−.35**	−.26**	−.18*
Change in area wage, 1982–85	.70**	.50**	.39**
Adjusted R^2	.33	.37	.20
Standard error	1.75	1.06	1.29
Number of observations	50	51	45

Source: See text and footnotes.
Note: Dependent variable is annualized percent change in monthly earnings of full-time government employees, October 1982 to October 1985, in each state at the level of government listed at the head of the column. The unionization rate is the proportion of full-time workers organized as of October 1982 in each state at the level of government listed at the head of the column. The change in government wage is the dependent variable during October 1979 to October 1982. Change in area wage is the annualized change in wages per employee covered by unemployment insurance in the state of the jurisdiction.
*Significant at 10 percent level.
**Significant at 5 percent level.

[9] For data sources and other information, see *supra* note 7.

cause of subsequent private-union wage concessions and membership losses. [10] The air traffic controllers' strike was a uniquely public-sector event; workers who did not have the legal right to strike were terminated for asserting that right. [11] If the dispute had any demonstration effects, they might have been expected to flow mainly into public labor-management relations.

Yet while some concession bargaining by unions in the 1980s occurred in the public sector, it was, as the author has noted elsewhere, a "lesser force" when compared with private-sector developments. [12] A substantial literature developed concerning private-sector concessions, but the literature on concessions in the public sector was quite limited, probably because of their lower frequency. [13]

Table 4 compares private with state and local union wage adjustments under major contracts. [14] The table indicates the proportions of workers covered by first-year wage freezes or cuts, a proxy for concession bargaining. Wage cuts were virtually unknown in major contracts in government, but could be found in such formerly "key" private industries as steel. Freezes in wages were more common than cuts in both sectors, but again the private sector featured such outcomes more prominently.

The Escalator Impact

Private-sector contracts were more likely than state and local contracts to have had cost-of-living escalator clauses prior to the concession period. Thus, in some cases wage freezes were partially alleviated by escalator increases under private agreements. Despite reduced inflation, private-sector union negotiators also held on to their escalators more tenaciously than did their government-sector counterparts. While some public-sector workers may have put a high priority

---

[10] It should be noted that the author does not view the results of the air controllers' strike as a major cause of concession bargaining. Other influences were much more important. However, the fact that the air controllers' dispute was popularly viewed as a cause of a private-sector phenomenon illustrates the growth in importance of the public sector in the field of industrial relations.

[11] Herbert R. Northrup, *The Rise and Demise of PATCO*, 37 Indus. & Lab. Rel. Rev. 167 (January 1984); Richard W. Hurd and Jill K. Krjesky, *"The Rise and Demise of PATCO": Reconstructed*, 40 Indus. & Lab. Rel. Rev. 115 (October 1986); Northrup, *Reply*, 40 Indus. & Lab. Rel. Rev. 122 (October 1986).

[12] Daniel J.B. Mitchell, *Concession Bargaining in the Public Sector: A Lesser Force*, 15 Pub. Pers. Mgmt. 23 (Spring 1986).

[13] For an exception, see David Lewin, *Public Sector Concession Bargaining: Lessons for the Private Sector*, Proceedings of the 35th Annual Meeting, Industrial Relations Research Association (Madison, Wis.: IRRA, 1983), 383.

[14] See the table for the definition of "major" contracts. It should be noted that the series on state and local wage settlements was one of the few areas of *expanded* collection by the U.S. Bureau of Labor Statistics of an industrial relations data source in a period when such information gathering was generally being trimmed. For details, see Edward Wasileski, *BLS Extends State and Local Government Bargaining Series*, 108 Monthly Lab. Rev. 36 (May 1985).

TABLE 4

Trends in Union Wage Adjustments in the
Private and Public Sectors, 1980–1986

	1980	1981	1982	1983	1984	1985	1986p
New union wage settlements							
First-year wage adjustments:							
Private	9.5%	9.8%	3.8%	2.6%	2.4%	2.3%	1.2%
State and local	7.5	7.4	7.2	4.4	4.8	4.6	5.7
Percent of workers with first-year wage cuts:							
Private	0%	3%	2%	12%	5%	3%	9%
State and local	0	0	0	0	0	*	0
Percent of workers with first-year wage freezes:							
Private:	*	5%	42%	44%	18%	33%	21%
State and local	10%	9	12	21	19	16	10
Percent of union workers with escalators:							
Private	57%	56%	58%	57%	57%	50%	40%
State and local	n.a.	21	2	1	2	2	2
Effective union wage adjustments:							
Private	9.9%	9.5%	6.8%	4.0%	3.7%	3.3%	2.3%
State and local	6.5	8.7	6.6	5.2	5.0	5.7	5.5
State and local wage adjustments according to employment cost index	n.a.	n.a.	6.5%	5.3%	5.9%	5.6%	5.4%

Source: Current Wage Developments, Monthly Labor Review, various issues.
Note: Private union adjustments refer to nonagricultural contracts covering 1,000 or more workers. State and local union adjustments refer to contracts covering 5,000 or more workers, 1980–83, and 1,000 or more workers, 1984–86. p = preliminary
*Less than 0.5%.

on contractual protection from inflation,[15] union bargainers in a few cases faced newly enacted legal bans on continuing such clauses for

---

[15] Sahab Dayal, *Unionized Professionals and Bargaining Priorities: An Exploratory Study of University Professors*, 13 J. Coll. Neg. Pub. Sector 55 (1984).

public employees.[16] Table 4 shows a spectacular drop in the proportion of union-represented public workers covered by escalators in 1982 in the major contract sector. This decline resulted from the elimination of escalators in 12 of the surveyed contracts, leaving escalator coverage in only three major agreements.

The fact that escalators were a relatively recent phenomenon in the public sector in most jurisdictions was undoubtedly a major factor in their elimination; they simply had not become as entrenched as they were in many private-sector bargaining units. In addition, as will be discussed later, union contracts are typically of shorter duration in government than in the private sector, making escalation less critical. With more frequent negotiations, unexpected inflation can always be reflected in a renegotiated contract, without substantial delay.

As Table 4 shows, even accounting for escalator wage increases, effective union wage adjustments in state and local employment still consistently exceeded those for private workers after 1982. But effective union wage adjustments were *not* out of line with general wage adjustments in that sector (union plus nonunion). Again, the lack of a public-sector union wage push in the 1980s is confirmed by the available data.

Fiscal Distress and Concessions

Thanks to the experiences of New York City's flirtation with bankruptcy in the mid-1970s and California's Proposition 13, the notion that union wage adjustments in the public sector are affected by fiscal crises is well established.[17] Workers may become angry and

---

[16] James J. Healy, *Confrontation in the Urban Mass Transit Industry: Is Legislation the Answer?*, Proceedings of the 36th Annual Meeting, Industrial Relations Research Association (Madison, Wis.: IRRA, 1984), 291; Richard U. Miller and James L. Stern, *A New Era in Transit Bargaining*, Proceedings of the 36th Annual Meeting, Industrial Relations Research Association (Madison, Wis.: IRRA, 1984), 278.

[17] It might be noted that Freeman found that public pay is responsive to economic conditions, although the timing in response may differ between the public and private sectors (Richard B. Freeman, How Do Public Sector Wages and Employment Respond to Economic Conditions? Working Paper No. 1653 (Cambridge: National Bureau of Economic Research, June 1985)). Annual regression analysis by the author, based on changes in compensation per full-time-equivalent employees in government and the private sector, revealed a mixed picture. For the period 1960–1985, the coefficients on annual price change (lagged one year) tended to be lower in government than in the private sector, i.e., 0.5 to 0.6 as opposed to 0.8. (The only exception was federal enterprises, which were dominated by the escalator clause applicable to postal workers.) To measure economic activity, the ratio of real GNP to its long-run trend was used. With regard to sensitivity of wage change to the level of economic activity, the private sector generally appeared more sensitive, but only because of the contribution of the 1980s and the accompanying concession bargaining. Significant coefficients were found for state and local enterprises and noneducational services. Other public subsectors produced "correctly" signed coefficients, but without high levels of statistical significance. These results reflect the fact that the public sector as a whole was less adversely affected by recessions in the 1960–1985 period (especially the economic slump of the early 1980s) than many private industries. Those government jurisdictions which did experience substantial fiscal distress are reflected in the coefficients of economic activity, but tend to become "lost" when their wage adjustments are mixed with those of other jurisdictions.

militant in the face of such experiences, but anger alone does not translate into big wage increases. Indeed, the major concern of unions in such situations may well shift to protecting employment rather than raising wages.[18]

Even when unions are negotiating to save jobs in the short run, there is always the hope on the employee side that concessionary wage losses may be made up in some future, more favorable period. As one local union president put it in late 1986, after obtaining job security guarantees in exchange for a wage freeze, "If we get logged in for two years, maybe there'll be a change in Washington. . . . Then we can get back to negotiating like we used to. Right now, people are concerned about keeping their jobs. . . ."[19] The evidence on catch-up tendencies in government wage setting suggests that this hope is not unrealistic.

Union "tastes" for employment versus wages in periods of fiscal distress will vary; the choice will not always be for the former over the latter.[20] Nevertheless, fiscal pressures do lead to reduced public pay settlements generally,[21] and there is an incentive for rival unions at least to coordinate their strategy when faced with a common budgetary threat.[22] Union leaders, if not members, have learned to associate periods of budget constraint with less favorable bargaining outcomes.[23]

The concession bargaining that did occur in the public sector in the 1980s was linked to fiscal distress of particular jurisdictions. Using a variety of data sources, the author developed a file of public-sector concession agreements (those involving first-year wage freezes or cuts) for the period of 1980–1986. This file permits a breakdown of concessions by government level, type of service provided, and other characteristics.[24]

Table 5 indicates that most state and local concessions were in fact negotiated at the local level, where most bargaining units are located.

---

[18] Gene Swimmer, *The Impact of Proposition 13 on Public Employee Relations: The Case of Los Angeles*, 11 J. Coll. Neg. Pub. Sector 13 (1982), and Swimmer, *The Impact of Proposition 13 on Municipal Police in California*, 12 J. Coll. Neg. Pub. Sector 127 (1983).

[19] *Omaha, Neb., Nonuniformed Workers Trade Freeze for Job Security*, 24 GERR 1437 (October 20, 1986).

[20] Raymond D. Horton, *Public-Sector Bargaining: Managing Labor Relations Under Conditions of Stress*, Proceedings of the 38th Annual Meeting, Industrial Relations Research Association (Madison, Wis.: IRRA, 1986), 304.

[21] Philip K. Way, *Public-Sector Pay Bargaining Under Government Financial Restrictions in the U.S. and the U.K.*, Proceedings of the 38th Annual Meeting, Industrial Relations Research Association (Madison, Wis.: IRRA, 1986), 260.

[22] David Lewin and Mary McCormick, *Coalition Bargaining in Municipal Government: The New York City Experience*, 34 Indus. & Lab. Rel. Rev. 175 (January 1981).

[23] *AFSCME President McEntee Reviews Union's Progress in Last Five Years*, 242 Daily Lab. Rep. A–6 (December 17, 1986).

[24] The file was drawn from articles appearing in Government Employee Relations Report, settlement listings in the Daily Labor Report (for publicly owned transit systems), and Current Wage Developments. See Mitchell, *supra* note 12, for use of an earlier version of the public-sector concession file.

TABLE 5

Characteristics of State and Local Union Wage Concession Sample, 1980–1986

Category	Proportion of Concessions in Category	Category	Proportion of Concessions in Category	Comparison Proportion of Agreements in Category[a]
Level:		State:		
State	13%	Oregon	15%	2%
Local	87	Michigan	14	9
Service:		Pennsylva-		
Education	27%	nia	10	7
Police	11	Ohio	8	5
Fire	10	Washington	7	4
Health	6	California	6	12
Transit	13	Other	40	61
Other	33	Union:		
Unit size:		AFSCME	19%	29%
Less than 1,000		NEA	18	6
workers	53%	IAFF	11	11
1,000 or more		ATU	10	2
workers	47	AFT	4	3
		Other	40	50

Sources: Author's public-sector concession file (see text and footnotes for details); U.S. Bureau of the Census, Labor-Management Relations in State and Local Governments, GC82(3)-3 (Washington: U.S. Government Printing Office, 1985), Table 3; U.S. Bureau of Labor Statistics, BLS File of State, County, and Municipal Collective Bargaining Agreements, Fall 1979, Report 598 (Washington: U.S. Government Printing Office, 1980), Table 2.

[a]Estimate of the proportion of agreements by state refers to labor-management agreements in effect as of October 1982. Estimate of the proportion of agreements by union refers to the number of state and local agreements on file with the Bureau of Labor Statistics as of Fall 1979.

The concession contracts split roughly 50-50 between large units (1,000 or more workers) and smaller units. Of course, the larger units account for the bulk of the affected workers.[25]

Education and transit were the services most commonly represented in the concession file; together they accounted for about 40 percent of the contracts included. There is no direct information source on the proportion of total state and local government contracts which fall into the education and transit sectors. Hence, by itself the 40 percent figure does not prove that these two sectors were more concession-prone than others within the public arena. But there is circumstantial evidence that they were, based on union affiliation.

---

[25] Ninety-three percent of the workers in the public-sector concession file were in units of 1,000 or more employees.

Table 5 compares the proportion of concessions associated with several public-sector unions with the proportion of all state and local contracts known to the Bureau of Labor Statistics (BLS) which were associated with those unions. The percentages of concession contracts associated with the National Education Association (NEA) and the American Federation of Teachers (AFT)—the two key unions in the education field—are disproportionately high. The Amalgamated Transit Union (ATU), the most important union in public transit, also shows a disproportionate rate of concession bargaining.

These results are indicative, but not conclusive, since the BLS comparison contract sample is incomplete with regard to agreements covering less than 1,000 workers.[26] The supposition that transit systems might be disproportionately represented among concession bargains is not especially jarring, since transit authorities often have private-sector attributes such as dependence on revenue from customers. Many publicly operated transit systems are descendents of earlier private enterprises. In a period when concession bargaining was widespread in the private sector, transit systems were the most likely places for a spillover of concessions into public negotiations.

The education sector, in contrast, seems a less likely place for a disproportionate amount of concession bargaining. As noted earlier, pay increases in public education generally outpaced those in both public and private employment. What must be stressed, however, is the relatively small proportion of workers covered by concessions in the public sector as compared with the private, and the lesser severity of those public concessions that were made. It is quite possible for public education to have had both disproportionate concession bargaining *and* higher average pay increases.

Six states—Oregon, Michigan, Pennsylvania, Ohio, Washington, and California—accounted for 60 percent of the wage concessions reported. Of these, all but California appear to have negotiated a disproportionate share of concessions, when compared with the number of union agreements falling within their boundaries. The budgetary problems of these states during the early 1980s are well known. Oregon and Washington suffered from declines in the lumber industry. Michigan, Pennsylvania, and Ohio became "rust belt" states, suffering lost tax revenues due to adverse trends in manufacturing. In short, the connection between public-sector concession bargaining and fiscal distress is clear.

---

[26] The Bureau of Labor Statistics file is described as containing virtually all agreements covering 1,000 or more workers and a small proportion of agreements covering fewer workers.

The Outcomes of Concession Bargaining

Table 6 compares various features of the government concession contracts to a similar sample covering the private sector.[27] The table indicates that many of the characteristics of private-sector concession bargaining in the 1980s could also be found in the public sector. For example, the increased use of profit sharing under private-sector concession contracts had a counterpart in contractual features linking pay to future available public revenues. Such share arrangements introduced an element of de facto wage flexibility into the agreement. But in neither public nor private employment did concession bargaining cause a substantial reduction in contract length compared with durational norms for the sector.[28] Thus, the added wage flexibility that might have been associated with shorter contracts did not develop.

Two-tier wage contracts became increasingly common during the mid-1980s in private employment, especially in concession situa-

TABLE 6

Union Wage Concessions in State and Local
Government and in Private Bargaining

	Private Sector	State and Local Government Sector
Percent of contracts in sample with:		
Escalator clause	20%	7%
Wage decrease	20	4
Two-tier wage plan	10	1
Profit sharing	5	–
Revenue sharing	–	5
Lump-sum wage plan	22	3
Mean contract duration in months	30	22
Settled by arbitration	–	6

Source: Author's concession files drawn from the Daily Labor Report, Government Employee Relations Report, and Current Wage Developments. See text and footnotes for details.
Note: Private-sector sample consists of over 1,800 settlements during 1981–1986 with first-year wage freezes or cuts. State and local sample consists of 182 settlements during 1980–1986 with first-year wage freezes or cuts.

---

[27] The private file was used (in an earlier form) in Mitchell, *supra* note 4. However, publicly owned transit system settlements have been deleted from the private file in Table 6 and appear instead in the public file shown on that table.
[28] Contract duration practices in the public sector will be discussed below.

tions.[29] These contracts also developed, but were less prevalent, in public employment; those that did exist appeared to be linked mainly to public enterprises. For example, at the federal level, the 1984 Postal Service contracts included a two-tier pay system,[30] and in the public concession sample, all of the contracts with reported two-tier plans involved transit systems. Where two-tier plans existed in public employment, unions pushed—sometimes successfully—to terminate them.[31]

Lump-sum pay systems were also found in concession agreements in both sectors.[32] However, these systems became widespread in private bargaining while remaining a relative rarity in government. Nominal wage decreases, the sample confirms, also were comparatively infrequent in government employment (and were found mainly for smaller bargaining units), but were more common in private concession bargaining.

The major difference between private and public concessions was probably their time profiles. Private concessions continued unabated into the mid-1980s, despite the general economic expansion after 1982. In contrast, the number of public concessions tended to taper off as the economy improved. Thus, the public-sector concessions that were negotiated seemed to be more transitory than their private counterparts and were linked to temporary fiscal distress in particular jurisdictions. Perhaps this transitory aspect is why, in most cases, the parties were able to reach a concession agreement without the intervention of interest arbitration. Apparently both sides understood the short-term fiscal dilemma they faced and adapted to it. Private concessions, however, represented a longer term weakening of union bargaining power, related to membership losses within industries and the rise of nonunion competition.

Pay Levels in Government

In one respect, the literature of the 1980s differed little from earlier research reports. Economists in the eighties were still trying to

---

[29] Under a two-tier pay plan, new hires are paid at lower rates than incumbent job-holders. See Sanford M. Jacoby and Daniel J.B. Mitchell, *Management Attitudes Toward Two-Tier Pay Plans*, 7 J. Lab. Res. 221 (Summer 1986), for more details.

[30] J. Joseph Loewenberg, *What's $13 Billion Among Friends? The 1984 Postal Arbitration*, Proceedings of the 38th Annual Meeting, Industrial Relations Research Association (Madison, Wis.: IRRA, 1986), 369.

[31] *City Workers in Detroit End Strike*, 109 Monthly Lab. Rev. 37 (October 1986).

[32] Lump-sum pay plans involve the paying of a designated bonus to employees which does not enter the basic rate of pay. Thus, the employer experiences lower labor costs during the contract life. For example, a two-year contract with annual 3-percent wage increases will raise the base wage (and the annual level of employer expenditure) by 6 percent during its life. In contrast, a two-year contract with 3-percent annual bonuses will not raise the base wage and raises annual expenditures by only 3 percent over its life.

pin down the impact of unions on public-sector pay. The question still was: Do unions make government pay levels higher? The answer still was, "Yes—somewhat."

"Rents" in Public Pay Determination

Before the union-wage-effect question can be addressed, however, it is important to develop some notion of what government pay levels would be like without unionization. Simple comparisons of pay levels in the unionized public sector with private pay could be misleading if government pay was inherently "too high"—that is, too high with or without a union. Thus, research on the union wage impact has been closely linked to the general question of whether public employees actually receive economic "rents"—premiums in pay above their alternative labor market value.

Table 7 provides a time-series comparison of pay levels on a total compensation basis between various public pay rates and a private-sector average.[33] Note that in the late 1970s and early 1980s, average federal pay levels, unadjusted for any occupational composition effects, were anywhere from 24 to 43 percent above those in the private sector. In contrast, state and local pay levels did not show such marked differences when measured against the private sector.

The simple ratio analysis of Table 7 has been reflected in more sophisticated comparisons in which controls were introduced for employee characteristics. Economists researching the issue of rents for public employees tended to conclude that federal workers (including the postal workers who dominate the federal enterprise column of Table 7) were "overpaid." But they were likely to find that state and local employees, as a group, were not overpaid, or were less overpaid.[34]

For demographic groups, researchers often found that those workers likely to receive lower pay in the private sector (women and minorities) received higher pay in public employment.[35] Whether this leveling effect of government was a "good thing," or whether government ought to be compared with private outcomes by demographic group, was much debated in testimony by economists in connection

[33] Comparisons of public and private total compensation figures are complicated by the inclusion of Social Security taxes. Private employers must pay such taxes; state and local governments may or may not be part of the Social Security system. Most federal employees are not under Social Security.

[34] Alan B. Krueger, Are Public Sector Workers Really Overpaid? Evidence from Longitudinal Data and Queues, Conference Paper on Public Sector Unionism (Cambridge: National Bureau of Economic Research, August 1986); D. Alton Smith, *Government Employment and Black/White Relative Wages*, 15 J. Hum. Resources 77 (Winter 1980); Sharon P. Smith, *Are State and Local Government Workers Overpaid?*, in The Economics of Municipal Labor Markets, *supra* note 3, at 59; Sharon P. Smith, *Prospects for Reforming Federal Pay*, 72 Am. Econ. Rev. 273 (May 1982).

[35] Morley Gunderson, *Public Sector Compensation in Canada and the U.S.*, 19 Indus. Rel. 257 (Fall 1980).

TABLE 7

Comparative Government and Private Pay Trends, 1950–1985

Year	Federal Enterprises to Private	Federal Civilian to Private	Federal Enterprises to Federal Civilian	State and Local Enterprises to Private	State and Local Education to Private	State and Local Noneducation to Private
1950	1.09	1.19	.92	1.02	n.a.	n.a.
1955	1.01	1.17	.86	1.01	.92	.90
1960	1.01	1.24	.82	.99	.99	.89
1965	1.07	1.33	.80	1.01	1.01	.89
1970	1.13	1.40	.81	1.06	1.10	.96
1975	1.25	1.43	.88	1.07	1.07	.97
1976	1.28	1.42	.90	1.07	1.07	.97
1977	1.28	1.43	.89	1.05	1.06	.97
1978	1.26	1.43	.88	1.02	1.03	.95
1979	1.24	1.39	.89	1.02	1.03	.95
1980	1.25	1.35	.93	1.01	1.02	.94
1981	1.30	1.36	.95	1.03	1.01	.96
1982	1.27	1.35	.94	1.04	1.03	.97
1983	1.30	1.36	.95	1.05	1.05	.99
1984	1.32	1.37	.97	1.06	1.06	1.01
1985	1.36	1.39	.98	1.09	1.09	1.04

Sources: U.S. Bureau of Economic Analysis, The National Income and Product Accounts of the United States, 1929–1982; Statistical Tables (Washington: U.S. Government Printing Office, 1986), Tables 6.4B and 6.7A; 66 Survey of Current Business 65–66 (July 1986).

Note: Data are ratios of compensation per full-time equivalent employee. Compensation includes wages, fringes, and payroll taxes.

with Postal Service wages.[36] However, "good thing" or not, the differential wage premiums are by now a well-documented fact.[37]

In making public/private wage comparisons, economists have tended to ignore employ*er* characteristics and to concentrate on employ*ees*. This tendency reflects the data sets which are most readily

[36] Martin Asher and Joel Popkin, *The Effect of Gender and Race Differentials on Public-Private Wage Comparisons: A Study of Postal Workers*, 38 Indus. & Lab. Rel. Rev. 16 (October 1984), and *Comment*, at 36; Jeffrey M. Perloff and Michael L. Wachter, *Wage Comparability in the U.S. Postal Service*, 38 Indus. & Lab. Rel. Rev. 26 (October 1984), and *Comment*, at 37.

[37] The fact that women and minorities are paid more in government than in the private sector does not necessarily mean that no discrimination occurs in public employment. For example, one detailed study indicated that male teachers earned more than females even within an identical salary schedule. Men seemed to be assigned to tasks involving extra compensation for out-of-school activities. It was difficult to determine whether this outcome was the result of discriminatory management preferences or whether it reflected employee preferences regarding assignments and time allocation. However, the authors suspected that it might reflect discrimination. See William A. Wines, Robert D. Ley, and Jack Fiorito, *Gender-Related Wage Differentials for Public School Teachers under Objective Salary Grids: Some Lessons on Comparable Worth*, 15 J. Coll. Neg. Pub. Sector 61 (1986).

available (such as the Current Population Survey), which focus on employee attributes. However, some evidence has developed indicating that a closer examination of employer attributes is needed.

It is known, for example, that larger firms in the private sector tend to pay higher wages than smaller firms. One study confirms a similar tendency for public employment; large public employers pay more than small ones.[38] This finding suggests that public/private comparisons should be standardized for size. Since government employees often work for relatively large employing units, arguments that prevailing wage comparisons—such as the National Survey of Professional, Administrative, Technical, and Clerical Pay (PATC) conducted for federal pay-setting purposes—*ought* to include more small firms need to be reexamined.[39] Including small firms in comparison surveys will obviously lower the average of pay levels gathered from the private sector. But whether such small firms are comparable to (generally larger) government employers is open to question.

Governmental units nominally operating within a single pay-setting system may be able to exercise some discretion over actual wage outcomes. It has been argued that, absent other pressures, such employing units will wish to pay "more" to their workers since high wages make for more contented workers.[40] But employing units will not typically have a totally free hand in such matters. However, they *may* be better able to pay higher wages if they service a politically powerful constituency and have that constituency behind them. One study based on federal civil service records, for example, found higher pay going to workers in agencies that were important to small, well-organized interest groups.[41]

Employee Turnover and Rents

Research on government pay differentials in the 1980s began to depart from the simple comparison approach. It has long been known (from sources such as area wage surveys) that in private employment, even narrowly defined jobs exhibit a broad range of pay levels within a local labor market. Private employers evidently follow a range of pay practices; some try to meet the average wage prevailing in the market, while others aim to pay above or below the average.

---

[38] Charles C. Brown and James L. Medoff, State and Local Government Wage Rates: Unions, Employer Size, and Ability to Pay, Conference Paper on Public Sector Unionism (Cambridge: National Bureau of Economic Research, 1986).

[39] The PATC survey is conducted annually by the U.S. Bureau of Labor Statistics.

[40] Stephen L. Mehay and Rodolfo A. Gonzalez, *The Relative Effect of Unionization and Interjurisdictional Competition on Municipal Wages*, 7 J. Lab. Res. 79 (Winter 1986).

[41] George J. Borjas, *Wage Determination in the Federal Government: The Role of Constituents and Bureaucrats*, 88 J. Pol. Econ. 1110 (December 1980).

It can be expected that relatively high wage-payers will experience lower employee turnover and greater ease of recruitment than will low-payers. High salaries are likely to attract a queue of job applicants, which the employer can screen for desired worker characteristics. Thus, jobs can be filled quickly, and, once filled, the new employees will be less likely to quit since outside opportunities at comparable wages will be difficult to locate.

This expectation about the effects of wage policy suggests that queues of job applicants and employee turnover rates could be scrutinized to determine the appropriateness of government pay levels. Put in its simplest terms, the argument is that government workers are overpaid if long queues exist for potential job vacancies and if incumbent workers are slow to turn over, relative to private employment. Several studies have referred to, or examined, public-sector queue and/or quit rate data and have concluded that overpayment exists in government, even at the local level.[42]

However, there is a conceptual difficulty with the queue/quit approach. Empirically, there are large firms, such as IBM, which are noted for high pay/low turnover policies. Usually it is concluded that such firms are following a rational, profit-maximizing strategy of careful screening, lower turnover costs, increased employee loyalty, etc. Because private firms are involved, economists *assume* that they are optimizing their pay policies. IBM is not seen as irrationally overpaying its work force.

But those analysts who apply the queue/quit approach to public employers are typically not willing to make the same presumption about government pay policies. Yet in the absence of a clear model of what queueing and quit rates are efficient for government, the appearance of long queues and low quits cannot be assumed to be less than optimal. Operational models that indicate optimal queues and quit rates for government are not readily at hand.

The queue/quit issue is particularly compelling during periods of high unemployment. In such periods, job applicants are often told by private employers that no vacancies exist. And workers with jobs during recessions are reluctant to quit. To be consistent, those analysts who take the queue/quit approach should argue, therefore, that private employers routinely overpay their workers during economic downturns.

---

[42] Krueger, *supra* note 34; Steven F. Venti, Wages in the Federal and Private Sectors, Working Paper No. 1641 (Cambridge: National Bureau of Economic Research, 1985); James E. Long, *Are Government Workers Overpaid? Alternative Evidence,* 17 J. Hum. Resources 123 (Winter 1982).

Of course, explaining this phenomenon, in which the typical private (and presumably profit-maximizing) employer cyclically becomes an overpayer, has long been a major challenge to economic theory. In recent years the paradox of private wage inflexibility in the face of labor surpluses has given rise to a substantial literature on "implicit contracting" in the labor market. Pending a resolution of this issue (and that may not occur for a long time!), the queue/quit approach at best serves as an indicator of overpayment in extreme cases. Even then, some kind of ad hoc adjustment for business cycle influences is necessary.

Nonwage Benefits

Wages are not the only job attribute relevant to the employee. In a world in which unemployment exists (even if economists cannot explain it very well), jobs that offer relative security from layoff are more attractive than others. Some researchers have analyzed unemployment probabilities and found—not surprisingly—that government jobs provide greater security on average than do private jobs.[43] Thus, even when wage comparisons do not show marked discrepancies between public and private pay (as is the case at the local level), factoring in job security as a benefit is likely to make government pay appear too high on an adjusted basis.[44]

Conventional employee benefits ought to be considered in public/private pay comparisons, although prevailing wage methodologies used by government pay-setters often omit fringes. As Table 8 shows, there is a tendency at all levels of government to devote a greater share of the compensation dollar to nonwage benefits, when compared with the private sector. Moreover, this tendency has been a longstanding practice. Thus, public employees are more likely to appear overpaid on a total compensation basis than on a wage-only basis.

However, there may be a size-of-employer problem inherent in such comparisons (as in the case of wages). Government employing units are often large and—it might be argued—should be compared with large private firms with regard to benefit policies. Indeed, some large employers, particularly those with strong unions, devote a substantially larger than average fraction of compensation to employee benefits.

But the impression of very large benefit-to-wage ratios in the private sector can be misleading. Often cited are Chamber of Com-

---

[43] Steven G. Allen, Unions and Job Security in the Public Sector, Working Paper No. 88 (Raleigh: Department of Economics, North Carolina State University, 1986).
[44] Don Bellanti and James Long, The Political Economy of the Rent-Seeking Society: The Case of Public Employees and Their Unions, 2 J. Lab. Res. 1 (Spring 1981).

TABLE 8

Ratio of Total Compensation to Wages and Salaries
in Public and Private Employment, 1960–1985

Year	Private	Federal Enterprises	Federal Civilian	State and Local Enterprises	State and Local Education	State and Local Noneducation
1960	1.06	1.08	1.08	1.09	1.09	1.09
1970	1.12	1.10	1.10	1.10	1.14	1.10
1975	1.16	1.16	1.15	1.14	1.18	1.15
1980	1.18	1.18	1.19	1.19	1.23	1.20
1981	1.19	1.18	1.19	1.20	1.24	1.21
1982	1.19	1.20	1.20	1.21	1.25	1.22
1983	1.19	1.21	1.22	1.21	1.26	1.22
1984	1.19	1.21	1.23	1.21	1.26	1.22
1985	1.19	1.23	1.24	1.22	1.26	1.23

Sources: U.S. Bureau of Economic Analysis, The National Income and Product Accounts of the United States, 1929–1982; Statistical Tables (Washington: U.S. Government Printing Office, 1986), Tables 6.4B and 6.5B; 66 Survey of Current Business 65 (July 1986).

merce surveys which, for example, reported a private-sector benefits-to-"payroll" ratio of almost 38 percent in 1985.[45] However, the Chamber's data do not suggest vast variations by firm size, although some differentials exist; the 1985 ratio for firms with fewer than 100 employees was 37.7 percent and the ratio for firms with 5,000 or more employees was 39.1 percent. (Medium-sized firms paid a little less than average.) Yet the greater problem is that the Chamber's benefit ratio is reported in a way that maximizes its size, presumably to demonstrate the generosity of employers and/or the burden upon them. But when adjusted to approximate the presentation format of Table 8, the Chamber's data indicate a benefit ratio of 20–21 percent—a figure roughly comparable to the 19 percent estimate shown on the table.[46]

Pensions

For current benefits, such as health insurance, employer expenditures represent the actual employer cost of the various plans offered

[45] U.S. Chamber of Commerce, Employee Benefits, 1985 (Washington: Chamber of Commerce, 1986).

[46] I have adjusted Chamber data by including as "benefits" only legally required benefits, pensions, insurance, and other agreed-upon payments (excluding meals, discounts on employer-produced goods and services, and miscellaneous payments), and profit-sharing and thrift plan contributions. Thus, I have excluded from benefits such important items as paid vacations (which are included as wages and salaries—not as benefits—in the Commerce Department figures of Table 8). When the excluded benefits are treated as wages and salaries, and not as benefits, the Chamber's benefit-to-wage ratio falls into the 20–21 percent bracket, as indicated in the text.

to workers. However, pensions, which represent a deferred benefit, have come in for special scrutiny by economists. Public pensions, unlike private, are not covered by the Employee Retirement Income Security Act (ERISA) of 1974, and thus may accrue large unfunded liabilities.[47] Future benefit payments which are unfunded do not show up as employer compensation expenditures, although they do represent potentially costly promises.

Analyses of public pension systems have generally found them to be more generous than private programs.[48] The degree of generosity is positively correlated with the employee's length of service and, during periods of inflation, the presence of an escalator clause in the pension benefit formula.[49] Some pension underfunding can be understood as an "optimal" shifting of burdens to future taxpayers, although short electoral horizons of political decision-makers may also be an important explanation.[50]

The issue of pension underfunding is likely to both reassert itself in the future and to complicate labor-management relations in the public sector. Taken as a whole, state and local pension systems have not been seen as in dire financial straits.[51] But state and local systems *cannot* be taken as a whole because they are not a single plan. Some plans have substantial underfunding problems; others do not. Underfunded plans cannot in general be "bailed out" by an infusion of assets from more healthy pension programs.

One employer solution to the underfunding problem has been to create a lower tier of pension benefits for new employees. Adding a lower tier reduces the increment of expected pension liability that would otherwise be associated with each hire. This two-tier approach was taken at the federal level in the 1980s.[52] However, two-tier pension plans and two-tier pay plans pose similar problems of cross-sectional equity. New hires work side-by-side with senior workers who earn higher rates of compensation for the same jobs.

---

[47] ERISA sets standards of funding, vesting, eligibility, and investment of plan assets for private pension programs and other deferred benefits.

[48] Joseph F. Quinn, *Pension Wealth of Government and Private Sector Workers*, 72 Am. Econ. Rev. 283 (May 1982).

[49] Formal escalation of pension benefits is virtually unknown in the private sector; see Bernard Jump, Jr., *State and Local Government Pension Benefits: Just Desserts or Just Rip-Offs?*, in The Economics of Municipal Labor Markets, *supra* note 3, at 212.

[50] Gene E. Mumy, *Pension Underfunding, Municipal Debt, and the Compensation of Municipal Employees*, in The Economics of Municipal Labor Markets, *supra* note 3, at 161; Robert S. Smith, *Salaries and Pension Funding: Are Public Safety Officers Given Preference over Taxpayers?*, in *id.*, at 188.

[51] Arden R. Hall and William D. Smith, *The Financial Condition of Public Employee Pension Plans*, in The Economics of Municipal Labor Markets, *supra* note 3, at 247.

[52] *New Retirement System for Federal Employees*, 109 Monthly Lab. Rev. 34 (October 1986).

Unions and Government Pay

Since merely having the government as employer may influence pay levels, one way to isolate the union effect is to confine union and nonunion wage comparisons solely to the public sector. Studies undertaken in the 1970s generally found that unions did have a pay-raising effect in government.[53] Table 9 suggests that similar results were likely to be found in the 1980s.

Simple Empirical Evidence

Table 9 reports results of cross-state regressions run in an attempt to explain government pay in 1982 by per capita income (a proxy for demand for government services), general area wage level (a proxy for labor market conditions and competition), and the government unionization rate.[54] The unionization coefficients are positive and, at the local and school district level, significant. While much criticism might be leveled at the specifics of the regressions, the results do suggest that more sophisticated studies will still find significant union wage impacts for local governments and school systems.

TABLE 9

Regressions Relating Government Wage Level to Unionization,
Per Capita Income, and Area Wage Level, 1982

	State Government	Local Government	School Districts
Constant	464**	− 239*	− 155
Unionization rate, 1982	1.58	4.64**	5.91**
Per capita income, 1982	.0098	.0317	.0250
Area wage level, 1982	.0597**	.0729**	.0678**
Adjusted R^2	.54	.81	.67
Standard error	149	136	149
Number of observations	50	51	45

Source: See text and footnotes.
Note: Dependent variable is average monthly earnings of full-time government employees in level of government listed at the head of the column. Per capita income refers to 1982 per capita income in state. Area wage level refers to 1982 wages per employee covered by unemployment insurance in state listed at the head of the column.
*Significant at 10 percent level.
**Significant at 5 percent level.

[53] Daniel J.B. Mitchell, *The Impact of Collective Bargaining on Compensation in the Public Sector*, in Public-Sector Bargaining, eds. Benjamin Aaron, Joseph R. Grodin, and James L. Stern (Washington: BNA Books, 1979), 118.
[54] The unionization rate refers to full-time workers. See *supra* note 7 for details on data sources.

Federal civil servants may have union representation, but the scope of their bargaining does not include pay. However, postal workers have been covered by a pay-bargaining system since the early 1970s. As has already been depicted in Table 7, postal pay began rising relative to private pay in the period after bargaining was adopted. It continued rising thereafter, except for a brief inflation-related lag in the late 1970s. Of more significance, postal pay also rose relative to (nonbargained) federal civil service pay during the 1970s and 1980s. Again, although these simple observations do not prove that there has been a union wage effect for postal workers, it would be most surprising—given the data in Table 7—if researchers hadn't found one.

Pay Research in the 1980s

In fact, a substantial body of literature in the 1980s concludes that unions typically have a wage-raising impact in government,[55] and researchers have usually found it to be smaller than private-union wage effects.[56] Some analysts have argued that union wage effects in the public sector have increased over time,[57] but others believe that the union wage effect appears early in the bargaining relationship and may actually diminish thereafter.[58]

Generally, it has been found that the wage effect depends on whether there is a contract, rather than on the mere presence of a union.[59] Whether there is a contract, and hence an effective union, depends crucially on the legislation covering the jurisdiction in question.[60] The presence of laws favorable to the introduction of collective

[55] See, for example, H. Gregg Lewis, Union/Nonunion Wage Gaps in the Public Sector, Conference Paper on Public Sector Unionism (Cambridge: National Bureau of Economic Research, August 1986); Freeman, supra note 3; Luis R. Gomez-Mejia and David B. Balkin, Union Impacts on Secretarial Earnings: A Public Sector Case, 23 Indus. Rel. 97 (Winter 1984); David P. Balkin, The Effect of Unions on the Compensation of Secretaries in Municipal Government, 13 J. Coll. Neg. Pub. Sector 29 (1984); Linda N. Edwards and Franklin R. Edwards, Wellington-Winter Revisited: The Case of Municipal Sanitation Collection, 35 Indus. & Lab. Rel. Rev. 307 (April 1982).

[56] William J. Moore and John Raisian, A Time Series Analysis of Union/Nonunion Relative Wage Effects in the Public Sector, Proceedings of the 34th Annual Meeting, Industrial Relations Research Association (Madison, Wis.: IRRA, 1982), 337.

[57] William H. Baugh and Joe A. Stone, Teachers, Unions, and Wages in the 1970s: Unionism Now Pays, 35 Indus. & Lab. Rel. Rev. 368 (April 1982).

[58] H. Kent Baker, The Short- and Long-Term Effects of Collective Bargaining on Faculty Compensation, 13 J. Coll. Neg. Pub. Sector 235 (1984).

[59] Richard B. Freeman and Robert Valletta, Does the Legal Environment Affect the Outcome of Public Sector Collective Bargaining? Conference Paper on Public Sector Unionism (Cambridge: National Bureau of Economic Research, 1986).

[60] Casey Ichniowski, Public Sector Recognition Strikes: Illegal and Ill-Fated, Working Paper No. 1808 (Cambridge: National Bureau of Economic Research, 1986); Ichniowski, Public Sector Union Growth and Bargaining Laws: A Proportional Hazards Approach with Time-Varying Treatments, Working Paper No. 1809 (Cambridge: National Bureau of Economic Research, 1986); Janet C. Hunt, Joseph V. Terza, Rudolph A. White, and Thomas A. Moore, Wages, Union Membership, and Public Sector Bargaining Legislation: Simultaneous Equations with an Ordinal Qualitative Variable, 7 J. Lab. Res. 225 (Summer 1986).

bargaining is associated with such variables as a prounion political climate, non-South location, and high local income levels.[61]

Some private-sector researchers have insisted that high wages may cause a demand for union services and, therefore, the seeming union-to-wage causality may be reversed. They argue that high wages may cause unions, rather than the other way around. To cope with this problem, these skeptics have used simultaneous-equation techniques and have included a demand-for-unionism equation. Often, the result is a reduced estimate of the union wage impact.

But there is reason to question this approach as applied to the private sector, where unionization patterns were established many years ago. Private-sector workers are more likely to be union members (or nonunion, as the case may be) because they happen to find work in a unionized workplace, not because they have made an individual choice about having union representation after they have a job. In the public sector, however, unionization is comparatively new and the simultaneity issue is more important. Government workers already in jobs have more of an effective choice concerning whether or not a union will represent them than do private-sector workers.

There have been only limited applications of the simultaneous-equation approach to government employees, but the finding in the studies that have been undertaken is that the simultaneous-equation methodology *increases* the estimated union wage impact.[62] It appears, therefore, that in public employment, low wages—not high wages— increase the demand for union services. Presumably, nonunion public workers vote for a union in the hope that it will raise their wages.[63]

Benefits and Unions

Research in the private sector has confirmed a special affinity of unions for fringe benefits. Various explanations have been given for this phenomenon. Probably the most convincing is that fringes are of

[61] Henry S. Farber, The Evolution of Public Sector Bargaining Laws, Conference Paper on Public Sector Unionism (Cambridge: National Bureau of Economic Research, 1986). However, other laws may interact with unionization in complex ways. For example, one study finds that residence laws (requiring civil servants to live in the city that employs them) seem to be associated with weakened union bargaining strength. See Hirsch and Rufolo, *supra* note 3.

[62] David Lewin and Harry C. Katz, *Payment Determination in Municipal Building Departments Under Unionism and Civil Service*, in The Economics of Municipal Labor Markets, *supra* note 3, at 90; Ann Bartel and David Lewin, *Wages and Unionism in the Public Sector: The Case of Police*, 63 Rev. Econ. & Stat. 53 (February 1981).

[63] However, one study of faculty bargaining (in a mix of public and private higher education institutions) did not find a tendency for lower wage institutions to unionize. See H. Kent Baker, *The Economic Impact of Collective Bargaining Across Academic Ranks*, 13 J. Coll. Neg. Pub. Sector 339 (1984).

special benefit to more senior workers, who will have an influential voice in union decision-making under "median voter" models.[64]

There is no reason to expect union preferences in the public sector to be notably different from those in the private sector with regard to benefits. Not all research concerning benefits in unionized situations in government has been aimed at specifically analyzing the union impact (as opposed to other variables which may influence benefit expenditures).[65] However, some studies undertaken in the 1980s suggest that (1) union bargaining increases employer expenditures on fringes,[66] and that (2) the union effect on fringes is larger than its impact on wages.[67]

Union Impacts on Management Strategy and Productivity

During the 1970s the U.S. Bureau of Labor Statistics (BLS) published various bulletins summarizing contractual features of both public and private union agreements. Budget cutbacks ended this program, and it is now more difficult to determine the union impact on items other than compensation levels. Unfortunately, lack of good data on public-sector contractual terms impedes research on the impact of bargaining on management and on the nature of the labor-management relationship.

Contract Duration and Union Security

Available studies indicate that union agreements in the public sector in the 1970s were typically shorter in duration than those in the private sector. Shorter durations, other things being equal, mean that management must devote more attention to bargaining, since negotiations will occur more frequently. In addition, it appeared that in the 1970s union security arrangements were less common in government (and generally weaker where they did exist) as compared with private employment. Absent union security arrangements, union financial resources may be scarce and organizing efforts will continue even after the union is officially recognized. There may be a more adversarial relationship—again, other things being equal—in such areas as griev-

---

[64] Median voter models are based on the observation that it is the inframarginal voter in a political decision-making system who casts the key vote. Thus, in a union setting a relatively senior worker will be the median voter, and median voter preferences will dominate union policy. See Richard B. Freeman and James L. Medoff, What Do Unions Do? (New York: Basic Books, 1984).

[65] See, for example, Marian M. Extejt and John I. Extejt, An Analysis of Fringe Benefit Levels Among Teacher Bargaining Units in Indiana, 12 J. Coll. Neg. Pub. Sector 143 (1983).

[66] Peter Feuille, John Thomas Delaney, and Wallace Hendricks, Police Bargaining, Arbitration, and Fringe Benefits, 6 J. Lab. Res. 1 (Winter 1985).

[67] Bartel and Lewin, supra note 62.

ance handling. Unions may be less willing to screen out frivolous grievances if the result might be loss of dues-paying members.

Available information, based on sources other than the BLS, suggests that the contract characteristics found in the 1970s carried over into the 1980s. Table 10 compares the results of a study of private union agreements undertaken by the Bureau of National Affairs, Inc., with those of a similar study of public-sector contracts in California. The table indicates that as of the mid-1980s, contract durations remained shorter in public employment than in private; contractual provisions associated with long-duration agreements (reopeners, escalators, and deferred pay adjustments) were also less common.

Union security was notably weaker in the California public-sector contracts than in the private sample. This tendency reflects state laws, which restrict the use of such clauses. However, although the figures would vary from employing unit to employing unit, there is other confirmation of weaker union security in the public sector. In 1985, 17 percent of government workers who were represented by unions were not union members, compared with only 10 percent in private

TABLE 10

Contractual Features of Labor-Management Agreements,
Public Sector (California) and Private Sector

	California Public-Sector Sample, 1984	BNA Private-Sector Sample, 1986
Mean contract duration (years)	1.8	2.9
Proportion of agreements with:		
Reopener	6%	14%
Escalator	12	42
Deferred wage adjustments	63	80
No strike/lockout clause	71	95
Union shop	1	60
Modified union shop	*	14
Agency shop	9	5
Maintenance of membership	6	4

Sources: California Department of Industrial Relations, Provisions of Public Sector Negotiated Labor Agreements in California, 1984 (San Francisco: Division of Labor Statistics and Research, 1985), Tables 1, 5, and 6; Bureau of National Affairs, Inc., Basic Patterns in Union Contracts, 11th ed. (Washington: BNA, 1986), 2–3, 101, 115.

Note: The California file consists of 757 agreements estimated to cover over one half of all full-time, state and local employees in the state. The BNA file consists of 400 contracts used periodically for surveys of contractual features. Contract durations were estimated from duration intervals.

*Less than 0.5

employment.[68] Published data do not permit the exclusion of federal workers from the 17-percent estimate for 1985, but data from 1980 indicate that their exclusion would probably cut the ratio only to about 14 percent, still well above the private-sector figure.[69]

Unfortunately, research into the implications of more frequent negotiations and weaker union security for management has been lacking. It is possible that such public/private differences, because of their impact on the overall labor-management relationship, could influence bargained wage outcomes and managerial strategies. But these effects, if they exist, are unknown.

Productivity, Resource Utilization, and Bargaining

The most commonly used measures of productivity for the private sector have been based on the national income (GNP) accounts. But measurement of productivity in government is difficult because the value of public services is assumed to be equal to the value of the labor input which produced them, according to national income methodology. Nonetheless, there may be ways to use national income data to estimate government productivity trends,[70] but finding more tangible and direct output measures would greatly ease the task.

Some progress was made by BLS during the early 1980s in estimating productivity trends at both the federal and the state and local levels, using information sources other than the national income accounts.[71] However, only limited aspects of government productivity could be monitored from these alternative sources. For example, the activities measured tended to be either government enterprises (such as state-owned liquor stores) or services for which there were usable output measures (such as the processing of unemployment insurance claims).

In the absence of readily available information on government efficiency in labor utilization, those researchers analyzing the union

---

[68] Gifford, *supra* note 2.

[69] U.S. Bureau of Labor Statistics, Earnings and Other Characteristics of Organized Workers, May 1980, Bull. 2105 (Washington: U.S. Government Printing Office, 1981). Unfortunately, the 1980 data do not separate the work force according to a public/private dichotomy with regard to membership versus representation. Instead, a break out is available only for "public administration," a category which excludes some public workers. Within public administration in 1980, about 17 percent of represented workers were not union members (the same proportion as in 1985). The state and local ratio was 14 percent; hence, the estimate in the text. (Federal employees presented a mixed picture; union-represented nonpostal workers were substantially more likely to be nonmembers than other government workers. But postal workers had nonmembership rates roughly comparable to the private sector.)

[70] Charles R. Hulten and James Robertson, *Labor Productivity in the Local Public Sector*, in The Economics of Municipal Labor Markets, *supra* note 3, at 342.

[71] U.S. Bureau of Labor Statistics, Measuring Productivity in State and Local Government, Bull. 2166 (Washington: U.S. Government Printing Office, 1983); Donald M. Fisk, *Productivity Trends in the Federal Government*, 106 Monthly Lab. Rev. 3 (October 1983); and Fisk, *Measuring Productivity in State and Local Government*, 107 Monthly Lab. Rev. 47 (June 1984).

impact on productivity have had to develop their own output measures. Studies in this field usually have found either no union/productivity effect or mixed effects (raising some output measures, lowering others).[72] These ambiguous findings mirror similar results obtained from microlevel research in private employment situations.

Public managers—certainly not an unbiased source of information—do not believe that collective bargaining enhances the *quality* of government service, but they are reluctant to say that unions decrease the *quantity* of services produced.[73] Unions may actually be able to obtain increased expenditures on services they represent through bargaining or lobbying.[74] Of course, added expenditure on production does not necessarily mean higher productivity.

Despite the fuzzy evidence on the union/productivity relationship, legislative authorities sometimes have acted in the belief that unions will lower productivity if not legally restrained by narrow scopes of bargaining. However, productivity issues and working conditions are intertwined. If unions are constrained from improving working conditions—lowering class sizes in schools, for example—they may simply exercise their bargaining power in the allowable arena of pay. Thus, in the school example, pay may be higher if class size cannot be lowered.[75]

Labor-Management Cooperation

Efforts to trade off higher pay for higher productivity have been made in private employment from time to time. During the 1980s, various quality of working life (QWL) arrangements were associated with private concession bargaining situations, but in these cases the real issue was not higher pay, but rather maintaining nominal pay (or limiting pay cuts) in exchange for more managerial flexibility regarding job assignments.

Where concession bargaining has occurred in government, there has also been heightened interest in QWL approaches.[76] However, employees are sometimes suspicious of management motives (and

---

[72] See, for example, Ronald G. Ehrenberg and Joshua L. Schwarz, *The Effects of Unions on Productivity in the Public Sector: The Case of Municipal Libraries*, in The Economics of Municipal Labor Markets, *supra* note 3, at 311; Ronald G. Ehrenberg, Daniel R. Sherman, and Joshua L. Schwarz, *Unions and Productivity in the Public Sector: A Study of Municipal Libraries*, 36 Indus. & Lab. Rel. Rev. 199 (January 1983); Randall W. Eberts, *Union Effects on Teacher Productivity*, 37 Indus. & Lab. Rel. Rev. 346 (April 1984).

[73] Dennis R. Howard and David F. Culkin, *Factors Affecting the Attitudes of Public Managers Toward Collective Bargaining*, 12 J. Coll. Neg. Pub. Sector 99 (1983).

[74] Allen, *supra* note 43; Randall W. Eberts, *How Unions Affect Management Decisions: Evidence from Public Schools*, 6 J. Lab. Res. 239 (Summer 1983).

[75] Stephen A. Woodbury, *The Scope of Bargaining and Bargaining Outcomes in the Public Schools*, 38 Indus. & Lab. Rel. Rev. 195 (January 1985).

[76] Lewin, *supra* note 13.

union leadership motives as well) in establishing cooperative ventures.[77] Yet quality circles and similar arrangements now have their advocates in public employment and at least limited effectiveness of such programs has been reported.[78]

Subcontracting and Union Wages

Union-represented workers in government have benefited, relative to many private-sector employees, from limited substitution possibilities for their services. The automobile consumers can purchase their cars from Detroit or Japan, but the driver's license needed to operate that car can come only from the state motor vehicle department.

Increasingly, however, there has been a greater interest by government managers in creating substitution possibilities through the mechanism of "contracting out." In principle, the computer operations underlying the issuance of driver's licenses could be subcontracted to a private firm. Managers might wish to contract out if, holding other influences constant, they believed that government productivity was lower than private productivity, or they might subcontract out if, other things being equal (including productivity), government wages were higher than private wages. Finally, they might want to use the *threat* of contracting out as a bargaining tool in an era of employee concerns about job security.

A productivity argument in favor of contracting out has developed from the economic theory of "shirking."[79] According to this theory, if government workers are more difficult to monitor than private-sector employees, they will shirk more than private workers.[80] Thus, the model suggests that where the service outputs of private subcontractors can be easily monitored, contracting out may improve productivity and efficiency.

The private firm which obtains a government contract at a fixed price has an incentive to monitor its employees carefully, since the firm retains the margin between price and cost as profit. Of course, this argument does not entirely lift the burden of monitoring from government. Absent careful scrutiny, the contractor has an incentive to shirk—that is, to produce a lower quality or quantity of service than is

---

[77] Daily Lab. Rep., *supra* note 23.

[78] Michael T. Boyce, *Can Quality Circles Be Applied in the Public Sector?* 14 J. Coll. Neg. Pub. Sector 67 (1985); George T. Sulzner, *The Impact of Labor-Management Cooperation Committees on Personnel Policies and Practices at Twenty Federal Bargaining Units,* 11 J. Coll. Neg. Pub. Sector 37 (1982).

[79] Hirsch and Rufolo, *supra* note 3.

[80] One study argues that even when government monitors employees through performance appraisals, the monitoring is only weakly reflected in employee rewards; see Bruce H. Dunson, *Pay, Experience, and Productivity: The Government-Sector Case,* 20 J. Hum. Resources 153 (Winter 1985). It should be noted, however, that similar results have been found in private employment.

desired by government managers. Thus, with contracting out, instead of monitoring its own employees, government must monitor the performance of subcontractors. If government managers were poorly motivated to do the former, they may not do a particularly good job at the latter.[81]

While advocates of subcontracting acknowledge this critique, the monitoring problem may simply lead them to demand a more complete "privatization" of public services. For example, government enterprises and quasi-enterprises could be sold to private companies, thus eliminating the government monitoring role altogether. Some evidence has been disseminated at the federal level suggesting that certain services are cheaper to obtain from the private market than from government.[82] These federal studies may further stimulate state and local managers to investigate the contracting-out option.

Whether the cost differentials which may exist between public and private service are based on productivity or compensation levels is an interesting question, but regardless of the answer, the possibility of substitution of private for public workers will tend to weaken union bargaining power in government.[83] Even where public-sector unions seek wage gains through means other than bargaining, the ability of management to contract out could limit their efforts.

For example, public unions have sought implementation of the principle of "comparable worth," which would raise the wages of jobs primarily held by women.[84] Although some of these efforts have been made through bargaining, litigation and lobbying have also been an important part of the strategy. There have been estimates that the job-displacement effect of raising wages in "female" jobs would be small, due to limited possibilities of cross-occupational substitution.[85] However, if government pay increases based on comparable worth raised wages relative to the *same* occupations in private employment, the

---

[81] Similarly, if governments tend to pay economic rents to their own employees, they might also pay such rents to subcontractors. Favoritism, kickbacks, and just sloppy purchasing of services are certainly not unknown in government contracting.

[82] James T. Bennett and Thomas J. DiLorenzo, *Public Employee Unions and the Privatization of "Public" Services*, 6 J. Lab. Res. 33 (Winter 1983).

[83] Not surprisingly, public-sector unions have strongly opposed contracting out, e.g., American Federation of State, County and Municipal Employees, Passing the Bucks: The Contracting Out of Public Services (Washington: AFSCME, 1983). It might be noted that some of the critiques made in this publication are based on the difficulty of monitoring contractor performance.

[84] Advocates of using comparable worth in setting pay argue that jobs of comparable value to the employer should be paid comparable wages. On the operational level, this idea is usually taken to mean that some type of job evaluation technique should be applied. Under job evaluation, jobs are broken down by attributes and, effectively, the various attributes are valued. Generally, the impact of such a technique is to raise pay in clerical occupations and certain professions (such as nursing) relative to blue-collar occupations.

[85] Ronald G. Ehrenberg and Robert S. Smith, *Comparable-Worth Wage Adjustments and Female Employment in the State and Local Sector*, 5 J. Lab. Econ. 43 (January 1987).

temptation to contract out would be increased. Thus, substitution effects and resulting employment displacement could be larger than anticipated.

Just as private-sector unions have sought anti-subcontracting provisions in their agreements with management, similar pressures can be expected in government. But the issue of contracting out and privatization is more than a labor-management issue; indeed, it is more than an issue of government costs. Contracting-out policy is interconnected with views on the appropriate role of government in the economy and with the opposing ideologies surrounding that role. Thus, the political climate will strongly influence the degree to which contracting out will be raised in the collective-bargaining arena in the future.

Strikes, Arbitration, and Wages

It is commonplace in analyzing private-sector collective bargaining to attribute the source of union negotiating strength to the strike threat. A credible strike threat represents a potential cost to management; management may be willing to pay a price in terms of improved pay and working conditions to avoid that cost. In the public sector, however, one of the characteristics of labor-management relations is a low strike propensity relative to private employment.[86]

The Empirical Strike Record

Tables 11A and 11B illustrate this tendency. The BLS stopped collecting detailed strike data in the early 1980s, but it is possible to compare public and private strike propensities in 1979—that is, just prior to the period of economic slump and concession bargaining. Table 11A compares strike rates in both sectors on a per-member basis rather than on the more commonly used basis of the entire work force. Union members are the more relevant base measure since nonunion workers rarely engage in significant strikes. And whether measured on a strike-per-worker basis or by the proportion of union workers involved in strike activity, strike propensities have been lower in public employment than in private.[87]

---

[86] The word "strike" in the text is used to represent any form of work stoppage, including lockouts.

[87] Strike propensities are especially low in federal employment. As Table 11A shows, there were no strikes at the federal level in 1979. One study of federal strikes covering 1962 to 1981 found that of the 39 recorded stoppages, 12 involved no union and consisted of very short spontaneous walkouts over local grievances; see Eugene H. Becker, *Analysis of Work Stoppages in the Federal Sector, 1962–81*, 105 Monthly Lab. Rev. 49 (August 1982). The limited scope of bargaining for federal employees (with the major exception of postal employees) undoubtedly contributes to this low strike propensity.

TABLE 11A

Strike Activity in the Public and Private Sectors, 1979

Sector	Work Stoppages Per 1,000 Union Members	Proportion of Union Members Involved in Work Stoppages
Private	.31	.11
Public	.13	.05
Federal	0	0
State	.06	.05
Local	.20	.08

Sources: Public-sector strike activity from U.S. Bureau of Labor Statistics, Work Stoppages in Government, 1979, Report 629 (Washington: U.S. Government Printing Office, 1981), 4; private-sector strike activity from U.S. Bureau of Labor Statistics, Analysis of Work Stoppages, 1979, Bulletin 2092 (Washington: U.S. Government Printing Office, 1981), 13; union membership from U.S. Bureau of the Census, Wage and Salary Data from the Income Survey Development Program: 1979, Series P-23, No. 118 (Washington: U.S. Government Printing Office, 1982), Table 1.

TABLE 11B

Strike Activity, 1982–1985

	1982	1983	1984	1985	1982–1985
Major government work stoppages as proportion of all major work stoppages	8%	15%	10%	13%	11%
Major work stoppages per 1,000 union-represented workers under major agreements:					
Public	–	–	–	–	.01
Private	–	–	–	–	.04

Sources: Work stoppages from preliminary monthly listings in Current Wage Developments, various issues. Estimate of workers represented under major agreements from U.S. Bureau of Labor Statistics, Bargaining Calendar, 1985, Bulletin 2231 (Washington: U.S. Government Printing Office, 1985), 3.

Note: Major work stoppages and major agreements are those involving 1,000 or more workers. Government stoppages and workers refer to state and local sector only.

During the 1980s, the only strike data available were for "major" work stoppages affecting 1,000 or more workers. Strike activity was especially quiescent in the private sector in the face of concession bargaining. But despite the calm in private negotiations, government work stoppages still accounted for only 11 percent of the major strikes between 1982 and 1985, according to Table 11B. Yet by 1985 public-sector union members accounted for one third of total union membership.[88] Stoppages-per-member were substantially lower in public than in private employment despite the fact that union members in the public sector were gaining larger wage settlements than their private counterparts.

Strikes, Wages, and Arbitration

The fact that strikes are often illegal in the public sector appears to account for their low frequency. Obviously, illegal strikes do occur, but the evidence suggests that work stoppages are more likely to take place in jurisdictions where strikes are legal than where they are illegal.[89] It is not surprising, however, to observe that what appears to raise wages is strike *usage* rather than the mere legality of the strike tactic.[90]

There is an ongoing search in the public sector for an alternative to the strike. It is not clear that this search is in response to a management preference. Managers in government may well prefer to negotiate with a strike threat in the background rather than rely on some other form of impasse resolution.[91] Nevertheless, there does seem to be a preference on the part of the electorate for avoiding strikes by government employees, and it is this preference that accounts for the various alternative dispute-resolution procedures found at the federal, state, and local levels.[92]

The available choices for impasse resolution other than the strike come down to fact-finding or some other form of interest arbitration. Fact-finding as the final step in the procedure has not been well received, either in the research literature or by the parties.[93] Where arbitration follows fact-finding, however, arbitrators may opt for the

---

[88] Gifford, *supra* note 2.

[89] Craig A. Olson, *Strikes, Strike Penalties, and Arbitration in Six States*, 39 Indus. & Lab. Rel. Rev. 539 (July 1986). Perhaps the more general result is that strikes occur more frequently in situations where the cost to the striker is relatively low. For example, it has been found that teachers in school districts which reschedule workdays to make up for days lost to strikes are more likely to strike than other teachers; see Olson, *The Role of Rescheduled School Days in Teacher Strikes*, 37 Indus. & Lab. Rel. Rev. 515 (July 1984). Presumably, in jurisdictions where strikes are illegal, the perceived cost is higher (due to the possibility of penalties) and therefore strike rates are lower.

[90] John Thomas Delaney, *Strikes, Arbitration, and Teacher Salaries: A Behavioral Analysis*, 36 Indus. & Lab. Rel. Rev. 431 (April 1983).

[91] One study of the Canadian experience suggests that management is more likely to prefer the strike to arbitration as an impasse resolution procedure than are unions; see Allen Ponak and Hoyt N. Wheeler, *Choice of Procedures in Canada and the United States*, 19 Indus. Rel. 292 (Fall 1980). A related study finds similar preferences among U.S. government managers; see Peter Feuille and John C. Anderson, *Public Sector Bargaining: Policy and Practice*, 19 Indus. Rel. 309 (Fall 1980).

[92] A listing of dispute resolution procedures in various jurisdictions can be found in Beth Walter Honadle, *A Model of the Public Sector Wage Determination Process—With Special Reference to Institutional Factors*, 10 J. Coll. Neg. Pub. Sector 105 (1981).

[93] Karen S. Gallagher and Donald L. Robson, *Factfinding in Indiana: A Study of Factfinding Frequency and Acceptance as an Impasse Resolution Procedure in Public School Negotiations*, 12 J. Coll. Neg. Pub. Sector 153 (1983).

fact-finder's views of an appropriate settlement rather than the views of either party.[94] Effectively, then, whether or not fact-finding occurs, the main alternative impasse resolution technique is interest arbitration, with or without an earlier step of fact-finding.

A substantial literature has developed concerning whether the use of compulsory arbitration is compatible with collective bargaining in government employment.[95] Generally, the argument is that the knowledge that impasses will eventually go to binding arbitration will "chill" bargaining. According to this view, the parties will fear that the arbitrator will "split the difference" between the labor and management proposals. Thus, each side will want to take extreme positions prior to arbitration, hoping to move the inevitable compromise (split) decision toward their position. Bargaining is likely to fail under these conditions and the parties will become addicted to arbitration (the so-called "narcotic" effect).

The debate over the use of arbitration up through the 1970s was based on a questionable model of arbitrator behavior. As Henry Farber pointed out, the fact that in a conventional arbitration setting, labor asks for more and management offers less than the eventual arbitrated decision does not necessarily mean that arbitrators split the difference.[96] In fact, the evidence suggests that arbitrators have their own norms concerning what an appropriate settlement should be. The parties, to appear reasonable, position themselves around the arbitrator's expected view, thus creating the illusion of split-the-difference decision making. Of course, the arbitrator's norm may be influenced by the parties' positions and their relative bargaining strength.

To the extent that a chilling effect does occur in the face of conventional arbitration, the final-offer form of arbitration has been proposed. Under the most common version of final-offer arbitration, the arbitrator is compelled to pick one party's offer or the other, with no compromise. There are variations under which the arbitrator may

[94] Daniel G. Gallagher and M.D. Chaubey, *Impasse Behavior and Tri-Offer Arbitration in Iowa*, 21 Indus. Rel. 129 (Spring 1982).

[95] See, for example, Frederic C. Champlin and Mario F. Bognanno, *"Chilling" Under Arbitration and Mixed Strike-Arbitration Regimes*, 6 J. Lab. Res. 375 (Fall 1985); James R. Chelius and Marian M. Extejt, *The Narcotic Effect of Impasse-Resolution Procedures*, 38 Indus. & Lab. Rel. Rev. 629 (July 1985); John C. Anderson, *The Impact of Arbitration: A Methodological Assessment*, 20 Indus. Rel. 129 (Spring 1981); David E. Bloom, *Is Arbitration Really Compatible with Bargaining?*, 20 Indus. Rel. 233 (Fall 1981); Richard J. Butler and Ronald G. Ehrenberg, *Estimating the Narcotic Effect of Public Sector Impasse Procedures*, 35 Indus. & Lab. Rel. Rev. 3 (October 1981); Thomas A. Kochan and Jean Baderschneider, *Estimating the Narcotic Effect: Choosing Techniques to Fit the Problem*, 35 Indus. & Lab. Rel. Rev. 21 (October 1981).

[96] Henry S. Farber, *Splitting-the-Difference in Interest Arbitration*, 35 Indus. & Lab. Rel. Rev. 70 (October 1981).

make a series of final-offer decisions on separate components of the offers. Or, the arbitrator may be able to pick a third proposal prepared by a neutral fact-finder.[97]

Use of arbitration as an impasse resolution technique seems to reduce the probability of a strike.[98] If this reduction is the primary goal, whether the parties settle disputes themselves or whether they are chilled into an addiction to arbitration, would not seem to be a major public policy concern. Although some have claimed that arbitration results in more costly settlements—which *could* be a legitimate public policy issue—the evidence for that position is quite mixed.[99] Labor and management practitioners in areas where arbitration is in use, moreover, do not seem to have unfavorable views toward it.[100]

There is some evidence that if the rules of final-offer arbitration are made clear, more "reasonable" offers from the parties result, at least under laboratory conditions.[101] However, the reactions of the parties in the real world where the final-offer technique is used pose analytical problems. It appears from one study of New Jersey police settlements that unions tend to ask for less (and get it) under final-offer arbitration relative to conventional arbitration.[102] But again, the studies are too limited to allow confident predictions of the effects of particular forms of arbitration on wages or other outcomes. The parties themselves may not have a clear-cut expectation of the impact of binding arbitration. As one local union president put it, "We went into arbitration, rolled the dice, and ended up with a three-year wage freeze."[103]

---

[97] David R. Friedman and Stuart S. Mukamal, *Wisconsin's Mediation-Arbitration Law: What Has It Done to Bargaining?*, 13 J. Coll. Neg. Pub. Sector 171 (1984). Apart from final-offer arbitration, there have also been proposals for "closed offer" submissions to arbitration. Under such a system, the parties would submit special offers to the arbitrator independent of their bargaining positions. To the author's knowledge, such arrangements have not been tried in the public sector. Practical barriers exist related to keeping closed offers confidential and separate from the bargaining process.

[98] Casey Ichniowski, *Arbitration and Police Bargaining: Prescriptions for the Blue Flu*, 21 Indus. Rel. 149 (Spring 1982).

[99] See Peter Feuille, John Thomas Delaney, and Wallace Hendricks, *The Impact of Interest Arbitration on Police Contracts*, 24 Indus. Rel. 161 (Spring 1985); Feuille, Delaney, and Hendricks, *supra* note 66; John Delaney, Peter Feuille, and Wallace Hendricks, *Police Salaries, Interest Arbitration, and the Leveling Effect*, 23 Indus. Rel. 417 (Fall 1984); George Saunders, *Impact of Interest Arbitration on Canadian Federal Employees' Wages*, 25 Indus. Rel. 320 (Fall 1986); Craig A. Olson, *The Impact of Arbitration on the Wages of Firefighters*, 19 Indus. Rel. 325 (Fall 1980).

[100] James Chelius and Marian M. Extejt, *The Impact of Arbitration on the Process of Collective Bargaining*, 12 J. Coll. Neg. Pub. Sector 327 (1983).

[101] Angelo S. DeNisi and James B. Dworkin, *Final-Offer Arbitration and the Naive Arbitrator*, 35 Indus. & Lab. Rel. Rev. 78 (October 1981).

[102] Orley Ashenfelter and David E. Bloom, *Models of Arbitrator Behavior: Theory and Evidence*, 74 Am. Econ. Rev. 111 (March 1984).

[103] *Pittsburgh, Pa., Transit Employees Get Arbitrated Cost-of-Living Raises*, 24 GERR 1438 (October 20, 1986).

Conclusions

When collective bargaining in the public sector was a comparatively new phenomenon, there were many observers who feared that the system would prove incompatible with the orderly functioning of government. This view is sometimes still expressed.[104] In general, however, the bargaining system in government has become so firmly ensconced that the basic issue of whether or not it should continue to exist is seldom discussed.

What is discussed is the impact of the system on labor costs and productivity. Concerning the former, it does appear clear that bargaining has some impact on wages and benefits, raising them above levels that would otherwise be set. That impact appears to be smaller in government, on average, than that found in the private sector. The evidence regarding the union impact on productivity in government is mixed, but the same ambiguous situation exists in the private sector as well.

Although the public sector experienced some concession bargaining in the 1980s, most such bargaining took place in private employment. The fact that the union wage effect in the private sector increased in the 1970s, and was larger than in government, may well have contributed to this differential outcome. Concession bargaining in the private sector represented an unraveling of previously achieved union wage advantages. Whether by intent or by accident, the public sector seemed better able to avoid this overshooting/unraveling development. In that respect, public-sector bargaining worked better than private-sector bargaining.

The public sector has also had a better record of avoiding strikes. While studies of the exact impact of arbitration (in its various forms) on wages and benefits as yet produce ambiguous results, it does not appear that arbitration is incompatible with bargaining. And even if a chilling effect occurs, there is no evidence that either the parties or the public are worse off for the experience. Yet private-sector folk wisdom persists in maintaining the paradoxical position that rights (grievance) arbitration has great merit, while interest arbitration has virtually none.

As part of the soul-searching process undertaken by organized labor in the face of the private-sector setbacks of the 1980s, the AFL-CIO made various recommendations for new approaches to worker representation.[105] After analyzing survey data, the Federation concluded, "Many workers, while supporting the concept of organization,

---

[104] Richard G. Neal, *It's Time to Cut Back on Collective Bargaining for Teachers and Other Public Employees*, 14 J. Coll. Neg. Pub. Sector 91 (1985).

[105] American Federation of Labor/Congress of Industrial Organizations, The Changing Situation of Workers and Their Unions (Washington: AFL-CIO, 1985).

wish to forward their interests in ways other than what they view as the traditional form of union representation—in their view, an adversarial collective bargaining relationship. . . ."[106] What might the substitute form of representation be? Various suggestions were offered, including "a bargaining approach based on solving problems through arbitration or mediation rather than through ultimate recourse to economic weapons. . . ."[107]

The implications are clear. Public-sector bargaining over wages and conditions is no longer the child of private-sector bargaining, even though it was originally its offspring. The now mature offspring has experience and lessons in the areas of pay-setting and dispute settlement of potential value to its parent.

---

[106] *Id.* at 18.
[107] Id.

CHAPTER 5

Dispute Resolution in the Public Sector

CRAIG A. OLSON*

Collective bargaining is now the dominant process for determining the employment conditions of state and local government employees in many jurisdictions. According to the 1982 Census of Governments, 39.5 percent of all state and local government employees were in bargaining units; in 15 states the proportion was over 50 percent.[1] The pervasive role of collective bargaining in the public sector and the importance of dispute resolution procedures in the bargaining process continue to generate interest in these processes among scholars, policy makers, and participants.

In this chapter we will review dispute resolution research and practice since the late 1970s with two objectives in mind. First, we will examine the research reports published since 1978 on public-sector dispute resolution. Second, we want to examine developments in the public sector during the same time period to identify any implications they might have for interpreting the existing research and for setting the agenda for future research. We attempt to achieve our objectives as follows: The first section is a discussion of public-sector strike activity and research on strikes; the second section reports on various aspects of interest arbitration.

Public-Sector Strikes and Their Regulation

Public Policy Trends

Controversy over the divergent paths taken by policy makers in different jurisdictions in their attempts to deal with public-sector strike activity has continued through the late 1970s and early 1980s with few new twists. Although some states did modify their policies, most of the existing legislation proved to be quite durable. States that

---

*University of Wisconsin, Madison.
[1] U.S. Bureau of the Census, 1982 Census of Governments, Labor-Management Relations in State and Local Governments, GC 82(3)-3 (Washington: U.S. Government Printing Office, 1985).

granted a limited right to strike to some employees maintained these policies despite developments at the federal level and, in some instances, numerous strikes within the states. For example, in Pennsylvania the right to strike is more restricted than in the private-sector model, but this law is more permissive than the models adopted by most states, which continue to outlaw strikes. Strikes by Pennsylvania public employees covered by Act 195, principally nonuniformed personnel, are permitted, provided they do not endanger the public health, safety, or welfare. Thus, legal strikes, especially by teachers, continue to be commonplace, especially when compared to the experience in many other jurisdictions.[2] The Pennsylvania Business Council cited this strike experience in a critical 1985 report which concluded that the state's labor relations impaired Pennsylvania's ability to attract business: "Labor relations remain a problem, largely because of the high number of public sector strikes in school systems."[3] Despite the strike experience and criticism of it, no major changes have been made in the strike provisions of the law since it was enacted in 1970.

The stability of the policy can be partially explained by the way the parties have adapted to the system. Teacher strikes occur frequently because the costs are typically low for both the teachers and the community. When teachers go on strike, the school days missed are usually rescheduled, so that students receive the prescribed number of days of instruction and teachers are paid for working the rescheduled days. Olson reports that in about two-thirds of the 305 teacher strikes during the decade of the 1970s, students received the mandated 180 days of instruction even though the mean strike duration was almost 13 days.[4] While this practice of making up missed days has important implications for the parties' bargaining behavior (discussed later), it certainly supports the view that many public-sector strikes do not present as great a risk to the public as is frequently assumed.

Another important factor, especially in the 1980s, is the apparent public support for the employer when strikes do occur. Since public-sector strike costs are primarily political in nature, the success of a strike for the employees and the union involved depends on their ability to generate political pressure on public officials that will cause them to make concessions to end the strike. This pressure has frequently been absent in recent years. For example, in 1986, 2,000

---

[2] Craig A. Olson, James L. Stern, Joyce M. Najita, and June M. Weisberger, *Strikes and Strike Penalties in the Public Sector*, Final Report to the U.S. Department of Labor, 1981; Craig A. Olson, *The Role of Rescheduled School Days in Teacher Strikes*, 37 Indus. & Lab. Rel. Rev. 515 (July 1984); Craig A. Olson, *Strikes, Strike Penalties, and Arbitration in Six States*, 39 Indus. & Lab. Rel. Rev. 539 (July 1986).
[3] 23 GERR 1216 (August 26, 1985).
[4] Olson, *The Role, supra* note 2.

nurses struck state-operated hospitals in Pennsylvania,[5] their major demand being a restructured wage scale. During the nine-day strike, management provided limited services using both management personnel and 25 to 40 percent of the bargaining-unit employees who chose not to strike. The demand for health care services was temporarily restricted through a variety of measures, including limiting new admissions, eliminating elective surgery, and transferring patients to other facilities. When the strike ended, not only had the union failed to achieve its major demand, but it also had to agree to a number of concessions. This result is not unlike developments in the private sector and demonstrates that even when strikes are legal, they involve risks for the unions and may not be an effective union strategy. It is ironic that the limited effects of the strike on the public contribute to the continued tolerance of the right to strike in Pennsylvania. Clearly, this is not the kind of scenario predicted by Wellington and Winter when they advocated a ban on all public-sector strikes.[6]

Other states continue to pursue policies that prohibit and, in some instances, penalize unions and employees who strike illegally. New York has had very few strikes during the 1980s even though interest arbitration has not been provided for the resolution of most employer-employee bargaining impasses. From 1981 to 1986 there were only 26 strikes among the roughly 3,500 bargaining units in the state.[7] While there may be numerous explanations of this experience, a key factor is undoubtedly the harsh Taylor Law strike penalties that have been consistently enforced.[8] The most significant deterrent in the law is the "two for one" penalty under which a striking employee is penalized one day's pay for each strike day, which is added to the day's pay the employee loses for not working. The most controversial feature of the penalty is that the struck employer is responsible for collecting the monetary penalty and also keeps the money. While the latter feature accounts for the high enforcement rate, it also raises serious questions about how the penalty affects the employer's interest in avoiding and settling strikes.[9] This issue has not been investigated.

Public-sector unions in the state have consistently opposed the strike penalty provisions of the law. The 1987 legislative program of the New York State Public Employee Conference included a proposal for three major changes in the Taylor Law, all of which address the strike

---

[5] 24 GERR 95 (January 27, 1986).

[6] Harry H. Wellington and Ralph K. Winter, Jr., The Unions and the Cities (Washington: Brookings Institution, 1971).

[7] 24 GERR 145 (February 3, 1986); 25 GERR 71 (January 19, 1987); U.S. Bureau of the Census, *supra* note 1.

[8] See Olson, *Strikes, Strike Penalties, supra* note 2.

[9] The "two for one" penalty was enforced in 72 percent of the strikes in the first 12 years of its existence. See Olson, *supra* note 2.

penalties.[10] If recent history is a guide, these proposed changes will not be implemented. The durability of the strike policies in New York reflects a variety of factors, an important one being the law's effectiveness in preventing strikes. Public support for changes in the law has been lacking precisely because there have been so few public-sector strikes in New York. The experience of the New York City transit workers, employees of the Metropolitan Transportation Authority (MTA), is instructive on this point. The MTA and the Transport Workers Union (TWU) have historically negotiated under the threat of a strike, and two major strikes occurred in 1966 and 1980. The 1966 strike was an important factor contributing to passage of the Taylor Law in 1967. The law's apparent failure to reduce the credibility of the strike threat and prevent the 1980 strike led the legislature to pass one-time arbitration statutes that covered the two subsequent bargaining rounds. Then, in December 1986 the legislature enacted a permanent tripartite interest arbitration statute covering 45,000 MTA employees.[11] This action suggests that where strike penalties have failed to prevent strikes, public and union support converged around a strike-prevention policy based on arbitration rather than employee and union penalties.

The different policies adopted in the neighboring states of New York and Pennsylvania and the political balance created by each of these policies have survived many challenges over the past 15 years. These thoughts are consistent with Kochan's theme in the earlier edition of this book.[12] States select different strike policies that reflect different emphases on strike prevention and/or the bilateral determination of working conditions. Furthermore, once adopted, changes in policy with respect to strikes rarely occur.

Other jurisdictions chose slightly different provisions regarding the legal status of public-sector strikes. Illinois and Ohio, the two major industrial states without comprehensive public-sector bargaining laws until fairly recently, enacted laws that included the limited right to strike for some employees and interest arbitration for others. These were policy changes, replacing laws that prohibited strikes and included penalties that usually were not enforced. Thus, the costs of striking changed very little substantively, as the parties moved from a de facto right to strike to a limited legal right to strike.

In contrast to the efforts taken by Illinois and Ohio, which modified the legal but not the substantive costs of striking, the actions by President Reagan in the 1981 strike of the Professional Air Traffic

[10] 25 GERR 269 (February 23, 1987).

[11] 24 GERR 1729 (December 29, 1986); 25 GERR 42 (January 12, 1987).

[12] Thomas A. Kochan, *Dynamics of Dispute Resolution in the Public Sector*, in Public-Sector Bargaining, eds. Benjamin Aaron, Joseph R. Grodin, and James L. Stern (Madison, Wis.: Industrial Relations Research Association, 1979), 150-190.

Controllers Organization (PATCO) dramatically raised the cost of striking in the federal sector without any change in the legal restrictions on strike activity. [13] This reaction would have been difficult to predict prior to 1980 because developments in labor relations regarding both postal workers and air traffic controllers during the 1960s and 1970s suggested a more tolerant attitude toward work stoppages by federal employees. The government's decision to discharge 12,000 air traffic controllers and decertify the union reflects, in part, a conservative government unsympathetic to the interests of organized labor. On the other hand, the action represented a reassertion of the historical policy against strikes by federal government employees that was still clearly favored by the electorate. Whether a Democratic administration would have acted differently remains an open question. As Northrup notes, the government's plan for operating during an air traffic controllers' strike was initially written during the Carter administration. [14]

The impact of the PATCO strike on public-sector dispute settlement is difficult to estimate, but it has probably been substantial. The precise effect is problematic because the action was correlated with other factors that may have influenced strike activity, including the high unemployment rate, employment cutbacks in the public sector, and a public more sympathetic to the position of employers in both the public and private sectors. Despite these qualifications, the action appears to have had a very direct impact on postal negotiations that were occurring during the summer of 1981. There is also some evidence that the action inspired other public-sector officials to take a more militant stance toward unions and public-sector strikes. [15]

The PATCO strike and similar, but less dramatic, strike experiences show the limited effectiveness of public-sector strikes in achieving trade union objectives in today's industrial relations environment. This suggests that researchers need to pay more attention to the role of the political climate when explaining public-sector strike activity. Since public-sector strike costs impose primarily political costs on employers, strike activity and outcomes negotiated under the threat of a strike ought to be sensitive to changes in the political environment. This issue has been largely ignored in the cross-sectional studies of strike activity, but could certainly be investigated by contrasting recent experience with the experience in the late 1960s and early 1970s

---

[13] Details of the strike can be found in Herbert R. Northrup, *The Rise and Demise of PATCO*, 37 Indus. & Lab. Rel. Rev. 167 (January 1984).

[14] *Id.*

[15] See, for example, summary reactions in U.S. Conference of Mayors, LMRS Newsletter, August 1981.

Public Policy and Strike Activity

Research on the effect of public policy on strike activity has been sparse when compared with research on either the use of interest arbitration or the effect of arbitration on compensation. This is regrettable since most states continue to pursue policies that have strike prevention as a major goal. Unfortunately, because the federal government no longer collects data on public-sector strikes, it is likely that additional research on this important topic will increasingly be confined to states that have bargaining legislation and an administrative agency responsible for the law's operation and the collection of strike statistics. This nonrandom sample of states for which data will be available will make it even more difficult to make inferences about the effects of public policy on strike activity. Since there probably will be less research on public-sector strikes in the future, it is useful to summarize what we know from existing research.

Three conclusions can be drawn from the presently available research. First, interest arbitration has been successful in reducing strike activity. The best work on this issue is Ichniowski's study of police strikes, using a pooled cross-section, time-series sample of municipalities.[16] He classified state laws into four groups: no bargaining law or a prohibition on bargaining, meet-and-confer laws, duty-to-bargain laws without compulsory arbitration, and duty-to-bargain with compulsory arbitration. He found that strikes were most likely to occur in states without a bargaining law and least likely to occur in states with a bargaining law that provided compulsory interest arbitration.[17] He also was able to determine if the lower incidence of strikes was related to some permanent, unmeasured features of the states that pass arbitration laws. This was done by examining the strike experience *within* jurisdictions that changed their laws during the study period. The predicted strike probability declined from 0.084 to 0.005 in municipalities that went from a duty-to-bargain law without arbitration to an interest arbitration law. These results are also consistent with Olson's finding that police and firefighter strikes were less frequent under compulsory arbitration than under any alternative policy in six states (Illinois, Indiana, New York, Ohio, Pennsylvania, and Wisconsin).[18]

---

[16] Casey Ichniowski, *Arbitration and Police Bargaining: Prescriptions for the Blue Flu*, 21 Indus. Rel. 149 (Spring 1982).

[17] The predicted strike probability for an "average" municipality for the four groups was 0.037 (no law), 0.009 (meet and confer), 0.027 (duty to bargain, no arbitration), and 0.009 (duty to bargain and arbitration).

[18] Olson, *Strikes, Strike Penalties, supra* note 2.

The second conclusion that can be drawn from existing research is that strike penalties, when they are enforced, can deter strikes. Olson found that New York's "two for one" penalty, described earlier, substantially reduced public-sector strike activity in that state.[19] On the other hand, the legal right to strike provided to nonuniformed municipal employees in Pennsylvania had no effect or only a modest effect on strike activity as compared to Illinois, Ohio, and Indiana where strikes were illegal but penalties for violating the prohibition were applied infrequently.

Third, state policies other than collective-bargaining policies can have an important impact on strike activity. One result of Pennsylvania's policy, under which school days missed because of teacher strikes are rescheduled, is a greater number of strikes in that state compared to the other five that Olson studied.[20] In addition, *within* Pennsylvania a school district's policy with respect to rescheduling school days has a substantial impact on whether strikes will occur. Strikes are less likely in districts where teachers do not expect the days to be rescheduled.[21] For example, 45 percent of the districts with strikes in 1970–1972 that did reschedule all the school days experienced strikes at least one more time in the subsequent six years, but only 9 percent of the districts with strikes in 1970–1972 that did not reschedule all school days experienced strikes again. These results demonstrate that the policies employers pursue during a strike can affect strike activity in subsequent bargaining and reinforce the earlier conclusion that the PATCO strike had a significant (though hard to quantify) effect on subsequent bargaining in the public sector.

An important caveat applies to the findings of this empirical research on public-sector strike activity. As with studies of private-sector strikes, there is no agreed-upon model explaining why public-sector strikes occur. Thus, researchers have had difficulty deciding what variables might be correlated with strike activity and the policy variables of interest and thus should be controlled for. While omitted variable bias is always a potential problem with any empirical research, it is especially difficult to evaluate when the theoretical model underlying the research is not well developed. The strength of the results of the studies cited above can only be tested with additional research using different models in other jurisdictions and time periods.

Interest Arbitration

Most research on public-sector dispute resolution in recent years has been on various facets of interest arbitration, and the issues studied include many topics other than the narcotic or arbitration-dependence

---

[19] *Id.*
[20] *Id.*
[21] Olson, *The Role, supra* note 2.

effects, the focus of much of the earlier research. Among the topics of recent interest are arbitrator decision making, the selection of arbitrators by the parties, theoretical models of bargaining behavior under different arbitration regimes, and the impact of arbitration availability and use on compensation. This latest research, which is reviewed in this section, contributes substantially to our understanding of interest arbitration.

Arbitration Usage

Some form of interest arbitration is available in more than 20 states for the resolution of impasses in negotiations between local governments and at least some of their employees. Police and firefighters are the groups most frequently covered by the procedure, although it is available to all public-sector employees in some states. Lester's data on arbitration usage in eight jurisdictions are summarized here in Table 1 and show usage rates as a percent of negotiated settlements in the 3.8 to 29 percent range.[22] The three lower figures are from states with either choice-of-procedure laws (Minnesota) or states that have combined arbitration with special fact-finding and mediation procedures (Iowa and Wisconsin). The low rate in Minnesota is partially attributable to the use of the right to strike in some disputes; in Iowa and Wisconsin the arbitration usage rates understate the direct impact of neutral decision making because of the special role of mediation and fact-finding in those states. In Iowa many disputes are settled after fact-finding because, under the law, the fact-finder's report becomes one of the final offers and communicates to the parties that selection of the report is the likely outcome of arbitration and, thus, that proceeding further would be futile. In Wisconsin, after an impasse is certified, the Wisconsin Employment Relations Commission appoints a mediator-arbitrator who first tries to mediate a settlement and then arbitrates if a mediated settlement is not achieved. The power of the mediators is enhanced by the prospect that they become arbitrators if the parties fail to resolve their differences. With the exception of Pennsylvania, usage rates in the other states fall in the 10 to 20 percent range, a rate roughly comparable to strike probabilities involving large bargaining units,[23] but higher than the approximately 2 to 3 percent strike rate across all private-sector negotiations.[24]

[22] See Richard A. Lester, Labor Arbitration in State and Local Government (Princeton, N.J.: Industrial Relations Section, Princeton University, 1984).

[23] Bruce E. Kaufman, The Propensity to Strike in American Manufacturing, Proceedings of the 30th Annual Meeting, Industrial Relations Research Association (Madison, Wis.: IRRA, 1978), 419.

[24] Thomas A. Kochan, Collective Bargaining and Industrial Relations (Homewood, Ill.: Richard D. Irwin, 1980).

TABLE 1

Arbitration Usage in Eight States

State	Years	Occupations	Procedures[a]	Arbitration Usage Rate
Iowa	1975–1977	All local employees	Tri-offer arb, with fact-finding	3.8%[b]
		"Local option" users	Vary	19%
Massachusetts	1974–1979	Police & firefighters	FOA by package	16%
Michigan	1970–1974	Police & firefighters	Conv (1970–1972) FOA by issue (1973–1974)	10–16%
Minnesota	1975–1983	Essential & nonessential	RTS, Conv, or FOA by issue	4–8%[c]
New Jersey	1978–1983	Police & firefighters	FOA or Conv	15%
New York	1974–1983	Police & firefighters	Conv	14%
Pennsylvania	1968–1976	Police & firefighters	Conv or FOA	29%
Wisconsin	1975–1983	Police & firefighters	FOA	10%
	1978–1982	Other local gov't employees	Med-FOA by package	6.6%[d]

Source: Richard A. Lester, Labor Arbitration in State and Local Government (Princeton, N.J.: Industrial Relations Section, Princeton University, 1984).

[a] FOA = final-offer awards, Conv = conventional, RTS = right to strike.

[b] But 13.5 percent were settled either by arbitration or after fact-finding where the fact-finder's recommendation is one of the three offers the arbitrator may select if the case goes to arbitration.

[c] There were also 99 legal strikes during this period (compared to the 391 awards). The lower figure is based on a very rough estimate of renegotiated contracts using Census of Government data while the upper bound estimate is awards as a percent of mediation petitions.

[d] This percentage reflects only final-offer awards and excludes the negotiated and consent awards reached after the appointment of the mediator-arbitrator.

There is surprisingly little research on the determinants of arbitration usage. No one has conducted a careful field investigation of whether settlement rates are higher under final-offer or conventional arbitration. Although this issue has been debated since 1966,[25] there have been no studies of arbitration usage that employ bargaining unit data from jurisdictions providing different forms of arbitration and that also control for other factors likely to lead to an impasse. Part of the problem facing researchers who attempt such a study is illustrated in Table 1 and in the caveats in the table notes. Across-state comparisons are difficult because each state has a slightly different procedure that applies to slightly different time periods, and the bargaining units at risk are frequently difficult to identify because most state data on

[25] Carl M. Stevens, Is Compulsory Arbitration Compatible with Bargaining? 5 Indus. Rel. 38 (February 1966).

contract negotiations are incomplete. While these factors may make across-state evaluations complex (and expensive), such an investigation is certainly worthwhile. Without such a study, any statement about what "the data say" about settlement rates under final-offer and conventional arbitration must be based on very gross data such as those summarized in Table 1. Apart from measurement error due to poor data on the number of negotiations, what data are available do not control for factors other than the procedure that might influence usage across jurisdictions.

Studies of arbitration usage since the late 1970s have been assessments of arbitration dependence *within* jurisdictions. The most important investigations in this set are the studies by Kochan and Baderschneider and by Butler and Ehrenberg,[26] all of whom used data collected in New York state by Kochan et al.[27] Kochan and Baderschneider tested a model of fact-finding and arbitration usage with data from police and firefighter negotiations over a period of years from the late 1960s to the mid-1970s. They were interested in two major issues: First, were certain bargaining relationships becoming dependent on third-party intervention? Second, was there a change in the use of third-party procedures when the 1967 law, which specified fact-finding, was replaced in 1974 by one requiring conventional interest arbitration?

To analyze dependence on third-party intervention, Kochan and Baderschneider compared the probability that fact-finding or arbitration was used in a later bargaining round with whether it had been used in earlier rounds. They found a modest dependence on third-party procedures in the first three rounds of bargaining after passage of the fact-finding law in 1967. For some parties this round occurred under the arbitration statute; for others, the fact-finding procedures of the older law were still in effect. They interpret their results as indicating that some relationships were developing a dependence on third-party intervention.

To examine the impact of the arbitration law on third-party usage, Kochan and Baderschneider examined the intercept in a linear probability model explaining third-party usage to see if there were any changes from the last bargaining round under fact-finding through the

[26] Thomas A. Kochan and Jean Baderschneider, *Dependence on Impasse Procedures: Police and Firefighters in New York State*, 31 Indus. & Lab. Rel. Rev. 431 (July 1978); Kochan and Baderschneider, *Estimating the Narcotic Effect: Choosing Techniques That Fit the Problem*, 35 Indus. & Lab. Rel. Rev. 21 (October 1981); Richard J. Butler and Ronald G. Ehrenberg, *Estimating the Narcotic Effect of Public Sector Impasse Procedures*, 35 Indus. & Lab. Rel. Rev. 3 (October 1981).

[27] Thomas A. Kochan, Mordehai Mironi, Ronald G. Ehrenberg, Jean Baderschneider, and Todd Jick, Dispute Resolution Under Fact-finding and Arbitration: An Empirical Evaluation (New York: American Arbitration Association, 1979).

first bargaining round under arbitration. The results showed a statistically significant increase of 17 to 22 points in the probability the parties used the new arbitration procedure rather than fact-finding in the last bargaining round under the old law.

The focus of Butler and Ehrenberg's reanalysis of Kochan and Baderschneider's data and Kochan and Baderschneider's reply was on the method used to analyze dependence on third-party procedures. Butler and Ehrenberg demonstrated that the conditional probability techniques used by Kochan and Baderschneider did not adequately test for the existence of third-party dependence where dependence is defined as the *causal* effect of using a procedure in one round on the chance that the procedure will be used again in a later round. They argued that a probability will be greater for bargaining relationships that have a greater propensity to use third-party procedures, but that this does not necessarily mean that using the procedure in one round *caused* the parties to be more likely to use the procedure in a later round. They then showed that their definition of dependence ("state dependence") can be distinguished from simply a higher propensity to use a procedure by comparing the frequency of different "runs patterns," or the coefficient on a dummy variable indicating previous usage that is estimated in a fixed-effect, linear-probability model.

The intuition behind the "runs test" was demonstrated using data on two bargaining rounds where 1 indicates the parties used arbitration and 0 indicates arbitration was not used. The 1/0 pattern should be observed as frequently as a 0/1 pattern if there is no causal effect of using a procedure in round one on round two usage because each pattern is equally likely, given some underlying propensity to use arbitration. Alternatively, if use in round one increases the likelihood of use in round two, then 1/0 should be observed less frequently than 0/1. Note that parties who always or never use arbitration (e.g., patterns 1/1 or 0/0) are ignored in this test of arbitration dependence. This is a natural result of Butler and Ehrenberg's definition of dependence because the frequency of 0/0 and 1/1 cannot be used to distinguish between different propensities to use procedures in all rounds and the causal effect of usage in round one on the second bargaining round. For example, if 1/1 is a more common pattern than 0/1, it may indicate arbitration dependence, a greater underlying propensity to use arbitration, or a combination of the two.

The results of their "runs test" agreed with Kochan and Baderschneider's results and detected a narcotic effect of the procedures for the first three bargaining rounds beginning with the passage of the 1967 law, but the runs test and the conditional probability tests produced different results for the last three rounds. The conditional probability tests continued to indicate a narcotic effect, but the runs test showed that use of the procedure actually reduced the chance that it would be used again, a "negative narcotic" effect.[28]

While demonstrating the distinction between arbitration dependence and arbitration propensity, the runs tests do not control for observable differences in the bargaining relationships that might account for different propensities to use arbitration. The fixed-effect, linear-probability model estimated by Butler and Ehrenberg controlled for both observed and unobserved variables influencing the chances the parties would use one of the procedures. This method produces estimates of the effect on usage of observed factors within bargaining relationships that changed across bargaining rounds. Unobserved factors or variables that were constant within bargaining relationships over bargaining rounds that might affect the propensity to use arbitration were controlled by first-differencing the independent and dependent variables. When data available for the last two rounds of bargaining were used as the dependent variable, the regression results showed a negative narcotic effect which is consistent with the runs results from the last three bargaining rounds.

A key point made by Kochan and Baderschneider in their reply to Butler and Ehrenberg was that the appropriate test for arbitration dependence depends on the definition of the construct. While recognizing the importance of the distinction between arbitration dependence and arbitration propensity, they argued that only testing for Butler and Ehrenberg's definition of dependence provides an overly narrow view of reliance on third-party procedures and that repeated use of a procedure, regardless of any causal factor, must be considered when evaluating the effect of a procedure on bargaining. Thus, because the methods proposed by Butler and Ehrenberg ignored the experience of the parties that always or never used the procedure, the methods cannot summarize the experience that all of the parties have had with it. For example, the city of Buffalo never achieved a bilateral settlement with police and firefighters during the 1970s. As the second largest city in the state, its experience is surely important in assessing dependence on third-party procedures even though data from Buffalo cannot be used to distinguish between the two competing explanations of reliance on third-party procedures.

Kochan and Baderschneider's analysis of the use of fact-finding and arbitration, the re-analysis of the data by Butler and Ehrenberg, and Kochan and Baderschneider's reply are required reading for any

---

[28] In their initial paper Kochan and Baderschneider did not report conditional probability results for the last three rounds.

student of interest arbitration. These studies illustrate many of the strengths and weaknesses of our understanding of arbitration usage. Most definitions of the narcotic effect of third-party intervention correspond to the definition of "state dependence" or the *causal* effect of using the procedure in one round on the chance the procedure is used in a later round. Butler and Ehrenberg's contribution is showing that a test of this effect must control for differences, due to measured and unmeasured factors, in the underlying probability of using third-party procedures. However, such an analysis may produce an incomplete assessment of third-party usage by the parties since many of the methods used to assess "state dependence" or the narcotic effect ignore information from certain bargaining relationships.

The Bernoulli-based runs test and the fixed-effect, linear-probability model are only two of several techniques that might be employed to control for various underlying propensities to use a third-party procedure. With respect to the runs test, looking at the first three and then the last three bargaining rounds separately is potentially misleading since each test ignores the experience in the other bargaining rounds. Chelius and Extejt took yet another look at the runs patterns from New York, using the first five bargaining rounds as well as additional data from Iowa, Indiana, and Pennsylvania.[29] They also offered another statistical technique for analyzing runs patterns that permitted one-tail tests of either a negative or positive narcotic or state dependence effect. In New York they found no narcotic effect associated with using either fact-finding or arbitration, but they did find a negative narcotic effect for teacher bargaining in Pennsylvania, Iowa, and Indiana. There was no evidence of state dependence for police, firefighters, and other government employees in Iowa. These conclusions were based on at least five rounds of data from each jurisdiction and occupational group.

Butler and Ehrenberg's fixed-effect, linear-probability model also has some limitations. First, like fixed-effect regression models using interval scaled dependent variables (i.e., wages), the estimated effect of variables that change over bargaining rounds is sensitive to measurement error in the independent variables.[30] Second, the effect of variables that are constant across bargaining rounds cannot be estimated by this method because their effect on arbitration usage is perfectly correlated with constant unobserved effects that are controlled for by the first-differencing or, equivalently, the set of bargaining unit dummies. Thus, theories about the effects of stable bargaining unit

---

[29] James R. Chelius and Marian M. Extejt, *The Narcotic Effect of Impasse-Resolution Procedures*, 38 Indus. & Lab. Rel. Rev. 629 (July 1985).
[30] See Richard B. Freeman, *Longitudinal Analyses of the Effects of Trade Unions*, 2 J. Lab. Econ. 1 (January 1984).

characteristics on dispute settlement usage cannot be tested. Third, the method is feasible with data for only a couple of bargaining rounds because the fixed effects are controlled for by first-differencing the variables from two rounds. Since data for more rounds are now available in many jurisdictions, this method ignores many years of experience. Future researchers might consider single-factor probit models developed since the early 1980s.[31]

Negotiating Under the Threat of Arbitration

Since the late 1970s a substantial amount of theoretical literature has emerged that has had, and will continue to have, a major impact on studies of interest arbitration. In one paper Farber and Katz develop a theoretical model of conventional arbitration that shows when arbitration can serve as an effective strike substitute by encouraging the parties to reach a bilateral settlement.[32] Their model assumes that an arbitrator of a dispute has a predetermined view of a fair award, that the parties do not know precisely what it is, and that actions the parties take will not affect it. Labor and management beliefs about what an arbitrator considers an appropriate award is described by a normal distribution centered on W^u and W^m for labor and management, respectively. The variances of these distributions describe each party's uncertainty about the arbitrator's position.

Farber and Katz show that a risk-averse party will concede to a wage beyond the expected arbitration award (W^{uc} and W^{mc}) to avoid the possibility of an unfavorable award from the arbitrator (see Figure 1a). The utility of these outcomes equals the expected utility of the uncertain arbitration award. If the parties' expectations about what an arbitrator will award converges to a common distribution ($f(W^*)$), a positive contract zone defined by W^{uc} and W^{mc} is created, provided risk-aversion dominates (see Figure 1b).

The contract zone grows larger as the risk aversion of each side increases, if the parties are uncertain about what an arbitrator will do. Similarly, risk-averse parties will be willing to concede more to avoid arbitration as the variance in $f(W^*)$ increases. Thus, uncertainty about the arbitrator's decision and risk aversion provide an incentive for the

[31] James J. Heckman, *Statistical Models for Discrete Panel Data*, in Structural Analysis of Discrete Data with Econometric Applications, eds. Charles F. Manski and Daniel McFadden (Cambridge, Mass.: MIT Press, 1981), 114-78; J.S. Butler and Robert Moffitt, *A Computationally Efficient Quadrature Procedure for the One Factor Multinomial Probit Model*, 50 Econometrica 761 (May 1982).

[32] Henry S. Farber and Harry C. Katz, *Interest Arbitration, Outcomes, and the Incentive to Bargain*, 33 Indus. & Lab. Rel. Rev. 55 (October 1979). See also Vincent P. Crawford, *Compulsory Arbitration, Arbitral Risk and Negotiated Settlements: A Case Study in Bargaining Under Imperfect Information*, 49 Rev. Econ. Stud. 69 (January 1982).

Figure 1 (a)

FARBER AND KATZ'S MODEL WHERE THE PARTIES
HAVE DIFFERING BELIEFS ABOUT THE AWARD

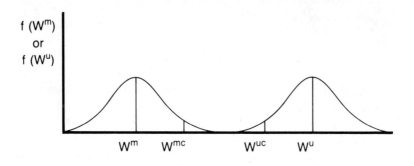

Figure 1 (b)

FARBER AND KATZ'S MODEL WHERE THE PARTIES
HAVE IDENTICAL BELIEFS ABOUT THE AWARD

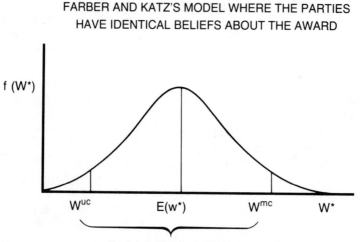

parties to reach a bilateral agreement in much the same way as the economic costs of a strike provide parties in the private sector with an incentive to reach a peaceful settlement.[33]

---

[33] The model also has implications for the negotiated agreements reached under the threat of arbitration. This is discussed later. Also, Bloom generalizes the Farber and Katz model to include arbitration costs other than uncertainty about what an arbitrator will do; see David E. Bloom, *Is Arbitration Really Compatible with Bargaining*, 20 Indus. Rel. 233 (Fall 1981).

One of the features of the arbitration process not considered by Farber and Katz is the offers the parties present to the arbitrator if a bilateral agreement is not reached. In a subsequent paper, Farber discusses the implications of this exogenous model for those offers and shows that the parties will position themselves around the expected arbitration award, with the more risk-averse party presenting an offer closer to $E(W^*)$.[34] When the parties are equally risk-averse, the mean of the offers equals the expected award. This is exactly what one would observe if arbitrators simply split the difference between the offers. Note, however, that the offers in this model are not motivated by any attempt to influence the arbitrator's decision. Thus, unlike Stevens' view of arbitration where arbitrators are influenced by offers and tend to split the difference between them,[35] in the Farber and Katz model the offers have no impact on arbitrator decisions and thus lack any strategic value to the parties. An important implication of these results is that a positive correlation between awards and the mean of the parties' offers cannot distinguish between Stevens's split-the-difference model and Farber and Katz's model of exogenous arbitrator decision making.

With this model, Farber and Katz have made a substantial contribution to our understanding of the interest arbitration process. If they are correct, then both conventional interest arbitration *and* final-offer arbitration can encourage bilateral settlements. This result has sharpened the debate over the relative merits of the two procedures by showing that the differences between them relate largely to the model of arbitrators' decision making. Since the advantage of final-offer arbitration rests on the assumption that arbitrators place substantial weight on the parties' offers, and if this assumption is incorrect, as in the Farber and Katz model, then the choice between the two procedures is not obvious. The empirical studies reviewed in the next section address this key issue.

A theoretical model of negotiations under a final-offer procedure is developed in another of Farber's papers where he shows that the contract zone and the offers the parties make under final-offer arbitration continue to be guided by risk aversion and uncertainty about what an arbitrator will do.[36] He develops three key results.

First, the more risk-averse party presents an offer closer to the mean of the distribution that describes the parties' beliefs about what the arbitrator will do. In other words, the party more fearful of what

---

[34] Henry S. Farber, *Splitting-the-Difference in Interest Arbitration*, 35 Indus. & Lab. Rel. Rev. 70 (October 1981).

[35] *Supra* note 25.

[36] Henry S. Farber, *An Analysis of Final-Offer Arbitration*, 24 J. Conflict Resolution 683 (December 1980); Vincent P. Crawford, *A Comment on Farber's Analysis of Final-Offer Arbitration*, 26 J. Conflict Resolution 157 (March 1982).

the arbitrator will decide will make the more reasonable final offer. If labor (management) is typically more risk-averse than management (labor), labor (management) will typically present the more reasonable final offer and have its offer selected more frequently. Thus, evidence that one side "wins" more final-offer cases than the other side does not necessarily mean that arbitrators favor one side over the other. Rather, it simply means that one side is more risk-averse and presents more reasonable final offers than does the other side.

Second, the final offers that the parties present to an arbitrator will be outside the contract zone, or more extreme than what the parties would be willing to accept in order to avoid arbitration.[37] As a result, the awards will also be outside the set of potential bilateral settlements defined by the contract zone.

Third, under the Farber and Katz model, the advantage of final-offer over conventional arbitration is clouded. The parties have an impact on the award through their offers under final-offer arbitration that is not available to them in the Farber and Katz model of conventional arbitration. They can reduce the risk of an unfavorable award by presenting a more reasonable final offer, an option that is not available in the Farber and Katz model in which offers have no impact on awards. Since the incentive to bargain and avoid arbitration in these models depends on uncertainty (and risk aversion), the contract zone created by final-offer arbitration may not be larger than that created by conventional arbitration.[38]

Given the implications of these theoretical models upon our view of different arbitration procedures, it is surprising that predictions from these models have not been tested. The empirical work that has been done (reviewed in the next section) tests an *assumption* of the models: Do arbitrators have an exogenous view of an appropriate award that is not influenced by the parties' offers? While it is important that this assumption be tested, other predictions about labor and management behavior implied by the models have been largely ignored.

Testing predictions about these models is important because of their implications for our evaluation of different dispute settlement procedures. For example, these theories and the indirect evidence from states that provide the parties with some flexibility in the design or choice of dispute-resolution procedures suggest that final-offer arbitration may not encourage bargaining any more than does conven-

---

[37] This assumes that uncertainty about what an arbitrator will do is the only cost of the procedure for a pair of risk-averse parties.

[38] Farber, *supra* note 36, does not directly compare conventional and final-offer arbitration. See also Steven J. Brams and Samuel Merrill, III, *Equilibrium Strategies for Final-Offer Arbitration: There is No Median Convergence*, 29 Mgmt. Sci. 927 (August 1983).

tional arbitration. According to the theoretical models discussed here, the parties will prefer a procedure where the risk of a very unfavorable settlement or, equivalently, the uncertainty of the outcome is minimal. Therefore, the parties should select the procedure where the result is least uncertain. If the final-offer process encourages bilateral bargaining more than does conventional arbitration because of greater risks, then the parties in states that offer a choice of procedure should be selecting conventional arbitration more often. But this has not been the case. In New Jersey, where the parties may jointly agree to substitute conventional for final-offer arbitration, only 23 percent of the interest arbitrations in the first three years were decided by the conventional procedure. Similarly, in Wisconsin few parties have opted out of the final-offer process in favor of conventional arbitration even though the local government's bargaining law provides the parties with wide latitude to design and agree upon their own procedure, which could be conventional arbitration. These data suggest either that predictions of the preferred procedure derived from the theory are wrong or that the alleged superiority of final-offer arbitration as a method for encouraging bargaining is overstated. Well-designed tests of the empirical implications of the models are required before we can make a judgment about which of these conclusions is correct.

Arbitration Decisions

Farber demonstrated that the split-the-difference model and the exogenous model of arbitrator decision making are special cases of a more general model where the arbitrator considers both the offers of the parties and the facts of the dispute before reaching a decision.[39] In this general model the arbitrator's award is a weighted average of both the facts and the average of the parties' offers.

A model that incorporates both the facts and the offers has considerable appeal. If an arbitrator mechanically splits the difference, then the parties have an incentive to present extreme offers. Since in actual cases they do not typically take extreme positions, the supposition ought to be that offers either do not influence arbitrators or have an influence only when they fall within a narrow range. The latter explanation seems to be the more reasonable. If the exogenous model is correct and the arbitrator ignores the positions of the parties, it is difficult to explain why they even bother to suggest an appropriate award. Finally, Bloom notes that offers may affect the award because they convey information to the arbitrator about the facts of the case that is not easily communicated any other way.[40]

---

[39] *Supra* note 34.
[40] David E. Bloom, *Empirical Models of Arbitrator Behavior Under Conventional Arbitration*, 68 Rev. Econ. & Stat. 578 (November 1986).

This issue has been investigated recently with experimental data. For one study Bazerman and Farber collected information from a sample of 64 arbitrators who were members of the National Academy of Arbitrators.[41] Each arbitrator was asked to evaluate each of 25 hypothetical disputes and then make an award. The positions or offers of the parties and the facts of the disputes varied.[42] The final offers in each case did not depend upon the facts. The authors used these data to estimate the relative weight placed on the offers versus the facts where the weight was a function of the difference between the parties' offers. The prediction was that as either side presented a more extreme position, the arbitrator would place less weight on the offers and more on the facts of the dispute. Their results showed that arbitrators consider both the facts and the offers but place substantially more weight on the facts. An average award predicted from the results equaled 0.92 of the award implied by only the facts plus 0.08 by the mean of the parties' offers.[43] The results also confirm that the importance of the offers declined as they diverged from one another or became more extreme.

A potential problem identified by Bazerman and Farber is that 38.3 percent of the awards in their study were either equal to or outside the boundaries defined by the parties' offers. They attribute these responses to the method used to construct the hypothetical disputes. Arbitrators were presented with simulated cases in which the facts and the offers were seemingly inconsistent, or "pathological" (the authors' terminology). This occurred because the offers were assigned to each scenario without regard to the facts of the case. When confronted with these inconsistencies, many of the arbitrators selected an award that appeared to them to be more consistent with the facts than with the parties' offers. All but one arbitrator made at least one award equal to or outside the boundaries of the offers. Bazerman and Farber assumed that these pathological cases had no impact on the decisions made in the other cases, and the pathological cases were effectively ignored when they estimated the weights placed on the offers and the facts.[44]

---

[41] Max H. Bazerman and Henry S. Farber, *Arbitrator Decision Making: When Are Final Offers Important?* 39 Indus. & Lab. Rel. Rev. 76 (October 1985). These data are also analyzed in Bazerman, *Norms of Distributive Justice in Interest Arbitration,* 38 Indus. & Lab. Rel. Rev. 558 (July 1985), and Farber and Bazerman, *The General Basis of Arbitrator Behavior: An Empirical Analysis of Conventional and Final-Offer Arbitration,* 54 Econometrica 1503 (November 1986).

[42] The scenarios varied across the following factors: inflation rate, comparable settlements, local and national average wages, economic condition of the firms, and the two offers presented by the parties.

[43] This result is obtained for the average difference between the offers of the parties.

[44] These awards are not omitted from the analysis; rather, they were included and treated as censored observations.

Since decisions that fall outside the boundaries of the offers are rarely observed in the real world, one must wonder why so many awards in the experiment did not fall within the parties' offers. There are two possible explanations. First, as Bazerman and Farber argue, pathological cases are seldom observed because the offers in real cases are correlated with the facts of the case, and they made no effort to correlate offers and facts in the experiment. Second, the willingness of the arbitrators to make awards outside the boundaries of the offers may indicate that the experiment lacked realism. Arbitrators participating in the experiment may have given less weight to the offers since it was unnecessary to signal any compromise to the parties by weighing the offers. Research by Bloom and Cavanagh on the parties' selection of arbitrators suggests that they share a common view of what makes an arbitrator acceptable,[45] and a part of this shared view may require that an arbitrator consider the positions of both parties and demonstrate this concern by viewing the offers as a constraint when making an award.

Whatever the reason for the "outlying" awards, the fundamental issue is whether these cases affect the extent to which the experimental results can be compared to actual interest arbitration decisions. Obviously, if the artificial nature of the experiment affected all of the decisions, then the estimates may not correspond to decisions in the real world. Alternatively, the results are more likely to generalize if the pathological cases were encountered only in the study because of its design and the arbitrators' decisions in other cases were unaffected by these scenarios. However, a convincing argument can be made that the seemingly pathological cases may have influenced the arbitrators' decisions in the other cases in the experiment.

The participating arbitrators knew that they were part of an experiment involving their decision-making skills and may have wanted to appear consistent across the scenarios. When confronted with a case where the offers did not fit the facts, they could ignore either the offers or the facts. Then, to remain consistent during the entire experiment, they might continue to deemphasize the dimension discounted in the pathological cases. Is there any reason to expect that these arbitrators ignored the offers rather than the facts in order to remain consistent? They certainly could have reasonably guessed the broad purposes of the study and they certainly knew that arbitrators are commonly criticized for "splitting the difference." This knowledge

---

[45] David E. Bloom and Christopher L. Cavanagh, *An Analysis of the Selection of Arbitrators*, 76 Am. Econ. Rev. 408 (June 1986).

may have prompted them to give the facts more weight than the offers in order to demonstrate that arbitrators do not simply split the difference between offers.

Bloom suggests a related explanation for why the offers were given little weight in the "normal" cases.[46] He argues that offers provide the arbitrators with additional information about the case that is not otherwise available because the offers are correlated (though imperfectly) with the facts. In the Bazerman and Farber experiment the pathological cases may have convinced these arbitrators to largely ignore the offers in all the scenarios because they contained no relevant information about the dispute.

In a second experimental study of arbitrator decision making in which he used another set of data collected from 55 National Academy arbitrators, Bloom reached a very different conclusion.[47] Four different cases involving a wage dispute were constructed for this study, each with a set of *different* offers that seemed plausible given the description of each case. One of the cases that included one of the plausible sets of offers was sent to each arbitrator, and the arbitrator was asked to make an award. In this design, variation in awards made by arbitrators who received the same case was attributable to differences in the offers and the arbitrators' different decision-making models. Bloom found that offers do affect awards and the weight given to the offers was very close to the weight the arbitrators gave to the facts in the Bazerman and Farber study.

Results of the Bloom study are consistent with the split-the-difference model of arbitrator behavior proposed by Stevens,[48] and are inconsistent with those of the Farber and Katz model in which offers do not influence the award. The coefficient on the mean offer was not different from 1, implying that a $1.00 increase in the average offer led to a $1.00 predicted increase in the settlement. However, there was substantial variation around this prediction. While supporting the split-the-difference model, Bloom's results have only limited implications for the practitioner who is trying to influence arbitrators. His results show that the parties should present offers that are as extreme as possible while still staying within the range considered "reasonable," based on the facts of the case. The study design precludes any assessment of the weight given to "unreasonable" offers or even of how an arbitrator decides whether or not an offer is unreasonable.

A third study of arbitrator decision making, this one by Ashenfelter and Bloom, used nonexperimental data from New Jersey.[49] Unre-

---

[46] Bloom, *supra* note 40.
[47] *Id.*
[48] *Supra* note 25.
[49] Orley Ashenfelter and David E. Bloom, *Models of Arbitrator Behavior: Theory and Evidence*, 74 Am. Econ. Rev. 111 (March 1984).

solved economic disputes involving police and firefighters are subject to final-offer arbitration in that state or, if both parties agree, to conventional arbitration. This system permits observations of both final-offer and conventional arbitration decisions made by a common set of arbitrators in the same jurisdiction over the same time period. Unfortunately, there are two problems that limit the value of the analysis of conventional awards. First, it was impossible to estimate the relative weights the arbitrators placed on the facts and offers under conventional arbitration because no offer data were available.[50] Therefore, the estimated weight placed on the facts will be biased because of the correlation between the facts and the offers.[51] Second, even if offer data were available for conventional arbitration cases, the simultaneity between decisions and offers would have to be accounted for in the estimation,[52] which is difficult because of the seemingly perfect overlap among the variables that affect both offers and awards.

While the Ashenfelter and Bloom study provides little insight into arbitrator decision making under conventional arbitration, it does give us empirical estimates of the factors arbitrators use when making final-offer decisions. The model assumes that neutral arbitrators under a final-offer procedure select the offer closest to their view of a fair award.[53] Building on the Farber and Katz model, the parties' beliefs about what an arbitrator thinks is fair is described by a normal distribution. When this model is combined with knowledge of the parties' final offers, the odds that the arbitrator will pick the union (or management) offer are defined. This is shown in Figure 2 where the shaded area represents the probability that management's offer will be chosen, and 1 minus this probability, or the unshaded area, represents the probability that the arbitrator will select the union's offer.

A more general specification permits the mean of $f(W^*)$ to be a weighted linear function of the facts of the case where the facts are observed by both the researcher and the parties. Such a specification implies a probit function where the weights assigned to the different dimensions of the case are estimated from the choices made by the arbitrators. The major difference between this probit model and most other probit models is that knowledge of the offers permits estimation of the error variance. In most probit models this parameter is not identified and is simply set equal to 1. Estimating this variance is important because it is an estimate of the parties' uncertainty about what arbitrators think is a fair award.

---

[50] Offers were available in final-offer cases.

[51] This assumes that the offers also play a role in the decisions and the facts aid the parties in determining their offers.

[52] See Bloom, *supra* note 40.

[53] This assumption can be and was tested. See Ashenfelter and Bloom, *supra* note 49, for details.

Figure 2

THE DISTRIBUTION OF FAIR SETTLEMENTS AND THE
PROBABILITY AN OFFER IS SELECTED UNDER FINAL-OFFER

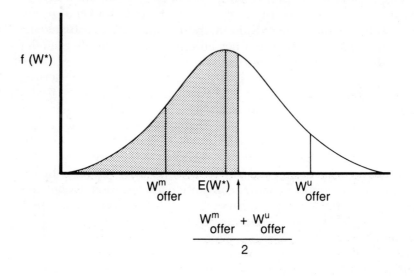

Unfortunately, the Ashenfelter and Bloom study did not produce reliable estimates of the role different factors play in arbitrators' decisions. The coefficient estimates were very unstable across the first three years of the New Jersey law. For two of the four variables, the estimated parameters were statistically significant in each year but did not have the same sign in all three years. The signs for the other two variables were the same across the three-year period, but the estimates for one year were at least half the size of those for the other years.

What should be done next in this area? Apart from simply replicating the Ashenfelter and Bloom analysis, three additional problems deserve attention. First, their model assumes that the variables the researcher includes are the same as those used by the parties when they estimate what an arbitrator will do. If this assumption is correct, then the variance in the error term that the researcher estimates represents both the parties' and the researcher's uncertainty about what an arbitrator will do (see Figure 2). But it is likely that estimates of both the weight arbitrators place on various factors and the estimated variance of the parties' beliefs about the underlying preferences of arbitrators will be biased if there are factors the parties considered when formulating their judgments of what an arbitrator will do that have not been observed by the researcher.

The sensitivity of the parameter estimates to omitted variable bias is illustrated using a random effects error structure that would not normally bias parameter estimates in a standard regression or probit model. Assume the model describing arbitrator decision making is

$$W^* = XB + v_i + e_{it}$$

where v and e are independent, normally distributed random variables and the X matrix is a set of variables determining W^* that is observed by both the parties and the researcher. The e variable, which varies across negotiations within bargaining relationships, reflects factors affecting an arbitrator's decision that are not observed by either the parties or the researcher. The v variable, which is constant over time within a bargaining relationship, reflects factors observed by the parties but not by the researcher. In a standard regression or probit model, failure to account for v in the estimation produces inefficient but not biased estimates of the remaining parameters. However, when analyzing arbitrators' decisions, omitting v will result in biased estimates because the parties consider v when formulating their final offers around $XB + v$. Therefore, even if v is independent of the Xs, it is correlated with the mean of the offers, and its omission will, in turn, produce biased estimates of both the parties' uncertainty about what an arbitrator will do (i.e., variance in $f(W^*)$) and the other parameters of the model that determine the mean of $f(W^*)$.

The preceding exercise has two implications. First, researchers should make sure that the variables considered by the arbitrator and known to the parties are included in their models. Given the absence of any clear theory about what other variables ought to be included, alternative plausible models should be estimated and reported. Second, omitted variables following the structure outlined in the preceding example can be estimated. A bivariate or trivariate probit model can be estimated with data from parties that have used the arbitration procedure two or three times.

A second area that has been largely ignored in work to date on arbitrator decision making, and one that is equally important, is how arbitrators decide cases under the final offer by total package procedure when a number of issues remains to be resolved. That procedure is used in several jurisdictions, including Wisconsin. In that state, between 1977 and 1985, in 61 percent of the cases involving teachers, the arbitrator was asked to resolve not only a dispute over a single year's salary, but also at least one other issue. Existing models, based on a single dispute over wages, implicitly assume that the positions of the parties on other issues have no impact on the arbitrator's decision—an assumption that certainly deserves careful investigation.

Finally, the process that arbitrators use in deciding cases should be examined in future studies. Several arbitrators have suggested that the offers of the parties play an important role not fully accounted for by the models we have developed. This role extends beyond the case under immediate consideration by informing the population of arbitrators what each side believes is "fair" in a particular dispute. For example, the major state teachers' organization in Wisconsin has established a set of bargaining goals for its affiliates that provides each local with an incentive to make a final offer that, if selected, will meet the union's statewide bargaining objectives. This policy is an explicit attempt by the union to shape arbitrators' view of what is appropriate in a particular context. If arbitrators come to believe that such a union goal is more important than they previously presumed, then they must either modify their presumptions or consistently reject the union's offer and thus run the risk of not being selected for another case. The latter position may be especially difficult to maintain when confronted with decisions supporting the union from other arbitrators. The implication that may be drawn from this discussion is that new models proposed for the study of the decision-making process in interest arbitration should include a dynamic feature not present in existing models.

Two of the three areas deserving attention from researchers can be addressed only with nonexperimental data. A model that specifies the factors which arbitrators actually consider when making decisions is best tested with field data since the experimental studies are necessarily confined to the particular issues the experimenter decides to manipulate, and an experimenter has no way of determining if this is an inclusive list of the factors considered by arbitrators in actual cases. The one area that is well suited for an experiment is the arbitral decision-making process in which the arbitrator must resolve multiple issues. This topic is especially appropriate for an experimental approach because the preferred position of the arbitrator on each issue as well as on the total package can be solicited. The position of the arbitrator on each of various issues is difficult to obtain from archival data on actual cases. Yet this information is needed if we are to determine how arbitrators weigh different issues when selecting a package.

Although another experimental study of arbitrator decision making has just been suggested, there are significant risks associated with using members of the National Academy of Arbitrators as subjects at any time in the near future in an experiment similar to the two studies reviewed earlier. Potentially serious problems of nonrandom sampling and response biases may be created by repeatedly returning to the same population of subjects to study the same set of issues over a relatively short time period. Bazerman and Farber had a very low response rate (64 out of 584) that may or may not have produced a representative sample of arbitrators deciding interest arbitration cases. Bloom also had a comparably low response rate (55 out of 527) even though the task he assigned was much easier and less time-consuming (evaluating one instead of 25 scenarios). These response rates suggest that arbitrators in the Academy, as a group, are now less willing to participate in experiments than they were several years ago, and it is problematic whether a mail survey, such as those used in the Bazerman and Farber and the Bloom studies, is even feasible today. However, the more important issue is how individuals in this population might be motivated to participate in yet another study and how this motivation might affect their responses. For example, those who respond might have a special interest in the topics reviewed in this section and may have read the studies (or this review), and their responses might be affected by their evaluation of this research, their guess about the intent of the experiment, and their own views about arbitrator decision making. Obviously, however, if these factors affect responses in an experiment, the study's contribution to an understanding of how arbitrators make decisions in actual disputes is seriously compromised.

Interest Arbitration and Outcomes

Two streams of research on interest arbitration and outcomes have developed since the late 1970s. One has its source in the theoretical results from the models developed by Farber and his colleagues, described earlier. In these models, settlement terms reached under the threat of arbitration are defined by the contract zone or the concessions the parties are willing to make to avoid arbitration (see Figures 1a and 1b). Thus, risk aversion and uncertainty about an arbitrator's award define the size and position of the zone of potential bilateral agreements. An implication of this result is that the distinction between bilateral and arbitrated settlements is overstated because bilateral agreements reached under the threat of arbitration are shaped by the parties' expectations of what an arbitrator might do. While none of these models provides guidance as to how the contract zone will be split when parties reach a bilateral agreement, the mean of the contract zone relative to the mean of $f(W^*)$ is biased against the more risk-averse party.

The empirical implications of these theoretical results have not been fully tested. In several studies the researchers found no difference between the intercepts in arbitrated and nonarbitrated settlements.[54] These results might be interpreted as consistent with the Farber and Katz model, but such a conclusion is valid only for the special case where there is no average difference in labor's and management's risk aversion. If the mean level of risk aversion is greater for one of the parties, then the model predicts that average negotiated settlements will be less favorable to that party relative to the average conventional arbitration award.

The absence of a difference in the intercept is also inconsistent with data from several jurisdictions showing that unions win more final-offer cases than do employers. But the implication drawn from Farber's research,[55] discussed earlier, is that unions are more risk-averse than employers and, therefore, when they negotiate under the threat of arbitration, the bilateral settlement should be less than a conventional arbitration award.

The apparent inconsistency between actual union win rates and empirical studies of arbitrated and negotiated settlements can be reconciled by noting that attempting to identify an intercept shift in a wage equation is a weak test of the model. The model implies that the effect of different variables on $f(W^*)$ should be identical in conventionally arbitrated and negotiated settlements. Thus, part of the test of this model is whether the vector of coefficients actually is the same. Such an investigation has not been reported in any of the published research.

A simple comparison between negotiated and arbitrated settlements in states that provide for final-offer arbitration also is not an appropriate test of the model, as the model produces predictions about how negotiated settlements compare with the mean of $f(W^*)$, or the expected awards from arbitrators if they are not constrained by the final-offer procedure. This value is not observed under final-offer arbitration because the award is the offer that is closest to the mean value, which introduces error in the measurement of what arbitrators think is a fair award. It is difficult to determine if the mean final-offer award is a biased estimate of $E(W^*)$. Two factors are biasing the mean final-offer award in opposite directions. If we assume that unions are more risk-averse than managements, then, according to Farber,[56] they will present more reasonable final offers. If the parties' offers were equally likely to be chosen, the mean of the award would be less than

[54] See David E. Bloom, *Collective Bargaining, Compulsory Arbitration and Salary Settlements in the Public Sector: The Case of New Jersey's Municipal Police Officers*, 2 J. Lab. Res. 369 (Fall 1981); John Thomas Delaney, *Strikes, Arbitration, and Teacher Salaries: A Behavioral Analysis*, 36 Indus. & Lab. Rel. Rev. 431 (April 1983): and Peter Feuille and John Thomas Delaney, *Collective Bargaining, Interest Arbitration, and Police Salaries*, 39 Indus. & Lab. Rel. Rev. 228 (January 1986).

[55] Farber, *supra* note 36.

[56] *Id.*

the mean of f(W*). However, union offers will be selected more frequently because arbitrators consider them more reasonable, and this will offset (or more than offset) the bias introduced by unions' more reasonable final offers. Whatever the bias created by using final-offer awards, it is clear that a comparison of awards and settlements in final-offer jurisdictions does not test the model.

The second stream of empirical research on the effect of interest arbitration on outcomes has investigated how its availability alters outcomes. These studies make comparisons across jurisdictions with different procedures or within jurisdictions at different points in time when different procedures were available. These studies have consistently identified small positive effects associated with the availability of arbitration, although in some of them and with some specifications the effects were not statistically significant.[57] Delaney's effects were the largest; he found that teachers covered by an interest arbitration law enjoyed a 10 percent wage premium over teachers not covered by arbitration and also not in a jurisdiction where there was a legal or a de facto right to strike. There was no difference between reported wages for teachers covered by arbitration and those with either the legal right to strike (Pennsylvania) or a de facto right to strike (Ohio).

The other studies, all analyses of police and firefighter settlements, found the mean wage effect of arbitration to be much less than Delaney's result for teachers.[58] Of this latter group, Feuille and Delaney's is the most comprehensive because of the time period covered (1971–1981) and the number of bargaining relationships in the sample (about 600). Depending on the year, the salary measure (minimum or maximum for patrol officers), and the specification, the estimated effect of arbitration ranged from 1.7 to 8.6 percent and was statistically significant.

Conclusions

Some very good research on public-sector dispute settlement has been conducted and reported since the previous edition of this book was published in 1979. New theories and a variety of research designs have been used to investigate a range of topics. Despite the lack of any agreed-upon theory on strikes in either the public or the private sector, research on the impact of public policy on strike activity has been able to progress because better data and more sophisticated

---

[57] See Craig A. Olson, *The Impact of Arbitration on the Wages of Firefighters*, 19 Indus. Rel. 325 (Fall 1980); Kochan, *supra* note 27; Delaney, *supra* note 54; Feuille and Delaney, *supra* note 54.

[58] Olson, *supra* note 57, and Feuille and Delaney, *supra* note 57, used panel data for their investigations.

analysis techniques have become available. Apparently interest arbitration and public policies that affect strike costs have an impact on the incidence of strikes. While there have been only a few studies of the effect of arbitration on strikes, what evidence there is shows that interest arbitration has effectively reduced strike activity. Where substantial strike penalties are enforced, as in New York, strike rates are very low. In contrast, the experience in Pennsylvania demonstrates that the policy of rescheduling school days missed during a teacher strike reduces the parties' strike costs and results in an increased incidence of strikes.

The theoretical work on arbitration by Farber and Katz and by Farber,[59] using basic techniques from economic theory, has provided many insights into interest arbitration. Although many readers may consider the mathematical models far removed from the practice of arbitration, these models do offer an array of hypotheses that can be empirically tested. For example, they showed that the bargaining behavior of the parties is influenced by the decision-making process of arbitrators, and this key insight was tested by Bazerman, Farber, and Bloom in their experimental studies of arbitrator decision making.[60] Many other implications of these models deserve attention in future research. Of particular interest would be more explicit tests of wage settlements reached under the threat of arbitration, as well as tests of the determinants of the offers the parties make under conventional and final-offer arbitration procedures.

---

[59] Farber and Katz, *supra* note 32; Farber, *supra* notes 34, 36.
[60] See *supra* notes 40 and 41.

CHAPTER 6

Public-Sector Labor Legislation—An Evolutionary Analysis

B.V.H. SCHNEIDER*

A reading of the history of employer-employee relations in the public service shows a consistent thread of concern that collective bargaining as we know it in the private sector is irreconcilable with the nature of government. This concern has been expressed in a variety of specific ways over the years, but in general it says that the complete transplantation of traditional collective bargaining into the governmental process would impair the decision-making power of elected officials as they seek to represent the public interest.

Resistance to collective bargaining in the name of the public interest, however expressed, can represent little more than a simple reluctance of an employer to share authority. Such a reaction is familiar in the private sector. But the problem is a larger one in the public sector. The political nature of government and its special relation to the public create a unique employment environment, one in which the sovereignty and nondelegation doctrines have been critical considerations in the creation of public-sector labor relations laws.

Early thought on the subject concluded that such mechanisms as exclusive recognition, binding agreements, and the strike or lockout were not transferable from the private to the public sector. Ida Klaus reported in 1959 that many governmental units had permitted their employees freedom of association and had accorded some degree of recognition to organizations of employees in the determination of employment conditions, but *at no level* had any government adopted "a thoroughgoing and systematic code of labor relations at all comparable in fundamental policy, basic guarantees and rights, and procedures

*University of California, Berkeley. I would like to thank Clara Stern, Librarian of the California Public Employee Relations Program, for her invaluable expert assistance. My thanks also to Sharon Melnyk. Bonnie Bogue, David Bowen, and Marla Taylor made helpful comments on an earlier version.

for their enforcement, with those of prevailing labor-relations laws in the private sector."[1] Such a system was generally viewed as inconsistent with government's sovereign decision-making status.

Nonetheless, when it became impossible to prevent strikes or to ignore the demands of public workers for participation in the setting of their terms of employment, policy makers turned hesitantly to the private-sector model. At a loss for workable alternative policy instruments, they diluted, stretched, and bent the system in attempts to make it fit government needs and employee expectations in hundreds of public agencies and dozens of states.

The result has been piecemeal adoption of traditional procedures, experimentation with new ones, and gradual abandonment of an unqualified sovereignty position. Concern with protecting government's ultimate authority (and, by extension, democratic processes) has come to be more narrowly focused on the need to guard political accountability.[2]

Neither the policy nor the philosophical process has been smooth or complete. The history of labor relations in the public sector is characterized by continuing tension between the drive for "real" (i.e., effective) collective bargaining, interpreted as equity by public employees, and the resistance of government as it strives to protect its decision-making power. From this comes the overriding "labor relations problem" in the public sector: the need to separate or reconcile political accountability and the bilateral authority inherent in the grant of collective-bargaining rights.

Accommodation has been achieved in regard to many elements of traditional (i.e., private-sector-like) collective bargaining.[3] In others, such as impasse resolution, the tension is unresolved, although the search for solutions has been intense.

In no case has a law been adopted which reproduces the National Labor Relations Act, although many approximate it. By 1987, 34 states had enacted collective-bargaining statutes covering all or some

---

[1] *Labor Relations in the Public Service: Exploration and Experiment*, 10 Syracuse L. Rev. 184 (1959).

[2] For an excellent treatment of the sovereignty and nondelegation doctrines, see James E. Westbrook, *The Use of the Nondelegation Doctrine in Public Sector Labor Law: Lessons From Cases That Have Perpetuated an Anachronism*, 30 St. Louis U.L.J. 331–384 (March 1986).

[3] The first question to be settled was the constitutional right of public employees to promote, associate with, and be represented by unions. The First Amendment has been held to protect these rights. However, it does not afford public employees the right to bargain or impose an obligation on the employer to recognize or bargain with their organizations, a distinction drawn by the U.S. Supreme Court in *Smith v. Arkansas State Highway Comm'n Employees Local 1315*, 441 U.S. 463, 101 LRRM 2091 (1979). See also Steven C. Schwab, *The Duty to Bargain in the Public Sector: Some Constitutional Considerations*, 16 New Eng. L. Rev. 397–412 (Summer 1981). Formerly, public employees in Alabama, Georgia, North Carolina, South Carolina, and Tennessee were statutorily prohibited from joining. These laws were struck down by court decisions. See, for example, *Atkins v. City of Charlotte*, 296 F. Supp. 1068, 70 LRRM 2732 (1969).

occupational groups,[4] two had statutes requiring the employer to meet

[4] For purposes of this listing, collective bargaining is defined as at least a legal compulsion on the employer to meet and confer in good faith with an exclusive representative in an endeavor to reach agreement on pay and conditions of employment. Alaska Stat., Title 23 § 23.40.070–23.40.260 (1972) as amended 1984 (all except teachers), Title 14 § 14.20.550–14.2.610 (1970) as amended 1975 (teachers); Cal. Ann. Codes, Government, Title 1 § 3500–3510 (1961) as amended 1986 (local employees), § 3512–3524 (1977) as amended 1986 (state), § 3525–3536 (1961) as amended 1983 (state exempt), § 3540–3549.3 (1975) as amended 1986 (public school employees), § 3560–3599 (1978) as amended 1983 (higher education), Labor Code § 1960–1963 (1959) (fire); Conn. Gen. Stat. Ann., Title 7, Ch. 113, § 7-467–7-479 (West 1965) as amended 1985 (local), Title 10, Ch. 166, § 10-153a–10-153g (West 1958) as amended 1984 (teachers), Title 5, Ch. 68, § 5-270–5-280 (West 1975) as amended 1986 (state); Del. Code Ann., Title 19, Ch. 13, § 1301–1312 (1965) as amended 1986 (all except teachers), Title 14, Ch. 40, § 4001–4019 (1969) as amended 1982 (teachers), Title 19, Ch. 477, § 1601–1618 (1986) (police and fire); Fl. Stat. Ann., § 447.201–447.609 (West 1974) as amended 1984 (all public employees); Hawaii Rev. Stat., Ch. 89, § 89-1–89-20 (1970) as amended 1986 (all public employees); Idaho Code, Ch. 18, § 44-1801–44-1811 (1970) as amended 1977 (fire), Ch. 12, § 33-1271–33-1276 (1971) as amended 1977 (teachers); Ill. Ann. Stat., Ch. 48, § 1601–1627 (Smith-Hurd 1983) as amended 1986 (all except schools and higher education), § 1701–1721 (Smith-Hurd 1983) (schools and higher education) as amended 1985; Ind. Code Ann., Title 20, § 20.7.5-1-1–20.7.5-1-14 (West 1973) as amended 1985 (teachers); Iowa Code Ann., Ch. 20, § 20.1–20.28 (1974) as amended 1986 (all public employees), Ch. 90, § 90.15–90.27 (1959) (fire arb.); Kan. Stat. Ann., Ch. 75, § 75-4321–75-4337 (1971) as amended 1981 (all except teachers), Ch. 72, § 72-5411–72-5437 (1970) as amended 1986 (teachers); Me. Rev. Stat. Ann., Title 26, Ch. 9-A, § 961–974 (1969) as amended 1985 (local), Ch. 9-B, § 979–979-P (1974) as amended 1985 (state), Ch. 12, § 1021–1035 (1975) as amended 1985 (higher education), Ch. 14, § 1281–1294 (1984) (judicial); Md. Ann. Code, Pub. Gen. Laws, Art. 77, § 160 (1969) as amended 1978 (teachers), § 160A (1974) as amended 1975; Mass. Gen. Laws Ann., Ch. 150E, § 1–15 (1973) as amended 1986 (all public employees), Ch. 1078, § 4A–4B (1973) as amended 1981 (police and fire disputes); Mich. Comp. Laws Ann., § 423.201–423.216 (1947) as amended 1978 (all; except state); § 423.231–423.246 (1969) as amended 1978 (police and fire arb.), § 423.271 (1980) (state police arb.); Minn. Stat. Ann., Ch. 179A, § 179A.01–179A.25 (West 1971) as amended 1985 (all); Mont. Rev. Codes, Title 39, Ch. 31, § 39-31-101–39-31-409 (1973) as amended 1985 (all), Ch. 32, § 39-32-101–39.32[ ] (1969) as amended 1983 (nurses), Ch. 472, § 39-34-101–39-34-106 (1979) (fire arb.); Neb. Rev. Stat., 1943, Ch. 48, Art. 8, § 48-801–48-838 (1947) as amended 1987 (all except certain teachers), Ch. 518, § 79-1287–79-1295 (1967) (teachers), L.B. 661 (1987) (state and higher education); Nev. Rev. Stat., Title 23, Ch. 288, § 288.010–288.280 (1969) as amended 1985 (local, schools); N.H. Rev. Stat. Ann., Ch. 273-A, § 273-A:1–273-A:16 (1975) as amended 1985 (all public employees); N.J. Stat. Ann., Title 34, Ch. 13A, § 34:13A-1–34:13A-13 (West 1941) as amended 1982 (all public employees), § 34:13A-14–34:13A-21 (1977) (police and fire arb.); N.Y. Civ. Serv. Law Ann., Art. 14, § 200–214 (Consol. 1967) as amended 1985 (all public employees); N.D. Cent. Code, Title 15, Ch. 15-38.1, § 15-38.1-01–15-38.1-15 (1969) as amended 1983 (teachers); Ohio Rev. Code Ann., Ch. 4117, § 4117.01–4117.23, and Secs. 4, 5, 7, and 8, as enacted by S.B. 133 (1983) (all); Okla. Stat. Ann., Title 11, § 51-101–51-113 (1971) as amended 1985 (municipal police and fire), Title 70, § 509.1–509.10 (1971) as amended 1986 (school employees); Or. Rev. Stat., Ch. 243, § 243.650–243[ ] (1963) as amended 1986 (all public employees); Pa. Stat. Ann., Title 43, Ch. 19, § 101–2301 (1970) as amended 1976 (public employees generally), Ch. 7, § 1–11 (1968) (police and fire); R.I. Gen. Laws 1956, Title 36, Ch. 11, § 36-11-1–36-11-12 (1958) as amended 1980 (state), Title 28, Ch. 9.4, § 28-9.4-1–28-9.4-19 (1967) as amended 1984 (local), Ch. 9.3, § 28-9.3-1–28-9.3-16 (1966) as amended 1986 (teachers), Ch. 9.1, § 28-9.1-1–28-9.1-17 (1961) as amended 1986 (fire), Ch. 9.2, § 28-9.2-1–28-9.2-16 (1963) as amended 1985 (police), Ch. 311, § 28-9.5-1 (state police) (1979); S.D. Comp. Laws 1967, Title 3, Ch. 3-18, § 3-18-1–3-18-17 (1969) as amended 1985 (public employees generally); Tenn. Code Ann., Title 49, § 49-5501–49-5516 (1978) (teachers); Vt. Stat. Ann., Title 6, Ch. 27, § 901–1006 (1969) as amended 1986 (state), Title 21, Ch. 20, § 1721–1735 (1973) as amended 1984 (local), Title 16, Ch. 27, § 1981–2010 (1969) (teachers); Wash. Rev. Code Ann., Title 41, Ch. 41.56, § 41.56.010–41.56.950 (1967) as amended 1985 (public employees generally), Ch. 58, § 41.58.005–41.58.803 (1975) as amended 1979 (public employment relations commission), Ch. 41.59, § 41.59.010–41.59.950 (1975) as amended 1983 (teachers), Title 28B, Ch. 28B.52, § 28B.52.010–28B.52.200 (1971) as amended 1975 (community college academic employees), Ch. 28B.16, § 28B.16.100 (1971) as amended 1983 (higher education classified), Title 53, Ch. 53.18, § 53.18.010–53.18.060 (1967) as amended 1975 (port employees), Title 47, Ch. 47.64, § 47.64.010–47.64.040 (1961) as amended 1979 (marine employees); Wis. Stat. Ann., Title 13, Ch. 111, § 111.80–111.94 (1966) as amended 1986 (state), § 111.70–111.71 (1959) as amended 1986 (local), 111.77 (1971) as amended 1978 (police and fire); Wyo. Rev. Stat., Ch. 197, § 27-10-101–27-10-109 (1965) (fire).

and consult with some groups,[5] three had authorized bargaining by statute for certain groups under restrictive circumstances,[6] and one had extended the right to bargain to state employees by executive order.[7] Ten states had no such statutes.[8]

What problems have arisen in the movement toward the private model? Which appear to have been solved? What problems remain? To what extent has the public sector been forced to build a new model? Using a broad brush, this chapter traces policy development on four major elements of collective bargaining—the right to bargain, impasse resolution, scope of bargaining, and union security.

The Right to Bargain

There was a time—spanning several decades before World War II—when even the act of joining or attempting to form a union for the purpose of self-protection was viewed with grave misgivings in many parts of the public sector. The right of public employees to associate might be constitutionally protected (although the law was not always clear on this, and statutory prohibitions on joining existed well into the sixties),[9] but such a right could not supersede the government employer's obligation to protect "the public interest." Although sovereign immunity had been delimited in other areas, e.g., immunity to suit, government authority in labor relations was viewed as absolute. It

---

[5] Ala. Code, Title 11, Ch. 43, Art. 7, § 11-43-143 (1967) (fire), § 16-8-10, 16-11-18, 16-22-6 (1973) (teachers); Mo. Ann. Stat., Title 8, Ch. 105, § 105.500–105.540 (1967) as amended 1969 (all except police and teachers).

[6] Ga. Code Ann., Title 54, Ch. 54-13, § 54-1301–1318 (1971) as amended 1976 (fire) [municipalities of 20,000 or more if implementing ordinance passed]; Ky. Rev. Stat., Ch. 345, § 345.010–345.130 (1972) as amended 1984 (fire), Ch. 78, § 78.400, 78.470, 78.480 (1972) (police) [municipalities of 300,000 or more]; Texas Rev. Civ. Stat. Ann., Title 83, Art. 5154c-1, § 1–20 (Vernon 1973) (police and fire) [municipalities where implementation approved by majority of voters].

[7] New Mexico, State Personnel Board regulations, September 30, 1983.

[8] Arizona, Arkansas, Colorado, Louisiana, Mississippi, North Carolina, South Carolina, Utah, Virginia, and West Virginia. Union organization occurs in all these states and collective-bargaining relationships are not uncommon, particularly in urban areas and in school districts, both urban and rural. Sometimes, municipalities create their own statutory systems; for example, the City of Tucson has enacted a bargaining ordinance. In Colorado, the state supreme court has held that a school board's participation in bargaining is not an unlawful delegation of authority (Littleton Educ. Ass'n. v. Arapahoe County School Dist. No. 6, 191 Colo. 411, 553 P.2d 793, 93 LRRM 2378 (1976)); see Mary Volk Gregory, Proposed Public Sector Bargaining Legislation for Colorado, 51 U. Colo. L. Rev. 107–133 (Spring 1980). After a 40-day recognition strike in Louisiana, a school district agreed to submit the question to a public referendum; the state supreme court held that the employer in this case did not have the authority to direct a referendum, but did have the implied power to bargain (St. John the Baptist Parish Ass'n. of Educ. v. Brown, 465 So.2d 674 [1985]). Widespread joint consultation, some bargaining, and numerous strikes take place in North Carolina, in spite of repressive legislation; for interesting background, see Michael G. Okun, Public Employee Bargaining in North Carolina: From Paternalism to Confusion, 59 N.C.L. Rev. 214–230 (October 1980). In West Virginia, the state supreme court held that a city was authorized to enter into a binding agreement with the union in that every municipality has the statutory authority "to contract and be contracted with," regardless of the absence of state collective bargaining legislation (State, County & Mun. Employees Council 58, Local 598 v. City of Huntington, 317 S.E. 2d 167, 119 LRRM 2797 [1984]).

[9] See supra note 3.

was joining for the purpose of bargaining that was the threat. In the absence of law specific to the subject, governments were successful in claiming in the courts that collective bargaining would amount to an abrogation of governmental discretion, that organization of personnel and determination of pay conditions were government functions, and that governmental functions might not be delegated. Bargaining, agreements, and/or force (strikes) would be "intolerable" invasions of the sovereign's absolute authority to act in the public interest.[10]

But World War II and its aftermath brought dramatic changes in circumstances and attitudes. The demand for more government services, sharp increases in the numbers of public employees, and inflation led to the growth of more militant and durable public-employee organizations, a rash of more effective strikes than had ever been experienced before, and, coincidentally but importantly, a resurgence of interest in the reform of public personnel administration.[11]

Public Policy and the Strike

Previously there had been no compelling reason for a review of public policy regarding the relationship between a government employer and its employees. Now, however, public and political concern over strikes gave rise to the first attempts to deal legislatively with a new labor problem in the public service.[12] In 1947, eight states passed antistrike laws.[13] In the same year, the Taft-Hartley Act banned strikes in the federal service and made such action a possible felony. Penalties in the state laws tended to be stiff, ranging from termination and ineligibility for reemployment for 12 months, to definition of striking as a misdemeanor, and to fines and imprisonment. New York's Condon-Wadlin Act required that rehired workers be placed on probation for five years and receive no pay increases for three years.

---

[10] The classic works on the early history of public-employee organizations and the problems that arose in the government context are Sterling D. Spero, Government as Employer, originally published in 1948 (Carbondale: Southern Illinois University Press, 1972), and Morton R. Godine, The Labor Problem in the Public Service (Cambridge, Mass.: Harvard University Press, 1951). Both are essential reading for those interested in the roots of public-employee organizations, which extend well back into the 19th century. It would be a serious error to assume, as much current work in this field does, that public-employee organizations were nonexistent or virtually impotent prior to World War II. Operating under constraints which normally foreclosed anything resembling a modern collective bargaining situation, they nonetheless pursued a variety of protective activities and, as David Ziskind has so well documented, were not reluctant to strike: One Thousand Strikes of Government Employees (New York: Arno, 1971) (reprint of 1940 ed.). See also Jean Couturier, Public Sector Bargaining, Civil Service, Politics, and the Rule of Law, in The Evolving Process—Collective Negotiations in Public Employment, 2d ed. (Fort Washington, Pa.: Labor Relations Press, 1985), 55–62.

[11] O. Glenn Stahl, Public Personnel Administration (New York: Harper & Row, 1962), 38–41.

[12] See Spero, supra note 10, at 16–43. For example, local government (excluding teachers) strikes increased from 39 in 1942 to 61 in 1946. See U.S. Dep't of Labor, Bureau of Labor Statistics, Work Stoppages in Government, 1972, Report 434 (Washington: 1974). Teachers' strikes rose from two in 1942 to 20 in 1947. See 90 Monthly Lab. Rev. 44 (August 1967).

[13] Michigan, Missouri, Nebraska, New York, Ohio, Pennsylvania, Texas, and Washington. Virginia led the way in 1946.

In spite of the harshness of the antistrike laws, a new trend was discernible. Some of the laws gave statutory recognition to the right of employees to communicate their views on employment conditions (Michigan, Ohio, Pennsylvania). Nebraska, in addition, created the industrial relations court to hear labor disputes and issue decisions regarding proprietary activities of the state. In Minnesota, public hospitals were covered by a law (1947) allowing for negotiations, exclusive representation, mediation, and binding arbitration as a tradeoff for a strike prohibition.

By 1950, the limitations of antistrike laws had become apparent. Many local governments had established bargaining arrangements with unions. Strikes were settled and penalties were ignored[14] as political bodies attempted to accommodate union aggressiveness and public demands for peace. An important straw in the wind was a recommendation of the first Hoover Commission in 1949 that "the heads of departments and agencies should be required to provide for the positive participation of employees in the formulation and improvement of federal personnel policies and practices."[15]

Cooperation in the Public Interest

Then, in the 1950s, came the second major public policy breakthrough: laws which reconceptualized the "labor problem"—i.e., strikes—as solvable by structured systems of labor-management cooperation. Cooperation as an assumption, if not a personnel technique, has a long history in the civil services. When service to the people is the objective, joint problem-solving is implied and the need for it was certainly made explicit in relation to service when employee organization was first condemned. "Cooperation in the public interest" was now resurrected to cope with demands by employees for a hand in determining employment conditions.

Starting with Illinois and North Dakota in 1951, six states passed laws which supported formal bilateralism for some groups of employees.[16] Each established the right of employees to join employee organizations. North Dakota and Minnesota placed an *obligation* on the employer to meet with representatives on employment problems. Illinois, New Hampshire, Wisconsin, and Alaska *authorized* employers to bargain collectively or to meet and confer. No law included a provision for exclusive representation or administrative machinery,

---

[14] Public Employee Labor Relations, Ill. Legislative Council, Pub. 132 (Springfield: 1958), 12–13.

[15] Kenneth O. Warner and Mary L. Hennessy, Public Management at the Bargaining Table (Chicago: Public Personnel Association, 1967), 398.

[16] Illinois and North Dakota (1951), New Hampshire (1955), Minnesota (1957), Wisconsin (1959), Alaska (1959). In Illinois the right was incorporated in a new state university merit system.

although exclusive representation was occasionally practiced locally here and there and had become standard practice in parts of the Illinois state service.[17] At the other end of the spectrum were laws by which Alabama barred state employees from joining labor organizations and North Carolina prohibited police and fire employees from joining a national labor organization.

In the early 1960s, California, Massachusetts, Oregon, and Rhode Island statutorily granted the right to organize. While California required all public employers to "meet and confer on request," Connecticut (municipal), Massachusetts (municipal), Oregon (municipal), and Rhode Island (police and fire) authorized "collective bargaining" on a permissive basis. No guidelines or standards were included.

Beginning of Collective Bargaining

The contention that any form of bargaining in the public sector was impossible was crumbling in the face of experience and political expediency. Or, to put it another way, the law was adjusting to changes in contemporary thinking. General acceptance of the concept of a legal duty on the part of the employer to bargain in good faith was facilitated by two events in 1962—President Kennedy's Executive Order 10988 covering the federal service and a new law in Wisconsin.

Executive Order 10988, although its scope of bargaining was limited, had the effect of legitimizing formal negotiating procedures, unit determination, exclusive recognition, and unfair practice procedures in the public sector.[18] The order also strongly emphasized participation for the good of the civil service. It wove together the objectives of the civil-service cooperation principle with procedural elements of the NLRA. Its preamble stated, in part:

> Participation of employees in the formulation and implementation of personnel policies affecting them contributes to effective conduct of public business, . . . the efficient administration of the Government and the well-being of employees require that orderly and constructive relationships be maintained between employee organizations and management officials, [and] effective employee management cooperation in the public service requires a clear statement of the respective rights and obligations of employee organizations and agency management . . . .

---

[17] Richard C. McFadden, Labor-Management Relations in the Illinois State Service (Urbana: Institute of Labor and Industrial Relations, University of Illinois, 1954), 18–21. See also, Public Employee Labor Relations, *supra* note 14. Collective bargaining in the Illinois state service can be traced back to 1919.

[18] For a description of the executive order and the history of employer-employee relations in the federal service, see B.V.H. Schneider, *Collective Bargaining and the Federal Civil Service*, 3 Indus. Rel. 97 (May 1964).

Of major importance in terms of impact was the adoption of exclusive representation and written agreements—steps toward the conventional private-sector bargaining model and away from the "government is different" syndrome, all of which would have seemed inconceivable 10 years earlier. Some court decisions in the 1940s had held that it was an abuse of discretion for a public employer to grant exclusive recognition to an employee representative if all employees concerned were not supporters of the representative. This position was slowly abandoned when governments began to move past the view that bargaining involves an impermissible illegal delegation of authority and came to rest on the rationale that agreements are an exercise of discretion rather than a delegation of authority.[19] Once written agreements were accepted as a desirable, if not inevitable, consequence of formalized relationships, exclusive representation became a logical prerequisite to orderly procedure. The prerequisite was that "fair" representation must be guaranteed, as it was in the executive order, by proof of majority support, by equal representation of all employees, and by assurance that individual representations could still be made to the employer.

The other public policy springboard of 1962 was the implementation of Wisconsin's pioneering law for municipal employees. It provided the sort of structure which the executive order did not—(1) a central administrative body, similar to the NLRB, to enforce and apply policies and procedures, and (2) a means for resolving impasses (mediation and fact-finding). Although exclusive representation was not specifically mentioned, the Wisconsin Employment Relations Board was mandated to hold elections and certify employee representatives, and employers were required to reduce agreements to writing in the case of negotiations with a majority representative.

NLRA Structure Minus the Strike

The years 1965–1967 brought a watershed in public-sector employment relations. Six more states—Connecticut, Delaware, Massachusetts, Michigan, Minnesota, and New York—moved by statute to a modified NLRA model, including a compulsion on the employer to bargain with certain groups of employees, machinery to administer and enforce procedures, and mediation-fact-finding mechanisms to resolve negotiations disputes. All included strike prohibitions.[20]

---

[19] See Richard F. Dole, Jr., *State and Local Public Employee Collective Bargaining in the Absence of Explicit Legislative Authorization*, 54 Iowa L. Rev. 539 (February 1969). A fascinating study of the "Missouri Trilogy" (*Missey, State ex rel. v. City of Cabool*, 441 S.W.2d 35, 70 LRRM 3394 [1969], *City of Springfield v. Clouse*, 206 S.W.2d 539 [Mo. 1947], and *Sumpter v. City of Moberly*, 645 S.W.2d 359, 112 LRRM 2787 [1982]) and the issues of governmental authority and binding agreements are included in Westbrook, *supra* note 2, at 337–352.

[20] Eleven other states adopted provisions or amended existing statutes to allow or mandate bargaining for certain groups: Alabama, Florida, Maine, Missouri, Montana, Nebraska, Oregon, Rhode Island, Vermont, Washington, Wyoming.

What were the reasons for this rush to an NLRA-type framework? Environmental conditions were of paramount importance. All seven states had influential labor movements and/or liberal political traditions, and a long history of public-sector employee organizations. Ad hoc bargaining arrangements had been developing steadily over the years. Perhaps the most critical factor of the time was the political-public realization that strikes were not a temporary postwar phenomenon or a condition which could be eradicated by law.[21] A statement of the American Federation of State, County and Municipal Employees (AFSCME) in 1966 set forth the union's insistence on the right to strike as essential to free collective bargaining. In July 1967, the traditionally conservative National Education Association (NEA) convention approved a policy statement that recognized strikes of NEA affiliates as likely to occur and worthy of support.[22] Clearly something more had to be done to counter the threat posed by the strike.

The situation in New York State in the mid-sixties exemplifies the kind of process going on somewhat less dramatically elsewhere. A critical trigger was the notoriety given the New York City transit strike in January 1966, along with Governor Rockefeller's appointment of the Taylor Committee the same month, and the committee's subsequent findings.[23] The committee's terms of reference focused on the twin policy goals which had been evolving since World War II: "protecting the public against the disruption of vital public services, while at the same time protecting the rights of public employees."[24] The committee, in its final report, came to grips with sovereignty and described the word as "scarcely an apt term to apply to a system of representative democratic government, such as our own, which is responsive to the electorate. It is more realistic to inquire as to the manner in which public employees can participate in establishing their employment terms within the framework of our political democracy."[25] The com-

---

[21] A total of 133 local government strikes were recorded in 1966. Work Stoppages in Government, 1972, BLS Report 434 (1974), 3.

[22] 90 Monthly Lab. Rev. III (September 1967). Thirty public-school strikes occurred in 1966, the largest number ever recorded. See 90 Monthly Lab. Rev. 44 (August 1967).

[23] Other important influences were a New York City welfare workers' strike in 1965 which was ended by the use of mediation and fact-finding; the ignoring of Condon-Wadlin strike penalties following New York City teachers' strikes; the waiving by legislation of strike penalties in various instances, including the New York City transit strike. See 89 Monthly Lab. Rev. III-IV (April 1966) and 90 Monthly Lab. Rev. 25 (December 1967).

[24] New York Governor's Committee (Taylor) on Public Employee Relations, Final Report (March 31, 1966), 9.

[25] Id. at 15. (For an interesting example of the speed with which opinion changed on this subject, see Railway Mail Ass'n. v. Murphy, 44 N.Y.S.2d 601, 13 LRRM 834 (1943), which states in part, "To tolerate or recognize any combination of Civil Service employees of the Government as a labor organization or union is not only incompatible with the spirit of democracy, but inconsistent with every principle upon which our Government is founded.")

mittee articulated the tradeoff which was to characterize public-sector legislation for the next few years: "It is elementary justice to assure public employees, who are stopped from using the strike, that they have the right to negotiate collectively."[26] What followed were recommendations for procedures based loosely on the NLRA model, but adapted to public sector differences—notably the substitution of mediation, fact-finding, and strike penalties for the right to strike.

By 1967, public policy in 21 states allowed participation of public employees in the determination of their pay and conditions of employment. Coverage of all public employees in a state was the exception, but coverage was slowly expanding and formal procedures and structures were increasingly common. The strike was still firmly rejected as incompatible with the nature of government employment. Modified bargaining systems were intended to make the strike unnecessary, and mediation-fact-finding procedures were expected to evolve into an acceptable substitute.

Impasse Resolution

When the Taylor Committee contended that the strike was inappropriate in the public sector, it based this view on two points. First, the strike is incompatible with the orderly functioning of our democratic form of representative government, in which relative *political*, rather than economic, power is the final determinant. Second, while admitting that some public employees are in nonessential services and others are engaged in work comparable to that performed in the private sector, it concluded that "a differentiation between essential and nonessential governmental services would be the subject of such intense and never-ending controversy as to be administratively impossible."[27] It also dispensed with compulsory arbitration as an option: "There is serious doubt whether it would be legal because of the obligation of the designated executive heads of government departments or agencies not to delegate certain fiscal and other duties. Moreover, it is our opinion that such a course would be detrimental to the cause of developing effective collective negotiations."[28]

---

[26] *Supra* note 24, at 20.
[27] *Id.* at 18–19.
[28] *Id.* at 46.

The Right to Strike

Pennsylvania proceeded to take a radically different line, moving directly from its 1947 no-strike statute to compulsory tripartite arbitration for police and firefighters in 1968,[29] to a comprehensive law and circumscribed right to strike for other public employees in 1970.[30] The commission that recommended the new approach stated:

> Twenty years of experience [under a no-strike law] has taught us that such a policy is unreasonable and unenforceable, particularly when coupled with ineffective or nonexistent collective bargaining. It is based upon a philosophy that one may not strike against the sovereign. But today's sovereign is engaged not only in government but in a great variety of other activities. The consequences of a strike by a policeman are very different from those of a gardener in a public park.[31]

Apparently collective bargaining was an idea whose time had definitely come in Pennsylvania; the commission reported that it could recall no witness who opposed the concept.[32] "Essentiality" as an insurmountable barrier to the right to strike was dismissed:

> The collective bargaining process will be strengthened if this qualified right to strike is recognized. It will be some curb on the possible intransigence of an employer; and the limitations on the right to strike will serve notice on the employee that there are limits to the hardships that he can impose . . . . Strikes can only be effective so long as they have public support . . . . We can look upon the limited and carefully defined right to strike as a safety valve that will in fact prevent strikes.[33]

Writing in 1967, only three years before passage of Pennsylvania's strike law, Andrew W. J. Thomson observed that no legislature "has yet permitted its employees to strike, and public opinion seems to indicate that such a development is not likely in the foreseeable future. The furthest that any legislative body has gone is to prohibit specifically only strikes which endanger the health, safety or welfare of the

---

[29] Awards are not subject to legislative approval.

[30] Under the general law, prison and mental hospital guards and court employees are covered by compulsory arbitration, but any part of an award requiring legislation is advisory. The courts have interpreted this to mean that an award is binding until the employer demonstrates that the legislative body responsible for providing funds has considered and rejected the award.

Strikes of other public employees are prohibited during statutory bargaining procedures (including mediation and fact-finding). An employer may seek an injunction to halt a strike where there is a clear and present danger to public health, safety, or welfare. The power to determine the latter is vested in the courts.

For an excellent study of public-sector strikes, see Antone Aboud and Grace Sterrett Aboud, The Right to Strike in Public Employment, 2d ed., Key Issues Series No. 15 (Ithaca: New York State School of Industrial and Labor Relations, Cornell University, 1982).

[31] Governor's Commission to Revise the Public Employee Law of Pennsylvania, Report and Recommendations (June 1968), 7.

[32] Id. at 9.

[33] Id. at 13–14. Hawaii took the same step in 1970 and for roughly the same reasons.

public as in Vermont . . . ."[34] A similar view was put forward by Ida Klaus who saw government as unyielding on the strike in part because of the unwillingness of the public to accept any action that would sanction strikes by public employees.[35] Both writers emphasized the difficulty of distinguishing between essential and nonessential services, the practical and philosophical point at which the New York and Pennsylvania legislatures chose to diverge, as noted above.

Fact-Finding

It is hardly surprising that heavy emphasis and high hopes were placed on mediation and fact-finding as procedural substitutes for strikes and lockouts. In 1973, Charles Rehmus reported that over 20 state statutes provided for fact-finding for some or all their public employees. He stated the reason for the attractiveness of the procedure: "If the issues in dispute and the recommendations for their resolution are clearly set forth and are well reasoned then the recommendations will be persuasive to all concerned."[36]

The problem with mediation and fact-finding, of course, is that they are not always persuasive, leaving the parties with the "finality" choices of an employer's unilateral action or an illegal employees' strike. In fact, it appears that 21 states now provide for fact-finding as a last step for one or more groups, an increase of only one since 1973. In these 21 states, there are 27 statutes that include fact-finding as a last step; 18 of the latter apply solely to schools (11), firefighters (3), police-fire (2), university (1), and state (1). The predominance of schools in this category is interesting and leads to speculation as to the possibility that there has been a trade-off of a more aggressive dispute resolution option for a broader scope of bargaining. It is true that 6 of the 11 either include professional objectives in scope or are less restrictive than other public-sector bargaining laws in the same state. However, with the exception of Alaska, Oklahoma, and Washington, these statutes are also either the only law in the state or the laws for other groups contain a similar impasse procedure.[37]

Strike Statutes

The critical question which the New York committee and Pennsylvania commission attempted to deal with—given the limitations imposed by the government's role in society, how do you accommo-

[34] Andrew W.J. Thomson, Strikes and Strike Penalties in Public Employment (Ithaca: New York State School of Industrial and Labor Relations, Cornell University, 1967), 8.
[35] Ida Klaus, A Look Ahead, in Labor-Management Relations in the Public Service, Part 6 (Honolulu: Industrial Relations Center, University of Hawaii, September 1968), 775–776.
[36] Charles Rehmus, The Fact Finder's Role, in The Public Interest and the Role of the Neutral in Dispute Settlement (Albany, N.Y.: Society of Professionals in Dispute Resolution, 1973), 37.
[37] California, Delaware, Idaho, Indiana, Kansas, Maryland, North Dakota, Tennessee.

date the pressure for finality in collective bargaining?—continues to absorb the parties, politicians, and public. More research has been carried out in this area than in any other in the field of public-sector labor relations. Legislative solutions, proposed and applied, have been imaginative and often daring.

For example, given the historical aversion to the strike in the public sector, one of the most interesting developments since 1970 has been the statutory granting of this right in 10 states.[38] The reasons seem to be basically those touched on by the Pennsylvania commission: a belief that bargaining will thereby be strengthened along with a belief that true essentiality of certain types of employees can be defined, and should be, to protect the interests of both public employees and the public. It is the latter objective which has most strongly marked these statutes. In no case is the right to strike unfettered. In all cases, a threat to the public health, safety, and/or welfare triggers a "no-strike" mechanism. In most cases, certain prestrike impasse procedures must be complied with.

Some of these procedures involve the passage of considerable time.[39] Others involve other kinds of devices to bring public pressure into the picture and to force harder bargaining. For example, after impasse, the Wisconsin law requires each party to submit a single final offer, which becomes a public document; a public hearing must be held if five citizens request one; if *both* parties withdraw their final offers, the labor organization may strike after giving 10 days' notice unless a court finds that a strike would pose an imminent threat to public health or safety. If *either* party does not withdraw its offer, the arbitrator proceeds. Essentiality is doubly protected in all 10 states by provision of compulsory arbitration for some group or groups of employees.[40]

The new law in Ohio contains a procedure which appears designed to provide particularly stringent safeguards for "democratic processes" and "accountability." The end of the routine negotiations process comes, at most, seven days after the fact-finders' recommendations. If both sides agree, the recommendations are accepted as is or as modified by the parties. If rejection is considered, votes must be taken. Either the employer or the union membership may reject the recommendations by a three-fifths majority of the total body. (In the case of the state, a 60 percent vote of the members of both houses is

---

[38] Alaska (1974), Hawaii (1970), Illinois (1983), Minnesota (1975), Montana (1969), Ohio (1983), Oregon (1973), Pennsylvania (1970), Vermont (1967), Wisconsin (1977).

[39] In Hawaii, the legislated procedure forbids a strike for 60 days after the fact-finding board has made public its findings and recommendations.

[40] All include compulsory arbitration for police *and* firefighters, except Montana which covers fire only and Vermont (municipal) where arbitration is voluntary for all units unless made compulsory by referendum.

necessary to reject a contract.) If the vote by both is at least 41 percent in favor, the contract is ratified. If either rejects the recommendations, an impasse exists and the findings are published. If there is still no agreement within seven days, designated safety services go to final-offer arbitration. Other employees may strike after 10 days' notice, unless they have selected another procedure (e.g., arbitration) in advance.[41]

Where there is no statute granting public employees a right to strike, the courts have generally held that no such right exists, citing four reasons for this common law position: strikes undermine governmental sovereignty;[42] they serve no purpose because employers lack authority to change legislatively determined employment conditions;[43] they give public employees excessive bargaining power because of the inelastic demand for public services;[44] and they threaten public health, safety, and welfare by interrupting essential services.[45] In dealing with the constitutional questions of equal protection, due process, and free speech, the courts have consistently held that the denial of the right to strike is not a violation.[46] On the other hand, where a statute grants the right to strike, the law has been declared not unconstitutional.[47]

In spite of the body of case law on the illegality of strikes where a statute does not permit them, 38 states currently carry no-strike laws on the books and 22 of these specify penalties. Twelve states specifically list strikes or unlawful strikes (where certain strikes are legal) as unfair practices in their employment relations laws.[48] Interestingly, seven states grant employees the right to engage in "concerted activities" (interpreted in the private sector to include the right to strike), while simultaneously prohibiting strikes.[49]

---

[41] See James T. O'Reilly and Neil Gath, *Structures and Conflicts: Ohio's Collective Bargaining Law for Public Employees*, 44 Ohio St. L.J. 891–942 (1983).

[42] *Norwalk Teachers' Ass'n. v. Board of Educ.*, 138 Conn. 269, 83 A.2d 842, 28 LRRM 2408 (1951).

[43] *City of Los Angeles v. Los Angeles Bldg. & Constr. Trades Council*, 94 Cal. App. 2d 36, 210 P.2d 305, 25 LRRM 2008 (1949).

[44] *City of New York v. De Lury*, 243 N.E.2d 128, 69 LRRM 2865 (1968).

[45] See Kurt L. Hanslowe and John L. Acierno, *The Law and Theory of Strikes by Government Employees*, 67 Cornell L. Rev. 1059–1066 (1982).

[46] See *City of New York v. De Lury*, supra note 44; *School Comm. Town of Westerly v. Westerly Teachers Ass'n*, 299 A.2d 441, 82 LRRM 2567 (1973); *Oneida County, Idaho, School Dist. No. 351 v. Oneida Educ. Ass'n*, 567 P.2d 830, 95 LRRM 3244 (1977); *Anchorage Educ. Ass'n v. Anchorage School Dist.*, 648 P.2d 993, 114 LRRM 3377 (1982).

[47] *Butler Area School Dist. v. Butler Educ. Ass'n*, 100 LRRM 2185 (Pa. 1978).

[48] Florida, Iowa, Kansas, Maine, Minnesota, Nebraska, New Hampshire, Ohio, Pennsylvania, Tennessee, Vermont, Wisconsin. For a comprehensive study of the treatment of unfair labor practices and strikes under the NLRA and state statutes applicable to public employees, see Benjamin Aaron, *Unfair Labor Practices and the Right to Strike in the Public Sector: Has the National Labor Relations Act Been a Good Model?* 38 Stan. L. Rev. 1097–1122 (April 1986).

[49] Connecticut, Florida, Iowa, Massachusetts, Michigan, Tennessee, Vermont.

The Right to Strike in the Absence of a Statutory Provision

Employees in three states have the right to strike without an explicit grant by statute. Montana is a special case in that its supreme court has chosen to accept the broad definition of "concerted activities" as including strikes. The court commented that no different interpretation is required where public employees are involved, particularly as nowhere in the municipal law are employees prohibited from striking.[50] (Nurses in Montana, however, do have a statutory right to strike.)

Idaho's law for firefighters prohibits strikes during the term of a contract. The state supreme court has ruled that firefighters have a "residual" right to strike after expiration and before a new contract is consummated, and "parties are free to negotiate one way or another depending upon their relative economic strengths."[51]

California is the newest addition to the right-to-strike group. In 1985, the state supreme court decided in *County Sanitation* (in a case covering employees under the local government statute) that the common law rule that public employees have no right to strike unless expressly authorized by legislation is "no longer supportable."[52] After reviewing the line of cases in which it had explicitly reserved judgment on the strike issue, and then describing its rejection in 1961 of the concept of sovereignty as a justification for governmental immunity from tort liability, the court went on to respond to the four traditional arguments against the strike right. On sovereignty: "the use of this archaic concept to justify a per se prohibition against public employee strikes is inconsistent with modern social reality and should be hereafter laid to rest." On strikes resulting in "government by contract" instead of "government by law": the local government act mandates bargaining rights nearly parallel to the private sector; by enacting these protections, the legislature "effectively removed many of the underpinnings of the common law per se ban against public employee strikes." On the inelastic demand for government services: "a key assumption . . . that all government services are essential—is factually insupportable." On the unacceptability of interruption of government services: "to the extent that the 'excessive bargaining power' and

---

[50] *State of Montana v. Public Employees Craft Council of Mont.*, 529 P.2d 785, 88 LRRM 2012 (1974).
[51] *Fire Fighters Local 1494 v. City of Coeur d'Alene, Idaho*, 100 LRRM 2079 (Idaho 1978).
[52] *County Sanitation Dist. 2, Los Angeles County v. Los Angeles County Employees Ass'n Local 660*, 38 Cal. 3d 564, 699 P.2d 835, 214 Cal. Rptr. 424, 119 LRRM 2433; *cert. denied*, 106 S. Ct. 408, 120 LRRM 3216 (1985).

'interruption of essential services' arguments still have merit, specific health and safety limitations on the right to strike should suffice to answer the concerns underlying those arguments."

The California court concluded that

> the common law prohibition against public sector strikes should not be recognized in this state. Consequently, strikes by public sector employees in this state as such are neither illegal nor tortious under California common law. We must immediately caution, however, that the right of public employees to strike is by no means unlimited. Prudence and concern for the general public welfare require certain restrictions.

This unprecedented decision caused a spate of reaction from legal scholars. A primary focus of attention was the *judicial* nature of the action and its infringement on the political accountability aspect of the nondelegation doctrine.

> The California Supreme Court failed to recognize judicial limitations when it embarked upon this policy analysis, an analysis that all other jurisdictions have reserved for the legislature.[53]
> The legislature necessarily had a purpose in expressly denying public employees the protections afforded private employees . . . . In reaching the opposite conclusion . . ., the court not only intruded upon determinations best left to the legislature, but also unnecessarily reconsidered a decision the legislature had already made. In doing so, the court misconstrued statutory provisions . . . .[54]
> [T]he California Supreme Court has obliterated any conceptual distinction between private sector and public sector impasse resolution. The consequence of doing so is to trivialize the influence of the citizen in public sector labor relations. When the right to strike is granted statutorily, the citizen is at least permitted a voice in designing the system, and that voice presumably assures that the interest of the citizen has been adequately protected. The California common law rule avoids even that degree of electoral power.[55]

On the other hand,

> The common-law rule . . . provided for a wholesale denial of the freedom of public employees to withhold their labor. Such denial is justified only where it has clearly been established that the public welfare is threatened. By granting . . . a limited right to strike, the . . . Court produced a decision worthy of consideration by courts currently advocating the abrogation of the common-law rule . . . . A number of courts are likely to follow the precedent set by this court.[56]

---

[53] Note, *California Public Employees Granted Right to Strike Without Legislative Authorization*, 64 Wash. U.L.Q. 269 (Winter 1986).
[54] G. Murray Snow, *County Sanitation District No. 2 v. Los Angeles County Employees Association, Local 660: A Study in Judicial Legislation*, 1986 B.Y.U. L. Rev. 206 (Winter 1986).
[55] Raymond L. Hogler, *The Common Law of Public Employee Strikes: A New Rule in California*, 37 Lab. L.J. 102–103 (February 1986).
[56] Lori E. Shaw, *Labor Law: The California Supreme Court Confers a Limited Right to Strike Upon Public Employees Through Judicial Fiat*, 11 U. Dayton L. Rev. 436 (Winter 1986).

Although some observers in California expected the legislature to respond by passing a no-strike law, this has not happened. Labor and management practitioners were more immediately interested in such questions as whether other public employees under similar California laws would by extension have the right to strike and how the health-and-safety standard would be applied.[57] Strikes have not increased. The Public Employment Relations Board (PERB), which does not have jurisdiction over local government, had already held under the public schools act that a strike before completion of impasse procedures does not constitute an unfair practice if provoked by the employer's unlawful activity; i.e., if provocation exists, such strikes may escape penalty.[58] In short, there is a good deal of interest in what *could* happen after *County Sanitation*, but so far nothing *has* happened.

The Trend Toward Compulsory Arbitration

Far more marked than the trend toward strike rights has been the trend to compulsory arbitration of bargaining impasses. In 1965, Maine[59] and Wyoming provided compulsory arbitration for firefighters. Two years later, Rhode Island, in education negotiations, had compulsory arbitration on all matters not involving the expenditure of money. In 1969, Nebraska expanded arbitration coverage from government proprietary services to all levels of government. In spite of a widely expressed concern of both employers and many AFL-CIO unions over the transfer of authority to third parties, 18 states had such laws by 1977. Nine years later, in 1986, there were 38 laws in 23 states which include compulsory arbitration in some form for some group or groups of employees.[60] All but three states cover both police *and* firefighters.[61]

Of the 38 statutes, 16 involve a variation on conventional arbitration, for example, last-best-offer by package or issue by issue, systems designed to shift responsibility for final terms to the parties and away

---

[57] See Bonnie G. Bogue, *The Supreme Court's Strike Decision: Implications and Ramifications*, Calif. Pub. Employee Rel., July 1985, 2–16. For background, see also Gregory Thomas Fain, *Local Public Employees Right to Strike After County Sanitation District*, 17 Pac. L.J. 533–552 (January 1986); Timothy M. Gill, *Public Employee Strikes: Legalization Through the Elimination of Remedies*, 72 Calif. L. Rev. 629–660 (July 1984); Hanslowe and Acierno, *supra* note 45.

[58] Calif. PERB Decs. 136 (1980), 208 (1982), 277 (1982), 291 (1983). However, in a recent order granting a school employer's request to seek an injunction against a teachers' strike, the board's new, more conservative majority has overruled its earlier ruling that a strike "provoked" by the employer's bad faith bargaining is permitted (PERB Ord. IR-50, 3-17-87).

[59] Repealed in 1969 and folded, as is, into a new municipal law.

[60] Alaska, Connecticut, Hawaii, Illinois, Iowa, Maine, Massachusetts (currently applicable to state police and Metropolitan District Commission officers), Michigan, Minnesota, Montana, Nebraska, Nevada, New Jersey, New York, Ohio, Oklahoma (binding only if accepted by employer), Oregon, Pennsylvania, Rhode Island, Vermont, Washington, Wisconsin, Wyoming.

[61] Firefighters, but not police, are covered in Montana and Wyoming. The statute in Massachusetts allows interest arbitration only for state police and Metropolitan District officers.

from the arbitrator, thereby extending the bargaining process.[62] Although more final-offer systems exist today than 10 years ago, it could not be said that there is a trend in that direction. Tanimoto's compilations for 1976 indicate that seven of 18 arbitration statutes at that time were based on final-offer, 39 percent of the total as opposed to 42 percent in 1986.[63] Currently, the breakdown by type is 22 conventional, 8 final-offer issue by issue, and 5 final-offer package; three offer a choice.

The overriding expressed consideration in the passage of these laws has been the need to develop peaceful procedures for resolving impasses. This objective appears over and over again in statutory policy statements and in the arguments of proponents of compulsory arbitration. By shifting finality to a third party, compulsory arbitration is intended to create a substitute both for the strike and for employer unilateralism. At one stroke a sort of balance is created between the parties by divesting them of their ultimate weapons, equity is achieved by settling impasses through a quasi-judicial forum, and the public interest is protected in that we have real collective bargaining, no strikes, and fair awards.

Few would argue that we have achieved this ideal. Compulsory arbitration is challenged most often on three grounds: (1) it does not deter strikes, (2) it has a chilling effect on the bargaining process, and (3) it involves an unacceptable delegation of governmental authority.

---

[62] Much has been written about such laws, experience under them, and the merits or drawbacks of different methods. See, for example: Paul F. Gerhart and John E. Drotning, *The Effectiveness of Public Sector Impasse Procedures: A Six State Study*, in Advances in Industrial and Labor Relations, Vol. 2, ed. David B. Lipsky (Greenwich, Conn.: JAI Press, 1985), 143–195; Robert G. Howlett, *Interest Arbitration in the Public Sector*, 60 Chi.[-]Kent L. Rev. 815–837 (1984); C. Craver, *Public Sector Impasse Resolution Procedures*, 60 Chi.[-]Kent L. Rev. 779–814 (1984); Daniel G. Gallagher and M. D. Chaubey, *Impasse Behavior and Tri-Offer Arbitration in Iowa*, 21 Indus. Rel. 129–148 (Spring 1982); Charles R. Greer and D. Scott Sink, *Oklahoma's Experience With a Unique Interest Arbitration Procedure for Fire Fighters and Police*, 37 Arb. J. 21–31 (December 1982); Frederic C. Champlin and Mario F. Bognanno, Compromise and Concession in Minnesota's Public Sector Under Strike and Arbitration Regimes, IRC Working Paper 82–15 (Minneapolis: Univ. of Minnesota, Industrial Relations Center, 1982); Jonathan Brock, Bargaining Beyond Impasse: Joint Resolution of Public Sector Labor Disputes (Boston: Auburn House, 1982); Janet Stewart Arnold, *The Historical Development of Public Employee Collective Bargaining in Nebraska*, 15 Creighton L. Rev. 477–497 (1981–1982); Henry S. Farber, *Does Final-Offer Arbitration Encourage Bargaining?*, Proceedings of the 33d Annual Meeting, Industrial Relations Research Association (Madison, Wis.: IRRA, 1981), 219–226; George R. Fleischli, *Some Problems With the Administration of Compulsory Final Offer Arbitration Procedures*, 56 Chi.[-]Kent L. Rev. 559–587 (Spring 1980); Thomas A. Kochan, Mordehai Mironi, Ronald G. Ehrenberg, Jean Baderschneider, and Todd Jick, Dispute Resolution Under Fact Finding and Arbitration: An Empirical Evaluation (New York: American Arbitration Association, 1979); Peter Feuille, Final Offer Arbitration (Chicago: International Personnel Management Association, 1975); James L. Stern et al., Final-Offer Arbitration (Lexington, Mass.: D.C. Heath and Co., 1975).

[63] Helene S. Tanimoto, Guide to Statutory Provisions in Public Sector Collective Bargaining: Impasse Resolution Procedures, 2d ed. (Honolulu: Industrial Relations Center, University of Hawaii, 1977).

Does it deter strikes? Most of the evidence available shows that arbitration has reduced strikes.[64] However, illegal strikes still occur where they are illegal under all circumstances and where they are legal under some circumstances regardless of the arbitration option.[65] Research on strikes has produced evidence that the introduction of public-sector labor laws can be correlated with an initial increase in strike incidence, but environmental and structural factors peculiar to the particular states appear far more likely to determine strike behavior, with or without arbitration.[66]

Does arbitration discourage true bargaining? The arguments that arbitration has, or does not have, a "chilling" effect on bargaining and that it has, or does not have, a "narcotic" effect on users have gone on for 20 years. Recent research data, based on reasonably long experience with a variety of systems, have been discussed thoroughly elsewhere.[67] Suffice it to say here that the trend in public-sector statutes

---

[64] Craig A. Olson, Strikes, Strike Penalties, and Arbitration in Six States, 39 Indus. & Lab. Rel. Rev. 539–551 (July 1986); Richard B. Freeman, Unionism Comes to the Public Sector, Working Paper No. 1452 (Cambridge, Mass.: National Bureau of Economic Research, 1984), 54–55; Craig A. Olson, James L. Stern, Joyce M. Najita, and June M. Weisberger, Strikes and Strike Penalties in the Public Sector, Final report for U.S. Dept. of Labor (Madison, Wis.: University of Wisconsin, 1981); Robert C. Rodgers, A Replication of the Burton-Krider Model of Public-Employee Strike Activity, Proceedings of the 33d Annual Meeting, Industrial Relations Research Association (Madison, Wis.: IRRA, 1981), 241–256; Hoyt N. Wheeler, An Analysis of Fire Fighter Strikes, 26 Lab. L.J. 17–20 (January 1975); John F. Burton, Jr. and Charles E. Krider, The Incidence of Strikes in Public Employment, in Labor in the Public and Nonprofit Sectors, ed. Daniel S. Hamermesh (Princeton, N. J.: Princeton University Press, 1975).

[65] See Aboud and Aboud, supra note 30, at 37–46; Robert E. Doherty, Public Policy and the Right to Strike, in The Evolving Process—Collective Negotiations in Public Employment (Fort Washington, Pa.: Labor Relations Press, 1985), 282–302. For strike statistics by state for 1970–80, see GERR Reference File, Tab 71, p. 1014; for 1978–1980, see U.S. Bureau of the Census and U.S. Dept. of Labor, Labor-Management Services Administration, Labor-Management Relations in State and Local Government, Special Studies Nos. 95, 100, 102 (Washington: 1980–1981).

[66] For an example, See Andrew A. Peterson, Deterring Strikes by Public Employees: New York's Two-for-One Salary Penalty and the 1979 Prison Guard Strike, 34 Indus. & Lab. Rel. Rev. 545–562 (July 1981), and Lynn Zimmer and James B. Jacobs, Challenging the Taylor Law: Prison Guards on Strike, 34 Indus. & Lab. Rel. Rev. 531–544 (July 1981).

[67] Daniel H. Kruger, Interest Arbitration Revisited, 36 Lab. L.J. 497–514 (August 1985); James R. Chelius and Marian M. Extejt, The Narcotic Effect of Impasse-Resolution Procedures, 38 Indus. & Lab. Rel. Rev. 629–638 (July 1985); Richard A. Lester, Labor Arbitration in State and Local Governments: An Examination of Experience in Eight States and New York City (Princeton, N.J.: Industrial Relations Section, Princeton University, 1984); Champlin and Bognanno, supra note 62; Richard J. Butler and Ronald G. Ehrenberg, Estimating the Narcotic Effect of Public Sector Impasse Procedures, 35 Indus. & Lab. Rel. Rev. 3–20 (October 1981); Thomas Kochan and Jean Baderschneider, Estimating the Narcotic Effect: Choosing Techniques That Fit the Problem, id. at 21–28; Henry S. Farber, Splitting-the-Difference in Interest Arbitration, id. at 70–77; Kochan, Mironi, et al., supra note 62; Thomas A. Kochan and Jean Baderschneider, Dependence on Impasse Procedures: Police and Firefighters in New York State, 31 Indus. & Lab. Rel. Rev. 431–449 (July 1978); Interest Arbitration: Can the Public Sector Afford It? Developing Limitations on the Process, Arbitration Issues for the 1980s, Proceedings of the 34th Annual Meeting, National Academy of Arbitrators, eds. James L. Stern and Barbara D. Dennis (Washington: BNA Books, 1982), 241–272; Arvid Anderson, Outer Limits of Interest Arbitration: The U.S. Experience, id. at 94–108.

toward arbitration suggests that chill and the narcotic effect are factors that can be dealt with or lived with. Certainly, reported instances of serious interference with the bargaining process are rare.

Far more important—because it goes to the heart of the public-sector employment-relations problem stated at the outset of this chapter—is the question of delegation of authority, or political accountability. So far 14 state high courts[68] have upheld compulsory arbitration statutes against state constitutionality claims that they improperly delegate legislative power and/or usurp home rule powers of municipalities.[69] Three state supreme courts have declared such statutes unconstitutional.[70] The decisions upholding constitutionality have most often found that there is a public interest in preventing strikes, that illegal delegation does not occur when there are statutory provisions of explicit standards and guidelines for arbitrators and procedural safeguards in the form of court review, and that the power to tax has not been transferred in that an arbitration act is regulatory and does not in itself impose a burden or charge.

But, as Joseph Grodin has pointed out,

> Whatever impact collective bargaining and strikes may have upon the political process . . . there is a qualitative difference between that impact and the effect of interest arbitration . . . . Even if it is assumed that arbitration generally deters strikes and that its impact on collective bargaining is benign or can be made benign, considerations of political responsibility remain. These considerations do not necessarily argue against a system of arbitration, but they do suggest that it be structured and limited in such a way as to preserve both the appearance and the reality of the democratic process in relation to important aspects of social planning.[71]

---

[68] All supreme courts except Oregon and Wisconsin where final ruling was at the appellate level.

[69] *Town of Berlin v. Santaguida*, 109 LRRM 2055 (Conn. 1980), remanding 98 LRRM 3259 (1978); *Carofano v. City of Bridgeport*, 196 Conn. 623, 495 A.2d 1011 (1985); *City of Biddeford Bd. of Educ. v. Biddeford Teachers Ass'n*, 83 LRRM 2098 (Me. 1973); *City of Bangor v. Bangor Educ. Ass'n*, 433 A.2d 383 (Me. 1981); *Town of Arlington v. Board of Conciliation & Arbitration*, 352 N.E.2d 914, 93 LRRM 2494 (Mass. 1976); *Dearborn Fire Fighters Local No. 412, IAFF v. City of Dearborn* and *Police Officers Ass'n, of Dearborn v. City of Dearborn*, 231 N.W.2d 226, 90 LRRM 2002 (Mich. 1975); *City of Detroit v. Detroit Police Officers Ass'n*, 105 LRRM 3083 (Mich. 1980); *City of Richfield v. Fire Fighters Local 1215*, 276 N.W.2d 42, 105 LRRM 3076 (Minn. 1979); *School Dist. of Seward Educ. Ass'n, v. School Dist. of Seward, Seward County, Neb.*, 188 Neb. 772, 199 N.W.2d 752, 80 LRRM 3393 (1972); *City of Amsterdam v. Helsby*, 37 N.Y.2d 19, 332 N.E.2d 290, 89 LRRM 2871 (1975); *Transit Union Div. 540 v. Mercer County Improvement Auth.*, 386 A.2d 1290, 98 LRRM 2526 (N.J. 1978); *Fire Fighters Local 1431 v. City of Medford*, 595 P.2d 1268, 102 LRRM 2633 (Ore. 1979); *Harney v. Russo*, 255 A.2d 560, 71 LRRM 2817 (Pa. 1969); *City of Warwick v. Warwick Regular Firemen's Ass'n*, 71 LRRM 3192 (R.I. 1969); *City of Spokane v. Spokane Police Guild*, 533 P.2d 1316, 93 LRRM 2373 (Wash. 1976); *Milwaukee Co. v. Milwaukee Dist. Council No. 48*, 109 Wis. 2d 14, 325 N.W.2d 350 (1982); *State of Wyoming ex rel. Fire Fighters Local 946 v. City of Laramie*, 437 P.2d 295, 68 LRRM 2038 (1968).

[70] *Greeley Police Union v. City Council of Greeley*, 191 Colo. 419, 553 P.2d 790, 93 LRRM 2382 (1976); *City of Sioux Falls v. Fire Fighters Local 814*, 90 LRRM 2945 (S.D. 1975); *Salt Lake City v. Fire Fighters Local 593, 1645, 1654, 2064*, 563 P.2d 786, 95 LRRM 2383 (Utah 1977).

[71] Joseph R. Grodin, *Political Aspects of Public Sector Interest Arbitration*, 1 Indus. Rel. L.J. 24 (Spring 1976).

Robert Howlett has said,

> Arbitration can change representative government . . . . It may result in
> a redistribution of government resources, change managerial authority,
> affect the cost of government, influence the amount of taxes required to
> operate government, impact on the quantity and quality of government
> public service, and allow government executives and legislators to
> escape responsibility for acts which they normally and should perform.

But he then asks rhetorically, "[I]f a legislature finds that the arbitration process is in the public interest, should there be objection to
interest arbitration?"[72]

Most legislatures have chosen to meet objection by incorporating
in the statutes criteria (often fairly detailed) which the arbitrators must
adhere to in making their decision; of the 38 statutes with compulsory
arbitration in 1986, 24 contained such standards. Several laws provide
specifically for judicial review.[73]

Raymond D. Horton, along with Grodin, was early in pointing out
the potential problems with interest arbitration: "By placing final
decisionmaking authority in the hands of persons not accountable to
the public, interest arbitration weakens political democracy."[74] He
suggested limiting and reforming the arbitration process, but, more
important: "The simplest and probably most desirable method . . .
would be to legalize *certain* public employee strikes."[75] This process
has, of course, been going on since Horton wrote in 1975.

Perhaps the most telling answer to the question of whether
arbitration constitutes an invalid delegation of legislative power came
from the Connecticut supreme court in 1985: "[T]he principle of
accountability remains viable in the ability of legislators to terminate or
modify any delegation of legislative power that has been made and in
the ultimate authority of the people to change the law by electing those
answerable to the public will."[76]

The following year, the Connecticut legislature amended the law
for state employees, dropping fact-finding and substituting final-offer,
issue-by-issue arbitration. Four safeguards of the public interest are
included:

1. The arbitrator is required to state the specific basis for each
decision.

---

[72] Howlett, *supra* note 62, at 821.
[73] Many do not, but judicial review has occurred nonetheless. Pennsylvania's limitation on
review in its police-fire statute has proved ineffective in numerous litigations. See Kochan, Mironi
et al., *supra* note 62, at 112–141; see also Stern et al., *supra* note 62, Anderson, *supra* note 67, and
Craver, *supra* note 62, at 787–802.
[74] Raymond D. Horton, *Arbitration, Arbitrators, and the Public Interest*, 28 Indus. & Lab.
Rel. Rev. 499 (July 1975).
[75] *Id.* at 505.
[76] *Carofano v. City of Bridgeport*, 196 Conn. 623, 495 A.2d 1016 (1985).

2. Criteria for decisions: history of bargaining, existing employment conditions of similar employee groups, prevailing wages, fringes, and working conditions in the labor market, overall compensation, ability to pay, cost of living, interests and welfare of employees.

3. The legislature may return an award to the parties for further bargaining if "it determines by a two-thirds vote, within 30 days of submission of the arbitration award, that there are insufficient funds for full implementation of said award." Failure to act within the 30 days makes the award binding.

4. A motion to vacate or modify an award may be filed with a court within 30 days of receipt. The court may vacate or modify if substantial rights of a party have been prejudiced because the award
   —violates the constitution
   —exceeds the arbitrator's statutory authority
   —was made on unlawful procedures
   —was affected by other errors of law
   —was erroneous based on substantial evidence of the whole record
   —was arbitrary or capricious.

The search for a satisfactory means of achieving finality goes on. Neither the strike nor compulsory arbitration is close to general acceptance, but arbitration has got the nod at the moment because, I would speculate, it seems controllable in form and it carries less emotional content than the strike. Compulsory arbitration is seen by many as the best available instrument for maximizing the potentialities of the collective bargaining process and minimizing illegal strikes and employer unilateralism.[77] In this sense, its proponents believe that it is "in the public interest." Continuing economic constraints, however, may yet cause governments to reevaluate the professional neutral as the channel through which they choose to see final decisions made. The pendulum may then swing to even greater experimentation with the legal strike, the absence of which, Horton has pointed out, removes "from management (and the public) one of its most important political resources—the opportunity to take public employee strikes."[78]

Scope of Bargaining

If public policy on dispute resolution is still in a state of evolution, this would appear to be even more true of statutory treatment of the scope of bargaining. We can see some consistency in the changes in

---

[77] See Arvid Anderson et al., *Impasse Resolution in Public Sector Collective Bargaining—An Examination of Compulsory Interest Arbitration in New York*, 51 St. John's L. Rev. 453 (Spring 1977).

[78] Horton, *supra* note 74.

laws regarding impasses. Trends are discernible, although a strong national consensus is absent. With scope, however, no long-term "trend" is apparent in the statutes. Twenty years ago there were wide differences from state to state in statutory law, and the same is true today. This is not to say that there are not similarities in practice or that there has not been a rigorous defining and redefining of what is bargainable. This activity has tended to take place idiosyncratically within each state and has rarely involved changes in the statutes. What is in fact bargainable is being determined by the parties, administering agencies, and the courts, and this is reasonable when one considers private-sector experience.

The definition of scope in the NLRA, as in most state public-sector statutes, is general. But scope is the area of labor relations in which the most vital interests of the parties and their constituencies are continually engaged. Scope in the area of bargaining represents a delicate power balance. Even where scope is most narrowly defined by public-sector labor law, the self-interest of the parties will tend to push toward pragmatic solutions, regardless of legal restrictions. Decades of controversy have attended the gradual creation of a definition of, and means for further defining, legal scope in the private sector; the process is still going on. Given the variety of statutory frameworks and the complication created by the government's being the employer, it is not surprising that the process in the public sector has had a kaleidoscopic quality.

Early Experience

In the 1950s and 1960s, many of the states that had statutes defined the scope of meet-and-confer or bargaining broadly in the manner of the NLRA, "Wages, hours and other terms and conditions of employment." In his study for the New York Public Employment Relations Board in 1970, Irving Sabghir found that statutory limitations on scope were not common. Those states which specifically restricted scope did so in the areas of management policies and civil service items, such as merit, recruitment, and classification. Furthermore, Sabghir could find no correlation between the types of bargaining relationship specified and scope provisions: "Thus, some meet and confer laws have a restrictive scope of bargaining provision and many which mandate a bargaining relationship are silent on the scope of bargaining."[79] By 1972, Lee C. Shaw[80] reported that a significant

---

[79] The Scope of Bargaining in Public Sector Collective Bargaining (Albany: New York State Public Employment Relations Board, October 1970), 5–21.
[80] *The Development of State and Federal Laws*, in Public Workers and Public Unions (Englewood Cliffs, N.J.: Prentice-Hall, 1972).

number of states were specifically exempting civil service systems and
the merit principle from scope[81] or were limiting scope by enumerat-
ing certain management rights or prerogatives.[82]

As employee organizations grew stronger and collective bargaining became more sophisticated, closer attention began to be paid by
scholars to the potential effects of bargaining on the political process.[83]
By 1973, Patricia Blair found that 23 states had legislation containing
language similar or identical to that used in the NLRA.[84] Her concern
was of a specific character, but one important to the broad, controversial area of delegation of authority. She found that the expansive NLRA
definition of scope was frequently combined with a definition of the
public employer which excluded the state's legislative body, thereby
requiring the courts, when construing the NLRA definition, to make
decisions which could reallocate the distribution of power between
state legislatures and executive officials and between state and local
governments. This effect was created by interjecting laws authorizing
or requiring bargaining into a structure of diffused power over public
employee working conditions.

The problem was recognized in the states. In order to avoid such
delegation, nine legislatures had provided that bargaining agreements
could not supersede state laws and/or that public employers might
conclude agreements on matters within their existing delegations of
power. Blair pointed out the critical incongruity: Although these laws

> will ensure against judicial interpretations that either expand existing
> delegations of power . . . or other laws that regulate public working
> conditions, this type of statutory scheme will restrict the scope of bar-
> gaining to less than that which prevails in the private sector. Restricting
> the number of subjects open to the collective bargaining process
> decreases the likelihood that collective bargaining will be an effective
> dispute settlement device, which is, of course, a primary reason for
> introducing bargaining into the public service.[85]

Meanwhile, lively action was taking place at the court and admin-
istrative-agency levels, as employee organizations pressed to bargain
over all matters affecting working conditions, and employers, with or

---

[81] *Id.* at 30. For example, Connecticut, Hawaii, Kansas, Maine, Rhode Island, Vermont, Washington, Wisconsin.

[82] *Id.* For example, Hawaii, Kansas, Nevada, New Hampshire, Wisconsin.

[83] See particularly, Harry H. Wellington and Ralph K. Winter, Jr., The Unions and the Cities (Washington: The Brookings Institution, 1971); Clyde W. Summers, *Public Employee Bargaining: A Political Perspective*, 83 Yale L.J. 1156 (1974), and *Public Sector Bargaining: Problems of Governmental Decisionmaking*, 44 U. Cin. L. Rev. 669 (1975).

[84] *State Legislative Control Over the Conditions of Public Employment: Defining the Scope of Collective Bargaining for State and Municipal Employees*, 26 Vand. L. Rev. 7 (January 1973).

[85] *Id.* at 17–18.

without a statutory management-rights clause, struggled to limit scope in their favor.[86] According to the American Bar Association Labor Relations Committee report of 1975, the

> trend has been to deem most topics bargainable, unless it can be demonstrated that the "extent and quality of service" to be rendered or "basic policy decisions as to the implementation of a mission of a government agency" [are] at stake. Even then the tendency is to find that the impact of managerial decisions on wages or working conditions is nevertheless a mandatory subject of bargaining.[87]

Three major questions were at issue: What should be the status of laws which provide conflicting methods of determining wages, hours, and other terms and conditions of employment (e.g., civil service and merit systems)? What rights should the government as management reserve to itself? How can bilateral decision making on certain issues by reconciled with the responsibility of government to the public? The first two questions are really of a piece with the third, that is, what happens to accountability? Unlike the private sector, in the public sector all employer (government) actions involve the "public interest," in the sense of *what* is decided, and "democratic processes," i.e., *how* actions are decided.

As the 1970s progressed, confusion and controversy over "competing systems," i.e., civil service and merit laws and the scope of collective bargaining, lessened. Wage, hour, and condition items were shifted into scope, but the merit principle itself was little affected.[88] New Hampshire's new law for state employees excluded the merit system from bargaining, as did laws in Florida, Hawaii, and Maine. The Pensylvania law was amended to allow contracts between the governor and state employees to supersede conflicting civil service rules on promotions and furloughs. California's 1977 law for state employees defined scope in the standard way and then listed conflicting code sections which could be superseded by agreement. A new law

---

[86] For a useful description of scope trends in Michigan, New Jersey, New York, Pennsylvania, Texas, and Wisconsin, see Walter J. Gershenfeld, J. Joseph Loewenberg, and Bernard Ingster, Scope of Public-Sector Bargaining (Lexington, Mass.: D.C. Heath and Co., 1977). See also Joan Weitzman, The Scope of Bargaining in Public Employment (New York: Praeger, 1975); Paul Prasow et al., Scope of Bargaining in the Public Sector—Concepts and Problems (Washington: U.S. Department of Labor, 1972).

[87] Part I, at 261.

[88] On this subject, see John F. Burton, Jr., *Local Government Bargaining and Management Structure*, 11 Indus. Rel. 123 (May 1972); David Lewin, *Local Government Labor Relations in Transition: The Case of Los Angeles*, 17 Lab. Hist. 191 (Spring 1976); David Lewin and Raymond D. Horton, *The Impact of Collective Bargaining on the Merit System in Government*, 30 Arb. J. 199 (September 1975); Milton Derber, Charles Maxey, and Kurt Wetzel, Public Management's Internal Organizational Response to the Demands of Collective Bargaining in the Twelve Midwestern States (Washington: U.S. Department of Labor, 1977); Donald Vial, *The Scope of Bargaining Controversy: Substantive Issues v. Procedural Hangups*, 15 Calif. Pub. Employee Rel. 2 (November 1972).

for teachers in Washington provided that negotiated agreements were to prevail over employer policies or regulations. No effort was made to deal with the merit issue in the Michigan, Minnesota, New York, and Nebraska laws; disputes were left to the agencies and courts.[89]

Another apparent statutory trend was toward inclusion of management-rights provisions. "The implicit theory is that certain subjects are so central to public policy and the public decisionmaking process that they cannot be determined bilaterally without involvement of others affected regardless of the momentary advantages perceived by management. . . . ."[90] Nevada narrowed scope for teachers by redefining class size, student discipline, staffing levels, and work loads as management rights. Florida, Iowa, Minnesota, and New Hampshire (state) included strong management-rights provisions in new laws. California's new law for teachers met the problem by specifically defining the phrase, "terms and conditions of employment,"[91] and reserving all other matters to management decision. In 1977, approximately 28 states were reported to have management-rights clauses of some type in one or more of their public-sector labor laws.[92]

In spite of statutory clarifications, legal tests continued to be the predominant means of sorting out what is, and what is not, bargainable. In 1977, R. Theodore Clark, Jr., made an impressive effort to come to grips analytically with what he described as the "staggering number of scope decisions [which] appear to be all over the lot."[93] As in the private sector, the mandatory/permissive/illegal approach to bargainability was being widely used. But because of the existence of conflicting systems, it was first necessary to determine whether an employer legally could agree to a given subject. If so, it then was necessary to determine whether the item was mandatory or permissible.[94] Clark found the mandatory-permissive dichotomy to be applicable under almost all the statutes.[95]

---

[89] See I.B. Helburn and N.D. Bennett, *Public Employee Bargaining and the Merit Principle*, 23 Lab. L.J. 618–629 (October 1972).

[90] American Bar Association, Labor Relations Law Committee Report, II (1976), 390.

[91] Health and welfare benefits, leave and transfer policies, safety, class size, evaluation procedures, union security, and grievance procedures.

[92] For an extensive source on statutory scope up to December 1980, see Joyce M. Najita, Guide to Statutory Provisions in Public Sector Collective Bargaining: Scope of Negotiations, 3d issue (Honolulu: Industrial Relations Center, University of Hawaii, 1981).

[93] R. Theodore Clark, Jr., *The Scope of the Duty to Bargain in Public Employment*, in Labor Relations Law in the Public Sector, ed. Andria S. Knapp (Chicago: American Bar Association, 1977). For a further discussion of scope litigation, see Joan Weitzman, Developments in Public Sector Labor Relations in the U.S., Occasional Paper (Ithaca: Institute of Public Employment, New York State School of Industrial and Labor Relations, Cornell University, January 1976), 23–29.

[94] A mandatory subject of bargaining is a subject on which the parties are required to negotiate; a permissive subject is one which they may negotiate but which neither party can insist on to the point of impasse.

[95] Clark, *supra* note 93, at 85.

Recent Experience

The phrase, "other terms and conditions of employment," has caused by far the most difficulty in resolving negotiability disputes. Several statutes which provide for NLRA-type scope also specify management prerogatives. This reservation creates, in many instances, an overlap problem, i.e., a given subject is arguably both a term or condition of employment and a prerogative which should be reserved to management. In fact, a management-prerogative provision need not exist at all for the management-reserve-rights doctrine to come into play.[96] (A classic example of such overlap is class size, which is both a working condition and an important element of educational policy.)

Two standards have been adopted by various state PERBs and courts to resolve this conflict. The overlap problem has been attacked by classifying a subject as mandatory if it is *significantly related* to wages, hours, and other terms and conditions of employment.[97] Clark saw this standard as inadequate because it does not properly recognize the competing interests at stake; undue weight is given to conditions of employment. However, a *balancing* test has rapidly emerged that acknowledges the overlap problem and involves a consideration of competing political interests. Courts and agencies in several states have combined these two standards.

For example, the Oregon PERB has interpreted its statute to allow a two-stage decision process. First, a determination is made as to whether a subject is of "like character" to enumerated mandatory items. Second, if it is of like character, PERB applies a balancing test to weigh inherent management rights involved against the effect the subject has on workers' employment. Where the latter is greater, the subject is mandatory; where the former is greater, the subject is permissive.[98]

The California courts and PERB have developed a set of tests for bargaining in public schools which attempts to cover all possible bases. First, a subject which is not specifically enumerated in the act is negotiable (1) if it logically and reasonably relates to an enumerated subject, (2) if conflict is likely and the "mediatory influence of negotiations is the appropriate means of resolving the conflict," and (3) if bargaining on the subject would not significantly abridge managerial

---

[96] *Fibreboard Paper Prods. Corp. v. NLRB*, 379 U.S. 223, 57 LRRM 2609 (1964).

[97] By this standard, class size, for example, has been determined to be both a mandatory and a prohibited subject of bargaining. Stephen A. Woodbury discusses the implications of the inclusion of class size in scope and how bargaining outcomes are affected, in *The Scope of Bargaining and Bargaining Outcomes in the Public Schools*, 38 Indus. & Lab. Rel. Rev. 195–210 (January 1985). For a good description and analysis of the courts' approach to the scope issue, see *Developments in the Law—Public Employment*, 97 Harv. L. Rev. 1611–1800 (May 1984).

[98] *IAFF Local 314 v. City of Salem*, Ore. ERB, No. C-61-83 (June 28, 1983).

prerogatives. Second, negotiation of subjects covered by other statutes is prohibited only if such other statutes would be "replaced, set aside, or annulled by the language of the proposed contract clause." Third, a party has the duty to clarify, through negotiations, any proposal which appears to be outside scope before it can refuse to bargain; failure to do so is a violation of the duty to bargain; however, this process does not compel the employer to engage in substantive negotiations on any subject not mandated.[99]

A look at the statutes as they stand today is not particularly revealing. Those which use only an NLRA definition of scope number about the same as they did 15 years ago—27 statutes in 21 states. Of these statutes, seven are teachers' laws and six are found in states with relatively less well-developed bargaining systems. On the other hand, 14 are in states with comprehensive bargaining laws, thus making it impossible to conclude that an NLRA-only definition may simply mean a system where the parties haven't got around to heavy power plays yet.

Eleven statutes contain very detailed clauses on scope, e.g., Iowa's with 17 specific subjects listed. Six teachers' statutes allow bargaining or consultation on professional objectives and policy-related matters. Eleven statutes contain what might be defined as traditional management-rights clauses. Fourteen statutes in 10 states include specific restrictions on bargaining on such matters as merit and classifications.

The two new Illinois statutes (1983) contain some very clear phraseology on the conflicting statutes problem.[100] That for education states: "§1717. In cases of any conflict between the provisions of this Act and any other law, executive order or administrative regulation, the provisions of this Act shall prevail and control," and "§1719. For purposes of this Act, the State of Illinois waives sovereign immunity." The statute for other Illinois employees makes the same statement on sovereignty (§1625), but goes into more detail on conflicting statutes:

> §1615. (a) In case of any conflict between the provisions of the Act and any other law, executive order or administrative regulation relating to wages, hours and conditions of employment and employment relations, the provisions of this Act or any collective bargaining agreement negotiated thereunder shall prevail and control . . . . (b) . . . any collective bargaining contract between a public employer and a labor organization executed pursuant to this Act shall supersede any contrary statutes,

---

[99] *CSEA v. Healdsburg Union High School Dist.; San Mateo Elem. Teachers Ass'n v. San Mateo City School Dist.*, Calif. PERB, Dec. 375 (January 5, 1984). See also *San Mateo City School Dist. v. Public Employment Relations Bd.*, 33 Cal. 3d 850, 663 P.2d 523, 117 LRRM 2195 (1983).

[100] See Michael Jenkins, *Collective Bargaining for Public Employees: An Overview of Illinois' New Act*, S. Ill. U. L. J. 483–514 (Fall 1983). Ohio also passed a new law in 1983; see James T. O'Reilly and Neil Gath, *Structures and Conflicts: Ohio's Collective Bargaining Law for Public Employees*, 44 Ohio St. L. J. 891–942 (Winter 1983).

charters, or ordinances, rules or regulations relating to wages, hours and conditions of employment and employment relations adopted by the public employer or its agents . . . . (c) It is the public policy of this State, pursuant to . . . the Illinois Constitution, that the provisions of this Act are the exclusive exercise by the State of powers and functions which might otherwise by exercised by home rule units.

More on the Accountability Factor

Current concerns over the scope of bargaining and government discretion and accountability arise in a context quite different from that of 20 to 30 years ago. Collective bargaining on wages, hours, and working conditions has become public policy, i.e., it is widely accepted as an institution and process consistent with the public's interest in equitable solution of labor problems. This shift has transformed the earlier concept of the government solely as sovereign into government as a dual entity: employer and sovereign. In the first role, we see the government delegating authority to bargain and reach binding agreements, shifting pay-hours-conditions items from civil service laws and personnel rules to the bargaining table, and concerning itself with its prerogatives as a manager.

In its other role as sovereign, the government retains the ultimate right to act and therefore the responsibility to resolve conflicts over issues which may be seen to fall within the scope of bargaining, yet which also concern wider political/public interests. There may be no question but that government must act in this capacity, but in the poorly defined, slippery area of scope of bargaining in public-sector labor relations, the questions are when and how.

Where statutory guidelines have been established, it is clear that role separation is taking place in an expeditious fashion. For example, the impetus behind the move to more detailed management-rights provisions in statutes is in large part a desire to wall off subjects considered inappropriate to insulated bilateral action, such as the mission of an agency or the extent and quality of service. But it is impossible to draw comprehensive and rational lines that will permanently prevent conflict between the elected official's need to be responsive to the "public interest" and the demands of public employees for influence over their conditions of employment. The pressure for such lines has been, and undoubtedly will continue to be, an ongoing characteristic of public-sector labor relations.

Sunshine laws are an excellent example of how strain in this area can produce experimentation and divergence from the private-sector model. The adoption of open-meeting or sunshine laws demonstrates an active need to somehow regulate the content of public-sector labor relations vis-à-vis the public interest, and in this case the public interest is increasingly associated with budget-allocation matters as well as questions of mission. The rationale appears to be that identifying and restricting unacceptable bargaining items is insufficient; the bargaining process should be open to the public, thereby ensuring access, exposure, and accountability.[101]

The public-sector labor laws of 11 states (13 statutes) now require some sort of sunshine. California (schools, state, higher education), Iowa, and Wisconsin (municipal) require that initial proposals be presented at a public meeting. Delaware (teachers) requires that fact-finding hearings be open; Vermont, the same if any party so requests. Four states require open negotiations: Alaska (unless the parties agree otherwise), Florida, Minnesota (except as provided by the Bureau of Mediation Services), and Texas. In Idaho (teachers), negotiations records must be made available to the public and ratification of final settlements occurs in open meetings. In Ohio, all hearings on complaints or petitions pursuant to the act are open.

In five other states, labor relations are affected by separate statutes: in Indiana the mediator's report is a public record and fact-finding is conducted in public; Kansas (teachers), Maryland, Montana (schools, local governments), and Tennessee (teachers) all require open negotiations.

Some laws state specifically that negotiations are to be closed (Iowa, Ohio) or are not subject to open meeting laws (Illinois).

Objections of the parties to bargaining in public have had their effect. A study of experience under Tennessee's law showed that often the parties felt they had to meet privately in order to come to an agreement at all, that in open meetings they were forced to play to their constituencies.[102] In Maryland, a state appeal court said that the fact that the parties had negotiated in private every year since 1968 did not preclude the employer from insisting on public meetings, but it would not be a violation of the open meeting act if both parties agreed to secret sessions.[103] Although the parties in California have expressed no objections to that state's public notice requirements, it is also true that with a few notable exceptions (e.g., the Los Angeles Unified School District) public interest in the process is minimal. In Min-

---

[101] See Summers, *supra* note 83, at 1197–1199; Harry T. Edwards, R. Theodore Clark, Jr., and Charles B. Craver, Labor Relations Law in the Public Sector: Cases and Materials, 2d ed. (New York: Bobbs-Merrill, 1979), 423–442; Robert Doherty, ed., Public Access: Citizens and Collective Bargaining in the Public Schools (Ithaca: New York School of Industrial and Labor Relations, Cornell University, 1979); Robert E. Doherty, *Bargaining and the Public: What's the Proper Role?* in The Evolving Process—Collective Negotiations in Public Employment, 2d ed. (Fort Washington, Pa.: Labor Relations Press, 1985), 303–315.

[102] Roger L. Bowlby and William R. Schriver, *The Behavioral Interpretation of Bluffing: A Public Sector Case*, 32 Lab. L.J. 469–473 (August 1981).

[103] *Carroll County Educ. Ass'n v. Carroll County Bd. of Educ.*, 448 A.2d 345, 114 LRRM 2048 (1982).

nesota, where the Bureau of Mediation Services, the administering agency, has discretion in the matter, practice has been to bar the public from most negotiation and mediation sessions.

A variation on the open-meeting or public-disclosure concept is the statutory provision which allows student input into negotiations in institutions of higher education. In California and Florida, students' representatives are allowed to attend negotiations. In Maine, students may meet and confer with the parties prior to bargaining and at reasonable times during negotiations. In Montana, students have the same rights as in Maine, plus that of meeting with the regents regarding terms of the agreement prior to execution.

Less widely used is the public referendum.[104] A couple of interesting litigations have taken place in California in the case of charter cities. In 1984, the state supreme court held that a charter city must meet and confer, under the local government bargaining act, with affected employee organizations before proposing to the voters charter amendments on matters within the scope of representation.[105] A somewhat different situation arose recently in San Francisco where, under the charter, the board of supervisors (the legislative body) has no power to provide employment benefits. The charter delegates final decision making to the electorate. The appeal court ruled that nothing in the language or purpose of the bargaining act preempts provisions of the city charter which already grant the electorate the right to approve any change in employee benefits. The court went on to say that the city's duty to bargain "is in no way infringed by the electorate's reservation of authority to approve any results of the bargaining process."[106]

Another example of how tension can arise from the bilateral authority/sovereign authority constraint is exemplified in the concern of many public employees, particularly professionals, with mission and quality of service. It is perhaps surprising that as these issues are being withdrawn or excluded from bargaining scope, there has been so little examination of the feasibility of alternate statutory formal joint-consultation schemes. Public employees traditionally have played a major consultative role in the provision of public services. The current lack of interest in formal consultation systems can probably be credited to the fact that the fight to transfer items formerly within the scope of informal consultation into the realm of bargaining is far from decided in many states.

---

[104] See Doherty, *Bargaining and the Public, supra* note 101, at 310–312.

[105] *Seal Beach Police Officers Ass'n, People, ex rel. v. Seal Beach, Cal.*, 36 Cal. 3d 591, 120 LRRM 2309 (1984).

[106] *United Public Employees Local 390/400 v. City and County of San Francisco*, No. A033767 (1st Dist.), March 19, 1987, *petition for reh'g filed.*

Union Security

Prior to the introduction of formal public-sector collective bargaining structures, the only form of union security was dues deduction, permitted by the employer and authorized by the employee. But once exclusive representation was accepted, with its companion obligation to represent all employees in a unit, union-security devices became a major employee-organization goal. One of the more interesting statutory developments of the seventies and eighties has been the rapid acceptance of union-security provisions, ranging from the fair-share service fee to, in a few cases, the union shop. [107]

The arguments presented in favor of union security are similar to those marshaled to support the transfer of other elements of traditional collective bargaining to the public sector, equity and stability: (1) as long as the exclusive representative must represent all employees in a unit equally, all employees should be obliged to pay their share of the cost of such services, and (2) the goal of constructive collective bargaining and peaceful settlements is substantially forwarded when a union has the security that flows from support of its full-unit constituency. These arguments are identical to those used to justify union security in the private sector.

The major objections to union security in the public sector have been grounded in the character of government employment: (1) discharge for failure to join and/or pay fees to an exclusive representative violates civil service laws based on merit principles, and (2) the right to associate or not associate is constitutionally protected against government infringement.

In spite of the force of these arguments, union security arrangements became fairly common in some states before laws were passed. In 1969, the year Vermont enacted the first statutory provision, union attorney I. J. Gromfine reported union shops in transit agreements in the cities of Chicago, Boston, Pittsburgh, St. Louis, and Memphis, among others; union-security agreements with public agencies in Michigan, New York, Missouri, Vermont, Indiana, and Illinois; and union shops for police and fire department employees in Rhode Island and Connecticut. [108] In some cases, such as in Michigan, the topic was

---

[107] Useful sources of information on union security in the public sector are Kurt L. Hanslowe, David Dunn, and Jay Erstling, Union Security in Public Employment: Of Free Riders and Free Association, Institute of Public Employment Monograph No. 8 (Ithaca: New York State School of Industrial and Labor Relations, Cornell University, 1978); Andria S. Knapp, ed., Labor Relations Law in the Public Sector, *supra* note 93, at 145–177; Charles M. Rehmus and Benjamin A. Kerner, *The Agency Shop After Abood: No Free Ride, But What's the Fare?*, 34 Indus. & Lab. Rel. Rev. 90–100 (October 1980); Edwards, Clark, and Craver, *supra* note 101, at 443–491.

[108] At New York University's 22d Conference on Labor. Reported in 304 GERR E9 (July 7, 1969).

held to be within the scope of bargaining.[109] More often, such agreements were the result of local innovation, normally correlated with high proportions of membership. By 1977, 17 state statutes included provision for some form of union security (beyond dues deduction) for all or some groups of employees.

The first challenge to these laws was on the question of right to associate. In *Matter of Farrigan v. Helsby* in 1973, the New York high court upheld PERB in finding that the agency shop violated the labor relations statute's guarantee to public employees of the right to refrain from joining or participating in an employee organization.[110] (Three years later, the legislature amended the law to authorize agency shop fees.) In 1974, the New Jersey supreme court ruled the agency shop illegal on the same ground[111] (the act was not amended to include an agency shop until after the *Abood* decision in 1977), as did the Maine Supreme Judicial Court in 1977[112] (the act still does not include a union-security section).

In a sweeping decision in 1977, the Washington supreme court ruled that the state law permitting the agency shop was constitutionally sound. It declared that the law did not violate the constitutional guarantees of freedom of speech, association, religion, due process, or equal protection, in that employees who objected to a union's political expenditures could obtain refunds under a publicized procedure and those who had bona fide religious objections could designate their fee for another purpose in harmony with the individual's conscience. At the same time, the court ruled that although the statute required "membership," the word was clearly defined as an obligation limited to contribution of dues in exchange for representation rights.[113]

In the same year, the Oregon appeals court ruled that statutory reference to an "all-union" type of security agreement was a drafting error and that although fair-share arrangements were permissible, union shops were prohibited, because under the statute employers could not discriminate to encourage or discourage union membership.[114]

---

[109] *Oakland County Sheriff*, 1968 MERC Op. 1.

[110] 42 A.D.2d 265 (3d Dep't).

[111] *Technical Eng'rs Local 194 v. New Jersey Turnpike Auth.*, 64 N.J. 579, 319 A.2d 224, 86 LRRM 2842 (1974); 123 N.J. Super. 46, 303 A.2d 599, 83 LRRM 2250 (1973); see also 117 N.J. Super. 349, 284 A.2d 566, 79 LRRM 2549 (1971).

[112] *Churchill v. Teachers, SAD 49*, 380 A.2d 186, 97 LRRM 2162 (1977).

[113] *Capitol Powerhouse Eng'rs v. Division of Bldgs. & Grounds, State of Wash.*, 570 P.2d 1042, 96 LRRM 3004 (1977).

[114] *Oregon State Employees Ass'n v. Oregon State Univ.*, 567 P.2d 1085, 96 LRRM 2555 (1977).

The Constitutional Issue

The central question the parties and the courts were wrestling with was, do union-security arrangements violate the public employee's constitutionally protected freedom of association? A person may not be compelled by the government to join an organization. This bar is embodied in the First Amendment which creates the right to associate or decline to associate. The right to associate is secured only against governmental infringement, and the Fourteenth Amendment extends that restraint to state and local governments.

The U.S. Supreme Court dealt with this issue in *Abood*.[115] When the *Abood* case reached the Court, the Michigan provision specifically permitted a union and a local government employer to agree to an agency-shop arrangement whereby every employee represented by a union—even though not a union member—must pay to the union, as a condition of employment, a service fee equal in amount to union dues. The issue before the Court was: "whether this arrangement violates the constitutional rights of government employees who object to public sector unions as such or to various union activities financed by the compulsory service fees." The Court ruled that negotiated agency-shop provisions are constitutionally valid as long as employees may refuse to pay that portion of the fee which the union uses for ideological purposes unrelated to its duties as exclusive bargaining representative.

Concerning the validity of the agency shop, the Court relied on the private-sector cases, *Hanson*[116] and *Machinists v. Street*,[117] which it had determined under the Railway Labor Act, and reiterated its view that such First Amendment "interference as exists is constitutionally justified by the *legislative* assessment of the important contribution" of union-security arrangements to labor relations systems [emphasis added]. "The desirability of labor peace is no less important in the public sector, nor is the risk of 'free riders' any smaller."

On the second issue—whether the union can constitutionally use compulsory fees for purposes other than collective bargaining—the Court accepted the teachers' argument that their right to associate was being violated and held that being compelled to contribute to the support of an ideological cause as a condition of employment violates rights of freedom of association and speech.

Of particular interest is the teachers' argument that collective bargaining in the public sector is inherently political and, therefore, the First and Fourteenth Amendments forbid coerced support of

---

[115] *Abood v. Detroit Bd. of Educ.*, 431 U.S. 209, 95 LRRM 2411 (1977).
[116] *Railway Employees Dep't. v. Hanson*, 351 U.S. 225, 38 LRRM 2099 (1956) (Congressional authorization of union shops appropriate under Commerce Clause to promote industrial peace).
[117] 367 U.S. 740, 48 LRRM 2345 (1961).

political activities. The Court answered that the constitutional inquiry evoked is whether a public employee has a "weightier First Amendment interest than a private employee"; the Court found that the public employee does not. "The differences between public and private sector collective bargaining simply do not translate into differences in First Amendment rights."

After Abood

The tidying up of agency shop or fee laws and the passage of new amendments which had commenced before *Abood* now accelerated. For example, in 1980, both Connecticut (schools) and New Jersey amended their laws. The former now permitted service fees to be negotiated as a condition of employment. The latter permitted service fees which were not to exceed 85 percent of regular dues, fees, and assessments and which would be subject to review on the request of the payer, ultimately by a three-member board appointed by the governor. The Connecticut supreme court validated a previously existing negotiated clause as a "proper exercise of public policy."[118]

Two states chose to allow fair-share fee systems in the absence of statutory authorization. Following an advisory opinion of the state supreme court, the Maine Labor Relations Board ruled that an 80 percent fair-share provision did not violate the act and was a mandatory subject of bargaining.[119] In an earlier decision, the Indiana court of appeals had ruled that payment of a service fee as a condition of employment, enforceable by discharge, was invalid as school employers could not bargain away their right to discharge.[120] The following year, the same court ruled that a fair-share fee was permissible and could be enforced through court action rather than discharge.[121]

The discharge problem was handled similarly in California under the schools law. The state supreme court recognized that the remedy to enforce agency-shop obligations is a proper subject of bargaining and addressed the issue of whether the phrase, "as a condition of continued employment," makes dismissal the exclusive remedy for failure to pay. The court found that the section in question merely defined organizational security without imposing a limitation on remedies. It found dismissal too drastic for it to endorse, given the availability of civil suit.[122] In Michigan, however, the supreme court decided

---

[118] *Dowaliby v. Hartford Fed'n of Teachers Local 1018*, 180 Conn. 459, 429 A.2d 950, 109 LRRM 3014 (1980).

[119] MLRB in *City of Bangor v. Bangor Fire Fighters Ass'n*, No. 83-06 (August 2, 1983). See *supra* note 112 and text.

[120] *Teachers Local 519 (Anderson) v. Alexander*, 416 N.E.2d 1327, 112 LRRM 2172 (1981).

[121] *Fort Wayne Educ. Ass'n v. Goetz*, 443 N.E.2d 364, 115 LRRM 2023 (1982).

[122] *San Lorenzo Educ. Ass'n v. Wilson*, 32 Cal. 3d 841, 654 P.2d 202, 115 LRRM 2347 (1982).

that its law permitted agency-shop agreements covering teachers when the remedy for nonpayment was discharge. It stated that the tenure law permitting discharge of tenured teachers only for reasonable and just cause must yield to the labor relations statute.[123] Ohio's new 1983 law permits payment of fees to be made a condition of employment.

Some states, and many local jurisdictions, have bypassed the condition of employment/discharge problem by providing, either by statute or agreement, for automatic deduction of fees for the exclusive representative. Four states provide for automatic deductions on certification—Connecticut (state), Hawaii, New York (state), and Rhode Island (state, teachers).

Statutes in eight states currently contain exemptions for religious reasons.[124] Hawaii's section includes a requirement that if the employees request the employee organization to use the grievance procedure on their behalf, the organization may charge the employees reasonable costs. In Washington, the supreme court, on remand from the U.S. Supreme Court, found that the statute must be read to allow a person to claim the alternative payment method based on personal beliefs that are deeply held, even if the person does not belong to a church or religious body.[125]

Procedural Issues: The Hudson Case

In *Abood*, the Supreme Court held that there were constitutional grounds for both the state's interest in authorizing the agency shop and the objecting employee's interest in not financing political positions. In *Hudson*,[126] the Court moved on to the constitutional requirements for union collection of agency fees.

The case arose out of a 1982 agreement under which the Chicago Board of Education would deduct "proportionate share" payments from the paychecks of nonunion members of the unit. These payments were 95 percent of regular dues, an amount the union estimated was spent on the bargaining and bargaining-related activities approved in *Abood*. If fee-payers objected to the amount, they could appeal to the union's executive committee, executive board, and outside arbitration, respectively (with the arbitrator selected by the union). If the fee was found by the arbitrator to be excessive, the balance was rebated. Hudson and others sued the union, arguing that the procedures violated their First Amendment rights.

---

[123] *Detroit School Dist. Bd. of Educ. v. Parks*, 335 N.W.2d 641, 114 LRRM 3269, aff'g 296 N.W.2d 815, 107 LRRM 2843 (Mich. 1983)
[124] California, Hawaii, Illinois, Montana, Ohio, Oregon, Washington, and Wisconsin.
[125] *Grant v. Spellman*, 99 Wash. 2d 815, 644 P.2d 1227 (1983).
[126] *Chicago Teachers Local 1 v. Hudson*, 106 S.Ct. 1066, 121 LRRM 2793 (1986).

The Court noted at the outset the contending interests which had to be balanced:

First, although the government interest in labor peace is strong enough to support an "agency shop" notwithstanding its limited infringement on nonunion employees' constitutional rights, the fact that those rights are protected by the First Amendment requires that the procedure be carefully tailored to minimize the infringement. Second, the nonunion employee—the individual whose First Amendment rights are being affected—must have a fair opportunity to identify the impact of the governmental action on his interests and to assert a meritorious First Amendment claim. [127]

The Court then framed the issue in two parts. Does the union procedure survive constitutional scrutiny because the procedure was sufficient, or, if not, did the "subsequent adoption of an escrow arrangement" cure remaining defects?

Its study of the original procedure led the Court to conclude that it "contained three fundamental flaws." Referring to its 1984 holding in *Ellis*, [128] the Court noted that pure rebate schemes fail because they allow, however temporarily, the use of dissenters' funds for purposes to which they object. Such "involuntary loans" are constitutionally defective, for protection of the "quality" of dissenters' interest is paramount regardless of the amount involved.

Second, the advance reduction of dues was inadequate "because it provided nonmembers with inadequate information about the basis for the proportionate share." The remaining flaw found by the Court in the union's initial procedure was its failure to "provide for a reasonably prompt decision by an impartial decisionmaker." The defect here, noted the Court, was that the appeal procedures—from hearings before union bodies to selection of an arbitrator—were entirely controlled by the union.

The Court next turned to the question of the effect of the union's later decision to escrow 100 percent of any fees collected from nonmembers who object. Escrow does not cure the defects, said the Court, since it does not address two of the three requirements, namely, adequate explanation of the advance reduction of dues and redress before an impartial decisionmaker. The union was not constitutionally required to escrow 100 percent of the agency fee in any event, since that requirement would deprive the union of the use of some funds to which it was indisputably entitled.

Summing up, the Court held that "the constitutional requirements for the Union's collection of agency fees include an adequate explanation of the basis of the fee, a reasonably prompt opportunity to

---

[127] Id., 121 LRRM at 2797.
[128] *Ellis v. Railway Clerks*, 466 U.S. 435, 116 LRRM 2001 (1984).

challenge the amount of the fee before an impartial decisionmaker, and an escrow for the amounts reasonably in dispute while such challenges are pending."

After Hudson

In the months following *Hudson*, the parties, the courts, and administering agencies have been busy reviewing procedures. The New York PERB is debating whether rule making, legislation, or a change in its case law is necessary to bring the state's fee requirements into conformity.[129] A federal appeals court has upheld as constitutional New Jersey's "demand and return" system, under which an objector must receive a refund of any part of the fee determined to be an overcharge. The statute requires that a system negotiated or adopted by unions must permit fee payers to obtain review "through full and fair proceedings placing the burden of proof on the majority representative." A dissatisfied payer is entitled to appeal to a board composed of a union representative, employer representative, and neutral third member.[130] Several decisions have been issued by other courts on various aspects of procedural requirements.[131]

The Statutes Today

In late 1986, 27 statutes in 19 states provided for agency-shop, fair-share fee, maintenance of membership, or union shop.[132] Kentucky (fire) and Vermont (municipal) permit union shops. An agency fee is mandatory on certification in Connecticut (state), Hawaii, New York (state), and Rhode Island (state, teachers). The agency shop is permitted for some group in 16 states; the fair-share fee is permitted for some group in five other states; maintenance of membership is permitted in three states.

Conclusion

The trend of law and public opinion in the United States has been toward more egalitarian interpretations of how employees and management should function within labor relations systems. But in the public sector, unlike the private, the equity goal constantly has had to

---

[129] 24 GERR 1292 (September 22, 1986). The PERB commissioned a study of the case law and the status of its statute. See Richard Briffault, The New York Agency Shop Fee and the Constitution (unpublished, August 8, 1986).

[130] *Robinson v. State of New Jersey*, 123 LRRM 3193 (3d Cir. 1986).

[131] Six of these are described in American Bar Association, Labor and Employment Law Section, Report (1986), 180–184.

[132] Alaska, California (4), Connecticut (2), Hawaii, Illinois, Kentucky, Massachusetts, Michigan, Minnesota, Montana, New Jersey, New York, Ohio, Oregon, Pennsylvania, Rhode Island (2), Vermont, Washington (3), Wisconsin (2).

be reconciled with the need to adjust to the special role of government. The descriptive material above traces some of the successes and failures of the reconciliation process.

In a significant number of states, the duty to bargain, exclusive representation, binding agreements, and union-security arrangments are now viewed as acceptable means to labor peace rather than as unacceptable "invasions of government authority." A similar core of acceptance underlies those more rudimentary systems that merely compel the employer to meet and confer with majority representatives. The trend is unmistakably toward bilateral responsibility for pay, hours, and working conditions.

This is not to suggest that all clashes with the sovereignty concept are likely to be resolved in due course. The nature of the conflict, rooted as it is in ideology, guarantees that the tension between sovereignty/accountability and bilateral authority can only be ameliorated, not eliminated. We will continue to see manifestations of the conflict whenever government's perceived need to have the last word intensifies (as is the case now regarding various scope issues, strikes, and compulsory arbitration).

Viewing public-sector labor relations in this manner points up the institutional barriers to full implementation of the traditional private-sector system, but fails to account for other factors influencing public-sector labor law. Economic conditions, for example, are of major importance. Following World War II, rising real incomes, the increased demand for government services and hence for government employees, and the improvement in private-sector pay and benefits relative to those in the public sector all contributed to militancy, public sympathy, and the subsequent passage of collective-bargaining laws. Demands for "equal treatment" fell on fertile soil.

The enigmatic economic circumstances of the last 15 years have had a different impact. An extended period of inflation, high unemployment, a slowdown in real wage growth, concerns over public budgets, and fiscal limitation measures have created an environment in which the demands of public employees are often greeted with public indifference, if not hostility. Where legislation has created a bilateral system of some kind, the public response appears to argue that public employees are as "equal" as they ought to be, at least for the time being. Where no statutory systems have been adopted (a handful of states mainly in the South and Southwest), economic pressures undoubtedly reinforce existing disinclination to experiment with increased labor rights.

Thirty years ago, no government had adopted a labor relations system similar in policy, rights, and procedures to that in the private sector. The change has been dramatic. But, although public-sector legal frameworks bear a strong resemblance to the NLRA, government remains the employer and has put its stamp on policy development. The public sector *is* different and the compromises and accommodations which have taken place suggest that this essential difference will continue to characterize trends in law and practice in the future.

CHAPTER 7

Judicial Response to Public-Sector Arbitration

Joseph R. Grodin* and Joyce M. Najita**

Binding arbitration of grievances that arise during the term of a labor agreement, once the exception in the public sector, is now the norm. A 1976 Bureau of Labor Statistics survey indicated that nine of every ten agreements contain some form of contractual grievance procedure, and of these, 85 percent culminate in arbitration.[1] Although comparable state and local government data of more recent origin are not available, a 1980 Office of Personnel Management survey shows that in the federal sector all agreements executed under the Civil Service Reform Act contain some form of contractual grievance procedure. Furthermore, all of the sampled agreements "provide for binding arbitration as the ultimate step in the grievance procedures as required by the Act."[2] Binding arbitration of interest disputes (i.e., disputes arising out of negotiations for a new agreement) has also proliferated. One review reports that 34 states and a number of local governments have enacted legislation either mandating or authorizing binding interest arbitration for some or all public employees.[3]

Not surprisingly, these phenomena have spawned a good deal of litigation in the courts. Parties have disputed over the validity of statutes or agreements calling for arbitration, over the role of the courts in determining prior to arbitration which particular issues are arbitrable, over the role of courts in reviewing arbitration awards, and over the relationship of arbitration to constitutional or statutory princi-

---

*Hastings College of Law, San Francisco, California.
**Industrial Relations Center, University of Hawaii.
[1] U.S. Department of Labor, Bureau of Labor Statistics, Collective Bargaining Agreements for State and County Government Employees, Bull. No. 1920 (Washington: 1976).
[2] U.S. Office of Personnel Management, A Survey of Negotiated Grievance Procedures and Arbitration in Federal Post Civil Service Reform Act Agreements, OLMR 81/02 (Washington: 1980), 41.
[3] Note, *Binding Interest Arbitration in the Public Sector: Is It Constitutional?* 18 Wm. & Mary L. Rev. 787 (1977). See also Richard B. Freeman, *Unionism Comes to the Public Sector,* 24 J. Econ. Lit. 41 (1986).

ples external to the agreement. As in other areas of public-sector labor law, the litigation typically turns on interpretation of statutory provisions that vary widely from state to state, so that it is impossible to generalize about "the law" of the subject. Looming beneath the surface questions of interpretation, however, are issues of public policy that often transcend the language of particular enactments and to that extent are susceptible to a comparative, if not generalized, examination of judicial response. That, at any rate, is the premise of this chapter. The focus will be on state law with passing reference to the recent problems arising out of federal-employee labor relations.

Grievance Arbitration

State and Local Government

The U.S. Supreme Court decisions in the famous *Steelworkers* Trilogy cases of 1960[4] marked the beginning of what David Feller has called the "golden age of arbitration" in the private sector.[5] Not only were agreements to arbitrate contract grievances valid and enforceable,[6] they were favored to the extent that special rules were devised for their protection and nurture. In determining whether a particular dispute fell within their scope, courts were not to pass upon the merits, but only to determine whether the party seeking arbitration was making a claim which "on its face is governed by the contract." An order to arbitrate such a claim was not to be denied "unless it may be said with positive assurance that the arbitration clause is not susceptible to an interpretation that covers the asserted dispute."[7] Finally, so long as the arbitrator's award can be characterized as drawing its "essence" from the agreement, the award is final and not subject to judicial review.[8]

The policy premises underlying these principles of judicial deference stemmed from the Court's perception of the role of arbitration in labor relations—a role different from and more expansive than that in the commercial arena, reflecting the unique characteristics of the collective-bargaining agreement. While commercial arbitration is the "substitute for litigation," labor arbitration is the "substitute for industrial strife," the agreement to arbitrate being the quid pro quo for the

---

[4] *Steelworkers v. American Mfg. Co.*, 363 U.S. 564, 46 LRRM 2414 (1960); *Steelworkers v. Warrior & Gulf Navigation Co.*, 363 U.S. 574, 46 LRRM 2416 (1960); *Steelworkers v. Enterprise Wheel & Car Corp.*, 363 U.S. 593, 46 LRRM 2423 (1960).

[5] Feller, *The Coming End of Arbitration's Golden Age*, in Arbitration—1976, Proceedings of the 29th Annual Meeting, National Academy of Arbitrators, eds. Barbara D. Dennis and Gerald G. Somers (Washington: BNA Books, 1976), 97.

[6] The validity and enforceability under federal law agreements to arbitrate were established prior to the Trilogy cases in *Textile Workers v. Lincoln Mills*, 353 U.S. 448, 40 LRRM 2113 (1957).

[7] *Steelworkers v. Warrior & Gulf Navigation Co.*, supra, note 4.

[8] *Steelworkers v. Enterprise Wheel & Car Corp.*, supra, note 4.

agreement not to strike. The labor agreement itself is "more than a contract," said the Court; it is a "generalized code to govern a myriad of cases which the draftsmen cannot wholly anticipate," an "effort to erect a system of industrial self-government" with grievance machinery at its core and arbitration as a dynamic process, "part and parcel of the collective bargaining process itself." It is for these reasons that disputes should be presumed arbitrable unless the parties have clearly provided otherwise. The processing of even unmeritorious grievances may have "therapeutic value." And arbitrators are not simply judges without robes. Chosen for their experience, their personal judgment, and their knowledge of the "common law of the shop," they perform functions "not normal to the courts," and indeed "foreign to the competence of the courts." It is their judgment that the parties have bargained for. These are the considerations which led to the rule that courts should withhold judgment on the merits in deciding whether to order arbitration, and should decline to review the merits of an award once rendered.

Feller has expressed concern whether Trilogy principles, premised as they are on the private nature of the collective-bargaining relationship, can survive the steady intrusion of public law into the collective-bargaining arena.[9] His thesis is that as arbitrators feel increasingly obliged to consider external law such as Title VII of the Civil Rights Act of 1964, the Occupational Safety and Health Act (OSHA), or the National Labor Relations Act (NLRA) itself, judges will feel less inclined to defer to their special competence.

But if the "golden age of arbitration" is becoming tarnished in the private sector, what of the public sector where arbitration has begun to take hold? Private-sector collective bargaining in the United States grew in an environment relatively free of statutory control; it supplanted a system in which terms and conditions of employment were determined largely by the individual "contract" of employment. In the public sector, however, collective bargaining arrived upon a scene saturated with public-law concepts. Government acts by definition through legislation or administrative regulation, and the authority of a particular governing body is in turn restricted or channeled by charter provision, statute, or constitution. Civil service systems and constitutional provisions accorded rights and procedures unknown to the private sector in its pre-collective-bargaining phase. Moreover, while the consequences of bargaining in the private sector have public impact, our traditions of free enterprise view that impact as being largely beyond public control, whereas the consequences of bargaining (and therefore arbitration) in the public sector are seen within a

---

[9] Feller, *supra* note 5. See also Feller, *Arbitration: The Days of Its Glory Are Numbered,* 2 Jud. Rel. L.J. 97 (1977).

democratic framework as being part of the public domain. Under such circumstances, have courts been willing to view public-sector griev- ance arbitration, through Trilogy-colored lenses, as an essentially autonomous institution?

Questions might also be raised as to the applicability of certain other premises underlying Trilogy principles. Since strikes are prohib- ited in most states, or limited, where permitted, and there is little in the history of public-sector labor relations corresponding to the mid- term work stoppages that characterized the prearbitration period in the private sector, can it be said that public-sector grievance arbitra- tion functions as the "substitute for industrial strife"? Since most arbitrators come to public-sector grievance arbitration from the pri- vate sector, should it be presumed that they possess special compe- tence with respect to the "common law of the shop"? Indeed, in view of the relative infancy of public-sector bargaining and the background of unilateral determination of employment conditions through ordi- nances and rules, does there exist a "common law of the shop" as to which special competence can be developed? Is the Trilogy view of the collective-bargaining agreement as an essentially open-ended process an appropriate model for the public sector? We do not mean to suggest the answers to these questions, nor to indicate that the answers should necessarily determine judicial response to public-sector grievance arbitration. On the contrary, we intend to argue that whatever the answers to these questions, grievance arbitration has a highly signifi- cant role to play in the public sector, and that courts should accommo- date to it in much the same way that they have in the private sector. We mean only to indicate that these are substantial questions, the answers to which are by no means self-evident, and that it is reasonable to expect that courts will be troubled by such questions as they approach the task of delineating the judicial role in relation to the arbitral process. The decisions are in accord with that expectation.

Validity of Agreements to Arbitrate

While it is sometimes said that courts at common law disapproved the arbitration of public-sector labor grievances as an unlawful delega- tion of governmental power,[10] close examination of the cases cited in support of that proposition reveal either that the court was not talking about arbitration at all,[11] or that it confused grievance arbitration with

---

[10] See, e.g., Note, *Legality and Propriety of Agreements to Arbitrate Major and Minor Disputes in Public Employment*, 54 Cornell L. Rev. 129, 130 (1968).

[11] E.g., *Mugford v. Mayor and City Council*, 185 Md. 266, 44 A.2d 745, 17 LRRM 690 (1945). Cited in Charles C. Killingsworth, *Grievance Arbitration in Public Employment*, 13 Arb. J. 3, 7 (1958) as the "leading case."

interest arbitration,[12] or that its objection to arbitration stemmed from the court's view that the underlying collective-bargaining agreement was itself beyond the authority of the public entity.[13] In any event, once legislatures in many states came to give their blessing to collective bargaining in the public sector, courts began to accept grievance arbitration as an appropriate means of giving effect to an otherwise valid contract even in the absence of express statutory authority. In the leading *City of Rhinelander*[14] case, for example, the Wisconsin supreme court held that a statute which authorized binding agreements by implication permitted binding agreements to arbitrate grievances, and it brushed aside the city's arguments based on sovereignty and home rule with the observation that the arguments failed to distinguish between grievance and interest arbitration. Similarly, in *Associated Teachers of Huntington*,[15] the New York court of appeals found that legislative authorization for unions to represent employees "in the administration of grievances" necessarily implies the legitimacy of arbitration, since (quoting from one of the Trilogy cases) "arbitration is, of course, part and parcel of the administration of grievances."[16] And like its sister tribunal in Wisconsin, the New York court dealt summarily with the school board's contention that its province was being invaded:

> Nor can we agree that a board of education is better qualified than an arbitrator to decide whether a teacher in its employ should be dismissed for incompetency or misconduct. It may not be gainsaid that arbitrators, selected because of their impartiality and their intimate knowledge of school board matters, are fully qualified to decide issues such as those under consideration.[17]

Many of the modern statutes explicitly authorize, and in at least two cases actually mandate, provisions for binding grievance arbitration.[18] Thus, except in states where collective bargaining agreements are

---

[12] *Cleveland v. Division 268*, 15 Ohio Supp. 76 (1975), distinguished on that ground in *Madison v. Frank Lloyd Wright Found.*, 20 Wis.2d 361, 122 N.W.2d 409 (1963).

[13] E.g., *Hayes v. Association of Classroom Teachers*, 76 LRRM 2140 (Cal. Super. 1970). Even in the absence of statute, some courts held collective-bargaining agreements and grievance arbitration to be valid, e.g., *Norwalk Teachers Ass'n v. Board of Educ.*, 138 Conn. 369, 83 A.2d 583, 28 LRRM 2408 (1951).

[14] *AFSCME Local 1226 v. City of Rhinelander*, 35 Wis.2d 209, 151 N.W.2d 30, 65 LRRM 2793 (1967).

[15] *Board of Educ. v. Associated Teachers of Huntington*, 30 N.Y.2d 122, 282 N.E.2d 109, 79 LRRM 2881 (1972).

[16] *Id.* at 2885.

[17] *Id.* at 2886.

[18] See Aaron, *The Impact of Public Employment Grievance Settlement on the Labor Arbitration Process*, in The Future of Labor Arbitration in America (New York: American Arbitration Association, 1976), 11–12. Aaron reported that as of September 1975 some 28 states and the District of Columbia had included some form of grievance procedure in their statutes.

not yet permitted,[19] there appears to be no question as to the general validity of agreements to arbitrate public-sector labor grievances.

There were, however, a number of cases, particularly early ones, in which courts refused to enforce arbitration agreements, or set aside arbitration awards, on the stated ground that some law or public policy external to the agreement precludes the public agency from "bargaining away" or "delegating" its authority or discretion with respect to the particular issue in dispute. In states where agreement is limited to mandatory subjects of bargaining, the limitation may be found in the statutory definition of bargaining scope;[20] in states where agreement is not so restricted, the limitation must be located elsewhere.[21] While the New York court of appeals, for example, spoke expansively in *Huntington* of the parties' freedom to contract over terms and conditions of employment "except in cases where some other applicable statutory provision explicitly and definitively prohibits the public employer from making an agreement," and in a subsequent decision declared that "arbitration is considered so preferable a means of settling labor disputes that it can be said that public policy impels its use,"[22] the same court two years later suggested that because of the "governmental interests and public concerns" which may be involved in school matters, "public policy, whether derived from, and whether explicit or implicit in statute or decisional law, or in neither, may also restrict the freedom to arbitrate."[23] That suggestion found its way into holdings in subsequent decisions to the effect that while a school board may commit itself to arbitrate over the application to probationary teachers of agreed-upon tenure-evaluation procedures, it may not arbitrate over the tenure decision itself,[24] or over whether school-board members are precluded by agreement from inspecting the files

---

[19] This was the situation, for example, with respect to bargaining between school districts and teachers in California prior to 1975. *Hayes v. Association of Classroom Teachers, supra* note 13.

[20] *Dunellen Bd. of Educ. v. Dunellen Educ. Ass'n,* 74 N.J. 17, 311 A.2d 737, 85 LRRM 2131 (1973) (school board could not be required to arbitrate dispute over consolidation of chairpersonship of two departments, that being a matter of "educational policy" and therefore excluded from the scope of bargaining); *Gorder v. Matanuska-Susitna School Dist.,* 84 LRRM 2683 (Alaska Sup. Ct. 1973) (discharge of probationary teacher not a matter involving continuous employment).

[21] See R. Theodore Clark, Jr., *The Scope of the Duty to Bargain in Public Employment,* in Labor Relations Law in the Public Sector, ed. Andria S. Knapp (Chicago: American Bar Association, 1977), 81, 85; Judith H. Toole, *Judicial Activism in Public Sector Grievance Arbitration: A Study of Recent Developments,* 33 Arb. J. 3, 6 (1978).

[22] *Associated Teachers of Huntington v. Board of Educ.,* 33 N.Y.2d 229, 306 N.E.2d 791, 85 LRRM 2795 (1973), known as the "second Huntington case."

[23] *Susquehanna Valley Cent. School Dist. v. Susquehanna Valley Teachers Ass'n,* 37 N.Y.2d 614, 90 LRRM 614 (1975). The suggestion was dicta, the court holding that the school district was obligated to arbitrate a grievance concerning staff reduction.

[24] *Cohoes City School Dist. v. Cohoes Teachers Ass'n,* 40 N.Y.2d 774, 358 N.E.2d 878, 94 LRRM 2192 (1976).

of individual teachers.[25] In both cases these actions were taken on the ground that such a commitment would be contrary to policy, which the court found to be implied in applicable statutes, that the board's discretion over such matters not be subject to such limitations.

The supreme judicial court of Massachusetts followed New York's lead in holding that a school committee "may not delegate to an arbitrator its authority to make decisions concerning tenure,"[26] and there are decisions in Montana,[27] South Dakota,[28] Washington,[29] and Florida[30] to the same effect, but the pattern of decisions is by no means consistent or symmetrical. Courts in Pennsylvania,[31] Michigan,[32] Maine,[33] Vermont,[34] Wisconsin,[35] and Hawaii,[36] for example, appear to accept arbitration over tenure decisions, whereas the Illinois supreme court holds that even the application of contractual evaluation procedures is an impermissible subject for arbitration.[37] The Massachusetts high court sustained the use of arbitration in a dispute over whether a school committee properly denied applications of school principals for transfer from one school to another, characterizing the issue as going to the "manner" of filling vacancies and therefore as not intruding upon the authority of the committee to exercise its discretion

---

[25] *Great Neck Free School Dist. v. Areman*, 41 N.Y.2d 527, 362 N.E.2d 843, 95 LRRM 2165 (1977). Cf., *Board of Educ. v. Yonkers Fed'n of Teachers*, 40 N.Y.2d 268, 386 N.Y.S.2d 657, 92 LRRM 3328 (N.Y. Ct. App. 1976) (upholding arbitration of layoffs under contractual "job security" clause, but suggesting decision might be otherwise if clause were not of "relatively brief" duration, or had been negotiated in a time of financial emergency or between parties of unequal bargaining power, or if clause did not explicitly protect teachers from layoff due to budgetary conditions).

[26] *School Comm. of Danvers v. Tyman*, 360 N.E.2d 977, 94 LRRM 3182 (1977). New Jersey's supreme court took a similar view. *Newark Teachers Union v. Board of Educ.*, 95 LRRM 2525 (1977).

[27] *Wibaux Educ. Ass'n v. Wibaux County High School*, 573 P.2d 1162, 97 LRRM 2592 (Mont. Sup. Ct. 1978).

[28] *Fries v. Wessington School Dist.*, 307 N.W.2d 875, 1981–1983 PBC ¶ 37,382 (S. Dak. Sup. Ct. 1981).

[29] *North Beach Educ. Ass'n v. North Beach School Dist.*, 31 Wash. App. 77, 639 P.2d 821 (1982).

[30] *Lake County Educ. Ass'n v. School Bd. of Lake County*, 360 So.2d 128, 99 LRRM 2493 (Fla. Ct. App. 1978).

[31] *Board of Educ. v. Philadelphia Fed'n of Teachers*, 346 A.2d 35, 90 LRRM 2879 (1975).

[32] *Kaleva-Norman-Dickson School Dist. No. 6. v. Kaleva-Norman-Dickson School Teachers Ass'n*, 393 Mich. 593, 227 N.W.2d 500, 89 LRRM 2078 (1975) (upholding propriety of arbitrating nonrenewal of probationary teacher's contract, but without considering delegation issue). Cf., *Brown v. Holton Pub. Schools*, 258 N.W.2d 51, 96 LRRM 2884 (1977) (holding school board's decision not to renew probationary teacher's contract was not arbitrable under the agreement).

[33] Cf., *Board of Directors v. Merrymeeting Educators' Ass'n*, 354 A.2d 169, 92 LRRM 2268 (Me. Sup. Ct. 1976) (issue of validity not raised).

[34] *Danville Bd. of School Directors v. Fibield*, 315 A.2d 473, 85 LRRM 2939 (Vt. Sup. Ct. 1974).

[35] *Joint School Dist. No. 10 v. Jefferson Educ. Ass'n*, 253 N.W.2d 536, 95 LRRM 3117 (Wis. Sup. Ct. 1977).

[36] *University of Hawaii Professional Assembly v. Univeristy of Hawaii* (4 cases), 659 P.2d 717, 720, 729, and 732 (Hawaii Sup. Ct. 1976).

[37] *Board of Trustees of Junior College Dist. No. 508 v. Cook County College Teachers Union*, 343 N.E.2d 473, 92 LRRM 2380 (1976).

in individual cases,[38] whereas the Minnesota supreme court declared that while a school district need not bargain over its "policy" of transferring teachers, the application of that policy to individual transfers is properly an arbitrable matter.[39]

The argument based on nondelegable discretion or authority has rarely been successful outside the field of education, but there are exceptions. The supreme court of Michigan, though apparently approving arbitration of disputes involving the nonrenewal of a probationary teacher's contract[40] and discharge of a police officer,[41] balked at arbitration over the dismissal of probation officers serving under the supervision of judges of the Recorders' court.[42] In a 4–3 opinion, a majority of the court, stressing the "sensitive" nature of the probation officer's function, argued that arbitration "could result in reinstatement of a probation officer in which the court could no longer place trust or confidence." One member of the majority, in a separate concurring opinion, even suggested that a statute which provided for arbitration of such disputes, in the absence of "standards" for decision, would pose a serious constitutional issue involving delegation of governmental authority. And in California, a court of appeals held that the City of Berkeley could not agree to arbitrate the dismissal of a city employee because its charter (which the court believed to be unaffected by the state public-employee bargaining law) vested the city manager with power to appoint, discipline, and remove all city employees, and in the court's opinion that power could not be "delegated" to an arbitrator.[43] While the case involved a police officer, the logic of the opinion would extend to any city employee, and to any city with a similar charter provision.

---

[38] *Bradley v. School Comm. of Boston*, 364 N.E.2d 1229, 96 LRRM 2542 (1977). The Massachusetts high court also sustained the use of arbitration in a dispute over a school committee's failure to hire sufficient substitutes to maintain agreed-upon limits on class size and teaching loads, where the committee acted not out of educational policy but because of financial strictures imposed by the mayor. *Boston Teachers Union v. School Comm. of Boston*, 350 N.E.2d 707, 93 LRRM 2205 (1976). That court held it beyond the authority of a school committee to agree to arbitrate over a decision to abolish a supervisory position, *Hanover School Comm. v. Curry*, 343 A.2d 144, 92 LRRM 2338 (1976), though an arbitrator's award with respect to such a dispute was sustained insofar as it ordered compensation to the supervisor whose position was abolished, *Braintree School Comm. v. Raymond*, 343 A.2d 145, 92 LRRM 2339 (1976).

[39] *Minneapolis Fed'n of Teachers v. Minneapolis Special School Dist.*, 95 LRRM 2359 (1977).

[40] *Kaleva-Norman-Dickson School Dist. No. 6 v. Kaleva-Norman-Dickson School Teachers Ass'n, supra* note 32.

[41] *Pontiac Police Officers Ass'n v. City of Pontiac*, 246 N.W.2d 831, 94 LRRM 2175 (Mich. Sup. Ct. 1976).

[42] *AFSCME v. Recorders Court Judges*, 248 N.W.2d 220, 94 LRRM 2392 (1976).

[43] On appeal, the California supreme court reversed, ruling that the city charter was not a bar to arbitration of dismissal actions and there was no unlawful delegation of the city manager's powers. *Taylor v. Crane; Berkeley Police Ass'n v. City of Berkeley*, 595 P.2d 129, 101 LRRM 3060 (1970).

The high court in Massachusetts suggested that the divergence of judicial opinion reflects "varying traditions and statutory provisions among the states."[44] There is clearly merit to that suggestion, but it is difficult to account for the results in terms of those factors alone. The tradition in all states prior to collective bargaining was that public bodies exercised virtually unfettered discretion with respect to nearly everything; the question is the extent to which that tradition should be deemed to survive a system of bilateralism imposed by law. And while the answer to that question is theoretically to be found in applicable statutes, the language of most of the statutes is singularly opaque. A statute that vests a school board with power to appoint for tenure "any or all of the persons recommended" by the superintendent of schools,[45] for example, does not necessarily imply that the power may not be limited through collective bargaining, or that the limitations may not be enforced through arbitration. If those results are found to be reflected in the statute, it is because in this, as in many areas of the law, the statute ultimately mirrors the policy predilections of the courts.

What those policy predilections are is not always easy to determine from the opinions. Analytically, the cases may be said to involve the validity of substantive contractual limitations upon the authority of the governing body rather than the validity of arbitration per se. From this point of view, if a public entity agrees to a particular limitation upon its authority, it should make no difference whether the limitation is to be enforced through arbitration or through the courts. It is difficult to resist the conclusion, however, that judicial perception of the nature of arbitration plays a role in the decisions. The word "delegation," for example, is not one that would be used in describing a system of norms to be judicially enforced, and the cases cited by the New York court of appeals as precedents for the proposition that some agreements to arbitrate ought not to be enforced are custody cases in which it was held that public policy required determination of the dispute by a judge.[46] What the judicial perception of the arbitral function is, and how it relates to the decisions rejecting arbitration of particular disputes, are matters best approached after completion of the survey.

---

[44] *School Comm. of Danvers v. Tyman, supra* note 26, at 3184. The court's reference was to the varying opinions in the tenure cases.

[45] New York Education Law, Sec. 2509. This was the statute the New York court of appeals held to preempt arbitration in *Cohoes, supra* note 24. Compare *Board of Police Comm'rs v. White*, 93 LRRM 2637 (Conn. Sup. Ct. 1976) (charter provision granting board of police commissioners power to remove police officers for cause held not to conflict with contractual provisions for arbitration).

[46] *Susquehanna Valley Cent. School Dist. v. Susquehanna Valley Teachers Ass'n, supra,* note 23.

Judicial Determination of Arbitrability

Assuming that the dispute is one which the parties may lawfully agree to arbitrate, a question may arise as to whether they have in fact done so. When this question arises in advance of arbitration in the private sector, courts are bound by the twin Trilogy principles precluding consideration of the merits and requiring the presumption of an affirmative answer.

In the early years of statutory-based public-sector collective bargaining, most state courts which had occasion to pass on arbitrability issues looked to Trilogy principles for guidance, and most applied those principles consistent with their underlying policy.[47] Some courts, however, intruded rather deeply into the merits in determining particular disputes to be nonarbitrable. The Connecticut supreme court, for example, held that although an agreement made reference to existing retirement plans, a dispute concerning those plans was not arbitrable under the agreement because the court considered it "impossible to say that the substantive provisions of the pension plan were made part of the agreement."[48] And an appellate court in Oregon held that teachers were not entitled to arbitrate a dispute over provisions of state administrative rules specifying class size, despite contract language which arguably incorporated those rules, on the ground that the "only rational interpretation" of the contract limited its scope to policies of the school district itself.[49]

Some courts went so far as to reverse the usual presumption of arbitrability. The highest court in Maine in effect took that position in a case involving arbitration over nonrenewal of probationary teacher contracts,[50] but decisions such as that are perhaps explainable in terms of judicial doubts concerning the validity of an agreement to arbitrate the particular dispute. More far-reaching was the New York court of appeals' 1977 decision in *Acting Superintendent of Schools of Liverpool Central School District v. United Liverpool Faculty Association.*[51] In that case, a union sought to compel arbitration of a grievance

---

[47] E.g., *Kaleva-Norman-Dickson School Dist. v. Teachers Ass'n, supra* note 32. *City School Dist. v. Poughkeepsie Pub. School Teachers,* 89 LRRM 2422 (N.Y. App. 1974). For discussion of the New York cases, see Gerard John DeWolf, *The Enforcement of the Labor Agreement in the Public Sector: The New York Experience,* 39 Albany L. Rev. 393 (1975).

[48] *Policemen's and Firemen's Retirement Bd., City of New Haven v. Sullivan,* 376 A.2d 399, 95 LRRM 2351 (Conn. Sup. Ct. 1977).

[49] *Portland Ass'n of Teachers v. School Dist. No. 1,* 555 P.2d 943, 93 LRRM 2879 (Ore. App. 1976).

[50] *Chassie v. Directors,* 356 A.2d 708, 92 LRRM 3359 (1976) (if the parties had intended to arbitrate such an issue, "certainly plainer language should have been employed"). Cf., *Brown v. Holton Pub. Schools, supra* note 32 (court, applying Trilogy language, concluded with "positive assurance" that contract language protecting teachers against unjust discharge was "not susceptible of an application" to the nonrenewal of a probationary teacher's contract.)

[51] 42 N.Y.2d 509, 399 N.Y.S.2d 189, 96 LRRM 2779 (1977). See William H. Englander, *The Liverpool Decision and Public Sector Arbitration: A Question of Nondelegable Responsibilities,* 33 Arb. J. 2, 25 (1978).

alleging that the school board violated the collective-bargaining agreement by refusing to allow a female teacher to return to work after sick leave unless she submitted to a complete medical examination by the school district's male physician, instead of permitting her to be examined by a female physician as she requested. The arbitration clause covered only "claimed violation, misinterpretation, or inequitable application of existing laws, rules, procedure, regulations, administrative orders or work rules of the District which relate to or involve Teachers' health or safety, physical facilities, materials or equipment furnished to teachers, or supervision of teachers," and the union argued that the dispute involved a claimed violation or inequitable application of existing laws and rules relating to the teacher's health. The agreement excluded from arbitration, however, "any matter involving a Teacher's rate of compensation, retirement benefits, disciplinary proceeding," and the district claimed that the dispute fell into the excluded category.

There was no doubt that the district could lawfully have agreed to arbitrate the dispute, and the court so held. There was also no doubt that under Trilogy principles the dispute would be held arbitrable, and the court impliedly conceded as much. The school board advanced an argument that the teacher waived her right to seek arbitration by filing an appeal under the state education law with the commissioner of education, and three judges of the court would have decided against arbitrability on that ground alone. A majority of the court, however, chose the occasion to announce new guiding principles for the determination of arbitrability in the public sector. Referring to the differences in perspective and approach that had evolved between commercial and labor arbitration, the former requiring (in New York) an "express, unequivocal agreement" to arbitrate the particular dispute, and the latter calling for application of Trilogy principles, the court reasoned that arbitration agreements pursuant to the Taylor Law cannot properly be characterized under either category:

> In the field of public employment, as distinguished from labor relations in the private sector, the public policy favoring arbitration—of recent origin—does not yet carry the same historical or general acceptance, nor, as evidenced in part by some of the litigation in our Court, has there so far been a similar demonstration of the efficacy of arbitration as a means for resolving controversies in governmental employment. Accordingly, it cannot be inferred as a practical matter that the parties to collective bargaining agreements in the public sector always intend to adopt the broadest permissible arbitration clauses. Indeed, inasmuch as the responsibilities of the elected representatives of the tax-paying public are overarching and fundamentally nondelegable, it must be taken, in the absence of clear, unequivocal agreement to the contrary,

that the board of education did *not* intend to refer differences which might arise to the arbitration forum. Such reference is not to be based on implication.

The guiding principle that emerged from the court's analysis was, in fact, the principle applicable to commercial arbitration: "the agreement to arbitrate must be express, direct and unequivocal as to the issues or disputes to be submitted to arbitration; anything less will lead to a denial of arbitration." The court concluded that a "very reasonable assertion can be made that this particular controversy falls within both the included and the excluded categories" and on that basis, and in light of the principle announced, concluded that arbitration should be stayed.[52]

In 1980 the New York court of appeals rendered three decisions which indicated a retreat from the restrictive view of *Liverpool*. In *Hannelore Lehnhoff v. Shepherd Nathan*,[53] the court of appeals found that the parties' collective bargaining agreement, which permitted the employer to suspend petitioner from employment in a state psychiatric center without pay if it determined that there was probable cause to believe that the employee's "continued presence on the job represents a potential danger to persons or property and would severely interfere with operations," contemplated that the issue of whether in fact there had been a probable-cause determination by the employer was to be submitted to arbitration. The court reversed a decision by the appellate division, which held that the arbitration clause did not even come into play until the suspending authority had made a finding of probable cause. Thus, the court of appeals held, judicial resolution of the merits of the dispute over the propriety of petitioner's suspension was foreclosed.

In the second case,[54] the court of appeals found the grievance of a probationary school teacher arbitrable within the meaning of the contract between the parties. Where the school district agreed to submit to arbitration all grievances involving "an alleged misinterpretation or misapplication of an express provision of [the] Agreement," it begs the question, said the court, to contend that the grievance is not arbitrable because it involves a dispute not unambiguously encompassed by an express substantive provision of the contract. The court distinguished *Liverpool* as requiring that arbitration be stayed only in cases where the parties' arbitration agreement did not unambiguously extend to

---

[52] *Liverpool* was followed by the California court of appeals in *Service Employees v. County of Napa*, 99 Cal. App.3d 946, 103 LRRM 2499 (1979), in which the senior author of this chapter, then an appellate judge, dissented.

[53] 48 N.Y.S.2d 990, 425 N.Y.S.2d 544 (1980).

[54] *Board of Educ. of Lakeland Cent. School Dist. of Shrub Oak v. Joseph Barni*, 49 N.Y.2d 311, 425 N.Y.S.2d 544, 103 LRRM 2903 (1980).

the particular dispute. Here, however, the parties' agreement to arbitrate the dispute was clear and unequivocal. The ambiguity surrounded the coverage of the applicable substantive provision of the contract which is a matter of contract interpretation for an arbitrator.

Finally, in *Board of Education of Middle Island Central School District No. 12 v. Middle Island Teachers Association*,[55] the court of appeals held that a probationary teacher who was denied tenure for alleged professional incompetence in the performance of his non-classroom duties had a right to arbitrate alleged breaches of contract evaluation procedures specifically referable to classroom performance. The court reversed a decision of the appellate division which had stayed arbitration on the grounds that the school board had denied tenure for reasons unrelated to the teacher's classroom performance. Citing *Liverpool*, the court of appeals found that the subject matter of the dispute was encompassed by the broad arbitration clause in the parties' collective-bargaining agreement. Since the school board is bound by an agreement which requires teacher evaluation procedures, failure to follow these procedures may form the basis for a grievance which may be submitted to arbitration. Even though the board had the right to deny tenure to a probationary teacher without an explanation, "the procedural aspect of the contract is discrete from the denial of tenure and should be so treated," said the court.

Judicial Review of the Award

The Trilogy principle of arbitral finality so long as the award draws its "essence" from the contract has been explicitly adopted by some state courts,[56] and statutory provisions in a number of states narrowly constrain the scope of judicial review.[57] The language which the courts use when asked to review arbitral awards is thus generally in accord with federal principles, but the application of that language is in some cases highly dubious, reflecting a significantly greater tendency to substitute the court's judgment for that of the arbitrator.

In some cases courts have set awards aside on the ground that the contract, or at least the contract as interpreted by the arbitrator, intrudes impermissibly upon an area of authority or discretion committed to the public agency by law or public policy. This category of cases has previously been discussed. In others, courts have set awards aside

---

55 50 N.Y.2d 426, 429 N.Y.S.2d 564, 1979–81 PBC ¶37,011 (1980).

56 E.g., *Board of Directors v. Merrymeeting Educators' Ass'n, supra* note 33; *Darien Educ. Ass'n v. Board of Educ.*, 374 A.2d 1081, 94 LRRM 2895 (Conn. Sup. Ct. 1977). Cf., *Beaver County Community College v. Faculty*, 96 LRRM 2375 (Pa. Sup. Ct. 1977) (applying statutory standard permitting review for awards "against the law," to require determination as to whether arbitrator's position could be "rationally derived from the agreement").

57 E.g., Wis. Stat. Ann. (Supp. 1973), §111.86.

on the ground that the contract as interpreted is in substantive conflict with the result dictated by an applicable law external to the agreement—as, for example, where the award enforces a contractual provision for parity pay found to conflict with the state public-employee bargaining law;[58] or orders reinstatement of an employee discharged for failing to reside within the city, contrary to the provisions of a city ordinance found to be controlling;[59] or directs payment of full pay to teachers during sabbatical leave in the face of a statute construed by the court as limiting sabbatical pay to one-half.[60] These cases involve the extent to which a collective-bargaining agreement is permitted to supersede the provisions of an otherwise applicable statute or ordinance. While one may quarrel with the answer that the court gives in a particular case, the proposition that the award should be set aside if the law be given superseding effect is unobjectionable. Far more debatable are the cases in which courts have set aside awards on grounds that the arbitrators have in some respect exceeded their authority under the agreement itself. While varying contract language and factual situations make generalizations difficult, several illustrative patterns emerge.

First, the courts appear less inclined to defer to an arbitration award where there exists a statute covering the subject matter, even if the statute is not deemed preemptive. The New Jersey supreme court recently held that where an award of back pay was not authorized by the collective-bargaining agreement, the arbitrator exceeded her authority by awarding back pay to grievants seeking retroactive pay for promotions. A number of employees whose names had been improperly removed from a promotions list grieved the matter, seeking back pay for the period of removal. The union demanded arbitration, but the county board resisted, claiming that the dispute was not arbitrable under the terms of the agreement. The court held that the grievance was arbitrable, however, and ordered arbitration, retaining jurisdiction. The arbitrator went on to award back pay to the aggrieved employees for "retroactive promotion," and the union moved to confirm. The court, however, vacated the award on the board's motion,

---

[58] *Fire Fighters Local 1219 v. Connecticut Labor Relations Bd.*, 370 A.2d 952 (Conn. Sup. Ct. 1977).

[59] *Wisconsin Employment Relations Comm'n v. Teamsters Local 563*, 250 N.W.2d 696, 94 LRRM 2849 (Wis. Sup. Ct. 1977).

[60] *Allegheny Valley School Dist. v. Allegheny Educ. Ass'n*, 360 A.2d 762, 92 LRRM 3536 (Pa. Comm. Ct. 1976). See also *Conley v. Joyce*, 366 A.2d 1292, 94 LRRM 2114 (Pa. Comm. Ct. 1976) (award regarding overtime pay modified to conform to statute); *Niagara Wheatfield Adm'rs Ass'n v. Niagara Wheatfield Cent. School Dist.*, 389 N.Y.S.2d 667, 94 LRRM 2682 (N.Y. App. Div. 1976) (award requiring continuance of fringe benefits after expiration of agreement modified to require continuance for reasonable time only, on grounds contract as arbitrator construed it was contrary to public policy). Cf. *Boston Teachers Union v. School Comm.*, *supra* note 38 (invalidating award which required payment of money to union scholarship fund as remedy for contract violation).

ruling that public officers were not entitled to compensation for services not rendered. The decision was reversed by the appellate division, which ruled that the employees were improperly characterized as public officers. The state supreme court focused its review on the scope of the arbitrator's authority, as limited by the collective-bargaining agreement, by the law, and by public policy. Finding that the contract did not contemplate such back-pay awards and that New Jersey law prescribed only narrow circumstances in which back pay could be awarded, the court ruled that the arbitrator exceeded her authority, and reversed the ruling below, reinstating the trial court's order of vacatur.[61] Such decisions reflect, perhaps, the unwillingness of courts to accept the full implications of collective bargaining and arbitration in an area still permeated by legislation.

Two recent cases, however, reflect greater understanding and acceptance of Trilogy principles. In *Board of Education, Dover Union Free School District v. Dover-Wingdale Teachers' Association,*[62] it was determined by the New York court of appeals that any limitation on the remedial power of an arbitrator must be clearly contained, either explicitly or incorporated by reference, in the arbitration clause itself. To infer a limitation from an ambiguous and general clause in the substantive provisions of the agreement would, in effect, require judicial interpretation and judicial interference with an arbitration award, which should be avoided unless that award is violative of a strong public policy, totally irrational, or in excess of a specifically enumerated limitation upon arbitral authority. Similarly, in *Garner v. City of Tulsa,*[63] the Oklahoma supreme court held that the arbitrator did not exceed his authority by considering a state statute governing firefighter pensions in resolving a dispute concerning the reinstatement of a firefighter.

Second, courts in the public sector appear less tolerant than those in the private sector of awards that rely on past practice to establish obligations not expressed in the agreement. In *Milwaukee Professional Fire Fighters v. City of Milwaukee,*[64] for example, an arbitrator relied upon past practice to find that the city's change in policies with respect to the scheduling of vacation days, days off, and special-duty overtime work for firefighters was in violation of the agreement, and ordered that past practice be resumed. The Wisconsin supreme court held that the arbitrator's reliance on past practice "did not draw its essence from

---

[61] *Communications Workers of Am. Local 1087 v. Monmouth County Bd. of Social Servs.*, 96 N.J. 442, 476 A.2d 777, 1984–86 PBC ¶34,238 (1984).
[62] 61 N.Y.2d 913, 463 N.E.2d 32, 474 N.Y.S.2d 716, 1984–86 PBC ¶34,145 (1984).
[63] 651 P.2d 1325 (Okla. 1982).
[64] 253 N.W.2d 481, 95 LRRM 2684 (Wis. Sup. Ct. 1977). See also *County of Allegheny v. Allegheny County Prison Employees*, 96 LRRM 3396 (Pa. Sup. Ct. 1977).

the agreement" because it was based upon his understanding of the "wishes of the parties" rather than upon the agreement itself. Where the arbitrator relied upon past practice to impose obligations at variance with the express terms of the agreement, judicial reaction is even more likely to be negative. In *Civil Service Employees Association v. City of Steuben*,[65] an arbitrator ruled that the county was precluded by past practice of many years from attempting to enforce a contract clause requiring that social workers obtain prior approval in writing in order to secure travel reimbursement from their homes to the homes of clients. The appellate division of the New York supreme court refused to enforce the award, stating that the arbitrator had "deliberately and intentionally" considered matters outside the agreement, and thereby "in effect wrote a new contract for the parties." While there are private-sector cases to similar effect, the prevailing view is to the contrary, and cases such as these may reflect a judicial assumption that in the public sector it is to be expected that limitations on managerial authority will be express rather than implied.

Finally, even where the arbitrator's award is based upon express contract language, courts in some cases have displayed a greater propensity than in the private sector to overturn the arbitrator's interpretation. In *Simpson v. North Collins Central School District*,[66] for example, an arbitrator interpreted a contractual provision requiring "just cause" for dismissal to require fair evaluation procedures for probationary teachers under consideration for tenure. Although the New York court of appeals had upheld the validity of arbitration over the application of evaluation procedures, as distinguished from arbitration over the substantive tenure decision, the appellate division of the New York supreme court found the arbitrator's interpretation of the agreement to be "irrational," and the imposition of what the court characterized as "ex post facto procedural standards" to be "tantamount to the making of a new contract for the parties."

Multiple Rights, Multiple Forums

In any system of grievance arbitration, private or public, questions arise as to the relationship between arbitration and other procedures for enforcement of rights created by the agreement or by

---

[65] 377 N.Y.S.2d 849, 91 LRRM 2916 (N.Y. App. Div. 1976). See *Lansing Fire Fighters Ass'n v. City of Lansing*, 97 LRRM 2857 (Mich. Cir. Ct. 1976) (arbitrator ruled city obligated by past practice to pay employees who retire during contract year a full food allowance, despite contract clause providing for pro rata amounts to employees who serve less than 12 months regular full-time duty. Held: Arbitrator exceeded his authority).

[66] 392 N.Y.S.2d 106, 95 LRRM 2083 (N.Y. App. Div. 1977). See also *Fairchild v. West Rutland School Dist.*, 376 A.2d 28, 95 LRRM 3006 (Vt. Sup. Ct. 1977) (arbitrator exceeded his authority by applying dismissal provisions of agreement to failure of school board to renew probationary teacher's contract). *Contra: Joint School Dist. No. 10 v. Jefferson Educ. Ass'n, supra* note 35.

external legal norms. Space does not permit a full exploration of this topic here,[67] but an attempt will be made to give some indication of the various contexts in which such questions arise in the public sector and of the nature of judicial response.

With respect to rights created by the agreement itself, it is well established in the private sector that the arbitral procedures are exclusive as regards disputes that the parties have agreed to arbitrate, and resort to the courts is generally not permitted. This is true not only for the employer and the union, but for the employee as well, unless the union is shown to have violated its duty of fair representation. There would appear to be no reason for not applying these principles to the public sector as well, and in general the courts appear to have accepted them.[68]

With respect to rights based on norms external to the agreement, the problem is more complex. Questions concerning the relationship of arbitration to rights and remedies created by such legislation as Title VII of the Civil Rights Act of 1964 and the National Labor Relations Act have been the subject of frequent litigation in the private sector with varying results.[69] In the public sector, the problem of relationship is accentuated by the multiplicity of statutory provisions which antedated collective bargaining and which provide employees with certain rights and remedies (e.g., protection against arbitrary discipline) that more closely parallel the typical content of collective bargaining agreements. May employees pursue such rights and remedies independently, or are they limited to the procedures which their union has agreed to? In some states the answer is contained in the collective-bargaining statute itself,[70] but in the absence of statutory guidance, courts have generally opted for a policy of coexistence: employees may elect to pursue statutory remedies despite the availability of contractual remedies,[71] and may even be permitted to pursue relief in one forum after losing in another.[72] The fact that the relief

---

[67] For more extensive treatment, see Aaron, *supra* note 18; Note, *Public Sector Grievance Procedures, Due Process and the Duty of Fair Representation*, 89 Harv. L. Rev. 752 (1976).

[68] See Note, *supra* note 67, at 782. The editors argue that due process may require a higher standard for the union's duty of fair representation. But see *Dade County Classroom Teachers Ass'n v. Ryan*, 225 So.2d 903, 71 LRRM 2958 (Fla. Sup. Ct. 1969) (nonconsenting teachers need not submit to union-controlled grievance procedure). See generally, Note, *The Privilege of Exclusive Recognition and Minority Union Rights in Public Employment*, 55 Cornell L. Rev. 1004 (1970).

[69] *Supra* note 67.

[70] E.g., Me. Rev. Stat. Ann. Title 26 §979-K (1964) ("any such grievance procedure shall be exclusive and shall supersede any otherwise applicable grievance procedure provided by law"); N.Y. Civ. Serv. Law, §74(4) (1973) (civil service remedies subject to terms of agreement).

[71] E.g., *Board of Educ. v. Associated Teachers of Huntington*, *supra* note 15.

[72] E.g, *City School Dist. v. Poughkeepsie Pub. School Teachers*, *supra* note 47 (school district obligated to activate at union's request over denial of teacher's transfer request, though teacher had maintained appeal to commissioner of education and lost). Cf., *Alexander v. Gardner-Denver*, 415 U.S. 36, 7 FEP Cases 81 (1974), holding arbitration award no bar to pursuit of remedies under Civil Rights Act.

sought from the arbitrator is asserted to conflict with statutory policy will not preclude arbitration, judicial review being available to test the validity of the ultimate award.[73]

The U.S. Supreme Court has held, in *McDonald v. City of West Branch, Michigan*[74] that an employee who claims he was discharged for exercising his First Amendment rights of freedom of speech, freedom of association, and freedom to petition the government for redress of grievances, must be permitted to pursue those claims in a federal court Section 1983 action notwithstanding an adverse arbitral award. The award could be introduced in evidence, the Court said, but it could not be accorded res judicata or collateral estoppel effect. Following the reasoning in *Alexander v. Gardner-Denver Co.*[75] which held that an employee could maintain an action under Title VII under such circumstances, and in *Barrentine v. Arkansas Best Freight Systems*[76] which reached the same conclusion under the Fair Labor Standards Act, the Court stressed (1) the lack of arbitral expertise with respect to the constitutional issues; (2) the focus of arbitration upon rights under the agreement; (3) the risk that a union with adverse interests may not pursue the employee's claim with sufficient vigor; and (4) the deficiencies in arbitral fact-finding compared to judicial fact-finding.[77]

Prior to *McDonald* the appellate division of the New York supreme court, in *Antinore v. State*,[78] upheld the constitutionality of New York's Civil Service Law permitting the substitution through collective-bargaining agreement of arbitral for statutory remedies in discharge and discipline cases on the ground that the union, as the employees' representative, could waive on their behalf whatever substantive and procedural constitutional rights they might have. The court's reasoning in that case is suspect after *McDonald*, though the supreme court did not have occasion to pass upon the plaintiff's claim, rejected by the jury, of due process denial. In the early *Huntington* case the New York court of appeals suggested in a footnote that where rights external to the agreement were involved, judicial review might extend to determining whether the arbitration proceeding was fair and

---

[73] *Pennsylvania Labor Relations Bd. v. Bald Eagle Area School Dist.*, 499 Pa. 62, 451 A.2d 671, 114 LRRM 2084 (1982) (courts have no reason to assume an arbitrator will ignore the law and award a payment based on a contractual interpretation which conflicts with a fundamental policy of this Commonwealth expressed in statutory law).

[74] 466 U.S. 284, 115 LRRM 3646 (1984).

[75] 415 U.S. 36, 7 FEP Cases 81 (1974).

[76] 450 U.S. 728, 24 WH Cases 1284 (1981).

[77] At least one state court has indicated that an arbitrator may not even consider and decide a constitutional claim—a result which goes beyond the reasoning of *McDonald*. *McGrath v. State of Minnesota*, 312 N.W.2d 438, 1981–83 PBC ¶37,318 (Minn. Sup. Ct. 1982).

[78] 371 N.Y.S.2d 213 (App. Div. 1975), *aff'd without opinion*, 40 N.Y.2d 921, 389 N.Y.S.2d 576, 94 LRRM 2224 (1976).

regular.[79] Such a standard, whether or not it goes far enough to meet constitutional requirements, clearly goes further than the normal scope of judicial review. Benjamin Aaron's prediction that judicial review of grievance-arbitration decisions in the public sector is likely to be "broader in scope than that prevailing in the private sector, especially in cases involving discipline or discharge,"[80] seems clearly on target.

Federal Government

In the federal sector the developing experience with judicial review shows that the review indeed is broader in scope than that prevailing in the state- and local-government sector. Under the federal-sector law, all decisions are subject to some kind of review by courts or administrative bodies, or both. As such, the law imposes new burdens on arbitrators and parties under a system that requires arbitrators to interpret external law and limits arbitrators' ability to fashion appropriate remedies.[81] Thus, it is not surprising to find that the federal-sector arbitration experience is criticized as marked by "judicial intrusion" that is "demeaning to the arbitration profession."[82]

The federal model is criticized for having strayed from the model of the traditional arbitration system. In the view of John Kagel, it falls short of traditional arbitration in several ways, though in several important respects it is better than what it supplanted. He explains:

> The federal-sector process may work in many instances to provide the kind of resolution of disputes that the traditional model does. But if either party chooses not to have it so work, then, unfortunately, there are numerous pitfalls and traps for the unwary—often for no apparent meritorious reason—written into the statute which can be used for delay or in other dilatory ways.[83]

---

[79] *Board of Educ. v. Associated Teachers of Huntington, supra* note 15. Footnote 8 of one opinion reads, "We assume, of course, that the arbitration procedure is fair and regular and free from any procedural inferences that might invalidate the award." (Cf., e.g., *Spielberg Mfg. Co.*, 112 NLRB 1080, 36 LRRM 1152 [1955].) Under the *Spielberg* doctrine, the NLRB will review arbitration awards involving mixed questions of contractual violations to determine not only procedural regularity, but also compatibility with statutory policies. As recently applied, the doctrine requires that the arbitrators have considered the statutory issue.

[80] Aaron, *supra* note 18, at 46–47.

[81] For an analysis of early FLRA decisions related to exceptions taken to remedies ordered by labor arbitrators, see Stephen L. Hayford, *The Impact of Law upon the Remedial Authority of Labor Arbitrators in the Federal Sector,* 37 Arb J. 28 (March 1982).

[82] See statement of Jean McKelvey before the Society of Federal Labor Relations Professionals conference, June 26, 1985, in 23 GERR 983 (July 15, 1985).

[83] Kagel, *Grievance Arbitration in the Federal Service: Still Hardly Final and Binding?* Arbitration Issues for the 1980s, Proceedings of the 34th Annual Meeting, National Academy of Arbitrators, eds. James L. Stern and Barbara D. Dennis (Washington: BNA Books, 1982), at 195.

On the other hand, it has been argued that while there are some similarities between the private-sector grievance arbitration system and the federal-sector system which has been patterned after it, the "differences are more significant and substantial." James M. Harkless contends:

> Grievance arbitration in the federal system is not a substitute for a strike because federal employees have never had that right. The grievance arbitration system in the federal sector is an adjudicatory one to secure compliance with the collective bargaining agreement, but it is more than that. As the Elkouris point out . . . it "is to review or police compliance with controlling laws, rules and regulations by federal agency employers and employees alike."

He goes on to quote the Elkouris further: "For some matters in the federal sector, the collective agreement and custom cannot be made the controlling 'law of the plant.'" Harkless concluded that because of these differences between federal- and private-sector grievance arbitration, federal-sector grievance arbitration decisions should not be accorded the same deference as in the private sector.[84]

Under the statutory scheme adopted in the Civil Service Reform Act (CSRA), negotiated grievance procedures cover a wide array of issues, including (1) "pure grievances" (those that do "not involve a reduction in grade or removal for unacceptable performance; a removal, suspension for more than 14 days, reduction in grade or pay, or furlough of 30 days or less; or a complaint of discrimination"),[85] (2) major personnel actions (adverse actions under Chapter 75 of the Code, and performance-based removals and demotions under Chapter 43), and (3) discrimination complaints. In the latter two cases the employee also has statutory appeal rights to the Merit Systems Protection Board (MSPB) and Equal Employment Opportunity Commission (EEOC), respectively. The adversely affected employee may choose either remedial route.[86] Arbitration awards involving "pure grievances" are subject to review only by the Federal Labor Relations Authority (FLRA), and the decision of the FLRA is final unless an unfair labor practice issue is involved. These grievances are the most numerous, and it is typically with the FLRA that arbitration awards run afoul in the application of external authority.

FLRA Review

When compared with a maximum of about 1½ percent of total cases which are appealed in the private sector, a rate of 17 percent—the proportion of cases in which exceptions were filed with the FLRA

---

[84] Harkless, *Comment*, Arbitration Issues for the 1980s, *supra* note 83, at 209.

[85] *Devine v. White*, 112 LRRM 2374, 2392 (D.C. Cir. 1983).

[86] Decisions of arbitrators and MSPB involving major personnel actions are subject to review by the U.S. court of appeals for the federal circuit. In discrimination cases, the arbitrator's award is subject to review by the FLRA, EEOC, and U.S. district court.

during the first three years of the CSRA—is substantial.[87] The degree
of penetration is to be found in the statistic that shows that in the first
seven years since the enactment of the statute, a total of 164, or
17.1 percent of the 963 awards to which exceptions were filed, were
modified or set aside, at least in part.[88]

The FLRA will review an arbitrator's award to determine if it is
deficient because "it is contrary to any law, rule, or regulation; or . . .
on other grounds similar to those applied by Federal courts in private
sector labor-management relations."[89] In its early cases, the FLRA
expressly recognized those grounds on which courts sustain challenges
to private-sector awards.[90] In more recent cases, awards have been set
aside by the FLRA because they were "contrary to any law, rule, or
regulation," including the Back Pay Act, the management-rights
clause applicable to federal-sector collective bargaining, and OPM and
agency regulations.[91]

The most common basis for exception taken to arbitrator awards is
remedies, usually the award of back pay within the context of the Back
Pay Act. Here, the FLRA has decided that to support an award of back
pay, as for example in lost promotion, denial of overtime, or reassign-
ment, the arbitrator must make an express finding that "but for" an
improper agency action, the grievant would have avoided the loss of
pay.[92]

Violation of the broad management-rights clause (5 U.S.C. Sec.
7106) is another basis for exception to be taken to an arbitrator's award.
In *Department of Housing and Urban Development and AFGE*,[93] for
example, the FLRA held that an arbitrator cannot order an agency to
assign specific duties or higher graded work to an employee because
this interferes with management's right to assign work. Management
rights are also significant in the performance appraisal area. Here, the
FLRA has held that an arbitrator may not find arbitrable a grievance
that challenges an agency's identification of job elements or establish-

---

[87] Ronald W. Haughton, *Arbitration in the Federal Sector*, 38 Arb. J. 55 (December 1983).

[88] 24 GERR 420 (March 31, 1986).

[89] 5 U.S.C. §7122(a).

[90] For citations to these cases, see Frank Elkouri and Edna Asper Elkouri, How Arbitration
Works, 4th ed. (Washington: BNA Books, 1985), 67. The grounds include the following: (1) the
arbitrator exceeded his authority; (2) the award does not draw its essence from the collective
bargaining agreement; (3) the award is incomplete, ambiguous, or contradictory, making implementation of the award impossible; (4) the award is based on a "nonfact"; (5) the arbitrator was
biased or partial; (6) the arbitrator refused to hear pertinent and material evidence.

[91] The following section is based on the excellent discussion by Herbert Fishgold and Mary
E. Jacksteit, *Implications of Cornelius v. Nutt for Federal Section Arbitrators*, a paper presented
before the National Academy of Arbitrators 1986 Continuing Education Conference in St. Louis,
November 1, 1986, 45–52.

[92] *Veterans Admin. Hosp.*, 5 FLRA No. 57 (1980); *American Fed'n of Gov't Employees*,
5 FLRA No. 66 (1981); *U.S. Army Missile Command, Redstone Arsenal and AFGE Local 1858*,
19 FLRA No. 38 (1985).

[93] 21 FLRA 413 (1986).

ment of performance standards; however, an arbitrator can ascertain whether a contractual requirement of "fairness and equity" has been met in the application of elements and standards and can order a reevaluation of the grievant's work using the proper standards or order that management's appraisal be assigned the rating provided for by the elements/standards.[94]

The Back Pay Act and management-rights clause are only two, but broad, restrictions on arbitral authority. Other specific legal authorities exist, including statutes governing entitlement to overtime, travel and pay differentials, and OPM and agency regulations as well.

Court Review

Cornelius v. Nutt,[95] a 1985 U.S. Supreme Court decision, is noteworthy because it marks a "significant erosion of the arbitrator's traditional independence"[96] in the determination of a dispute falling within the dual jurisdiction of the negotiated grievance procedure and the statutory appeal process administered by the MSPB. The issue presented to the Court was whether or not it was permissible for an arbitrator to apply a "harmful error" standard different than that used by the MSPB in a case falling within this dual jurisdiction. Holding that the MSPB's standard was binding upon arbitrators, the Court decided the issue in favor of consistency.[97]

The *Nutt* case involved an arbitrator who found that the grievants had engaged in misconduct normally worthy of dismissal, but because the employer had violated the collective-bargaining agreement by failing (1) to provide the employees with an opportunity for union representation and (2) to bring charges within a reasonable period of time, set aside the removal of the employees. The arbitrator found these contract violations constituted harmful error despite his conclusion that the procedural errors had no potential of having affected the agency's removal decision. The removals were reduced to suspensions as a sanction against the employer for violating the collective-bargaining agreement. The federal circuit affirmed, holding that an arbitrator could make a finding of harmful error and set aside agency action where the error involved no harm to the employee, but rather harm to union rights from significant violations of the collective-bargaining

---

[94] *Bureau of Engraving and Printing and Washington Plate Printers Union*, 20 FLRA No. 39 (1985).

[95] 472 U.S. 648, 119 LRRM 2905 (1985). For an excellent discussion of the case and other cases affecting federal sector arbitration, see Fishgold and Jacksteit, *supra* note 91.

[96] Fishgold and Jacksteit, *supra* note 91, at 52.

[97] It is important to note that the FLRA has not adopted the concept of consistency between arbitration and statutory appeals. Further, the vast majority of grievances do not involve adverse actions and performance-based removals and demotions.

agreement. Thus, the appeals court was prepared to permit arbitrators to fashion a standard for harmful error, not accepted or used by the MSPB.

The Supreme Court disagreed, holding that Congress intended for arbitrators, in matters heard under Section 7121(e), to apply the same "substantive standards" as would be applied by the MSPB were it hearing the case. The Court also found that consistency with the MSPB's harmful error rule, in particular, was required by the desire of Congress to give agencies greater ability to remove employees committing misconduct, or failing to perform adequately. The substance of the arbitrator's harmful error standard was found repugnant to that purpose, since admittedly guilty and unprejudiced employees would go unpunished for the sake of vindicating union rights. The undeniable interests of the union in arbitration, and the traditional role of arbitrators as vindicators of the collective-bargaining process, were seen as of lesser importance to Congress than these other purposes.

The Court specifically rejected the D.C. Circuit's earlier conclusion in *Devine v. White*[98] that there could be circumstances where no effect on the outcome need be shown. The Court's decision thus raises concern whether it intends for arbitrators to adhere to every standard used by the MSPB, whether or not derived from the statute, and whether or not enunciated by regulation or by case precedent. Further, in *Devine v. Sutermeister*,[99] a case the federal circuit court decided a few months after it considered *Nutt*, the court in dicta said that arbitrators are not bound by MSPB precedent (in this instance governing the mitigation of penalties). In July 1984, in *Devine v. NTEU*,[100] the same court rejected an OPM request to disavow the language from *Sutermeister* and reaffirmed its previous statement that there is no support for a requirement that arbitrators follow MSPB precedent.

Fishgold and Jacksteit feel the *Nutt* decision does not represent a radical departure.

> Authority external to the collective bargaining agreement has always been the rule, not the exception. But viewed from the standpoint of traditional labor arbitration practice, it does mark a further significant erosion of the arbitrator's independence in at least one class of federal sector cases. The extent to which arbitrators will be expected to sit "like common law judges" and concern themselves with the ever-expanding body of MSPB case law remains to be seen. But a requirement of consistency in basic areas seems inevitable.[101]

---

[98] 697 F.2d 421, 112 LRRM 2374 (1983).
[99] 724 F.2d 1558, 116 LRRM 2495 (1983).
[100] 737 F.2d 1031, 84 FLRR 1-8017 (1984).
[101] Fishgold and Jacksteit, *supra* note 91, at 52–53.

The Postal Service

Brief mention should be made here about the U.S. Postal Service, where collective bargaining for employees is subject to the provisions of the private-sector National Labor Relations Act but with two major exceptions: a ban on strikes and union shop provisions. In contrast to workers covered by the CSRA, postal workers enjoy a greatly expanded scope of bargaining which includes "wages, many benefits, and most working conditions."[102] The Postal Reorganization Act also provides for final and binding arbitration to resolve impasse disputes.

In its review of postal employee grievances, courts have held that a postal employee is bound by an arbitrator's decision upholding her dismissal,[103] and once an arbitrator has made a threshold determination that an employee has participated in a strike against the government, no mitigation of the discharge penalty is possible.[104]

Interest Arbitration

State and Local Government

Interest arbitration, involving the binding determination of contract terms, has some private-sector roots, but is mainly a public-sector phenomenon, developed in response to the legal prohibition against strikes by public employees.[105] While a number of statutes authorize interest arbitration by agreement between a public entity and a union, in fact such agreements are rare, and most interest arbitration takes place pursuant to legislative mandate.[106] Thus, while grievance arbitration is primarily consensual and based upon procedure and criteria contained in agreements, interest arbitration is primarily statutory and based upon procedure and criteria specified by law. The differences go deeper than that, however. The grievance arbitrators' business is to pass upon the claims of the respective parties to rights under the agreement, and while their decisions may entail discretion, that discretion is typically channeled within a relatively narrow range of criteria and touches upon only a relatively small portion of the parties' relationships to one another. The interest arbitrators' business is to make a contract for the parties, at least with respect to the issues in dispute, and while the governing statute or agreement may prescribe

---

[102] J. Joseph Loewenberg, *The U.S. Postal Service*, in Collective Bargaining: Contemporary American Experience, ed. Gerald G. Somers (Madison, Wis.: IRRA, 1980), 435–485.

[103] *Smith v. Daws*, 614 F.2d 1069, 103 LRRM 3055 (1980).

[104] *American Postal Workers v. United States Postal Serv.*, 104 LRRM 3115 (1980).

[105] See Charles J. Morris, *The Role of Interest Arbitration in a Collective Bargaining System*, in The Future of Labor Arbitration in America (New York: American Arbitration Association, 1976), 197.

[106] *Id.* at 230.

standards to guide their determinations, these are typically designed so as to allow discretion to be exercised over a broad range. At the risk of some oversimplification, the difference is between norm application and norm creation.

Validity of Interest Arbitration

Statutes mandating interest arbitration for public employees have been challenged on a variety of state constitutional grounds, most of them involving either the relationship of state to local authority, the relationship of arbitration to the legislative process, or a combination of the two. The first category of challenge—that the statute intrudes impermissibly upon the autonomy of a "home rule" city or county— has been uniformly rejected by the courts and need not concern us here. [107] The second category, involving the relationship of arbitration to the legislative process, may take a variety of forms: that the statute constitutes an unlawful delegation of legislative power to private parties, that the statute contains insufficient standards or safeguards to guide or check arbitral discretion, that it represents an unconstitutional delegation of the taxing power, or that the method by which arbitrators are chosen violates the "one man, one vote" principle. [108] The third category of challenge stems from the provisions, known as "ripper clauses," found in 18 state constitutions and prohibiting the legislature from delegating to a "special or private body" any power to interfere with "municipal moneys or to perform municipal functions." [109]

Prior to 1975, Pennsylvania was the only state in which interest arbitration was held constitutionally impermissible, and that was on the basis of a ripper clause that has subsequently been amended to permit arbitration. [110] After that amendment, the state interest-arbitration statute was sustained. [111] The supreme court of Wyoming upheld that state's interest-arbitration statute despite a ripper clause in the state's constitution, [112] and the courts of Rhode Island, [113] Maine, [114] and Nebraska [115] (which have no ripper clauses) rejected constitutional challenges based on other grounds. The supreme court of Maine was equally divided on the question of unlawful delegation,

---

[107] Notes, *supra* note 3, at 787, 814.

[108] *Id.* at 818.

[109] *Id.* at 797.

[110] *Erie Fire Fighters Local 293 v. Gardner,* 406 Pa. 395, 178 A.2d 691 (1962).

[111] *Harney v. Russo,* 435 Pa. 183, 255 A.2d 560, 71 LRRM 2817 (1969).

[112] *State ex rel. Fire Fighters Local 946 v. City of Laramie,* 437 P.2d 295, 68 LRRM 2038 (1968).

[113] *City of Warwick v. Warwick Regular Firemen's Ass'n,* 106 R.I. 109, 256 A.2d 206, 71 LRRM 3192 (1969).

[114] *City of Biddeford v. Biddeford Teachers Ass'n,* 204 A.2d 387, 83 LRRM 2098 (Me. 1973).

[115] *School Dist. of Seward Educ. Ass'n v. School Dist. of Seward,* 188 Neb. 772, 199 N.W.2d 752 (1972).

but since the lower court had sustained the statute, the effect of the division was to affirm. Thus, by the end of 1974 the score stood 5–0 in favor of constitutionality.

Since that time, interest arbitration's constitutional batting average has been rising. The highest courts in Connecticut,[116] Maine,[117] New Jersey,[118] Minnesota,[119] New York,[120] Massachusetts,[121] Washington,[122] and Michigan[123] have sustained the constitutionality of interest arbitration in those states; and courts in South Dakota,[124] Colorado,[125] Utah,[126] and Maryland[127] have reached the opposite conclusion. While each of the latter state constitutions contains ripper clauses, the decisions in Colorado and Utah went beyond those clauses to rely generally on unconstitutional delegation doctrine. In California, the supreme court in a footnote in one case rather summarily dispensed with a constitutional attack raised by an amicus curiae to the constitutionality of a city-charter provision calling for binding interest arbitration;[128] however, the vitality of that footnote is dampened somewhat by the reasoning of the same court in an opinion which holds that an arrangement by a general-law city for interest arbitration would constitute an impermissible delegation of wage-fixing authority under a state statute providing that "by resolution or ordinance the city council shall fix the compensation of all appointive officers."[129]

The delegation issue is the most formidable of the constitutional issues, and its various ramifications are best reflected in the diverse opinions that comprise the Michigan supreme court's decision in

---

[116] *Town of Berlin v. Frank Santaguida*, 435 A.2d 980, 109 LRRM 2055 (1980).

[117] *School Comm. of Bangor v. Educ. Ass'n*, 433 A.2d 383, 1981–83 PBC ¶37,319 (1981).

[118] *Division 540, Amalgamated Transit Union v. Mercer County Improvement Auth.*, 386 A.2d 1290, 98 LRRM 2526 (N.J. Sup. Ct. 1978).

[119] *City of Richfield and Fire Fighters Local 1215 and State of Minnesota*, 276 N.W.2d 42, 1979–80 PBC ¶36,501 (1979).

[120] *City of Amsterdam v. Helsby*, 37 N.Y.2d 19, 332 N.E.2d 290, 89 LRRM 2871 (1975); *City of Buffalo v. New York State Pub. Employment Relations Bd.*, 37 N.Y.2d 19, 332 N.E.2d 290, 89 LRRM 2871 (1975).

[121] *Town of Arlington v. Board of Conciliation and Arbitration*, 352 N.E.2d 914, 93 LRRM 2494 (1976).

[122] *City of Spokane v. Spokane Police Guild*, 87 Wash.2d 457, 553 P.2d 1316, 93 LRRM 2373 (1976).

[123] *Dearborn Fire Fighters Local 412 v. City of Dearborn*, 394 Mich. 229, 231 N.W.2d 226, 90 LRRM 2002 (1975); *City of Detroit v. Detroit Police Officers Ass'n*, 294 N.W.2d 68, 105 LRRM 3083 (1980).

[124] *City of Sioux Falls v. Sioux Falls Fire Fighters Local 814*, 234 N.W.2d 535 (S. Dak. Sup. Ct. 1977).

[125] *Greeley Police Union v. City Council*, 553 P.2d 790, 93 LRRM 2382 (1976); *City of Aurora v. Aurora Fire Fighters Protective Ass'n*, 566 P.2d 1356, 96 LRRM 2252 (Colo. Sup. Ct. 1977).

[126] *Salt Lake City v. International Ass'n of Fire Fighters*, 563 P.2d 786, 95 LRRM 2383 (Utah Sup. Ct. 1977).

[127] *Maryland Classified Employees Ass'n v. Anderson*, 93 LRRM 2997 (Md. Cir. Ct. 1976).

[128] *Fire Fighters Local 1186 v. City of Vallejo*, 12 Cal. 3d 608, 526 P.2d 971, 87 LRRM 2453 (1974).

[129] *Bagley v. City of Manhattan Beach*, 18 Cal. 3d 22, 553 P.2d 1140, 93 LRRM 2435 (1976).

Dearborn Fire Fighters Union v. City of Dearborn.[130] The Michigan statute mandates interest arbitration for police and fire department labor disputes; like most interest-arbitration statutes, it provides for a tripartite arbitration panel composed of one delegate named by each of the parties and a neutral member to be selected by those two. In the event they fail to agree upon selection, then the neutral is appointed by the chair of the Michigan Employment Relations Commission (MERC). The city of Dearborn, at impasse in negotiations with both police and fire department employees, declined to designate a delegate to the arbitration panels, and so the MERC chairman appointed the neutral for each panel, and the two-person panels proceeded to consider and issue awards. The city refused to comply with the awards, and litigation ensued.

The four justices sitting on the case each wrote a separate opinion. Justice Levin, joined by Chief Justice Kavanagh, summarized their argument for the unconstitutionality of the statute as follows:

> The arbitrator/chairman of the panel is entrusted with the authority to decide major questions of public policy concerning the conditions of public employment, the levels and standards of public services and the allocation of public revenues. Those questions are legislative and political, not judicial or quasi-judicial. The act is structured to insulate the arbitrator/chairman's decision from review in the political process. It is not intended that he be, nor is he in fact, accountable within the political process for his decision. This is not consonant with the constitutional exercise of political power in a representative democracy.[131]

Although the statute contained both standards to guide the exercise of the delegated power and procedural safeguards such as provisions for hearing, statement of findings and conclusions, and judicial review—characteristics generally considered adequate to validate the delegation of legislative authority—Justices Levin and Kavanagh considered the statute defective because it allocated such authority to private persons who did not have continuing responsibility for its exercise, ad hoc and "expendable" arbitrators who were not accountable in any meaningful way. The fact that the neutral arbitrator in the *Dearborn* case happened to have been appointed by the MERC chairman did not make the arbitrator any more accountable in their view, since the statute called for the MERC chairman to appoint an "impartial" person rather than someone who would seek to render a decision "which will have the support of the electorate or of their elected representatives." The availability of judicial review of the

---

[130] *Supra* note 123.
[131] *Id.* at 2003.

award, while possibly assuring against the arbitrary exercise of discretionary power, could not in their opinion fulfill the constitutional need for "review and accountability through the political process":

> It is the unique method of appointment, requiring independent decision makers without accountability to a governmental appointing authority, and the unique dispersal of decision-making power among numerous *ad hoc* decision makers, only temporarily in office, precluding assessment of responsibility for the consequences of their decisions on the level of public resources and the cost of government, which renders invalid this particular delegation of legislative power.[132]

The two remaining judges, whose combined opinions carried the day, agreed upon the conclusion in the particular case, but for quite different reasons. Justice Coleman adopted a pragmatic approach, reasoning that some system of interest arbitration was clearly called for if strikes were to be avoided and that the choice between ad hoc arbitrators and a permanent arbitration board involved a balancing process that should be left to the legislature. Justice Williams, in a lengthier and more analytical opinion, argued that whether a person to whom power is delegated should be characterized as "a private person, or better . . . a non-politically accountable person" should depend, not upon the label the person wears, but upon the "underlying reality"; and this reality, in the justice's opinion, should be viewed from the perspective of four criteria:

> First, how close by appointment is the person or agency to the elective process and political accountability? . . .
> Second, how clearly restricted is the operation of the person or agency by standards written into the law and the possibility of judicial review?
> Third, how much is the person or agency held to public accountability by the length of tenure on and the public exposure of the job?
> Fourth, . . . the importance and breadth of power granted.[133]

Applying these criteria, Justice Williams found:

1. While selection of the arbitration panels is outside the ordinary political processes, appointment of the neutral by the MERC chairman "guarantees high public visibility and accountability."

2. While operators operate independently, the statute's specific and ample standards plus provision for judicial review assure a "high degree of legal accountability."

3. While tenure of arbitrators is brief, arbitrators are motivated both by professional dedication and concern for continuing acceptability; they operate in the focus of "intense public and media scrutiny"; and they are subject to legal standards, all evidencing a "considerable degree of personal accountability."

---

[132] *Id.* at 2013.
[133] *Id.* at 2029.

4. While the job is important, the areas of discretion are "suitably delimited."

Justice Williams concluded that while selection of the arbitrator by the parties would pose serious constitutional doubt, so long as the MERC chairman appointed the arbitrator, the statute was constitutional.

The accountability issue was later treated in detail in the June 1980 decision of the Michigan supreme court in *City of Detroit v. Detroit Police Officers Association.*[134] In that decision, the majority held that the 1976 amendments changing the method of appointing the neutral chairperson of the arbitration panel removed any doubts regarding the panel's accountability that existed after the *Dearborn* decision. Chairpersons are now appointed by the MERC from its permanent arbitration panel. The court reasoned that persons whose names appear on that panel will be concerned with the long-term impact of their decisions because they must be residents of Michigan and because they remain on the panel until removed by MERC. They serve in many disputes, so they are not "hit-and-run arbitrators," the court stated. As appointees of MERC the arbitrators acquire a kind of political accountability they would not have if appointed by the partisan members of the arbitration panel. The majority believed that the "tension" between independence and political accountability was balanced by the act's standards to guide the panel, by the public atmosphere in which the act operates, and by the act's provision for judicial review. In deciding whether the arbitration panel's award was supported by the evidence, the court tackled the extremely important matter of the weight to be given to each of the eight factors which the law requires the arbitration panel to consider. The court held that the legislature mandated the arbitration panel to weigh the factors and that such was a constitutional delegation of authority. Listing the factors may be necessary before courts will uphold the constitutionality of interest-arbitration statutes, but the weight to be given each factor must be determined on a case-by-case basis before a decision can be reached.

Determinations of Arbitrability

While in some states the scope of issues subject to arbitration appears to be narrower than the scope of issues over which bargaining is required, in most states the two scopes are congruent so that determining what issues are required to be arbitrated poses essentially the same task as determining the area of mandatory negotiation. Question has arisen, however, concerning the proper role of the court in passing upon disputed issues of arbitrability in advance of arbitration.

---

[134] *Supra* note 123.

In *Fire Fighters Local 1186 v. City of Vallejo*,[135] the California supreme court was confronted with issues of arbitrability under a city-charter provision calling for arbitration in disputes over "wages, hours and working conditions," but excluding "the merits, necessity, or organization of any service or activity provided by law." The union sought to require arbitration of four issues labeled "Reduction of Personnel," "Vacancies and Promotions," "Schedule of Hours," and "Constant Manning Procedures." The scope of the actual disputes underlying certain of these labels, however, was somewhat obscure. With respect to "Constant Manning Procedures," for example, the union's initial proposal sought to add one engine company and to increase the personnel assigned to existing engine companies, but it subsequently modified its position to require only the maintenance of the existing manning schedule for the term of the agreement. The city contended that even the revised proposal fell within the exclusionary clause as a matter relating to "merits, necessity or organization." The court, applying federal precedent, decided that the manning schedule would be subject to arbitral determination insofar as it may be found to relate to questions of employee work load and safety, and that was a factual finding that should appropriately be made by the arbitrator in the first instance. However, the court declared,

> the parties themselves, or the arbitrators, in the ongoing process of arbitration, might suggest alternative solutions for the manpower problem that might remove or transform the issue. Indeed, the union in the instant case has already abandoned one position and assumed another. These are the elements and considerations that argue against preliminary court rulings that would dam up the stream of arbitration by premature limitations upon the process, thwarting its potential destination of the resolution of the issues.[136]

Similar reasoning with respect to the "Reduction of Personnel" and "Vacancies and Promotions" issues, and a finding that the "Schedule of Hours" issue was clearly arbitrable, led the court to order arbitration with respect to all the issues in dispute.

The court's opinion seems to call for deferral to the arbitrator where determination of arbitrability depends upon disputed factual questions or, in any event, where the identification of the issue is ambiguous and susceptible to change in the dynamic process of negotiation of which interest arbitration is viewed as an integral part. The result is a presumption of arbitrability somewhat analogous to that which exists in most states for grievance arbitration, but with this significant difference: whereas in the case of grievance arbitration the

---

[135] *Supra* note 128.
[136] *Id.* at 2459–2460.

question of arbitrability depends upon the agreement of the parties and normally does not involve any question of public policy, in the case of interest arbitration the question is one of statutory (or charter) interpretation and involves limitations presumably imposed by the legislature or the electorate for policy reasons. The court made clear that after arbitration, judicial review would be available to determine whether the arbitrators had exceeded their powers.

Judicial Review

A considerable body of law is developing with respect to the proper scope of judicial review once an interest award has been rendered.[137] Some statutes purport to preclude review entirely, or to limit review to the grounds available for setting aside an award rendered pursuant to consensual agreement, such as partiality, fraud, or acts in excess of the arbitrator's authority.[138] Interest arbitration arguably requires a broader scope of review, however, at least to the extent that the applicable statute specifies procedures or criteria for decision, since these presumably reflect public-policy judgments that are binding upon the arbitrator.

In New York, the court of appeals held in a case involving interest arbitration for hospitals in the private sector that the legislature's attempt to limit review to the narrow grounds applicable in ordinary arbitration cases was unconstitutional, and that due process requires review at least to the extent of determining whether the arbitrator acted in a manner that was "arbitrary or capricious."[139] The New York court has since applied similar reasoning and the same standard to arbitration for firefighters and police under the Taylor Law, which contains no provision for review.[140] In Pennsylvania, where the interest-arbitration statute provides that the tribunal's determination is to be final and binding without appeal, the supreme court has held that due process considerations require review on questions of jurisdiction, the regularity of procedures, whether the arbitrator exceeded his powers, and questions of constitutional dimension.[141]

Predictably, courts are reluctant to overturn arbitral judgments as to the propriety of particular wage or benefit adjustments. In New York, for example, the appellate division of the supreme court vacated

---

[137] See, generally, Note, *Compulsory Arbitration: The Scope of Judicial Review,* 51 St. John's L. Rev. 604 (1977).

[138] *Id.* at 619ff

[139] *Mt. St. Mary's Hosp. v. Catherwood,* 26 N.Y.2d 493, 260 N.E.2d 508, 74 LRRM 2897 (1970).

[140] *Caso v. Coffey,* 41 N.Y.2d 153, 359 N.E.2d 683, 93 LRRM 2133 (1976) (rejection review based on "substantial evidence"). See Arvid Anderson, Eleanor Sovern MacDonald, and John F. O'Reilly, *Impasse Resolution in Public Sector Collective Bargaining—An Examination of Compulsory Interest Arbitration in New York,* 51 St. John's L. Rev. 453, 468 (1977).

[141] *City of Washington v. Police Dep't,* 436 Pa. 168, 259 A.2d 437, 72 LRRM 2847 (1969).

an award granting salary increases to police in the city of Buffalo on the ground that the city was without means to fund the increase, but the court of appeals reversed this decision. The police association, the court noted, had introduced evidence showing that Buffalo police officers' wages and working conditions compared unfavorably with those of police in other areas and that cost-of-living increases had diminished their real wages. While the city pointed to a variety of fiscal problems, there were differences between the parties as to available revenues, and in any event the arbitration panel took fiscal problems into account, weighing them against the factors of entitlement relied upon by the police. That, the court said, was all the statute required when it called for consideration of ability to pay as well as other criteria:

> On this record, it cannot be said that the panel's award was irrational. It was within its province, under the applicable statute, not only to judge the facts but choose the priorities to which, in its judgment, some matters were entitled to over others. It had a right to balance this ability of the City to pay against the interests of the public and the PBA members. . . .[142]

The statute, the court declared, "vests broad authority in the arbitration panel to determine municipal fiscal priorities within existing revenues."[143]

Courts have, however, overturned or modified awards which order a result found to be in substantive conflict with some constitutional or statutory provision, as for example where the award changed the retirement age in a pension plan without benefit of the actuarial study mandated by statute,[144] or imposed a contractual obligation beyond the one-year limit permitted by statute,[145] or awarded overtime pay for work in excess of 320 hours in an eight-week period without taking into account a statutory prohibition against requiring an officer to work more than 8 hours in a 24-hour period,[146] or established impermissible limitations upon the school district's authority to terminate probationary teachers.[147] In this respect, the nature of judicial review for interest awards is the same as for grievance arbitration.

The right of legislative bodies to countermand "final and binding" arbitration decisions was tested in two states, and the legislative bodies prevailed in each case. In Minnesota the issue went to the state supreme court, while in Hawaii it remained with the Public Employment Relations Board.

---

[142] *City of Buffalo v. Rinaldo*, 95 LRRM 2776, 2778 (N.Y. App. 1977).
[143] *Id.*
[144] *In re Montgomery Township Police Dep't*, 91 LRRM 2815 (Pa. Comm. Ct. 1976).
[145] *City of E. Providence v. Fire Fighters Local 850*, 94 LRRM 2571 (R.I. Sup. Ct. 1976).
[146] *Conley v. Joyce, supra* note 60.
[147] *Superintending Schools Comm. v. Town of Winslow*, 93 LRRM 2398 (Me. Sup. Jud. Ct. 1976).

A 1977 salary dispute between the Minnesota Education Association and the Minnesota Community College System was submitted to binding arbitration. The parties then signed a contract incorporating the award. The legislature subsequently funded less than the contractual increases, based on increases granted to state university faculty. The education association filed suit at the district-court level where the state argued that both the contract and the law require wage agreements to be approved by the legislature. The lower court accepted the union's right to bring suit and the validity of an unfair labor practice charge in not complying with the arbitration award.[148] The court distinguished between voluntary bilateral agreements and arbitrated settlements, and ordered $1,500,000 in back pay.

On appeal, the Minnesota supreme court reversed the district court, determining that the "intent of the legislature was to reserve the right to review all salary provisions of contracts with state employees, however arrived at."[149]

In the Hawaii case a final-offer arbitration panel in 1979 awarded firefighters a cost-of-living adjustment along with specified wage increases over two years. Taking issue with the COLA provision, the governor failed to submit the award to the legislature as required for funding, and the legislature adjourned without acting to fund the "binding" award.

The firefighters voted to strike and also filed unfair labor practice charges with the Hawaii Public Employment Relations Board. The board, in a split decision, dismissed the charges, finding that the "final and binding" arbitration provisions really meant "advisory arbitration." The parties reached a settlement with more money and no COLA in the second year, thereby averting a strike, but leaving the statutory issue of finality unsettled.[150]

Federal Government

Final and binding arbitration is still used sparingly in federal-sector negotiations; in 1982 the Federal Service Impasses Panel (FSIP) used it in less than 7 percent of the 800 sets of negotiations that took place.[151] It is one part of FSIP's "arsenal of weapons," which includes fact-finding (with or without recommendations), conventional arbitration, final-offer arbitration, "med-arb," written submissions in lieu of a hearing, and sending the parties to an outside arbitrator. The statute permits the parties to use an agreed-upon binding-arbitration pro-

---

[148] *Minnesota Educ. Ass'n v. State of Minnesota*, 804 GERR 17, 101 LRRM 3068 (1979).

[149] *Minnesota Educ. Ass'n v. State of Minnesota*, 282 N.W.2d 915, 103 LRRM 2195 (1979).

[150] *Hawaii Fire Fighters Ass'n Local 1463 and George R. Ariyoshi*, 2 HPERB No. 111 at 286 (1979).

[151] Haughton, *supra* note 87, at 55–56.

cedure if the Panel approves the procedure.[152] If an outside binding-arbitration procedure is used by the parties, an exception to the arbitrator's award may be filed with the FLRA by either party. The Authority applies the same criteria to determine if the award is deficient, namely, (1) it is contrary to any law, rule, or regulation, or (2) other grounds similar to those applied by federal courts in private-sector labor-management relations.

The limited recourse to the Panel so far is explained by the parties' lack of familiarity with the Panel and their lack of sophistication in bargaining, the limited scope of bargaining permitted by the law, and the broad management-rights clause. These limitations serve to reduce the stakes at the bargaining table and promote possibility of voluntary settlements.[153]

Decisions of the Panel are not subject to direct judicial review,[154] nor are they subject to direct review by the FLRA.[155] The exclusive means of obtaining review by the FLRA requires the dissatisfied party to refuse to comply with the Panel decision, accept an unfair labor practice charge, and litigate the matter before the FLRA, whose decisions are reviewable.

Concluding Observations

State and Local Government

At the outset of the statutory era of public-sector labor relations, state courts were almost uniformly receptive to grievance arbitration on the basis of principles analogous to those developed in the private sector. Then in the mid-1970s their enthusiasm appeared to wane and decisions reflected a marked reticence toward arbitral determination of certain issues, particularly where it is unclear whether the parties contemplated arbitration of the issue, where the issue calls for the exercise of discretion not governed by explicit contractual criteria, or where the award is seen as having potential impact upon the level or quality of service or upon financial resources. This reticence is displayed through rulings that limit the power of the parties to agree to arbitrate certain matters, interpret narrowly the scope of matters that the parties have agreed to arbitrate, and subject the arbitral award to a

---

[152] Howard G. Gamser, *Statement*, in Federal Labor-Management Relations and Impasse Procedures, Hearings, House Subcommittee on Investigations of the Committee on Post Office and Civil Service, Serial No. 97-50 (Washington: 1983), 67.

[153] Beverly K. Schaffer, *Negotiation Impasses: The Road to Resolution*, J. Air L. & Com. (June 1982), 294.

[154] *Nevada Nat'l Guard v. United States*, No. 79-7235 (9th Cir., Dec. 14, 1980).

[155] *California Nat'l Guard*, 2 FLRA No. 21 (1979).

broader judicial review than is permitted normally in labor arbitration cases. Subsequent and recent decisions present a mixed picture, reflecting in part a retreat to the basic private-sector principles.

Why this trend has developed is unclear. Perhaps courts were responding to the tides of public opinion in the mid-1970s that ran against public-employee bargaining. Perhaps also the decisions reflected a belief that public entities, often inexperienced in labor relations matters, required some degree of insulation from their own errors of judgment in bargaining.[156] As these groups become more practiced, they may come to rely on traditional methods without resort to judicial avenues of dispute resolution. More fundamentally, perhaps the trend is indicative of a reaction to an earlier premise of identity between public- and private-sector labor relations that has proved difficult to maintain. Importation of private-sector labor relations principles to the public sector is a little like the transplantation of American labor law to Japan after World War II. There was nothing wrong with American labor law, but it was not immediately adaptable to the semifeudal system of labor relations upon which it was sought to be imposed. While the differences between the private and public sectors are not that great, differences do exist and may take some time to overcome. Indeed, in some respects the gap may never be entirely closed.

But if courts are reacting to the realization of the differences between the public and private sectors, their reaction in the case of grievance arbitration is excessive. While all of the premises stated in the Trilogy cases for judicial deferral may not be present in the public sector,[157] certain crucial premises are as follows: that effective labor relations requires a dynamic view of the collective-bargaining agreement as establishing a process for resolution of a wide range of disputes, and that arbitration can be an effective method for resolving disputes quickly, peacefully, and in a manner most likely to be in accord with the ongoing relationship of the parties. The presumption-of-arbitrability and the finality-of-awards principles for grievance arbitration would appear to be principles as justifiable for grievance arbitration in the public sector as they are in the private.

---

[156] Prior to its recent decision imposing strict standards in determining arbitration, the New York court of appeals often chided public entities concerning their obligation to protect their interest in bargaining. E.g., *City School Dist. v. Poughkeepsie Pub. School Teachers, supra* note 47.

[157] Some of the premises stated in the Trilogy cases (e.g., presumed special competence of the arbitrator) are subject to question even in the private sector. See Feller, *Arbitration: The Days of Its Glory Are Numbered*, 2 Indus. Rel. L.J. 97, 98 (1977).

The grievance-arbitration experience in the federal sector is unique because it is used to review or police compliance with controlling laws, rules, and regulations by the agency and employees. This broader scope invites judicial review and increases the number of forums where relief may be sought. Arbitrators must make a full examination of relevant external authority and require advocates to present evidence and argument regarding the effect of relevant statutes and regulations upon potential remedy orders. Unfortunately, the shadow of judicial review may influence the nature of arbitral opinions and decisions.

The experience so far shows little likelihood of transfer of private-sector principles and practices. How much uniformity with the Merit Systems Protection Board will be sought by the Federal Labor Relations Authority is not yet evident, so how much consistency will be achieved is still unclear. Finally, given the limitations on the scope of bargaining, it does not appear likely that the practice of interest arbitration will develop in the federal sector as it has at the state and local government level.

Interest arbitration poses more difficult policy questions, the full extent of which have just recently begun to be recognized by the courts. As opinions in the Michigan case suggest, and as the 1975 New York case involving the City of Buffalo demonstrates, the interest arbitrator may be called upon to make decisions that go far beyond the scope of expertise which we normally attribute to a labor arbitrator, and which may intrude heavily upon areas of public policy normally considered appropriate for resolution by persons or tribunals more directly accountable to the political process. While courts early in the process tended to validate interest-arbitration statutes rather mechanically or formalistically, without significant analysis, more recent opinions reflect concern, sometimes resulting in a negative constitutional response.

The concern expressed by the courts is justified, but on the whole their analysis seems to miss the mark. Their complaint that the arbitrator's award lacks the support of the electorate (or their elected representatives) overlooks the source of the dispute which arbitration is intended to resolve. It is precisely because the interests of the voters as expressed by their elected officials clash in certain respects with the interests of the employees as expressed by their union that there exists a controversy to submit to arbitration.

The hypothesis underlying interest arbitration is that public employees, or at least certain public employees, should not be permitted to strike and that arbitration is necessary to protect their interests against the unilateral imposition of terms by the governing body.

Clearly, therefore, one would not expect the arbitrator to be politically responsive to the local electorate which, ultimately, constitutes the employer. Moreover, at least under the systems of interest arbitration so far utilized in this country, the arbitrator's role is not primarily to implement some neutral state policy as to what the wages and working conditions of local employees ought to be, but rather to function as an extension of the negotiating process in such a manner as to accommodate the interests of the public employer with the interests of the employees involved in the dispute. For this reason, the suggestion of Justice Williams in the Michigan case that the problem of delegation is solved so long as the neutral is appointed by a state official seems artificial. It is likely that the MERC chairman, recognizing the accommodative function of arbitration, would appoint arbitrators from the same list the parties would use in selecting them, and would consult with the parties in the process of doing so.

Similarly, Justice Levin's proposal that the problem can be solved by the establishment of a permanent state panel of arbitrators creates tension with the underlying premise that arbitrators are not expected necessarily to produce decisions acceptable to the appointing authority or to administer some overriding public policy with respect to the content of agreements; their political independence is an essential ingredient of the interest-arbitration process as presently conceived. In these respects, interest arbitration is sui generis, and not amenable to the sort of constitutional analysis normally brought to bear upon the delegation of power to administrative agencies.

Perhaps a better analysis would be as follows: interest arbitration, for the reasons already mentioned, does pose problems in terms of the values of the democratic process. It appears, however, to be the only workable and just alternative to the strike as a means of accommodating the interests of public employers and their employees. Whether on balance it is preferable to a policy of permitting public employees to strike is debatable. That debate, however, is one that should be carried on in the legislature rather than in the courts.

If the legislature opts for interest arbitration, its option is not irrevocable; process values are ultimately preserved by the ability of the legislature to change its mind. Meanwhile, an acceptable degree of protection against arbitrary or unjust results can be secured through clear description of the issues subject to arbitration, and through standards and safeguards subject to judicial review.

Interest arbitration is still at an experimental stage in this country, and courts should not terminate the experiment before the results can be determined.

CHAPTER 8

Public-Sector Labor Relations in Canada

SHIRLEY B. GOLDENBERG*

The public sector is an area in which Canadian labor relations have broken new ground, in contrast to the private sector where they have developed in large measure on the pattern established in the United States. Collective bargaining in the public sector, broadly defined, has a considerably longer history in Canada than in the United States and is currently more varied and more extensive. Given the unique relationship between private-sector labor relations in these two countries and their generally similar philosophy of collective bargaining, in spite of some recent differences,[1] lessons learned from Canadian policy initiatives and bargaining experience in the public sector may be equally relevant in the United States. In both countries, the problem of reconciling the rights that have so long been available to workers in the private sector with the particular characteristics and constraints of public employment is a serious issue on the labor relations scene.

Evolution and Present Status of Collective Bargaining in the Public Sector

In contrast with the United States, where some of the most bitter recognition disputes have involved employees of municipal governments, municipal workers in Canada apart from police and firefighters[2]

---

*McGill University.
[1] The most striking difference is in the position of the organized labor movement. In contrast with the dramatic decline in union membership in the United States in recent years, the rate of union organization in Canada has remained relatively stable. Approximately 40 percent of paid nonagricultural workers in Canada were members of trade unions at the beginning of 1985, the latest date for which figures are available. Directory of Labour Organizations in Canada (Ottawa: Minister of Supply and Services Canada, 1985).
[2] Police and firefighters acquired the right to strike under the British Columbia Labour Code (1973), with voluntary arbitration as an alternative at the discretion of the bargaining agent. However, this right was seriously limited by the Essential Services Disputes Act (1977), which now gives the Cabinet discretion to stop a strike involving police and firefighters. Four other

have, from the outset, enjoyed the same rights under general provincial labor legislation as employees in the private sector. This has meant, among other things, a virtually blanket right to strike over impasses in contract negotiations. Recognition strikes by municipal employees are prohibited by law, as they are in the private sector, as a quid pro quo for formal certification procedures. Municipal workers in Canada have been exercising their bargaining rights for several decades. At the present time, almost all municipal corporations with a total of 50 or more employees and a population in excess of 10,000 have a collective-bargaining relationship with at least one unit of their employees.

Collective bargaining is also practiced on a very wide scale by workers in the health and education sectors. While some provinces deny or otherwise restrict the right to strike of teachers and/or hospital workers, others allow these occupational groups, like municipal employees, to bargain under general labor legislation without any particular limitations.[3] Workers performing a broad range of other

provinces (Saskatchewan, Manitoba, Nova Scotia, and New Brunswick) give members of the protective services a legal right to strike without any particular restrictions. The remaining provinces provide for arbitration as the ultimate procedure for dispute resolution.

Police have exercised their right to strike more often than have firefighters. There have been several lawful police strikes in Nova Scotia and New Brunswick, but only one in western Canada (Regina). Montreal police and firefighters have struck on a number of occasions, although they are prohibited from doing so by the Labour Code of Quebec. Each time they were forced back to work by emergency legislation.

[3] Teachers are specifically excluded from the coverage of labor legislation and, consequently, from the right to strike in Prince Edward Island, British Columbia, and Manitoba. The School Act of Prince Edward Island and the Public Schools Act of British Columbia and Manitoba provide for collective bargaining with binding arbitration of unresolved disputes. Although teachers in Saskatchewan are not excluded from the Trade Union Act, they bargain under different legislation, the Teacher Collective Bargaining Act, which provides for binding third-party determination if a negotiated agreement is not reached. Although teachers have had the right to strike under the Quebec Labour Code since 1965, teacher strikes in that province have almost invariably been ended by special legislation. Ontario teachers, who previously lacked the right to strike because of their exclusion from labor legislation, acquired this right in 1975 by virtue of a separate statute, the Education Relations Act. However, the government has power to terminate a strike if advised by the Education Relations Commission, appointed under the act to supervise negotiations, that the school year of a group of students is in jeopardy.

Hospital workers other than doctors are generally included in labor legislation, but are subject to particular restrictions in some of the provinces. While Section 163 of the Alberta Labour Act (1973) gave the government discretion to forbid a strike or lockout in the hospital sector, the act was amended in 1983 to prohibit all strikes by hospital employees and to impose binding arbitration of unresolved disputes. Section 44 of the Labour Relations Act of Prince Edward Island substitutes binding arbitration for the right to strike in disputes involving hospital workers. While Ontario and Newfoundland do not exclude hospital employees from their general labor legislation, both the Hospital Labour Disputes Arbitration Act (1965) in Ontario and the Hospital Employees Employment Act (1966–67) in Newfoundland prohibit strikes and lockouts in the hospital sector and provide for arbitration as a substitute. The British Columbia Labour Code permits a hospital union, like the police and firefighter unions, to elect arbitration at the point of impasse in negotiations as an alternative to exercising their right to strike. However, the Essential Services Disputes Act now qualifies the right to strike by hospital employees, as it does in the case of police and firefighters. The Quebec Labour Code, as enacted in 1964, gave hospital employees the right to strike, but qualified this right, under Article 99, by giving the government discretionary power to delay a strike for up to 80 days by appointing a board of inquiry into the dispute and taking an injunction to prevent or terminate a strike. Subsequent legislative initiatives to protect public services, whether under private or public ownership, as well as employees of many federal and provincial government agencies and boards, have also enjoyed full collective bargaining rights under general labor legislation in Canada as long as such legislation has existed. Thus workers in sectors such as railways, airlines, longshoring, and broadcasting, at the federal level and those employed by hydroelectric commissions, liquor boards, and so on, at the provincial level enjoy and use the bargaining rights that are available to employees in the private sector, including the right to strike.

Although the right to bargain collectively, including the right to strike, has long been taken for granted in Canada by employees of municipal governments as well as by workers in other areas of public-service employment, the federal government and all but one of the provinces were still resisting the extension of this right to their own employees as late as the middle 1960s. The exception was the province of Saskatchewan where a socialist government included its own employees in the coverage of its original labor legislation, the Trade Union Act, as far back as 1944.

The historical resistance to collective bargaining for federal and provincial civil servants was based largely on the principle of the sovereignty of the state. As in the United States, collective bargaining and its corollary, the strike, were considered imcompatible with this principle, with the obligation of public service inherent in government employment, and with the essential and monopoly nature of many of the services involved. Moreover, with the relative security of civil service employment to compensate for lagging wage levels, and a tradition of patronage appointments in certain areas of public employment, civil servants themselves were not inclined to assert the rights that workers were demanding and achieving in other sectors of the economy. The practice of unilateral decision making by the government as employer, except in the case of municipal government, was not seriously challenged before the early 1960s. Since that time, however, civil servants have discarded their traditional docility in favor of collective action.

Spurred on by successfully negotiated settlements in the private sector, and in certain areas of public employment, civil servants in a number of jurisdictions began to challenge the government as employer to grant them the right to bargain collectively that the law guaranteed to other workers and imposed on other employers. In 1965

---

essential services in the event of a strike by hospital employees have proved ineffective in practice. But the most recent amendments to the Quebec Labour Code (Bill 37, 1985), requiring between 80 and 90 percent of the employees to remain on the job in the event of a strike (the percent depending on the category of hospital affected) has effectively removed the right to strike in this sector.

the government of Quebec took a lead over the other provinces and the federal government by granting broad collective-bargaining rights, including the right to strike, to employees in the civil service.[4] The federal government followed suit in 1967,[5] New Brunswick in 1968,[6] and British Columbia in 1973.[7] Public-service bargaining legislation introduced in Newfoundland in 1970 ostensibly included the right to strike but, until it was amended in 1973, imposed far greater restrictions on the exercise of this right than did other jurisdictions.[8] The remaining provinces, beginning with Ontario as early as 1963, have also granted their employees bargaining rights but deny them the legal right to strike.[9]

While collective bargaining came latest to employees at the senior levels of government, it is at this level that its coverage now is most complete. Virtually all federal and provincial government employees eligible to bargain are covered by collective agreements.[10] The replacement in all jurisdictions of informal consultative relationships by genuine bilateral negotiations between associations of public servants and the governments that employ them, and the affiliation of the majority of these associations with the mainstream labor movement, was one of the most interesting developments in labor relations in Canada in the 1960s and 1970s. Among other things, it had an important impact on the rate of unionization and on the composition of the organized labor movement.

---

[4] Civil Service Act, S.Q. 1965, c. 14, now the Public Service Act, S.Q. 1983, c. 55.
[5] Public Service Staff Relations Act, S.C. 1967, c. 72.
[6] Public Service Labour Relations Act, S.N.B. 1968, c. 88.
[7] Public Service Labour Relations Act, S.B.C. 1973, c. 144.
[8] Public Service (Collective Bargaining) Act, S. Nfld. 1970, c. 85, as amended 1973. The 1970 act was never proclaimed. The labor movement had protested that broad discretionary powers given to the government to make regulations with respect to application of the act could, in practice, nullify the rights, in particular the right to strike, that the act purported to give.
[9] The Public Service Act of Ontario, as amended in 1963 (S.O. 1962–63, c. 118), and with some slight revisions a few years later (S.O. 1966, c. 130), established a negotiating arrangement that fell far short of the bargaining model that already existed in Saskatchewan and that eventually would be adopted, with some modifications, in other jurisdictions, including Ontario. However, it constituted a major step forward at the time by providing for binding arbitration of unresolved disputes which were previously settled unilaterally by the employer. The Crown Employees Collective Bargaining Act a decade later (S.O. 1972, c. 67) replaced the earlier negotiating arrangement with a formal collective bargaining regime but retained the strike prohibition. The Alberta Public Service Act was amended in 1971 (S.A. 1971, c. 89) to provide for arbitration of unresolved disputes which, as in Ontario, were previously settled unilaterally by the employer. The Alberta Public Service Employee Relations Act, enacted in 1977 (S.A. 1977, c. 40, now R.S.A. 1980, c. P-33) made no change in this respect. Arbitration was introduced in Manitoba in 1969 by amendments to the Civil Service Act (S.M. 1969, c. 3) and in Prince Edward Island in 1972, the latter case being by special Regulations (O.C. No. 958/72) under the existing Civil Service Act (S.P.E.I. 1962, c. 5) rather than by new legislation. Nova Scotia government employees were given limited bargaining rights by the Joint Council Act (R.S.N.S. 1967, c. 35), since replaced by the Civil Service Collective Bargaining Act (S.N.S. 1978, c. 3). The latter act and subsequent amendments have retained arbitration as the ultimate procedure for dispute resolution.
[10] See the section below, The Bargaining Unit, for a discussion of professional and managerial exclusions.

Public-Sector Unions

The upsurge in union membership in Canada in the decade after the mid-1960s, following a period of relative stagnation if not actual decline, may be attributed almost entirely to the adoption of collective bargaining by government employees at the federal and provincial levels. This increase may also be partially ascribed to the considerable increase in collective bargaining in the health and education sectors, particularly by nurses and teachers.[11] These developments have brought into the ranks of organized labor large numbers of white-collar and professional workers, groups that have been traditionally resistant to unionization in the private sector. They have also been a major factor in reducing the numerical dominance of U.S.-based unions, long a feature of the Canadian labor movement.[12] The vast majority of workers in these new areas of collective bargaining were organized in exclusively Canadian unions, as was already the case for municipal employees.

Teachers, Hospital Workers, and Municipal Employees

Apart from a few rather interesting exceptions in the province of Quebec,[13] Canadian teachers and nurses have resisted joining the mainstream labor movement. Some bargain through independent associations of employee members, organizationally separate from, but with close links to, their respective professional associations. In a number of provinces, particularly where negotiations are conducted on a centralized basis, the professional association itself may be the certified bargaining agent.

Unlike nurses and teachers, and police and firefighters whose right to union affiliation is generally restricted by law, most municipal employees who bargain collectively are in unions affiliated with the mainstream labor movement. The majority are members of the Canadian Union of Public Employees (CUPE), an affiliate of the Canadian Labour Congress (CLC), the main exception being some municipal workers in the province of Quebec who have been organized by the Confederation of National Trade Unions (CNTU), a provincially based

---

[11] Union membership as a percentage of total paid nonagricultural workers rose from 30.7 in 1966 to 38.2 in 1977. Labour Canada, Labour Organizations in Canada (Ottawa: 1977).

[12] Unions with headquarters in the United States accounted for 49 percent of total Canadian union membership in 1977, compared with 70.8 percent in 1966. By 1985, even before the breakaway of the Canadian automobile workers from the United Automobile Workers, membership in international unions had dropped to 39.4 percent of total union membership in Canada. Labour Canada, supra note 11, for 1966 and 1977, and Directory, supra note 1, for 1985.

[13] The largest group of teachers in Quebec, the Centrale des enseignants du Québec (CEQ), considers itself an integral part of the trade union movement and has, on several occasions, formed a common front with other unions in public-sector negotiations. One group of nurses was originally affiliated with the Confederation of National Trade Unions (CNTU), a militant Quebec-based labor federation, but now is independent.

labor federation. CUPE is the largest union in Canada. Its membership, apart from municipal employees, is drawn largely, though not exclusively, from nonprofessional hospital workers and employees of public utilities. It is the certified bargaining agent for one unit of provincial government employees in New Brunswick and for one unit in Nova Scotia. It also represents a police unit in Nova Scotia.

Provincial Government Employees

Unions of government employees in most provinces have evolved from associations of civil servants that were in existence prior to the bargaining legislation. A number of these associations, almost all of which were previously unaffiliated, applied for and received local charters from the CLC by the early 1970s, which reflected a growing feeling of affinity by government employees with the mainstream labor movement. Following a resolution adopted at its 1974 convention in response to protests by CUPE, which claimed jurisdiction over government employees, the CLC called a moratorium on future direct affiliations of provincial associations and laid down as a condition of continuing affiliation with the CLC the formation, within two years, of a national union grouping the provincial associations. The National Union of Provincial Government Employees (NUPGE) was formed in 1976 by grouping five provincial government employee unions already affiliated with the CLC—those of British Columbia, Alberta, Saskatchewan, Manitoba, and Prince Edward Island. At this time it was the fifth largest union in Canada. With the affiliation of the Newfoundland and Nova Scotia associations in 1977 and 1978, respectively, and the Ontario association in 1980, NUPGE became the second largest union in Canada, representing government employees in all provinces but New Brunswick and Quebec. Associations of government employees in both these provinces have remained outside the ambit of NUPGE. However, the fact that government employees in Quebec did not affiliate with NUPGE and have had no affiliation with the CLC has not isolated them from the mainstream labor movement. Government employee associations in Quebec affiliated with the CNTU in 1965, which was as soon as the law permitted it. They broke ties with that central labor organization in 1972 as a result of ideological differences. [14] In February 1986 NUPGE signed an agreement with the union representing professional employees of the government of Quebec, giving it "associate status" within NUPGE. [15] While this may

---

[14] The break came following a general strike of public and parapublic employees with which the civil servants were not in accord.

[15] While the Syndicat de professionnelles et professionnels du gouvernement du Québec (SPGQ) did not become an actual NUPGE component, the "associate status" agreement gives the SPGQ full participation in NUPGE committees, observer status at national executive board meetings and NUPGE conventions, and access to a variety of NUPGE services, including research, publications, and educational programs.

be considered a breakthrough that gives NUPGE a "window on Quebec," there is no sign of any relationship developing between NUPGE and the union representing the majority of Quebec government employees.[16]

It was not easy for this "union of unions" to strike a balance between autonomy for its components and the establishment of a strong and effective national organization. Each of the provincial associations has retained its own identity and executive and exercises full autonomy with respect to collective bargaining and contract administration. The national union plays a significant role in providing bargaining information and coordinating bargaining strategy. A Collective Bargaining Advisory Committee, made up of the chief negotiators of the provincial components, meets at the national headquarters on a regular basis to share information and discuss strategy. NUPGE has coordinated national support in case of strikes by its components, assists components in making representations with respect to particular legislative proposals, and has on a number of occasions taken complaints to the International Labour Organisation on behalf of an affiliate. NUPGE also considers itself as a voice for the components at the CLC and with the federal government.

Federal Government Employees

The majority of federal government employees belong to the Public Service Alliance of Canada (PSAC) which was formed in 1968 by the merger of two associations of federal civil servants. PSAC is composed of a central administration and 17 relatively autonomous components organized on departmental lines. The central administration has full responsibility for collective bargaining because of a statutory requirement that national bargaining units be organized on an occupational group basis, which, in most cases, cuts across departmental lines. However, the components make a considerable contribution to the preparation and conduct of negotiations and are also largely responsible for the administration of the collective bargaining agreements at the departmental level, with greater or less assistance, as may be required, from regional representatives of PSAC. The membership of PSAC is confined to public employees, most of whom are employed directly by the federal government.[17] Like CUPE and NUPGE, the Alliance is affiliated with the CLC. It is now the third largest union in Canada.

---

[16] Le Syndicat des fonctionnaires provinciaux du Québec (SFPQ) represents all blue-collar and nonprofessional white-collar government employees in Quebec.

[17] Over 173,000 of the Alliance's 175,000 members are employed in government departments; the rest are distributed among "separate employers" that bargain under the Public Service Staff Relations Act. See *infra* note 38.

None of the other bargaining agents in the federal public service is nearly as large as the Alliance.[18] The next largest is the Professional Institute of the Public Service of Canada (PIPSC).[19] Unlike the Alliance, it is not affiliated with a central labor organization. PIPSC has a long history of organization as a professional association and represents a majority of the employees with professional training or other academic degrees. PIPSC is organized on an occupational basis that cuts across departmental lines, each occupational group being virtually identical in composition to the certified bargaining units it represents. The membership of PIPSC, like that of the Alliance, is confined to public employees, the majority of whom are employed directly by the federal government.

Of the 76 bargaining units of federal government employees, 39 are represented by PSAC, 26 by PIPSC. Most of the other bargaining agents do not represent more than a single bargaining unit. Their bargaining strength, however, has depended less on the numbers they represent than on the nature of the work performed. The air traffic control and electronics units, for example, though relatively small in numbers, have frequently exercised greater clout in negotiations than some of the larger bargaining units.

Bargaining rights for employees in the federal public service are held, with very few exceptions, by Canadian-based unions. The exceptions are in the electronics unit, the printing-operations unit, the ship-repair units, and some very small units of the Staff of the Non-Public Funds, Canadian Forces,[20] which are represented by locals of international unions.

----

[18] Of approximately 215,600 employees bargaining under the Public Service Staff Relations Act at the beginning of 1986, 207,880 were employed in the central administration (i.e., departments of government) and were represented as follows: Public Service Alliance of Canada, 173,374; Professional Institute of the Public Service of Canada, 18,471; International Brotherhood of Electrical Workers, Local 228, 2,970; Economists', Sociologists', and Statisticians' Association, 2,477; Canadian Air Traffic Control Association, 2,049; Canadian Merchant Service Guild, 1,474; Federal Government Dockyards Trades and Labour Council East, 1,431; Federal Government Dockyards Trades and Labour Council (Esquimalt, B.C.), 797; Canadian Association of Professional Radio Operators, 1,218; Canadian Union of Professional and Technical Employees, 1,133; Professional Association of Foreign Service Officers, 928; Council of Graphic Arts Unions of the Public Service of Canada, 1,049; Aircraft Operations Group Association, 509. Of approximately 7,725 employees of "separate employers," about half are represented by PSAC and PIPSC together. The rest are distributed, in small numbers, among a number of other bargaining agents, none of whom represents employees in the central administration. Among employees of the National Film Board, 326 are represented by Le Syndicat général du cinéma et de la télévision, an affiliate of the CNTU. Nineteenth Annual Report, Public Service Staff Relations Board (Ottawa: 1985–1986).

[19] The Canadian Union of Postal Workers (CUPW) and the Letter Carriers' Union of Canada (LCUC) were the next largest bargaining agents until 1981. The enactment of the Canada Post Corporation Act in October of that year transformed the post office into a Crown corporation, thereby removing post office labor relations from the jurisdiction of the PSSRA. Post office labor relations are now governed by provisions of the Canada Labour Code.

[20] Civilian employees at army bases operating canteens and other services.

It is clear that the vast majority of workers in government employment and other areas of public service, such as health and education, with which this chapter will be concerned, have been organized by all-Canadian unions operating virtually exclusively in the public sector. On the other hand, in the case of railways, airlines, broadcasting, and even some municipal transportation commissions, a variety of national and international unions may be found. These sectors have long-established bargaining relationships in Canada, as in the United States, and while they might be included under a very broad definition of public service, they are beyond the scope of this study.

Management Organization in the Public Sector

Only those aspects of management organization in the public sector that are relevant to the bargaining function and the administration of collective agreements will be considered here. The problems of management organization with respect to collective bargaining vary between levels of government and are becoming particularly complex in the health and education sectors.

The Municipal Sector

Even at the municipal level, where collective bargaining is a long-established practice, the question of who will represent the municipal corporation as an employer in the conduct of negotiations remains a problem. A variety of practices may be found.

Negotiations in smaller municipalities are frequently conducted by a committee of the municipal council, assisted by a senior staff official such as the municipal clerk or treasurer. While this practice may reflect the reluctance of some small municipal councils to delegate authority, sometimes these councils simply do not have a senior officer with sufficient skills in negotiation to assume the bargaining function. The members of municipal councils themselves, more often than not, are lacking in negotiating skills, and the uncertainty of elected office may contribute to discontinuity on the management team; these situations have not enhanced the effectiveness of negotiations on the employer side. While medium to large municipalities usually have a personnel department and frequently assign the responsibility for negotiations to the personnel director, the effectiveness of this practice depends, as it does at other levels of government, on the mandate that is given to the negotiator. When a union has reason to believe that the employer spokesperson lacks authority to make a final decision, particularly on monetary matters, it is likely to resort to pressure on elected officials to conclude an agreement rather than continuing serious negotiations at the bargaining table. The implications for good-faith bargaining are self-evident.

Where municipalities have more elaborate administrative structures involving a chief executive officer or agency—a city manager, city administrator, or board of commissioners, for example—such officers usually have responsibility for the negotiations, even though they may delegate the actual bargaining to a personnel director or labor relations officer. The negotiator in such cases usually has a fairly clear mandate from the chief executive officer who will have obtained a mandate from the municipal council as to the limits within which to negotiate.

There have been some initiatives toward coordinating bargaining efforts of municipal managements in large metropolitan areas to avoid whipsawing tactics by unions. The Vancouver Municipal Labour Relations Bureau provides an interesting example of bargaining on a single-city basis. The Bureau conducts negotiations for the city of Vancouver and several surrounding municipalities which finance it and give it a mandate to bargain on their behalf.

While there is no single pattern of employer organization for collective bargaining at the municipal level, at least one common management problem may be identified. As creatures of their respective provincial legislatures, municipalities in Canada, large or small, operate on a limited tax base, although the services they are required to provide are steadily increasing. When negotiations reach a point where a choice must be made between a wage increase that a municipality feels unable to pay and a work stoppage that would have adverse effects on the public, the locus of decision making may shift to the provincial government which will ultimately finance all or part of the settlement.

Hospitals and Schools

Local hospital managements and boards of school trustees in most jurisdictions are still legally autonomous units for the purpose of labor negotiations. In practice, however, there has been a noticeable trend toward centralization of bargaining structures. Hospital and school boards, more often than not, delegate responsibility for negotiations to their respective regional or provincial associations. Responsibility for administration of the resulting agreements is retained in such cases by the individual hospitals and school boards, most of which have personnel or industrial relations divisions for this purpose.

Whatever the level of bargaining—local, regional, or provincial—the central role of government in distributing funds to hospitals and schools has seriously undermined their autonomy as employers. Thus, while local hospitals and school boards by and large have retained their positions as legal employers, provincial governments are increasingly becoming the effective employer where financial matters are concerned. In most provinces, government influence over the results of negotiations is still exercised indirectly, by virtue of the financial constraints they place on hospital and school administrations. However, four provinces—New Brunswick, Quebec, Prince Edward Island, and Newfoundland—have put an end to the fiction of employer autonomy in labor negotiations in the health and education sectors by including government representatives, by statute, on the management side of the bargaining table at which a province-wide agreement must be negotiated, at least on the major financial issues. The role of the government representatives in these negotiations is best described by the maxim, "He who pays the piper calls the tune," but contract administration remains the responsibility of local hospitals and school boards.

The Senior Levels of Government

A major problem in management organization at senior levels of government, federal and provincial, has been the need to accommodate the functions of long-established administrative structures to the demands of a collective-bargaining regime which, it should be noted, has not replaced the traditional "merit system" as a basis for selection, promotion, etc., in government employment but coexists rather uneasily with it. Public service commissions, the centralized personnel agencies originally established to enforce the merit system, therefore prevail in all jurisdictions. In some provinces the adoption of collective bargaining has actually resulted in an accretion of the commissions' functions by the addition of the responsibility for negotiations. However, with decisions that were previously made unilaterally now subject to the provisions of negotiated agreements, public service commissions find their functions considerably reduced in jurisdictions that have assigned the responsibility for bargaining to another agency of government—a separate civil service department, a management committee of the Cabinet, or a staff relations division of the Treasury Board.[21]

Some provincial governments still seem to consider it most appropriate for the agency formally responsible for staffing, that is, the Public Service Commission, to be the employer spokesperson in nego-

---

[21] The collective-bargaining function is vested in the Public Service Commission or its chairperson in Alberta, Saskatchewan, and Nova Scotia. In Prince Edward Island, representatives of the Treasury Board and line departments sit with representatives of the Civil Service Commission on the government negotiating team. As in the federal jurisdiction, Quebec, New Brunswick, and Newfoundland designate the Treasury Board as employer for the purpose of collective bargaining. The negotiating function in British Columbia is assigned to the Government Employee Labour Relations Bureau, a division of the Treasury Board. A Management Committee of Cabinet is responsible for negotiations with government employees in Ontario and Manitoba. For a detailed discussion of the evolution of the personnel function in the provincial public service, see J.E. Hodgetts and O.P. Dwivedi, Provincial Governments as Employers (Montreal: McGill-Queen's University Press, 1974).

tiations. Others, as well as the federal government, see more logic in entrusting the negotiating function to an agency like the Treasury Board which is responsible for overall budgetary decisions, including those related to personnel policy. Experience has shown, however, that effective bargaining depends more on the mandate that is given to the government negotiators than on the agency to which the negotiations have been entrusted. The most successful bargaining experience has been in cases where governments have delegated to experienced negotiators sufficient authority, within previously defined limits, not only to make a deal, but, equally important, to inspire confidence in the union negotiators that they have the authority to do so. Where, however, government negotiating committees lack a precise mandate to effect a settlement, particularly on monetary issues, they may require constant recourse to the political authority for which they are simply the spokesperson. When it comes to the "crunch" in these situations, decisions are made at the Cabinet level rather than at the bargaining table. This particular problem has emerged where governments have established a bargaining relationship with their own employees before defining a clear-cut policy on the issues that are likely to arise; therefore, it should be amenable to solution through experience. On only rare occasions have the politicians themselves come to the bargaining table. Although this is generally considered to be an undesirable practice, it has happened in at least two provinces, Quebec and British Columbia, in recent rounds of negotiations.

Finally, with respect to management organization, the fact that the negotiating function, like the staffing function, is formally assigned in all jurisdictions to a central agency of government has not precluded some departmental input into the negotiating process. At the federal level in particular, suggestions from the various "user" departments play a significant role in the development of the employer bargaining position. Departmental input may also take the form of representation and active participation on the management negotiating team, although the Treasury Board negotiator is always the principal spokesperson. There is also considerable departmental influence in most jurisdictions over the hiring of personnel, subject to the monitoring authority of public service commissions. There is full departmental autonomy in the administration of collective agreements, including the handling of the grievance procedure.

The Determination of Compensation Through Collective Bargaining

The dollar cost of remuneration in the public service, largely borne by the taxpayer, strikes an emotional chord in the public mind. This, in turn, has raised important policy questions, as has the potential pattern-setting effect of highly visible settlements in the public sector. Some settlements have been atypical. However, when made for high-profile groups, often after the threat or use of a strike, these settlements have reinforced a popular perception that wage increases in the public sector have been out of control and that collective bargaining has been the cause, particularly when accompanied by the right to strike.

Trends in Compensation: Public- and Private-Sector Comparisons

Although it is difficult, if not impossible, to separate the impact of collective bargaining from other variables in the wage-determination process, there is some evidence that it was important in raising wages in the public sector, particularly in the initial stages when catch-up with the unionized private sector was a factor. The experience was similar in the private sector when collective bargaining was first adopted. One study shows, for example, that wage increases in first collective agreements in the public sector were approximately 4 percent higher than corresponding increases in renewed agreements in all years from 1968 to 1975, when the first peacetime wage control legislation was enacted.[22] It also shows that the largest negotiated increases in that period were effected in the lower wage categories. Since the distribution of workers on the basis of wages tends to be pyramidal, the lower wage category would include the majority of newly unionized workers. The union argument that the public employer should set an example in compensation was probably most convincing at this level where the potential for exploitation had been greatest.

None of the serious comparative research on wage developments in the private and public sectors bears out the popular perception, shared by the policy makers in a number of jurisdictions, that overall negotiated increases in the public sector have significantly outpaced those in the private sector either in the decade prior to the imposition of wage and price controls in 1975 (the period on which most of the research has been based) or in the years that have followed.[23] As seen

---

[22] Jean-Michel Cousineau and Robert Lacroix, Wage Determination in Major Collective Agreements in the Private and Public Sectors (Ottawa: Economic Council of Canada, 1977). The federal government introduced a three-year program of mandatory wage and price controls in October 1975 (Anti-Inflation Act, S.C. 1974–75–76, c. 75). The program, popularly known as the AIB, after the Anti-Inflation Board that was mainly responsible for administering it, was introduced in large measure because of concern that wage settlements were rising at an unacceptable rate, particularly in the public sector. For wage guidelines under the Anti-Inflation Act, see infra note 29.

[23] The argument, largely undocumented, that negotiated increases in the public sector, particularly at the provincial and local levels, had created an inflationary pattern for the rest of the economy, stimulated an interest in objective research on comparative compensation trends. See, for example, Allan M. Maslove and Gene Swimmer, Wage Controls in Canada, 1975–1978 (Montreal: Institute for Research on Public Policy, 1980); Douglas A.L. Auld, L. Christofides, R. Swidinsky, and D. Wilton, The Determinants of Negotiated Wage Settlements in Canada

in Tables 1 and 2, in some years, base-rate increases in settlements in the public sector, broadly defined, have been marginally lower than in the private sector.[24]

Table 1 shows that the rate of increase for the public sector as a whole was highest in 1975, with base-rate increases approximately 4 percent higher than in the private sector. However, a careful exam-

TABLE 1

Average Annual Base Rate Increases Negotiated in
New Settlements in Canada, 1967–1985[a]

| Year | Private | Components Within the Public Sector | | | | |
		Public	Federal	Provincial	Local	Education, Health and Welfare
1967	7.8	9.6	n.a.	8.5	12.5	9.4
1968	8.1	7.6	7.0	8.3	7.0	10.0
1969	8.6	7.2	6.3	8.5	11.4	6.9
1970	8.6	8.4	8.4	7.2	9.9	8.9
1971	8.0	7.6	6.6	7.9	9.4	8.4
1972	9.2	7.2	8.9	8.0	7.6	6.5
1973	10.1	10.6	12.3	10.1	9.9	10.2
1974	14.4	14.8	11.3	15.1	12.7	17.8
1975	14.4	18.6	14.3	20.0	17.8	21.3
1976	9.3	10.7	11.9	11.1	10.4	10.2
1977	7.3	7.9	9.6	7.8	7.8	6.7
1978	6.9	6.9	6.8	7.0	6.7	6.4
1979	8.2	7.8	7.4	6.8	8.4	8.0
1980	9.9	7.8	10.1	10.3	10.1	5.6
1981	11.5	12.7	11.9	13.4	12.8	13.2
1982	8.2	10.2	8.3	11.7	11.1	11.0
1983	4.6	4.0	5.4	4.0	5.6	2.7
1984	2.5	3.9	5.0	5.1	3.1	3.1
1985	2.5	3.6	3.2	3.7	4.6	3.2

Sources: 1967–1978, from Morley Gunderson, *Public Sector Compensation in Canada and the U.S.*, 19 Indus. Rel. 266 (Fall 1980). 1979–1985, courtesy of Pradeep Kumar, Industrial Relations Centre, Queen's University. Primary source for all data, Labour Canada.
   [a] From collective agreements covering 500 or more employees, excluding construction.

(1966–1975): A Microeconometric Analysis, a study prepared for the Anti-Inflation Board (Ottawa: Minister of Supply and Services Canada, 1979); Morley Gunderson, *Public-Private Wage and Non-Wage Differentials in Canada: Some Calculations from Published Tabulations*, in Public Employment and Compensation in Canada; Myths and Realities, Vol. 1 of the series on Public-Sector Employment in Canada, ed. David K. Foot (Toronto: Butterworth, for the Institute for Research on Public Policy, 1978), 127; Government of Canada, Agenda for Cooperation (Ottawa: 1977); and Cousineau and Lacroix, *supra* note 22.
   [24] The figures in Table 1 represent the only available comparative data for the whole time period under consideration. They do not include the effect of COLA clauses. Table 2 shows the *effective* average base-rate increase, i.e., including COLA. Calculation of effective average base-rate increase including COLA was introduced by Labour Canada in 1978.

TABLE 2

Average Annual Effective Wage Adjustments in New Settlements
in Canada, Life of Contract, 1978–1985[a]

		Components Within the Public Sector				
Year	Private	Public	Federal	Provincial	Local	Education, Health and Welfare
1978	8.7	7.1	7.2	7.8	7.3	6.8
1979	10.8	9.2	8.4	9.1	9.4	8.2
1980	11.6	10.9	11.3	11.3	10.8	10.8
1981	12.7	13.2	12.7	13.5	12.8	13.5
1982	9.5	10.4	8.3	11.1	11.9	11.4
1983	5.3	4.5	5.4	4.9	5.7	3.5
1984	3.2	3.9	5.0	5.2	3.4	3.1
1985	3.3	3.8	3.2	4.1	4.6	3.3

Source: From Labour Canada data, courtesy of Pradeep Kumar, Industrial Relations Centre, Queen's University.
[a] From collective agreements covering 500 or more employees, excluding construction. Effective wage adjustments include payments generated from cost-of-living clauses.

ination of the figures shows that whatever public-sector advantage there may have been was the result of exceptionally high settlements in the provincial and local public services and in the parapublic sector, which includes services in health, welfare, and education. The federal increase in 1975 was, in fact, significantly lower than the increase for the public sector as a whole and virtually identical to, or even slightly below, the increase in the private sector. The figures for 1975 in particular, but also for the overall period, illustrate the importance of distinguishing among the various components of the public sector in comparing compensation trends. One pattern that emerges when these distinctions are observed is the volatile nature of the settlements made at the provincial and local levels, including those for health, welfare, and education where there was a virtual explosion over a number of years in demand for these services. Even in those sectors, moreover, the figures show that unusually high settlements in some years have tended to be dissipated over time.

The effect of a work stoppage on the public would be less in most of the federal services than in many provincial or municipal services, and this fact might well have made it easier for the federal government to hold the line. However, caution must be exercised in interpreting the developments in base-wage rates on which most of the available comparative data have been calculated. For one thing, they fail to take account of the phenomenon of "classification creep" which has been an important factor, particularly in the larger public jurisdictions, in increasing individual incomes at the lower levels through promotion and reclassification, for example. This phenomenon, along with other aspects of wage drift such as overtime pay, can increase the total wage bill of the employer without showing a corresponding increase in base-wage rates. Base-rate trends also fail to take account of exceptional increases for particular groups and of differences in compensation trends both among and within occupational classifications. They completely ignore developments in professional and upper bargaining-unit salaries although, as will be discussed below, these developments raise some basic compensation issues. They also have a significant impact on the total wage bill of the employer.

Levels of Compensation: Private- and Public-Sector Comparisons

To avoid the distortions that can arise from confining comparisons to base-rate trends, some attempts have been made to compare actual wage levels for similar occupations in the private and public sectors. Such comparisons, of necessity, are limited to a specific point in time. The findings are interesting nonetheless, and they do confirm the importance of distinguishing between the various levels of government for purposes of comparison.

Studies comparing private- and public-sector wage and salary levels indicate only a small public-sector wage advantage, confined largely to entry level positions in the lower paying occupations and for female employees. While pay has tended to be higher in the public than in the private sector for workers holding unskilled, semiskilled, and skilled blue-collar jobs and for certain entry and intermediate level white-collar positions, for the bulk of the professional, managerial, and executive positions government pays less—often far less—than industry. Moreover, as base rate increases have leveled out over time, the public-sector wage advantage for some of the lower level occupations may have dissipated as well.[25] The limited evidence also suggests that the largest wage advantage, where it does exist, is at the provincial and local levels, with little or no advantage at the federal level. A study prepared for the Conference Board in Canada on the basis of mid-1978 statistics, and comparing job categories on a highly disaggregated level, concluded,

> With the exception of certain jobs at the entrance or junior levels, especially within the professional and technical categories, the maximum hourly rates of pay in the federal government are approximately the same as, and in some cases less than, the average pay rates in the private sector.[26]

---

[25] Morley Gunderson, *Public Sector Compensation in Canada and the U.S.*, 19 Indus. Rel. 257 (Fall 1980).

[26] Marc J. Daniel and William E.A. Robinson, Compensation in Canada: A Study of the Public and Private Sectors (Ottawa: The Conference Board in Canada, 1980), 24.

Compensation Restraint Programs

Neither levels of remuneration nor rates of increase in the federal public service had generally been out of line, either with the private sector or with other areas of public employment, and this fact was recognized by the federal government when it introduced the Public Sector Compensation Restraint Act (PSCRA)[27] in the summer of 1982 as part of its program to control inflation, which was then running at double-digit levels. In defending the proposed wage-restraint legislation in the course of the budget debate, the Honorable Donald J. Johnston, then president of the Treasury Board, noted that a major purpose of the legislation was to set a pattern of restraint for other sectors:

> [W]e do not like singling out government employees whose pay increases have not been noticeably out of line. . . . But leadership must begin at home. . . . It must begin here by those employees who are affected by our own legislation and by our own benefit programs. We are hoping to see the . . . objective which we are introducing adopted by other sectors, by other governments, by other businesses and by the private sector.[28]

The PSCRA extended, for a period ranging from two to three years, all collective agreements and arbitral awards in the federal public service. Negotiations over wages and all other aspects of compensation were, in effect, placed "on hold" for the period during which the act was applicable to any particular bargaining unit. Wage increases were limited to the ceilings the act imposed and other aspects of the compensation package were frozen at their existing levels. In addition to suspending negotiations for the renewal of agreements, the PSCRA rolled back any increases under existing agreements that exceeded the allowable limit. This provision was in contrast to the anti-inflation legislation of 1975, which had neither prohibited negotiations for new or renewed agreements nor interfered with the provisions of existing agreements.[29] In substitution for any increase in

---

[27] S.C. 1980–81–82, c. 122.

[28] House of Commons Debates, June 30, 1982, at 18965.

[29] The Anti-Inflation program of 1975 established a range of permissible increases for new contracts, i.e., contracts to be negotiated following the expiration of existing collective agreements. Wage guidelines under the act provided for a basic increase of 8, 6, and 4 percent in the first, second, and third years, respectively, added to a 2 percent "national productivity factor," plus or minus up to 2 percent depending on a group's recent wage settlements in relation to other groups. The formula could produce variations of up to 4 percent between groups, with permissible increases ranging between 8 and 12 percent, 6 and 10 percent, and 4 and 8 percent in the three years the program was to be in effect. The Anti-Inflation Act also provided an exemption for low-paid workers and a ceiling ($2,400) on increases for higher-paid workers. Negotiated increases were to be monitored by the Anti-Inflation Board (AIB) and could be rolled back if they exceeded the permissible limits.

In contrast with the PSCRA which applied to the federal public sector, broadly defined, and to corporations that bargained in conjunction with federal Crown corporations, the Anti-Inflation Act included in its coverage all private-sector firms employing over 500 workers (20 or over in the

wage rates called for under an existing collective agreement or arbitral award, the PSCRA established the following pattern of increases: in the first 12-month period, an increase of 6 percent, and for the second 12-month period, an increase of 5 percent. The first 12-month period was to be calculated as of the day immediately prior to the date on which the first increase in wage rates would, but for the PSCRA, have occurred under a collective agreement or other compensation plan in the absence of a collective agreement.[30] The act contained a transitional provision for increases of up to 9 percent for the 12-month period following the expiration of a collective agreement which had expired prior to the enactment of the PSCRA and had not yet been renegotiated.

The PSCRA had its intended pattern-setting effect in other areas of public employment and in the private sector as well. The federal restraint legislation, combined with a variety of provincial programs of wage restraint in a wide area of public services,[31] and coinciding with the worst economic recession since the 1930s, resulted in a dramatic decline in the rate of inflation and in the rate of wage increases which, in some cases, were replaced by wage freezes and even wage roll-backs. With the expiration of formal wage restraint legislation and/or other programs of public-sector wage control (with the exception of one province, British Columbia, where the wage-restraint legislation is extended indefinitely), and the gradual, though uneven, recovery from the recession, negotiated wage increases have again become a characteristic of collective agreements in both the private and public sectors. These increases, however, still reflect a psychology of restraint. Negotiated wage increases since the formal end of wage controls have, on the whole, done no more, and sometimes even less, than keep pace with the rate of inflation which stabilized, in this period, at around 4 percent.

---

construction industry) even if they would normally fall under provincial jurisdiction. The Anti-Inflation Act also contained an "opting-in provision" for provincial governments. All provinces but Saskatchewan and Quebec elected to opt into the program. Quebec established a provincial board, patterned on the AIB, to monitor wage increases for its public employees.

[30] The Public Sector Compensation Restraint Act applied to a wide range of public employees, many of whom are not engaged in collective bargaining. The term "compensation plan" was defined in subsection 2(1) of the PSCRA as "the provisions, however established, for the determination and administration of compensation [including] such provisions contained in collective agreements or arbitral awards or established bilaterally between an employer and an employee, unilaterally by an employer, or by or pursuant to any Act of Parliament."

[31] Seven of the 10 provinces (British Columbia, Alberta, Ontario, Quebec, Nova Scotia, Newfoundland, and Prince Edward Island) enacted wage restraint legislation. The details of the provincial legislation varied considerably, but all had the purpose—and the result—of keeping wage increases down. Three provinces (Saskatchewan, Manitoba, and New Brunswick) managed to keep negotiated increases within stated policy guidelines, short of legislated controls.

Compensation Issues in the Public Service

When senior levels of government extended bargaining rights to their own employees, they accepted, as a general principle, that wages and salaries in the public service should be fair in comparison with the private sector where they are determined largely through economic bargaining power. With the adoption of the Public Service Staff Relations Act (PSSRA) in 1967, fair comparison with the private sector as well as between the various parts of the federal public service was, by implication at least, written into the law. Section 68 of the Public Service Staff Relations Act specified the following criteria to guide arbitrators of interest disputes:

(a) the needs of the Public Service for qualified employees;
(b) the conditions of employment in similar occupations outside the Public Service, including such geographic, industrial or other variations as the Arbitration Tribunal may consider relevant;
(c) the need to maintain appropriate relationships in the conditions of employment as between different grade levels within an occupation and as between occupations in the Public Service;
(d) the need to establish terms and conditions of employment that are fair and reasonable in relation to the qualifications required, the work performed, the responsibility assumed and the nature of the services rendered; and,
(e) any other factor that to it appears to be relevant to the matter in dispute.

Similar provisions were written into the original public service bargaining statutes of a number of provinces.[32]

While the general principle of fair comparison was endorsed by public service unions and employers alike, no consensus was ever reached as to its interpretation and application. The unions, on the one hand, have maintained from the outset that a public employer should be the best employer, that its wage policy should be based on the highest rates being paid for comparable work in the private sector. Some even argue that governments should assume the lead. Most governments, on the other hand, have favored a comparison with the "average" outside employer, or even with those who pay slightly above the average. The federal government in particular has maintained that anything more would be inflationary, thus incompatible with its overriding responsibility for the economy as a whole.

Apart from the philosophical differences between the parties as to the appropriate level at which comparisons should be made, there have also been serious practical problems in applying the com-

---

[32] Recent proposals to amend the PSSRA, if enacted, would instruct arbitrators of interest disputes to take into account the government's economic and fiscal policies in making their awards. There have been statutory provisions to this effect in Alberta and British Columbia since 1983.

parability principle, especially where public services are monopoly services and thus lack private-sector comparisons. The air traffic controllers are a classic example. For while acceptable substitutes for direct comparisons may be worked out on the basis of the skills they require and the time it takes to acquire them, it has been more difficult to agree on the weight to assign to the particular responsibility involved in the job and the psychological tensions flowing from it.

Some public-service wage demands in Canada have been based on comparisons with the same or similar occupational groups in different parts of the country. Demands have frequently been made by police, firefighters, employees of municipal transportation commissions, teachers, and nurses, among others, for parity with their counterparts in cities and provinces where prevailing rates are higher. The employers, on the other hand, have pleaded differences in ability to pay.

The one area in which regional disparities have been ignored, by and large, is the federal public service, but this too has raised problems. While regional rates, based on various systems of pay zones, are negotiated for a few federal bargaining units,[33] most federal government employees are paid on the basis of a national wage, regardless of the location of their employment. As a result, wages in a federal bargaining unit may compare favorably with external rates in some parts of the country while placing employees at a relative disadvantage in others. The question of recognizing regional differences in national bargaining units still produces more controversy than consensus.

The difficulty of applying the comparability principle is self-evident where public-service occupations, by virtue of their monopoly character, are lacking in private-sector counterparts. But even where external comparisons exist, putting regional differences aside, other problems have arisen, as in the case of construction. While the unions argue on the basis of equal pay for equal work, public employers who give year-round employment have been reluctant to be bound by wage rates that have been negotiated in the private sector to compensate for the seasonal nature of the industry. The construction case is one illustration of the distortions that can result if comparisons are limited to wages and salaries and fail to take account of factors such as job security as well as benefits outside the collective agreement—medical, surgical, and superannuation plans, for example—that may be superior to those negotiated in the private sector. The experience with public-sector bargaining suggests that if comparison with the private sector is to be realistic as a guide to pay determination, it should

---

[33] General labor and trades, general services, ship repair and ships' crews, and some hospital and teaching units.

include, at the very least, all the elements in the compensation package that involve a measurable monetary value. This, in turn, raises another problem—the difficulty of securing information, particularly consistent information, on the cost of fringe benefits to private employers. At least part of that problem flows from the difficulty of computing the cost of benefits, some of which, such as holidays, vacations, and sick leave, must be evaluated in conjunction with age, seniority, and other relevant factors; others, like overtime, are difficult to measure in advance. A fully reliable measurement of total compensation still remains to be developed.

Although formal wage-restraint programs have come to an end in all jurisdictions but British Columbia, where they have been extended indefinitely, it would appear that wage determination in the public sector, for the time being at least, is being tied far more closely to government fiscal policy than to the principle of external comparisons. However, the question of internal relativities within the public service, some of which have become distorted in the course of bargaining, raises other compensation issues. At the federal level, for example, where the government's wage policy, before the enactment of the PSCRA, was based primarily on outside comparisons for both national and regional rates, developments in the outside labor market brought higher increases for some groups than for others; given also the differences in bargaining power among different occupational groups within the federal public service, developments in negotiated rates of pay were bound to differ among groups, to some extent at least. Even where percentage increases have been the same, the effect has been different for higher- and lower-paid occupational groups, resulting, in fact, in widening the gap between them. In some cases a system of percentage increases also enlarged disparities among various levels in a single bargaining unit.

Two basic compensation issues came to the fore in the public service a few years prior to the enactment of the PSCRA. One of them involved the declining position of managerial salaries relative to bargaining-unit wages, a matter which is also of some concern in the United States. The other stems from complaints under human rights legislation.

Concern over the declining position of managerial salaries relative to salaries at the upper level of bargaining units, as well as the declining position of the former group of salaries relative to those for comparable positions in the private sector, appears to have been one factor, at least, in the federal government's decision in 1980 to establish a separate management category. One of the objectives, clearly stated, in establishing this category was to ensure that managers would be paid more than their immediate subordinates who are subject to collective bargaining. To this end, the official compensation policy was to provide "for aggregate compensation comparability between the federal Public Service and the average salary provided by the private sector for all management levels up to and including the lowest level of the Executive group."[34]

It should be noted, however, that this policy was not intended to apply at the level of the more senior executives and deputy ministers whose salaries would continue to reflect "a policy of internal relativities, with appropriate salary differentials between successive executive and deputy minister salary ranges, with the upper limits of the ranges being set by the government."[35]

Human Rights Legislation: Impact on Compensation Policy

A relatively new compensation issue, but one with potentially far-reaching implications, arises out of the provisions for equal pay for work of equal value in the human rights legislation of a number of jurisdictions.[36] Adjustments under these provisions have, in general, been exempted from the provisions of public-sector wage restraint programs. In the federal public service in particular, where bargaining units have been certified on an occupational basis, most of the allegations of wage discrimination under the Canadian Human Rights Act have been made on behalf of bargaining units composed principally or entirely of women.[37]

Public-Sector Legislation

Although virtually all public employees in Canada now enjoy the right to bargain collectively, the extent of their bargaining rights and the conditions under which these rights are exercised vary considerably among jurisdictions. It goes almost without saying that the legal framework within which negotiations take place can have an important bearing on their outcome.

As has already been noted, workers in municipal employment and in the parapublic sector are covered, by and large, by the provisions of the general labor legislation that applies in the private sector, with

---

[34] News release, July 10, 1980.

[35] *Id.* For a discussion of the private-sector advantage in executive compensation, see Morley Gunderson, *The Public/Private Sector Compensation Controversy,* in Conflict or Compromise: The Future of Public Sector Industrial Relations, eds. Mark Thompson and Gene Swimmer (Montreal: Institute for Research on Public Policy, 1984), 25–26.

[36] The federal jurisdiction, Quebec, Manitoba, and Ontario have incorporated the principle of equal pay for work of equal value into the law. The statutory provision for equal pay for work of equal value is applicable to both the private and public sectors in the federal jurisdiction and in Quebec, but is applicable only to the public service in Manitoba and Ontario. The other jurisdictions provide for equal pay for equal work.

[37] For a discussion of some of these cases, see Jacob Finkelman and Shirley B. Goldenberg, Collective Bargaining in the Public Service: The Federal Experience in Canada, Vol. 1 (Montreal: Institute for Research on Public Policy, 1983), 387.

occasional restrictions on the right to strike. Collective bargaining by employees at senior levels of government, on the other hand, has most often been subject, from the outset, to special legislation. In seven of the ten provinces—New Brunswick, Newfoundland, Ontario, Prince Edward Island, British Columbia, Alberta, and Nova Scotia—labor relations for government employees are governed by special statutes, as is the case in the federal jurisdiction. British Columbia differs from the others, however, in that some provisions of its Labour Code also apply, provided that they are not in conflict with or inconsistent with any provision of the Public Service Labour Relations Act, in which case the provisions of the latter act would prevail.

In three provinces, Saskatchewan, Quebec, and Manitoba, the general labor legislation has been made applicable to public service. But while government employees have, from the outset, enjoyed full collective-bargaining rights under the general labor legislation of Saskatchewan, apart from a prohibition on negotiations on classification, these rights are circumscribed by special provisions in the case of Quebec and Manitoba as they are, by definition, in jurisdictions where separate public-service bargaining enactments exist. The Quebec Civil Service Act of 1965, which extended the provisions of the Labour Code to government employees, modified those provisions with respect to a number of matters—recognition procedures, the scope of negotiable items, and the procedure to be followed when bargaining breaks down before the right to strike may be exercised.

There has also been special legislation prior to practically every round of public-service bargaining in Quebec. This has had implications for the structure of bargaining, the timetable of negotiations, dispute resolution procedures, and so on. In addition, there have been several instances of back-to-work legislation when bargaining has broken down. The laws of exception in Quebec have, in some ways, been more significant than the standing legislation they have amended or temporarily replaced. Similarly in Manitoba, the rights of public employees under the Labour Relations Act, which was made applicable to them in 1972, are limited by other legislation. The fact that public servants are also subject to the provisions of the Civil Service Act, under which they were originally granted bargaining rights in 1965, places serious limitations on the rights they might otherwise enjoy under the Labour Relations Act. This is the case, among other matters, with respect to recognition procedures, scope of bargaining, and the procedures available for the resolution of disputes. For while the Labour Relations Act gives the right to strike to employees under its coverage, the Civil Service Act states clearly that unresolved negotiating disputes must be settled by arbitration. The Manitoba Government Employees' Association actually went to court for an interpretation of these conflicting provisions, but the judge refused to rule on a "hypothetical" case.

Statutory provisions affecting collective bargaining by government employees reflect a range of alternatives on a number of major policy issues, in particular the choice of a bargaining agent, the structure and composition of the bargaining unit, the scope of negotiable issues, and the settlement of interest disputes. There are also considerable differences between jurisdictions that have separate public-service labor legislation, both in the coverage of the legislation and in the machinery to implement its provisions.

Most provinces include the employees of at least some government agencies, such as provincially operated vocational schools and mental hospitals, in addition to the employees of government departments, under their public-service bargaining legislation. The federal Public Service Staff Relations Act (1967), like some of the provincial statutes, covers labor relations in a considerable number of government agencies and boards in addition to the civil service. These are listed in the act as "separate employers" for the purpose of collective bargaining.[38] Only four provinces, Manitoba, Saskatchewan, Quebec, and Nova Scotia, allow employees of all government agencies and boards to bargain under general labor legislation. Employees of Crown corporations, on the other hand, enjoy full collective-bargaining rights under labor legislation in all jurisdictions but Newfoundland. In that province, any Crown corporation may be placed under the Public Service Collective Bargaining Act (1973) at the discretion of the cabinet.

New Brunswick, Quebec, Newfoundland, and Prince Edward Island are the only provinces in which the government is directly involved in collective bargaining in the entire health and education sectors. By providing for government participation in collective bargaining in hospitals, schools, and community colleges as well as in the civil service and certain government agencies and boards, these provinces have, to a large extent, eliminated the demarcation line between the public service as traditionally defined and the so-called parapublic services as far as labor relations are concerned. While the statutes governing labor relations in the health and education sectors

---

[38] "Separate Employers" bargaining under the PSSRA include the Office of the Auditor General, the National Film Board, the National Research Council, the Social Sciences and Humanities Research Council, the Medical Research Council, the Northern Canada Power Commission, the Communications Security Establishment of the Department of National Defense, the Staff of the Non-Public Funds of Canadian Forces, and the Canadian Advisory Council on the Status of Women.

are different in each of the above-named provinces, the fact that the government is a party to the bargaining relationship in all cases and that negotiations are carried out on a province-wide basis has introduced an element of consistency, within each province, in the treatment of workers in these sectors.

The Bargaining Agent

When public-service bargaining legislation was introduced at the federal level and in the provinces of New Brunswick, Newfoundland, and British Columbia, government employees in those jurisdictions acquired the right to associate in unions of their choice, subject to regular certification procedures, as was already the case in Saskatchewan. (Certification is handled by separate boards at the federal level and in New Brunswick and by the Labour Relations Boards of the other provinces.) But when the governments of Alberta, Manitoba, Ontario, Prince Edward Island, and Nova Scotia granted bargaining rights to their employees, they gave statutory recognition to the associations of civil servants with which they already had informal consultative relationships. Quebec awarded statutory recognition to one group of civil servants and freedom of association to others. The Civil Service Act (1965) designated an existing association, Le Syndicat des fonctionnaires provinciaux du Québec, as bargaining agent for the largest group of civil servants (clerical and blue-collar employees) but left others, notably the professionals, relatively free to organize in unions of their choice.

The law was eventually amended in Manitoba, Ontario, Prince Edward Island, and Alberta to allow government employees to replace the Civil Service Association originally recognized by statute should it (the association) cease to represent the majority in the bargaining unit. While such amendments appear to be a concession to the principle of freedom of association, their practical application is virtually nil in view of a continuing provision in the laws of these provinces for service-wide bargaining units. The practical difficulty of displacing the bargaining agent of a service-wide bargaining unit is self-evident. The "no-raiding" provision under the CLC constitution (as in the AFL-CIO constitution) is an additional impediment to displacing the existing bargaining agents in these provinces, all of which are now components of NUPGE and, through it, are affiliated with the CLC.

The Bargaining Unit

The criteria for determining appropriate bargaining units and the mechanisms by which they are established vary among jurisdictions, as do the means and criteria for the selection of bargaining agents.

Although workers employed in a managerial or confidential capacity tend to be excluded, by definition, from collective bargaining, as in the private sector, there has been remarkably little controversy over these excluded categories in the public sector. The line for managerial exclusions has generally been drawn at a higher level in public employment, particularly government employment, than in private industry, with the result that employees performing a variety of supervisory functions are frequently included in public-service bargaining units. The federal and New Brunswick statutes grant privileges to supervisory employees that are absent in other jurisdictions. They make specific provision for supervisory employees to be included in public-service bargaining units, either with other workers in their occupational group or in separate units of their own; the latter option has frequently been selected.

There are more policy differences among jurisdictions with respect to the appropriate occupational composition of bargaining units than over the criteria for managerial exclusions. Saskatchewan alone has no statutory restrictions on the formation of bargaining units in the public service. At the federal level and in some of the provinces, the law requires bargaining units to be certified according to predetermined occupational classifications. A number of alternatives exist. For example, the Quebec Public Service Act requires only separate bargaining units for professional and nonprofessional employees, whereas both the New Brunswick and federal statutes establish five occupational classifications—scientific and professional, technical, administrative, administrative support, and operational (and separate groups within each classification)—for certification purposes. At the federal level this has resulted in the certification, on a national level, of 76 occupational bargaining units for which the Treasury Board is the employer. The British Columbia Act requires three bargaining units in the public service, one for licensed professionals, one for registered nurses, and one for all the others combined. However, British Columbia has also introduced an innovative system of two-tier bargaining within each of these broad classifications. The act provides for every collective agreement to consist of two or more parts: a master part covering the terms and conditions of employment that are common to all employees in the bargaining unit, and a subsidiary part for each occupational group within the unit, covering the terms and conditions that apply only to employees in the specific group. The act provides for the separate occupational groups within the three broad bargaining units to be determined by negotiation between the parties. No serious complications appear to have been encountered in the application of this provision.

A system of two-tier bargaining was worked out in 1986 between the federal Treasury Board and the Public Service Alliance of Canada. The parties have agreed to negotiate a master agreement, the terms of which will be applicable to all 39 units represented by the Alliance, along with separate agreements on a limited number of specific topics that will continue to be negotiated on a unit-by-unit basis. PSAC has given up the right to strike over negotiations for the master agreement but retains the right to strike over disagreement on issues to be negotiated by the individual bargaining units. This new arrangement for two-tier bargaining represents a marked departure from previous practice where collective agreements have been negotiated, by and large, on an individual bargaining-unit basis, according to the formal bargaining structure envisaged in the act and implicit in the certificates of certification. PIPSC has also worked out some new bargaining arrangements with the Treasury Board. However, in contrast with PSAC, which will be negotiating on a limited number of issues for all its bargaining units in the central administration, PIPSC has agreed to negotiate on all issues in dispute for a limited number of bargaining units—18 of the 26 units it represents.[39]

Where governments have granted bargaining rights to their own employees by formalizing a de facto negotiating arrangement with an existing association of public servants—in other words, by statutory recognition—the practice has usually been to entrench all-inclusive bargaining units, covering the entire public service, in the provisions of the law. Although negotiating structures have generally been established, in practice, to accommodate the interests of different occupational groups in the context of these service-wide units (with a master agreement for the overall bargaining unit and subsidiary agreements for different occupational groups), some groups, notably the professionals, have occasionally objected to being included in a unit against their will. In one province, Alberta, the legislation recognizes this objection by allowing the professionals in the public service to opt out of the general bargaining unit if a majority so desires; if they do so, however, they forfeit their bargaining rights, which is what has happened in practice. Two provinces exclude the members of certain professions from any bargaining rights. All licensed professionals in Ontario are excluded from the coverage of the public-service legislation and members of the legal profession are excluded in British Columbia.

---

[39] For a few previous experiments with multiunit bargaining and for a discussion of bargaining unit structure, see Finkelman and Goldenberg, *supra* note 37, at 283–285.

Limitations on the Scope of Bargaining

The legislation in all jurisdictions has permitted government employees to negotiate over wages and working conditions such as hours of work, holidays, vacations and other leave entitlements, and various aspects of occupational health and safety. However, full collective bargaining on the private-sector pattern is denied in government service, more often than not, by a considerable list of management rights. These management rights have continued to be exercised by Public Service Commissions, and are protected under public-service legislation and/or specifically excluded from bargaining by the applicable labor relations legislation.

While the permissible scope of public-service bargaining varies among jurisdictions, the personnel functions of recruitment and classification are excluded from negotiation as a general rule; certain personnel functions with implications for job security such as promotion, demotion, transfer, layoff, and recall are subject to negotiation in some jurisdictions and specifically excluded in others. The applicable bargaining legislation in a number of provinces has permitted the negotiation of provisions for the recognition of seniority with respect to some of these matters, all of which, however, are treated as exclusive management rights under the federal legislation. Provisions for the exercise of seniority rights for reasons other than vacation entitlement are conspicuous by their absence in federal agreements. As in the case of job security, any provisions for union membership security, that is, for union membership as a condition of employment, are precluded from the scope of bargaining in the federal jurisdiction where they would be considered contrary to the "merit principle" as a condition of employment and, consequently, contrary to the law. The applicable bargaining legislation in most of the provinces, on the other hand, either permits or even requires certain union security provisions, subject in some cases to exemption on grounds of religious objection. Items such as superannuation plans, which are covered by separate legislation, are generally excluded from collective bargaining in all jurisdictions. The PSSRA and a few provincial statutes specifically prohibit collective agreements from altering, eliminating, or introducing terms or conditions of employment which "would require or have the effect of requiring the enactment or amendment of any legislation . . . except for the purpose of appropriating moneys required for its implementation. . . ."[40]

---

[40] Public Service Staff Relations Act, S.C. 1967, c. 72, s. 56(2)(a).

When the legislation specifies a limited list of negotiable items such as wages, working conditions, and holidays, all other issues would appear to be taboo, by implication at least. In practice, however, some of the excluded issues have found their way to the bargaining table when unions have been strong enough to insist. In Quebec, for example, some issues such as job security which were "non-negotiable" under the original Civil Service Act (1965) were not only discussed at the bargaining table, but appeared as clauses in the first negotiated agreements. When the act was amended in 1969, it broadened the scope of negotiable issues for the purpose of future bargaining. In addition, the new legislation validated all items in collective agreements that had already been negotiated. This was particularly significant, as many of the provisions in those collective agreements went beyond the legally negotiable issues under the original Civil Service Act.

There have been cases where "non-negotiable" items have been handled separately, with an agreement taking the form of a "letter of understanding" between the parties rather than forming part of the collective agreement. However, a serious problem flowing from the limitations on bargainable issues is the fact that items not covered by a collective agreement are usually not subject to the grievance procedure. The fact that appeals on classification, and even on suspension and dismissal, other than dismissal for disciplinary reasons, are decided in many jurisdictions by a Public Service Commission which may have been responsible for the original decision, does little to inspire employee confidence in the objectivity of the system.

The federal jurisdiction and some of the provinces have retained the mechanism for consultation through joint councils[41] that preceded the adoption of formal collective bargaining as a means of dealing with nonnegotiable items. While most unions do not consider this an acceptable substitute for the right to bargain over the excluded issues with a view to including them in collective agreements, the mechanism can be useful for dealing with issues of service-wide interest that transcend individual bargaining units, even when such issues are negotiable under the law. In the federal jurisdiction, agreements on bargainable issues of service-wide interest reached in the National Joint Council are incorporated in collective agreements under a formula agreed to by the parties in December 1978. National Joint Council clauses are binding, as part of collective agreements, and are subject to the regular grievance procedure.

---

[41] Joint councils are consultative bodies made up of equal numbers of employer and employee representatives.

Provisions for Dispute Resolution

The most contentious issue facing the policy makers is the procedure to be followed when negotiations break down. This is the aspect of public-service labor relations in which the most significant differences still occur and in which considerable experimentation undoubtedly must take place before an acceptable formula is found. The subject still provokes more controversy than consensus.

Half the provinces in Canada (Nova Scotia, Prince Edward Island, Ontario, Manitoba, and Alberta) deny the right to strike to government employees under any circumstances. The others (Saskatchewan, Quebec, New Brunswick, Newfoundland, and British Columbia) as well as the federal government, allow them to strike after observing prescribed conciliation procedures and occasionally other delays. British Columbia is the only jurisdiction that grants a government employer the right to lock out as a counterpart to the unions' right to strike. This right has not been exercised in practice. In an extensive review of the federal legislation,[42] Jacob Finkelman, first chairman of the Public Service Staff Relations Board (PSSRB), recommended the addition of a lockout provision to the PSSRA. No action has been taken on that recommendation which was also supported by the Joint Parliamentary Committee that was subsequently appointed to consider the Finkelman Report.[43] While the question of a lockout by a government employer was virtually unthinkable when the early public-service legislation was being drafted, experience suggests that the right to a lockout, judiciously exercised, might expedite the settlement of certain disputes. The Finkelman recommendation was undoubtedly influenced by the experience of rotating strikes in the Post Office, which at the time was still subject to the Public Service Staff Relations Act. Those rotating strikes caused disruption of service to the public comparable with the effects of a general strike, at minimal financial loss to the membership.

The jurisdictions that grant the right to strike allow voluntary arbitration as an alternative, with the notable exception of Quebec where successive governments have consistently refused to permit a third-party decision on matters affecting the provincial budget. The federal situation is unique in that the employee bargaining agent must decide on the ultimate method of dispute resolution before serving

---

[42] Jacob Finkelman, Employer-Employee Relations in the Public Service of Canada (Ottawa: Information Canada, 1974). Supplementary Observations and Recommendations, 1975.

[43] Government of Canada, Report to Parliament of the Special Joint Committee on Employer-Employee Relations in the Public Service of Canada (Ottawa: Information Canada, 1976).

notice to bargain. Two options are available: referral of a dispute to a conciliation board with the ultimate right to strike, or binding arbitration. Whichever option is chosen, conciliation officers may be named to assist the parties to reach agreement prior to the ultimate step in the process. Once the process is specified, it is binding for the round of negotiations following such specification, but may be altered by the bargaining agent before any succeeding round of negotiations begins. It is interesting to note that the bargaining agent has the sole right of choice of method, and this choice cannot be vetoed by the employer.

Procedural Delays. Most provinces that permit strikes by government employees require specific conciliation procedures before a legal strike may take place, these procedures as a rule being virtually the same as those required in the private sector. Employees who choose the conciliation-strike option at the federal level only acquire the right to strike after an ad hoc conciliation board appointed by the chairperson of the PSSRB has tried and failed to effect a settlement. The New Brunswick statute, however, sets out a specific timetable for negotiation, conciliation, and other procedures before the right to strike may be exercised. Given the innovative nature of these procedures, it may be of interest to examine them in some detail.

There is a 45-day statutory limit on public-sector negotiations in New Brunswick unless the parties agree otherwise. The chairperson of the Public Service Labour Relations Board (PSLRB) *may* appoint a conciliator to assist in the negotiations if asked to do so by either of the parties. However, if it appears that the parties are not likely to reach agreement, the chair *must* appoint a conciliation board within 15 days of the statutory or agreed-upon time limit on the bargaining. A conciliation board consists of a member selected by each of the parties who, in turn, select a chairperson, as is the case at the federal level.

A conciliation board must submit a report to the chairperson of the PSLRB if it fails to effect a settlement, but if the parties do not settle following the report, they are still not free to strike. At this stage, either party may request the chairperson of the PSLRB to declare that a deadlock exists. If the chair is satisfied that the required conciliation procedures have been observed, the chairperson declares a deadlock and asks the parties if they are prepared to submit the dispute to arbitration. If either party rejects arbitration, the union is free to conduct a vote among its members "to determine whether they desire to take strike action." A majority vote in the affirmative gives the union the legal right to strike. Should a majority vote against a strike, the chairperson of the PSLRB orders the parties to resume negotiations for a period of 21 days after which, if agreement has not been reached, either party may again request the chairperson to declare that a deadlock exists. The process continues to repeat itself until the parties either reach a negotiated settlement, agree to submit to arbitration, or the bargaining agent secures a majority strike vote after which a legal work-stoppage may take place.

The New Brunswick statute made an interesting modification to the federal act on which it was patterned. For while the federal act requires the bargaining agent to choose between conciliation with the ultimate right to strike and binding arbitration prior to any negotiations, this decision may be taken at any time in New Brunswick and may actually be changed as negotiations proceed. There have been some occasions, in practice, where after the completion of conciliation-board procedures the union has indicated a willingness to accept binding arbitration. However, the employer has consistently refused to agree to arbitration.

New Brunswick differs from the other jurisdictions in which a strike is permitted by requiring a strike vote after all other legal delays have been exhausted. A noted Canadian expert on labor relations, H.D. Woods, made the following comment on this particular feature of the New Brunswick legislation:

> The compulsory strike-authorization vote in New Brunswick introduces an element of realism in that province's procedure. It is the membership of the unit of employees, acting after an impasse has been reached and at least one party has rejected arbitration, who really make the strike decision. On balance, the option of voting for a strike or for further negotiations can probably be expected to have a conservative effect since the voter will be concerned with an imminent strike situation, whereas in the federal procedure the decision has been taken when those who take it are protected by a very considerable period of time from the strike itself. Also in New Brunswick a vote against a strike does not carry with it a repudiation of the strike procedure, but only an instruction from the membership to their bargaining agent to have another try. If this leads to failure the membership may revise their vote after a relatively short period of time.[44]

Protection of Essential Services. Although the federal government and half the provinces have now accepted the strike as a legitimate element of the bargaining process, all of them except Saskatchewan have special provisions in their statutes for the protection of essential services. At the federal level and in New Brunswick, agreement must be reached, before conciliation procedures can be invoked, on a list of "designated employees" to remain on the job in the event of a legal strike; the public service labor relations boards in these jurisdictions make the final decision on designated employees in the absence of agreement by the parties. Newfoundland has a special

---

[44] H.D. Woods, Labour Policy in Canada, 2d ed. (Toronto: Macmillan of Canada, 1973), 315.

provision, which is absent in the other jurisdictions, whereby the right to strike is removed from an entire bargaining unit if 50 percent or more of its members are designated as performing essential services. This provision can be a serious practical constraint on the legal right to strike.

The legislation that granted public employees the right to strike in British Columbia (Public Service Labour Relations Act, 1973) made no provision with respect to essential services. However, the situation changed in 1977 with the enactment of the Essential Services Disputes Act. That act, with subsequent amendments to broaden its coverage, now empowers the government to intervene in a wide range of public services when, in its opinion, the interruption of these services or part of them would be a threat to life, health and safety, or the economy and welfare of the public, or might result in a substantial reduction in the delivery of educational services.[45] The act provides a choice of procedures in such cases: the government could direct the Labour Relations Board to designate the services that must be maintained for the protection of life, health, safety, etc.; it could order a suspension of a strike or lockout for a nonrenewable period of up to 90 days, with the possibility of an extension not exceeding 14 days; or it could appoint a special mediator to assist the parties in reaching a settlement.

A "Taft-Hartley" provision, designed to safeguard essential services, was included in the original legislation granting the right to strike to public employees in Quebec. Article 99 of the Labour Code allowed the Cabinet to seek a court injunction suspending the right to strike when, in its opinion, "a threatened or actual strike in a public service endanger[ed] public health or safety or interfere[d] with the education of a group of students."[46] The injunction would be for a nonrenewable 80-day period, following which the right to strike would again accrue to the union.

Article 99 was repealed in 1983. An amendment to the Labour Code in 1982 established a Council of Essential Services, with the function of ensuring the continuation of essential services in the event of a strike. This amendment covered a wide range of public services to which Article 99 originally applied, including the hospital and educa-

---

[45] The Essential Services Disputes Act (R.S.B.C. 1979, c. 113, as amended by S.B.C. 1984, c. 26, s. 66) applies to the government of British Columbia, various government agencies and Crown corporations, colleges, schools, and universities, health services and municipalities, and any employer of members of firefighter, police, and health care unions.

[46] The following categories of employers were listed as "public services," subject to Article 99, in the Quebec Labour Code: municipal and school corporations; hospitals, sanitoriums, and institutions for the mentally ill; orphanages; universities and colleges; telephone and telegraph companies and companies providing boat, tramway, bus, or railway transportation; enterprises for the production, transportation, distribution, or sale of gas, water, or electricity; garbage removal undertakings; and the services of the government of the province and all other agencies of the government except the Quebec Liquor Board.

tion sectors and government employment as such. The council is responsible for approving a list of services to be maintained before a legal strike may occur and for monitoring the adequacy of the services that are maintained during a strike, with a right to amend the list of services to be maintained should it judge this to be necessary. The council is to inform the government if, in its judgment, the agreed-upon services are insufficient or are not being adequately maintained to protect public health and safety, in which case the government, without further legislative action, could terminate or suspend the strike. Further amendments to the Labour Code in 1985 strengthened the powers of the council by giving orders issued by the council the force of a judgment of the superior court. While Article 99 of the Labour Code provided for the suspension of a strike in particular circumstances for all members of the bargaining unit concerned, the essential services provisions that replaced it are based on the principle, already established in some other jurisdictions, that only employees whose services are essential to public health and safety should be forbidden to go on strike, while other members of the same bargaining unit may be permitted to do so.[47]

Administration of the Procedures. In addition to differences between jurisdictions on the contentious issue of the right to strike and the measures to protect essential services, significant differences may also be noted in the administration of conciliation and arbitration procedures. In some provinces, the Minister of Labour still appoints the conciliation officer or board in public-service labor disputes as he does in the private sector. Public-service unions have complained of the conflict of interest inherent in a system in which the minister who administers the conciliation machinery is also a member of the government which is a party to the dispute. However, while all unions have recognized this problem, they have reacted differently to it in different jurisdictions. Much depends on the general climate of labor relations. For example, while the unions in Saskatchewan have drawn attention to the problem, they have never made a serious issue of it. In Quebec, on the other hand, unions have sometimes refused to use the conciliation machinery provided in the law on the ground that the minister, being a party to the dispute, could not be trusted in the appointment of a conciliator. The federal and New Brunswick statutes, from the outset, removed the decision on conciliation procedure from all political influence by entrusting this function to the chairperson of independent boards (the Public Service Staff Relations Board at the federal level and

---

[47] But see *supra* note 3 for the high proportion of employees now required to remain on the job in the event of a strike in the health and social affairs sector.

the Public Service Labour Relations Board in New Brunswick) that also handle certification procedures and administer the machinery for arbitration and adjudication of grievances. While British Columbia has not set up a separate public service board, the Labour Relations Board of that province performs the same functions.

In the case of arbitration, whether voluntary or compulsory, confidence in the impartiality of the system is of particular importance. This was recognized in the federal statute which was the first to provide for a permanent tribunal for interest arbitration.[48] The pattern has since been followed in other jurisdictions, like New Brunswick, where arbitration is voluntary and in others, like Ontario and Alberta, where it is compulsory.

Impasse Procedures in Practice

The experience in Canada, as in the United States, provides conclusive evidence that laws alone will not determine the course of events in labor relations. The variety of experience, particularly in jurisdictions that grant the right to strike, shows that the socioeconomic and political environment and the historical context of the bargaining relationship have at least as important an impact on the dynamics of dispute resolution as the impasse procedures provided in the law.

The Provincial Experience

The provinces that have extended the right to strike to government employees have not, on the whole, suffered the dire consequences that some observers predicted. In Saskatchewan, for example, there was never even a threat of a strike by government employees for 30 years after the law allowed it. There have been a few strikes in that province since 1973 over lagging negotiations, but these have usually involved small numbers of employees and have been of very short duration. The first strike by a substantial number of employees, on a service-wide basis, occurred in 1975. It lasted 11 days and was settled by mediation. In 1979 the government took court action to bring a month-long, service-wide strike to an end. Rotating strikes in

---

48 The PSSRA provided for the establishment of a permanent arbitration tribunal consisting of a neutral chairperson, appointed by the government for a five-year term, and two panels of "partisan" members appointed by the PSSRB to represent the interests of the parties. The act provided for the chairperson of the PSSRB to select one member from each panel to sit on the arbitration tribunal when a dispute was referred to arbitration. The arbitration tribunal has since been absorbed into the structure of the PSSRB by amendments to the PSSRA (S.C. 1974–75–76, c. 67). In respect of each dispute referred to arbitration, an arbitration board now consists of a member of the PSSRB, acting as chairperson, and two other members from the panels representative of the interests of the parties. As a result of this amendment there is now a pool of alternate chairpersons and several arbitration boards may sit concurrently. The amendment was recommended in the Finkelman Report as a means of expediting the arbitration procedure which had become seriously bogged down by delays.

1986 were ended by legislation. Saskatchewan was a so-called "have not" province until the middle 1970s after which the discovery of potash, uranium, and eventually oil altered the financial picture. The union strategy may well have changed with the increase in the employer's ability to pay. In New Brunswick, too, the experience has been generally peaceful under nearly two decades of permissive legislation, with only one brief strike by a small unit of government employees, the veterinarians, and one strike by school board employees who, like hospital employees, bargain with the government under the Public Service Labour Relations Act. Although government employees in Newfoundland have the right to strike, a recent strike in that province fell into the unlawful category because of the failure of the union to observe the requirement of the law for the maintenance of essential services.

The right to strike by public employees in British Columbia had existed for more than a decade before the first significant strike occurred over an impasse in negotiations. The British Columbia Government Employees Union struck for a period of seven weeks in the summer of 1982. However, there were only eight days in which all bargaining unit members were on strike. The strike was generally of a rotating character, with varying numbers of workers on strike at any one time; the union wished to bring public attention to the issues involved without unduly inconveniencing—or antagonizing—the public. Accordingly, the union made a point of ensuring that essential services were maintained and that essentiality was broadly defined. A few brief work-stoppages by government employees in British Columbia, beginning in 1980, involved small numbers of workers and were over matters such as backlog of grievances, reorganization procedures involving layoffs and transfers, legislation limiting indexing of pensions, and so on, rather than over negotiating disputes. As such, they were not within the law.[49] A two-week strike over the government's restraint program occurred in 1983. There were a couple of very short stoppages by small numbers of workers in 1986 during the course of negotiations for a new contract; the negotiations were eventually settled peacefully.

Of all the provinces that have extended the right to strike to public employees, the most frequent, and serious, strikes against the government have been in Quebec where a rash of public-sector strikes followed the granting of the right to strike. Such strikes have occurred repeatedly. However, the majority of these have been by workers in

---

[49] A lawful strike cannot occur in Canada under any circumstances other than a negotiation dispute. Disputes arising during the term of a collective agreement must be resolved by grievance arbitration.

the health and education sectors, who bargain directly with the government, rather than by government employees as such. Their strikes have invariably been ended by special legislation. It is generally agreed that the unstable climate of labor relations in Quebec, in both the private and public sectors, has had more to do with social and political factors than with the statutory right to strike.[50] When a "common front" of public-sector unions entered negotiations in 1972 when the slogan of *Cassez le système* (down with the system), they surely would not have felt inhibited by a legal prohibition on the strike, any more than they felt obliged to comply with a court injunction to maintain essential services when their leaders decided, for political reasons, that the injunction should be defied. When negotiations were politicized to the point that the legitimacy of the system itself was being questioned, it could hardly be expected that the law would be observed.

There have been brief work-stoppages on a few occasions, but no major strikes, by government employees in provinces where strikes are prohibited. In the occasional instances where they have occurred, they have been of very short duration; most often they have involved liquor board employees or employees in correctional institutions or medical services rather than government employees more narrowly defined. Work-stoppages by government employees in the provinces that prohibit them have most often been for reasons other than a breakdown in negotiations. Short stoppages have occurred, for example, over the question of bargaining unit structure, the imposition of wage controls, accumulated grievances, and so on. Strikes of this sort would be unlawful even in jurisdictions where the right to strike over negotiating disputes exists. There have been signs, however, that civil servants in some of these provinces could become increasingly militant, in both demands for changes in the law and occasional threats to defy it. Some threats of illegal action have not been without effect. In one province at least, an eleventh-hour settlement on the eve of a strike deadline, at a figure far higher than the government was originally prepared to consider, indicates that the threat of a strike that would have been illegal was nevertheless taken seriously by the

---

[50] For a discussion of public-sector negotiations in Quebec and the centralization and politicization of negotiations in that province, see Gérard Hébert, *Public Sector Bargaining in Quebec: A Case of Hypercentralization*, in Conflict or Compromise: The Future of Public Sector Industrial Relations, eds. Mark Thompson and Gene Swimmer (Montreal: Institute for Research on Public Policy, 1984). For the sociopolitical context of public-sector labor relations in Quebec and a detailed account of each round of bargaining from 1964 to 1982–1983, see Maurice Lemelin, *Les négociations collectives dans les secteurs public et parapublic* (Montreal: Les Editions Agence d'Arc, Inc., 1984).

employer. Conversely, ad hoc legislation to end or prevent particular strikes, notably in the province of Quebec, has contained such extreme penalties for noncompliance that it has had the desired effect.[51]

The Federal Experience

As in the case of the provinces where the right to strike exists, the experience under the Public Service Staff Relations Act has not borne out the forebodings of the early prophets of doom. Although the federal service has not been entirely free of strikes since the right to strike was granted, neither was it before. Legal strikes have been few and far between, and some of the strikes that have occurred have involved groups that previously struck illegally. Postal workers and air traffic controllers, for example, had struck in Canada when the law did not allow it, as they have done in the United States.

From the time the Public Service Staff Relations Act was enacted in 1967 up to the enactment of the Public Sector Compensation Restraint Act in 1982, when collective bargaining was put on hold, there had been 710 sets of negotiations between the government of Canada and units of its employees; in only 27, or less than 4 percent, did a strike occur. Only two of these strikes were ended by legislation. One, in 1977, involved air traffic controllers; the other, in 1978, was over a dispute in the Post Office. The other strikes were allowed to run their course—that is, until a negotiated settlement was reached. There have been no strikes by federal government employees since the resumption of negotiations following the expiration of the Public Sector Compensation Restraint Act.

The 27 strikes over negotiating disputes under the PSSRA have involved employees in only 14 bargaining units. Seven of the strikes were by employees in the Post Office, who are no longer covered by the Public Service Staff Relations Act. There have been a half-dozen other repeaters, among them the air traffic controllers, but none of the repeaters other than the postal unions has struck more than twice. The duration of the strikes has ranged from 1 day to 101 days, with the median point at 21 days. With few exceptions, the longer ones have

---

[51] This was the case in the most recent round of public-sector negotiations in Quebec. Bill 160, enacted in November 1986 to end an illegal strike of hospital workers and to head off plans for continuing rotating strikes in hospitals and health centers, imposed such heavy penalties that the unions had no choice but to retreat. Under the bill, which did not remove the health care workers' existing limited right to strike, illegal strikes would mean loss of wages and seniority for workers; two days' pay would be docked for each day on strike, and one year of seniority would be lost for each day or part of a day on an illegal strike. It would open unions to lawsuits by patients and would allow hospitals to hire nonunion workers to replace strikers. The bill provided for fines up to $100 a day for workers, $25,000 a day for union leaders, and $100,000 for the unions. As a further financial penalty to the unions, the government would stop collecting union dues for three months for every day of an illegal strike.

been either rotating strikes (as the 101-day strike of postal employees in 1970) or strikes in which a relatively small number of employees in a unit took part. This was the case, for example, in the 31-day strike by the General Labour and Trades Unit in February and March of 1975. The only members of that unit likely to cause serious inconvenience to the public by withdrawing their services were the employees who normally manned the heavy equipment for removal of snow on airport runways. These were the only ones the union called out on strike as their services, though not necessary to the safety or security of the public, could cause major inconvenience or cost if discontinued. To the good fortune of the government employer, the weather was remarkably clear for most of the time this particular unit was on strike. A strike in 1980, by employees in the Clerical and Regulatory Unit, which continued for 30 days, did cause major inconvenience, even though not all employees in the unit were on strike at any one time. Adding significantly to the impact of the strike was the fact that the strike itself affected virtually every department of government and that employees in other bargaining units, who were not entitled to strike at that stage, refused, on instructions of the Public Service Alliance, to cross picket lines established by the Clerical and Regulatory Unit. But what was even more significant about the strike was the change in attitude it represented by a traditionally docile group which, until that time, had always selected the arbitration option for a resolution of bargaining impasses. The placards they carried on the picket lines read: "The worm has turned."

But while legal strikes have been relatively rare under the PSSRA, unlawful strikes have been more common. Some, by postal workers in particular, have occurred during the term of collective agreements, the so-called "closed period" during which strikes are prohibited. Others have involved refusal to work by "designated employees"—those required to maintain previously defined "essential services." The refusal to work by designated employees has given some public-service strikes a greater impact than they otherwise might have had. The report emanating from a public inquiry into the experience under the Public Service Staff Relations Act recommended stricter enforcement procedures with respect to designated employees and increased penalties for noncompliance.[52] No action has been taken on these recommendations.

The Choice of Procedures

The Public Service Staff Relations Act has undoubtedly been the most innovative piece of public-sector labor legislation in Canada. It broke new ground in a number of respects, one of the most important

---

[52] Government of Canada, Report, *supra* note 43.

being the establishment of an independent board to administer it. Its most original contribution, however, was its built-in choice of procedures for dispute resolution, including the unique requirement that the choice be made, by the bargaining agent, prior to the start of negotiations.

As expected and hoped by the policy makers, the initial choices of impasse procedure leaned heavily in favor of the arbitration option, the few exceptions being the postal units, the air traffic control unit, the ship-repair and printing units, and the unit of electronic technicians. The first two, as noted earlier, had already struck before the law allowed it. The others, being represented by unions with long experience under private-sector labor legislation, could hardly have been expected to voluntarily relinquish the right to strike. The Public Service Alliance of Canada and the Professional Institute of the Public Service which, together, represented the vast majority of employees in the service, continued to specify arbitration as the method of dispute resolution for all the units they represented for several rounds of bargaining. By the mid-1970s, however, a number of bargaining units (including the formerly docile Clerical and Regulatory group) began to digress from their original option, and although a few groups have switched back and forth a number of times, the trend since then has clearly been away from the arbitration option. By early 1986, the most recent date for which figures are available, 64 bargaining units, representing 190,064 employees in the Central Administration, had specified the conciliation-board route; 12, representing 17,816 employees had specified the arbitration route.[53] Thirty-six of the 39 bargaining units in the Central Administration for which PSAC is the bargaining agent and 22 of the 26 units represented by PIPSC are among those now on the conciliation-board/strike option.[54] That such a significant number of bargaining units repudiated their original option, with the result that the majority of employees in the federal public service are now in bargaining units committed to the conciliation-board route, with the possibility of a strike at the end of the road, indicates that the

---

[53] The proportions are different in the case of the employees of the "Separate Employers," with 5,334 in bargaining units that have specified the arbitration option and 2,390 in units on the conciliation board/strike route. Nineteenth Annual Report, Public Service Staff Relations Board (Ottawa: 1985–1986).

[54] Some of the largest bargaining units represented by PSAC altered their dispute-resolution specification in the latter half of the 1970s. By 1980 a significant majority of its members were already on the conciliation-board route. At PSAC's 1982 convention, a resolution was adopted recommending "to all its members" that they "opt for the conciliation/strike route as the dispute settlement method." Although a few PIPSC units had switched to the conciliation-board option by the end of the 1970s, the major move away from the arbitration option by units represented by PIPSC dates from 1981. The argument supporting this development was that there would be no need for the employees to resort to a full-scale strike; pressure would be exerted on the employer through rotating strikes. For alterations in dispute procedures in various years, see Annual Reports of the PSSRB.

confidence in arbitration was short-lived.[55] The strike statistics cited above, however, show that neither the right to strike per se nor the move away from the arbitration option has brought the wheels of the federal government to a halt.

The pronounced shift away from the arbitration option undoubtedly reflected a growing militancy in certain groups and was encouraged by some new leaders. However, some of the switches may reflect problems with the arbitration process as such. Apart from complaints about delays in the system and dissatisfaction with particular awards, the bargaining agents have been particularly critical of the statutory limitations on the matters that may be taken to arbitration. Observers concerned with the apparent rejection of the arbitration option have suggested that the law be amended to bring the scope of arbitration into line, as far as possible, with the matters that are bargainable. As the law now stands, some of the issues that can, and have been, discussed in the course of conciliation-board procedures cannot be raised before an arbitration board.[56]

While the trend in the past decade has clearly been away from arbitration as the method of dispute resolution, a particularly significant recent switch has occurred in the opposite direction. The choice of the arbitration option by the air traffic control group, and the reason that provoked it, raises serious questions concerning the designation of "essential employees" which, as the quid pro quo for the right to strike, was one of the most innovative features of the PSSRA. There have been differences between the parties from the outset concerning the number of employees to be designated in particular circumstances and the tasks that designated employees should be required to perform. It

---

[55] For a discussion of the early movement away from the arbitration option, see L. W. C. S. Barnes and L.A. Kelly, Interest Arbitration in the Federal Public Service (Kingston, Ont.: Industrial Relations Centre, Queen's University, 1975). For the effect of impasse procedures on bargaining processes and outcomes, see John C. Anderson and Thomas A. Kochan, *Impasse Procedures in the Canadian Federal Service: Effects on the Bargaining Process*, 30 Indus. & Lab. Rel. Rev. 283 (April 1977); Bryan M. Downie, The Behavioral, Economic and Institutional Effects of Compulsory Interest Arbitration, Discussion Paper No. 147 (Ottawa: Economic Council of Canada, 1979); and George Saunders, Interest Arbitration and Wage Inflation in the Federal Public Service, Discussion Paper No. 162 (Ottawa: Economic Council of Canada, 1980).

[56] The PSSRA is very specific on the subject matter of arbitral awards, and also on matters that may not be included. The act specifies rates of pay, hours of work, leave entitlements, standards of discipline, and other terms and conditions of employment directly related thereto as permissible subject matter of arbitral awards. No arbitral award may deal with the standards, procedures, or processes governing the appointment, appraisal, promotion, demotion, transfer, layoff, or release of employees (none of which are bargainable) or with any term or condition of employment that was not a subject of negotiation between the parties before arbitration was requested. Although the PSSRA provides that a conciliation board report may contain recommendations only on matters that are within the scope of bargaining, it has been the practice to permit a conciliation board to discuss with the parties some nonbargainable issues to see if a solution can be found for them. This cannot happen in arbitration, as an arbitration ruling that exceeds the scope permitted in the act undoubtedly would be overturned on review. See Finkelman and Goldenberg, *supra* note 37, at Ch. 4, *Scope of Bargaining*, for a comparison of the scope of bargaining under the conciliation-board and arbitration options.

has also become apparent in the light of experience that there are deficiencies in the designation provision itself, in particular the rather narrow definition of the services to be protected in the event of a strike and the lengthy procedure for designation. However, in spite of some deficiencies in the legislation and differences relating to its application, it appeared until 1980 that a modus vivendi had been reached that was reasonably acceptable to all sides. As for the Public Service Staff Relations Board, it made clear from the outset that if it were to err at all, it would prefer to do so on the side of caution; in other words, it would rather designate too many than too few where public safety and security are concerned.[57]

The last bargaining experience of the air traffic control unit under the conciliation-board option was the first incident in which the policies the parties themselves had followed for over a decade and on which the board had based its decisions on designation was brought into serious question by the employer. The decision by the employer to keep all commercial flights in operation in the event of a strike and, accordingly, to designate all operational air traffic controllers as essential to public safety and security, effectively removed the right to strike, or at least to conduct an effective strike, from the air traffic control unit. The "designation" of over 1,700 air traffic controllers in that round of negotiations was in sharp contrast with all previous rounds in which approximately 200 had been designated to keep emergency flights in operation. With a new government policy of keeping all commercial air traffic operational, even in the event of a strike, all operational air traffic controllers had become essential to the "safety or security of the public," the criterion for designation under the PSSRA.

The employer's list was challenged by the bargaining agent, the Canadian Air Traffic Control Association (CATCA). The PSSRB held unanimously in a preliminary decision that it was not bound to take into account ministerial or government pronouncements on the level of services to be maintained. It found, instead, that implicit in making its determination on the number or classes of air traffic controllers to be designated was the requirement that it decide the level of services by air traffic controllers that must be maintained at federal government airports in order to ensure the safety and security of the public in the event of a lawful strike by members of the unit. The board's decision was set aside by the federal court of appeal which found, in part, that the board had no right, under the act, to determine the level of service,

---

[57] The Board has even gone beyond the strict literal language of the law by holding in some cases that certain social services, such as the services of clerks processing welfare and welfare-related checks, fall within the phrase "the safety or security of the public."

since that matter was a policy decision for which the government alone was responsible. The judgment of the federal court of appeal was upheld by the Supreme Court of Canada.

The employer's use of the designation provision in the air traffic control case, and the decision of the courts upholding the employer's position, could create a "whole new ballgame" with respect to designation under the PSSRA. The CATCA case has complicated the already difficult task faced by the PSSRB in interpreting and applying the designation provision. Past agreements of the parties and past decisions of the board can no longer be relied on for guidance. The courts' decisions have indeed already had an impact on other units as well as the air traffic control unit, as the government has been designating a significantly higher proportion of employees in some other units than used to be the case. It has been suggested that the law be clarified with respect to the designation principle and its implications for the right to strike in the light of the CATCA case since the courts have ruled, in effect, that the right to strike under the PSSRA, as presently worded, is not necessarily a right in practice. It has also been suggested that the law be amended to permit the bargaining agent to alter its option from reference to a conciliation board to reference to arbitration at any stage of the process. Otherwise, if a large number of employees are designated and the capacity of a bargaining agent to conduct an effective legal strike is destroyed, the bargaining agent would be deprived of any effective method in law for resolving an impasse in negotiations.[58] Because of the present provision in the PSSRA that prohibits a bargaining agent from changing its dispute resolution process in the course of any given round of negotiations and because of its own experience in the last round, CATCA, in spite of its long-time reputation for militancy, felt obliged to switch to the arbitration option. Only one other group, the meteorology unit, has since done likewise. All other switches since the CATCA case have continued the trend away from the arbitration option.

Public-Service Labor Relations and the Courts

There have been some instances of court review of rulings of administrative tribunals and of arbitral awards. More often, however, resort to the courts in public-sector labor relations has taken the form of injunctions to prevent or terminate a strike, prosecutions for failure to observe such injunctions, and prosecutions for calling or engaging in strikes specifically prohibited by law. This situation has occurred in the

---

[58] Finkelman and Goldenberg, *supra* note 37, Vol. 2, at 702.

case of police and firefighters in some of the provinces and designated employees at the federal level and in the case of failure to comply with legislation enacted to end or prevent a particular strike.

Potential Impact of the Charter of Rights and Freedoms

A recent development may well give the courts a far more significant role in labor relations than they ever had in the past. The proclamation of the Canadian Charter of Rights and Freedoms[59] has enhanced the role of the courts by providing them with a mandate to overrule legislation if it is found to conflict with the fundamental values promulgated by the Charter. Some of the values proclaimed in the Charter have particular application to Canadian labor law in both the private and public sectors—among them such fundamental freedoms as freedom of conscience and religion, freedom of thought, belief, opinion, and expression, and freedom of association, all of which are articulated in Section 2, as well as the guarantee, in Section 15, of equality rights and protection against discrimination. Some of these provisions are not too different from those already contained in human rights enactments of the federal and various provincial jurisdictions. However, a major difference lies in the fact that the Charter is part of the Constitution of Canada. Other laws may now be challenged in light of the Charter and their legitimacy must be judged against the fundamental rights and freedoms guaranteed under the Charter. The only limitation on the exercise of rights guaranteed by the Charter appears in Section 1, which provides that such rights are "subject only to such reasonable limits prescribed by law as can be demonstrably justified in a free and democratic society." While Section 33 allows a legislature to exclude the operation of certain parts of the Charter, by a legislative declaration to that effect, such a declaration could last for only five years after which it would have to be reenacted.[60]

A noted scholar of Canadian labor law, Donald Carter, has characterized this new development as the "Charterization" of the labor law system, in view of the fact that "all Canadian labour legislation and the exercise of powers derived from that legislation must be re-examined in the light of the Charter."[61] Referring to the fact that Charter values are subject to "reasonable limits prescribed by law," he points out that

---

[59] Set out in the Constitution Act 1982 (Schedule B of Canada Act, 1982 [U.K.] 1982, c. 11).

[60] Section 33, frequently referred to as the "notwithstanding clause" (i.e., notwithstanding the provisions of the Charter), was used by the Saskatchewan government to ensure the validity of the legislation enacted in 1986 to end rotating strikes by public employees.

[61] Donald D. Carter, The Changing Face of Canadian Labour Relations Law (Kingston, Ont.: Industrial Relations Centre, Queen's University, 1985), 2. Reprint No. 54, reprint of a paper presented at the Annual Fall Industrial Relations Seminar, Oct. 20–25, 1985.

such reasonable limits and the level of justification required for them are not spelled out specifically in the Charter but are left to be determined primarily by the courts:

> The Charter now creates the potential for virtually every labour relations issue to be outfitted in constitutional clothing, handing over to constitutional lawyers and judges a wide discretion to reshape the Canadian labour law system. Once an issue becomes fitted in constitutional cloth, it then becomes a matter for the courts since the judiciary are the ultimate arbiters of constitutional matters. Thus, the most immediate effect of the Charter is to enhance the authority of the courts at the expense of the legislatures and administrative tribunals. . . . The effect of the Charter is to give the courts the final say . . . unless the legislature is prepared to face the political risks of expressly overriding the Charter.[62]

Carter predicts, in addition, that the courts are less likely than they have been in the past to show restraint in review of decisions of labor relations boards:

> Once an issue is regarded as a constitutional matter, . . . the justification for judicial restraint disappears. After all it is the judges, and not the labour boards, who are experts in constitutional law and so the matter must be decided ultimately by the courts. The effect of the Charter is to transform what would otherwise be a labour relations issue into a constitutional question with the result that the matter becomes one for ultimate resolution by the courts. The growing use of Charter arguments by both trade unions and employers means that, increasingly Canadian labour law will be shaped by the courts rather than by legislatures and labour boards.[63]

There clearly is considerable potential conflict between the Charter emphasis on individual rights and the collective rights that are at the basis of Canadian labor law and practice. This could have implications, depending on the interpretation of the courts, for the various provisions for union security that are now permitted, and in some jurisdictions even required, by law. Some "Charter challenges" on these and related matters, such as the payment of union dues to a political party, are currently proceeding through the various levels of the judicial system. The outcome of these cases will be felt equally in the private and public sectors. The Charter guarantees of equality and the prohibitions on discrimination, likewise, could affect numerous aspects of the employment relationship in both sectors.

Among the Charter cases to date with broadest ramifications for the public sector have been the challenges to wage restraint legislation, federal and provincial, as a violation of the Charter guarantee of

---

[62] *Id.* at 3.
[63] *Id.*

freedom of association. These challenges pose the question of the extent to which the guarantee of freedom of association includes protection for the purposes of an association or the means of achieving such purposes which, in the case of a labor union, include, in addition to the right to organize, the right to bargain collectively and to strike; all of these rights were suspended for a limited period by the legislation in question. Various court decisions to date have produced conflicting answers to this question. It now rests with the Supreme Court of Canada to decide to what extent free collective bargaining, including the right to strike, is included in the guarantee of freedom of association under the Charter and whether or not the abrogation of some of these freedoms for a limited period could be considered to be reasonable limits upon freedom of association that could be justified in a free and democratic society. Other Charter cases have involved challenges to legislation imposing compulsory interest arbitration in place of strikes and lockouts for certain public employees, and some have dealt with the constitutionality of ad hoc legislation prohibiting particular strikes. The ultimate disposition of such cases by the Supreme Court of Canada could have broad ramifications for public-sector labor law and practice.

It is still too early to determine the extent to which the "Charterization" of the law will affect the Canadian system of labor relations in both the private and public sectors. However, one thing is certain. The Charter has given the courts a role with respect to labor relations that few could have anticipated. It remains to be seen what the ultimate impact will be.

Concluding Observations

The inconsistencies in policy and practice among jurisdictions and the reevaluations that continue to take place reinforce the conclusion that labor relations in the public sector are still in a fluid state in Canada. The only prediction that can be made with certainty is that public-service bargaining, in one form or another, is definitely here to stay. But it will be a long time, if ever, before a consensus can be reached as to the most appropriate mechanism, at each stage of the bargaining relationship, by which to accommodate the rights that are available to workers in the private sector to the particular characteristics and responsibilities of public-service employment.

Of all the issues that have plagued the policy makers and the parties, as well as the public, the question of dispute resolution remains paramount and one of the most difficult to resolve. However, if there is one lesson to be learned from the Canadian experience, it is that laws alone will not determine the form that labor relations will take. This has been demonstrated by the variety of experience in jurisdictions that have granted the right to strike, and also by cases of defiance of the law in certain instances.

Jurisdictions that currently prohibit strikes in the public service seem unlikely to change their position on this matter, at least in the foreseeable future. Most of them, however, have recognized the importance of providing impartial mechanisms, in the form of independent boards, to administer the dispute-resolution machinery. There is a growing realization that unions must at least be assured of the impartiality of the available impasse procedures if a prohibition of the strike is to be respected.

In jurisdictions that grant the right to strike, a crucial problem is the definition of "essential services" and the guarantee that these will be maintained. There appears to be a growing inclination by governments to curb the power of the unions to disrupt essential services, short of withdrawing the right to strike as such. Policy makers in some jurisdictions have recently broadened the definition of essential services,[64] and at least one province, Quebec, has also tightened enforcement measures. There have been recommendations to do likewise in other jurisdictions. Experience has shown that the present statutory penalties for noncompliance are not always a deterrent if workers are sufficiently determined to defy them.[65] Unless the problem of enforceability of the essential services provisions is satisfactorily resolved, and it is unlikely that it can be entirely, ad hoc legislative measures appropriate to particular circumstances, and usually with stricter penalties for noncompliance than those provided in the existing statute, remain the last resort. The elected representatives of the people have the ultimate power and responsibility to respond to a threat to the public welfare. This presumes, of course, that the federal Parliament or provincial legislature, as the case may be, is in session or available for recall when an emergency arises, or that the Cabinet can act to protect essential services without resort to the legislature—as it can in

---

[64] There has been a notable increase in the number of designations in federal bargaining units since the CATCA case. Proposals to amend the PSSRA, announced by the government in January 1987, would add "public health and the protection of federal public property and long-term research and experiments" to the current statutory criteria of "safety and security of the public" for designating employees as "essential." Recommendations to this effect were made by the Joint Parliamentary Committee in 1976 (Government of Canada, Report, *supra* note 43). As noted earlier, in Quebec the high proportion of employees now designated as essential in the hospital sector makes it virtually impossible for them to conduct an effective legal strike.

[65] The Joint Parliamentary Committee noted that the refusal to work by designated employees had given some federal public service strikes a greater impact than they otherwise might have had. Accordingly, it recommended that the penalties for noncompliance with the law be increased in the case of designated employees. Moreover, to avoid the temptation of the employer to secure the termination of unlawful strikes by designated employees in exchange for a waiver of prosecution or disciplinary action, the committee recommended the appointment of an independent commissioner with responsibility for initiating legal proceedings in the absence of such action by the employer. No action has been taken on these recommendations, made nearly 10 years ago.

British Columbia, under the Essential Services Disputes Act, and in Quebec, on advice of the Council of Essential Services. Suggestions have been made in other jurisdictions to amend the applicable legislation to empower the Cabinet to suspend the right to strike during the election period following the dissolution of Parliament or a provincial legislature where, in its opinion, a strike would be against the public interest. There has been a provision to this effect in Saskatchewan since 1982,[66] and in the federal jurisdiction, under the Canada Labour Code, since 1972. The latter statute, however, is not applicable to the public service.[67]

On another matter of particular public interest, wage determination in public employment, it is impossible to predict how the policy makers would react if the bargaining position of the unions were to improve (as it probably would under more favorable economic conditions) and if negotiated and arbitrated wage increases were then to get out of line with government fiscal and economic policies to which they have been kept so closely tied since the end of the formal controls programs. One astute observer suggests that it is "premature to predict that we have seen the end of legislated wage restraint in the public sector."[68] Time alone will tell. However, the recent and current behavior of the policy makers in a number of jurisdictions reflects a determination to hold the line on public-sector wages as well as to take a harder line on various matters related to dispute resolution, particularly where "essential services" are involved. Finally, there is the question of the constitutionality of the various legislated restraint programs, both temporary and permanent, which is still to be decided by the Supreme Court of Canada. The interpretation that the Court places on freedom of association and whether or not it upholds the various restraints as "reasonable limits in a free and democratic society" will have important implications for the future course of public-sector labor relations in Canada. Other Charter cases, particularly insofar as they concern the competing values of individual and collective rights, could have a major impact on the labor-management relationship in both the private and public sectors.

---

[66] The Labour-Management Dispute (Temporary Provisions) Act, S.S. 1981–82, c. L-0.1., allows the Cabinet to forbid or halt a strike during a provincial election if, in its opinion, the dispute creates a situation of pressing public importance or might endanger the health or safety of any person in the province.

[67] In the absence of such a provision in the PSSRA, and in anticipation of an early dissolution of Parliament, a special law to the same effect was enacted in April 1978 to avert a threatened postal strike during the election.

[68] Carter, *supra* note 61, at 13.

CHAPTER 9

The Future of Collective Bargaining in the Public Sector

BENJAMIN AARON*

Collective bargaining in the public sector[1] was in its infancy in the 1960s; it has now come of age. Only seven states[2] have no statutes dealing with collective bargaining for any group of government employees. The United States,[3] the District of Columbia, and all but two other states[4] authorize and regulate collective bargaining either for government employees generally or for specific categories of such employees.[5] The federal government and a significant number of states have single statutes applicable to collective bargaining by all govern-

---

*Professor of Law, Emeritus, U.C.L.A. School of Law. *Note:* Parts of this article have previously appeared in Aaron, *Unfair Labor Practices and the Right to Strike in the Public Sector: Has the National Labor Relations Act Been a Good Model?* 38 Stan. L. Rev. 1097 (1986)

[1] By "public sector," I mean only government employment, whether on the federal, state, or local level.

[2] Alabama, Arizona, Arkansas, Colorado, Louisiana, Mississippi, and West Virginia.

[3] 5 U.S.C. §§7101-7135 (1982).

[4] North Carolina and Texas are the exceptions. A North Carolina statute specifically prohibits collective bargaining between any state, county, or municipal agency and any organization of government employees. N.C. Gen. Stat., §95-98 (1985) (effective June 7, 1982). The constitutionality of this provision was upheld in *Winston-Salem Ass'n v. Phillips*, 381 F. Supp. 644, 648, 87 LRRM 2925 (M.D.N.C. 1974). Another provision, §95-97, prohibiting government employees from joining labor organizations, was held unconstitutional on its face in *Atkins v. City of Charlotte*, 296 F. Supp. 1068, 1075, 70 LRRM 2732 (W.D.N.C. 1969).

A 1947 Texas statute declares it to be against public policy for any state, county, or municipal official to enter into a collective bargaining agreement with a labor organization. Texas Stat. Ann., art. 5154c (Vernon 1971). In 1973, however, Texas enacted the Fire and Police Employees Relations Act, Texas Rev. Stat. Ann., art. 5154c-1 (Vernon 1985), which grants local police and firefighters the right to bargain collectively.

[5] Of the 41 states in this category, two do not authorize collective bargaining, but instead establish grievance procedures. The South Carolina statutes neither authorize nor prohibit collective bargaining by government employees. In *Holder v. City of Columbia*, 71 LC ¶53,128 (D.S.C. 18, April 1972), the city's regulation prohibiting battalion chiefs and captains from associating with a firefighters' union was enjoined, in the absence of proof that the unionization of these employees would adversely affect fire protection services or lead to disciplinary problems. Similarly, Virginia has no statute relating to collective bargaining by government employees. In *Commonwealth of Virginia v. Board of Arlington County*, 217 Va. 558, 232 S.E.2d 30, 94 LRRM 2291 (1977), the Virginia supreme court held that in the absence of express statutory authority, neither a local government body nor a school board may engage in collective bargaining with a labor organization. Virginia has, however, enacted statutory grievance procedures for state and for county and municipal employees.

ment employees;[6] the remainder have one or more statutes dealing with specific categories of government employees. These statutes cover virtually all government employees at the state and municipal levels.[7]

Bargaining Organizations

Although the organization of public-sector employees has not maintained the rapid pace of the 1960s and early 1970s, the proportion of government employees who are members of bargaining organizations[8] is now about 35.8 percent, which compares favorably to a corresponding figure for the private sector of about 17.5 percent. About 43 percent of government employees are covered by collective agreements.[9]

The outlook for government bargaining organizations, in my opinion, is for slow but continuing growth or, at the worst, for the maintenance of a steady state. The assault on unions being waged by many of the nation's private employers has no counterpart in most of the public sector. In the private sector, antiunion employers are stirred to action by the smell of blood of a wounded and weakened labor movement, but in the government employment sector, most unions are healthy and strong. Moreover, government employers are less concerned about "competitiveness" than are their private-sector counterparts, and, thanks in some instances to statutory limitations on the scope of bargaining, they are less often confronted by demands of bargaining organizations for a voice in basic policy decisions reserved to management. That is not to say, however, that this particular front will remain quiet; one may anticipate that bargaining organizations and their supporters will continue to seek judicial decisions or amendments to existing statutes that would increase the number of issues subject to mandatory bargaining. On the other hand, I think it less likely that government employers will seek amendments restricting still further existing statutory limits on the scope of bargaining.

---

[6] Alaska, Delaware, Florida, Hawaii, Illinois, Iowa, Kansas, Massachusetts, Michigan, Minnesota, Missouri, New Hampshire, New Jersey, New York, Ohio, Oregon, Pennsylvania, South Dakota, and Washington. All of these statutes, as well as the federal law, exempt certain categories of employees from coverage.

[7] E.g., California and Wisconsin.

[8] Employees in the public sector are represented in some cases by unions and in others by associations. Although the differences between the two types of organizations, in respect of collective bargaining attitudes and tactics, are gradually disappearing, some associations still object to being called unions. The term "bargaining organizations" employed in this chapter is designed to overcome this difficulty.

[9] Daily Lab. Rep., No. 29, February 12, 1986, B–1.

Strike Rights

The impact of the dismissal of some 12,000 air traffic controllers, following the illegal PATCO strike in 1981, which sent a shock wave throughout all government employment, seems to have diminished considerably. Indeed, a new bargaining organization of air traffic controllers, the National Air Traffic Controllers Association (NATCA), rising Phoenix-like from the ashes of PATCO, now represents those employees. Significantly, the new organization counts among its leaders and strongest supporters many who refused to go on strike in 1981, and it was selected as bargaining representative by better than a two-to-one margin.[10] NATCA has said it will eschew the strike weapon, which is certainly prudent; there seems to be no foreseeable prospect that Congress will remove the present ban against strikes by federal employees or moderate the Draconian penalties for violations of that prohibition.[11] In the federal sector, therefore, bargaining organizations will have to continue to rely upon impasse procedures and legislative lobbying to achieve their objectives.

No such confident predictions can be made in respect of strikes by state and municipal government employees. A brief look at the present situation will indicate just how varied the existing laws are. Although most state statutes[12] specifically forbid government employees to strike, 11 states[13] now permit strikes by some government employees in certain circumstances. In most states whose statutes are silent on the subject, however, the courts have ruled that strikes by government employees are illegal.[14]

---

[10] Daily Lab. Rep., No. 112, June 12, 1987, A-9–A-10.

[11] The federal law prohibits strikes by government employees unless the strikes are explicitly authorized by statute. See, e.g., *United Fed'n of Postal Clerks v. Blount*, 325 F. Supp. 879, 882, 76 LRRM 2932 (D.D.C.), *aff'd mem.*, 404 U.S. 802, 78 LRRM 2463 (1971). Congress has reinforced the common law prohibition against strikes. Federal government employees participating in a strike are permanently barred from federal employment, see 5 U.S.C. §7311 (1982), and are guilty of a felony. 18 U.S.C. §1918 (1982). It is also a crime to aid or abet strikers. 18 U.S.C. §1231. Moreover, strikes against the federal government are unfair labor practices under Title VII of the Civil Service Reform Act of 1978 (CSRA), 5 U.S.C. §7116(b)(7)(A) (1982) (Federal Services Labor-Management Relations), and bargaining organizations engaging in such strikes can be decertified, see *id.* at §7120(f) (1982). Finally, all federal employees are required by statute to take an oath not to strike, see *id.* at §3333(a) (1982).

[12] The following jurisdictions make it an unfair labor practice to instigate or engage in a strike or other concerted refusal to work: District of Columbia, Florida, New Hampshire, Ohio, Tennessee (teachers), Vermont (state employees), and Wisconsin (state employees). A few states with no laws permitting or regulating collective bargaining by government employees (e.g., Georgia and Texas) have particularly harsh punitive statutes applicable to strikers. Bargaining organizations that call illegal strikes are punished by fines (e.g., Nevada), withdrawal of recognition or certification (e.g., Minnesota), or revocation of dues deductions or checkoff privileges (e.g., New York).

[13] Alaska, California, Hawaii, Idaho, Illinois, Minnesota, Montana, Oregon, Pennsylvania, Vermont, and Wisconsin.

[14] See, e.g., *Steelworkers v. University of Alabama*, 430 F. Supp. 996 (N.D. Ala. 1977), *aff'd*, 599 F.2d 56 (5th Cir. 1979); *Potts v. Hay*, 318 S.W.2d 826, 827, 43 LRRM 2327 (Ark. 1958) (dictum); but see, *County Sanitation Dist. No. 2 v. Los Angeles County Employees' Ass'n Local 660*, 38 Cal. 3d 564, 592, 699 P.2d 835, 854, 119 LRRM 2433 (1985).

Even in states that expressly protect the right of government employees to strike, certain strikes are not allowed. Typically, the state statute divides government employees into categories on the basis of whether the services they provide are "essential." Government employees who provide essential services are rarely, if ever, permitted to strike.[15] States differ as to which government employees may strike. Teachers may not strike in Alaska,[16] but they may do so in Hawaii,[17] Minnesota,[18] and Vermont.[19] Firefighters have a limited right to strike in Idaho;[20] Pennsylvania forbids employees necessary to the functioning of the courts to strike,[21] and Minnesota specifically denies the right to strike to professional engineers.[22]

Strikes by government employees are also unprotected unless the employees follow designated statutory procedures. Many states require that the employees be organized into a collective bargaining unit with an exclusive representative.[23] Often, they must exhaust fact-finding and mediation procedures[24] and give notice before they may

---

[15] See e.g., Alaska Stat., Sec. 23.40.200(a)-(d) (1984) (dividing government employees into three categories having either a right to strike, a limited right to strike, or no right to strike); Hawaii Rev. Stat., §89-12(b) (1970), §89-12(c)-(e) (Supp. 1984) (denying right to strike to designated "essential employees" by the Public Employment Relations Board); Idaho Code, §44-1181 (1977) (limited right to strike for firefighters); Ill. Ann. Stat., Ch. 48, §1603(o), 1617(a) (Smith-Hurd Supp. 1985) (listing essential government employees and forbidding them to strike); Minn. Stat. Ann., §179A.18, subd. 1, 179A.03, subd. 7 (West Supp. 1985) (denying the right to strike to confidential, essential, and managerial employees, and defining "essential employee"); Mont. Code Ann., §§39-31-103(2)(a), 39-31-201, 39-32-102(5), 39-34-105 (1985) (separate statutes applying to government employees, nurses, and firefighters authorize strikes for the first group but limit the right to strike for the other two); Oregon Rev. Stat., §§243.726(6), 243.736 (1981) (forbidding certain government employees to strike, but specifying that financial inconvenience normally incident to a strike is not a threat to public welfare); Pa. Stat. Ann., §1101.1001 (Purdon Supp. 1985) (listing government employees who may not strike); Vt. Stat. Ann., Title 21, §1730 (1978) (limited right of government employees to strike); Wis. Stat. Ann., §111.70(1) (nm) (West 1974) (permitting all municipal employees except police and firefighters to strike); state employees are forbidden to strike by §111.84(2)(e) (West. Supp. 1984). In California, where the right of government employees to strike was created by a court rather than by a legislature, strikes are forbidden if they pose "an imminent threat to public health or safety." *County Sanitation Dist. No. 2 v. Los Angeles County Employees' Ass'n Local 660, supra* note 14.

[16] *Anchorage Educ. Ass'n v. Anchorage School Dist.*, 648 P.2d 993, 114 LRRM 3377 (Alaska 1982).

[17] *Board of Educ. & Hawaii State Teachers' Ass'n*, No. S-05-16, 3 HPERB No. 186 (1984).

[18] Minn. Stat. Ann., §179A.18, subd. 2 (West Supp. 1985).

[19] *Green Mountain Union High School v. Chester Educ. Ass'n*, No. 78-112R (VLRB 1979).

[20] *Fire Fighters Local 1494 v. City of Coeur d'Alene, Idaho*, 99 Idaho 630, 586 P.2d 1346, 100 LRRM 2079 (1978) (firefighters may strike outside the term of a collective bargaining agreement, but they must bargain in good faith).

[21] Pa. Stat. Ann., Title 43, §1101.1001 (Purdon Supp. 1985).

[22] Minn. Stat. Ann., §179A.18, subd. 1 (West Supp. 1985) (definition of "essential employee").

[23] E.g., Alaska Stat., §23.40.200 (1984) (majority in collective bargaining unit must authorize strike by secret ballot); Hawaii Rev. Stat., §89-12(a) (Supp. 1984) (employees must belong to a bargaining unit for which an exclusive representative has been certified); Ill. Ann. Stat., Ch. 48, §1617(a) (Smith-Hurd Supp. 1985) (striking employees must be represented by an exclusive bargaining agent); Oregon Rev. Stat., §243.726(1)-(2) (1981) (employees must belong to an appropriate bargaining unit with an exclusive representative).

[24] Hawaii Rev. Stat., §89-11(b)(1)-(2) (Supp. 1984) (requiring up to 33 days of mediation and fact-finding); Minn. Stat. Ann., §179A.18, subd. 1-2 (West Supp. 1985) (if there is no collective bar-

strike.[25] Many statutes provide that a government employer may petition a court for an injunction against a strike that endangers public welfare.[26] Like substantive limitations on government employees' right to strike, procedural restrictions vary from state to state.

It is clear that public opinion generally supports restriction, if not outright prohibition, of strikes by government employees. Nevertheless, as noted above, the restriction is not absolute in 11 of the 50 states. There is at least a possibility that additional states will join the minority of those permitting a limited right to strike; indeed, it seems more likely that this will occur than that the limited right, having once been granted by statute, will be repealed. There is the further possibility that states permitting a limited right to strike by government employees may, perhaps borrowing from each other, add to or subtract from the categories of those employees regarded as "essential" and thus not permitted to strike.

Dispute Resolution Procedures

Meanwhile, the emphasis remains on alternative methods of dispute resolution. As Joseph Grodin and Joyce Najita point out in their chapter, binding arbitration of grievances that arise during the term of a labor agreement has now become the norm in governmental, as well as private, employment. The pressure to strike over such disputes has thus been almost totally relieved. The remaining problem is what to do about so-called interests disputes, that is, those arising out of negotiations over new terms and conditions of employment. The standard procedures offered or prescribed as alternatives to the strike are mediation, fact-finding, and various forms of arbitration, all reviewed in the Grodin-Najita chapter. Even when resort to mediation and fact-finding is compulsory, the results of those procedures—formal or informal recommendations—are not binding upon the parties. One reason why the results of such proceedings are frequently disappointing, it seems to me, is that the procedures of mediation and fact-finding have been

---

gaining agreement in effect, employees must participate in mediation for at least 45 days); Oregon Rev. Stat., §243.726(1)-(2) (1981) (requiring up to 50 days of mediation and fact-finding); Pa. Stat. Ann., Title 43, §1101.801-.802 (Purdon Supp. 1985) (statutory mediation and fact-finding procedures lasting as long as 81 days); Wis. Stat. Ann., §111.70(4)(cm)(6)(b)-(c) (West Supp. 1984) (employees may strike only after exhausting statutory procedures and if both parties withdraw their final offers).

[25] Hawaii Rev. Stat., §89-12(b) (1970) (10 days' notice to board and to employer); Ill. Ann. Stat., Ch. 48, §1617(a) (Smith-Hurd Supp. 1985) (5 days' notice to employer); Oregon Rev. Stat., §243.726(2)(d) (1981) (10 days' notice to employer and board).

[26] E.g., Ill. Ann. Stat., Ch. 48, §1618 (Smith-Hurd Supp. 1985) (government employer *must* petition if Illinois State or Local Labor Boards find clear and present danger to health of community; court need not grant injunction against strike if it can fashion another remedy); Pa. Stat. Ann., Title 43, §1101.1003 (Purdon Supp. 1985) (either employer or attorney general may sue for injunction in an appropriate case); Wis. Stat. Ann., §111.70(7m)(a) (West Supp. 1984) (employer or any citizen directly affected may petition for injunction).

treated as separate stages on a continuum, instead of being combined in a single, more dynamic process, as for example, in the Michigan model of final-offer selection in state police compulsory arbitrations.[27] Although the procedure does not specifically call for mediation activities by the panel, the tripartite structure of the panel and its power to remand the dispute for further collective bargaining suggest that mediation does, or at any rate can, play a role in the fact-finding and final-offer selection functions of the panel.

Now that the constitutional objections to compulsory arbitration of interests disputes in the public sector have been largely overcome, I would anticipate an increasing resort to this form of settlement. Charges that compulsory arbitration tends to have a "narcotic" effect on collective bargaining, whatever their merit, are likely to carry less weight with state legislatures than will the prospect of strike-free, definite, and certain disputes resolutions brought about by compulsory arbitration. A greater concern, perhaps, is the ever-present danger that arbitrators will grant wage awards that are unacceptably high or will decide noneconomic issues in ways that impermissibly intrude in areas intended to be the exclusive preserve of government management. Those fears can be assuaged, however, by the appropriate statutory restriction of arbitral powers and by the exercise of judicial review in cases in which arbitrators have clearly exceeded the limits of their legal authority.

Employee Privacy Rights

In the area of basic constitutional rights, the outlook in the public sector is somewhat mixed. On the one hand, the very nature of government employment insures that most employees will continue to be protected by constitutional guarantees of individual rights, such as the privilege against self-incrimination, freedom of expression, substantive and procedural due process, and the like.[28] On the other hand, mounting public concern over problems of alcohol and drug abuse among certain categories of government employees, that is, those in the various areas of public transportation, may ultimately lead to

---

[27] 1980 Mich. Pub. Act 17, §8 provides in part: "At anytime before the rendering of an order, the chairperson of the arbitration panel, if he or she believes it would be useful or beneficial to do so, may remand the dispute to the parties for further collective bargaining for a period not to exceed 3 weeks." Sec. 10, indicating the factors to be considered in deciding disputed issues, sets forth eight criteria, including "(b) other factors, not confined to those listed in this section, that normally or traditionally are taken into consideration in the determination of wages, hours, and terms and conditions of employment through voluntary collective bargaining, mediation, fact-finding, arbitration or otherwise between the parties, in the public service or in private employment."

[28] See Aaron, *The Impact of Public Employment Grievance Settlement on the Labor Arbitration Process*, in The Future of Labor Arbitration in America (New York: American Arbitration Association, 1976), 1, 21-36.

judicial or statutory requirements of mandatory, random testing without probable cause that up to now have generally been regarded as violative of individual constitutional rights.

Indeed, the extent to which a government employee's basic right of privacy is entitled to protection was placed in issue in the recent case of *O'Connor v. Ortega*, decided by the U.S. Supreme Court.[29] There a state-employed psychiatrist, who had been placed on administrative leave while certain alleged improprieties by him were being investigated, was held to be reasonably free from work-related invasions of privacy in his workplace, but the issue of what is a reasonable expectation of privacy and what is a justified search and seizure by a government employer was held to be determinable on a case-by-case basis. In this type of case, said a majority of the Court, what is a reasonable search depends on the context within which the search takes place, and requires balancing the employees' legitimate expectation of privacy against the government's need for supervision, control, and the efficient operation of the workplace. The Court has thus introduced substantial flexibility into the application of the Fourth Amendment's guarantee against unreasonable searches and seizures in so far as government employees are concerned.

AIDS Testing

Another straw in the wind is the recent decision by the Court of Appeals for the District of Columbia Circuit in *Local 1812, American Federation of Government Employees v. United States Department of State*.[30] In that case the testing of State Department foreign service employees for the presence of AIDS virus (HIV) in their blood was held not to be a violation of their constitutionally protected rights of privacy and freedom from unreasonable searches and seizures. The court refused to grant a preliminary injunction, as requested by the AFGE. It held that the inclusion of the blood test for the HIV virus in the routine medical examinations given to foreign service personnel to determine eligibility for placement abroad, depending upon the adequacy of the medical care available, was reasonably related to the individual's fitness for duty. Particularly in dealing with the raging epidemic of AIDS, one may expect that the balance between broad public concerns about public safety and the government employee's right of privacy and security against searches and seizures will increasingly be struck in favor of the former.

---

[29] 107 S. Ct. 1492 (1987).
[30] 2 Individual Employment Rights Cases 47 (1987).

Generally, however, government employees, whether organized or not, will continue to remain more secure from arbitrary discipline or dismissal than are the great majority of unorganized employees in the private sector. The issues of unjust dismissal and employment at will, which currently loom so large in the private sector, simply have no substantial counterpart in government employment.

Pay Equity

In one area of employment relations, bargaining organizations of government employees have played a leading role and will probably continue to do so for the foreseeable future. I refer to the subject of pay equity for women and comparable worth. In a policy statement entitled "Comparable Worth and Equal Employment of Women," issued in 1985,[31] the National Council on Employment Policy stated in part:

> The threat of court challenge, along with the political clout of labor and women's organizations, has prompted most state governments to address the concept of comparable worth in some form during the last three years. State pay systems have proven vulnerable to political pressure as well as legal challenge for several reasons. Information regarding state pay-setting mechanisms is readily available and subject to scrutiny. In addition, state employees are frequently represented by unions or professional organizations who advance comparable worth claims. Finally, state officials are held accountable for wage structures which appear to discriminate against women. Not surprisingly, almost all pay equity initiatives in the early 1980s have been launched at the state level.[32]

Some states have established statutory policies regarding comparable worth. A few examples will suffice. Minnesota was the first state to enact and implement a comprehensive pay equity policy for state government employees. It completed in 1985 full implementation of the plan it began in 1982 when the personnel law was amended to provide for compensation based on "comparability of the value of the work in relationship to other positions in the executive branch."[33] In 1982, California established such a policy for the setting of state salaries for female-dominated jobs on the basis of "comparability of the value of the work."[34] In 1984, Iowa enacted a statutory policy that a state department, board, commission, or agency "shall not discriminate in

---

[31] Daily Lab. Rep., No. 181, September 18, 1985, D-1–D-5.
[32] *Id.* at D-3.
[33] Minnesota Statutes 1982, Ch. 43A, sub. 3.
[34] Cal. Government Code, §19827.2 (Deering).

compensation for work of comparable worth between jobs held predominantly by women and jobs held predominantly by men."[35] In 1983, Oregon adopted a law declaring it to be the public policy of the state "to attempt to achieve an equitable relationship between the comparability of the value of work performed by persons in state service and the compensation and classification plans within the state system." To this end, Oregon created a Task Force on State Compensation and Classification Equity.[36] Finally, in 1983 and 1985, Washington passed laws requiring the adoption of a comparable worth pay adjustment plan and calling for affirmative action within Washington state government employment and institutions of higher education.[37]

Besides being active on the legislative front, public-sector bargaining organizations have been involved in most of the litigation involving comparable worth. Although neither federal nor state courts have been particularly receptive to the concept of comparable worth, litigation, or the threat of it, has led to important settlements in a few significant cases. One such case involved the state of Washington and the American Federation of State, County and Municipal Employees (AFSCME). The state commissioned an independent study of civil service positions which concluded that clear indications of pay differences existed between job groups predominantly held by men and those predominantly held by women, and that the jobs were of comparable worth. The report also computed the cost of eliminating the discrimination. The state, however, took no action to implement the report, and AFSCME brought suit to compel such implementation. A federal district court held that the state's failure to eliminate an admittedly discriminatory compensation system constituted an intentional violation of Title VII of the Civil Rights Act of 1964[38] because it did not present convincing evidence of a good faith reason for the failure to pay women their evaluated worth.[39] Despite the reversal of this decision on appeal, the parties eventually reached an out-of-court settlement in which the state agreed to spend $482.4 million, between 1986 and 1992, for pay increases for state employees at certain levels below the "comparable worth line."[40]

In my judgment, despite the hostility of the courts to theories of comparable worth, the idea will continue to spread, with bargaining organizations such as AFSCME and others representing nurses and

---

[35] Iowa Code, §79.18.
[36] S.B. 484, Oregon Laws of 1983.
[37] Wash. Rev. Code Ann., §28B.16.020.
[38] 42 U.S.C. §§2000e–2000e-17 (1982).
[39] AFSCME v. State of Washington, 578 F. Supp. 846, 33 FEP Cases 808 (W.D. Wash. 1983), rev'd, 770 F.2d 1401, 38 FEP Cases 1353 (9th Cir. 1985).
[40] Daily Lab. Report, No. 36, February 24, 1986, A–6.

teachers taking the lead in both lobbying for legislation and suing for judicial relief. The effects will be felt not only in the public sector but in the private sector as well.

A National Law?

Although the states have gone their separate ways in enacting collective bargaining legislation for government employees, agitation for a uniform federal statute binding on the states has never completely disappeared.

In the summer of 1974, two prototype bills dealing with federal standards for state and local government labor relations were pending in Congress. The first would simply have amended the definition of "employer" in the NLRA[41] by deleting from the exclusion clause the words "or any state or political subdivision thereof," thereby making state and local government employees subject to the provisions of the NLRA.[42] The second was more ambitious: Among other things, it would have extended the organizational and collective bargaining rights guaranteed by the NLRA to "employees of the States, territories, and possessions of the United States and the political subdivisions thereof" and would have established a National Public Employment Relations Commission (NPERC) with powers similar to those of the NLRB.[43] The bill specified a number of "unlawful acts," some applying to employers, others applying to employee organizations.[44] With regard to strikes, the bill contained a general provision that, except for the express limitations on strikes set forth in the bill, no federal or state law would restrict the right to strike. A federal district court could issue an injunction against a strike only after making findings of fact, after due notice and hearing, that the commencement or continuation of the strike would pose a "clear and present danger to the public health or safety" and that the exclusive representative had failed to make a reasonable effort to use the statutory voluntary impasse-resolution procedures of mediation and fact-finding.[45] Courts could also enjoin strikes involving violations of any lawful provisions of collective agreements, such as no-strike clauses. Finally, the bill would have prece-

---

[41] NLRA §2(2), 29 U.S.C. §152(2) (1982).

[42] H.R. 9730, 93d Cong., 1st Sess., 119 Cong. Rec. 27,062 (1973); S. 3294, 93d Cong., 1st Sess., 120 Cong. Rec. 18,250 (1973).

[43] H.R. 8677, 93d Cong., 1st Sess., 119 Cong. Rec. 19,271 (1973); S. 3295, 93d Cong., 2d Sess., 120 Cong. Rec. 18,250 (1973).

[44] These lists correspond, respectively, to NLRA §§8(a)(1)-(5) (employers' unfair practices) & 8(b)(1)-(3) (employee organizations' unfair practices). The bill would have given NPERC power to award damages.

[45] A novel feature of the fact-finding procedure was that the findings could be made binding at the option of the employee organization, but not at that of the employer.

dence over all federal, state, and other laws inconsistent with it. A coalition of unions, whose members consisted exclusively or in part of federal, state, and local government employees, backed the bill.

Congress considered neither prototype bill seriously. Two years later, remaining support for the prototype bills eroded when, in *National League of Cities v. Usery*,[46] the Supreme Court held unconstitutional the 1974 amendments to the Fair Labor Standards Act,[47] which extended the Act's minimum wage and maximum hour provisions to almost all employees of states and their political subdivisions.[48] Subsequently, however, in *Garcia v. San Antonio Metropolitan Transit Authority*,[49] the Supreme Court overruled *National League of Cities* and rejected, "as unsound in principle and unworkable in practice, a rule of state immunity from federal regulation that turns on a judicial appraisal of whether a particular governmental function is 'integral' or 'traditional.' "[50] The Court instead found limits on the federal government's power to regulate state functions in the political process of the federal government itself, concluding that "State sovereign interests . . . are more properly protected by procedural safeguards inherent in the structure of the federal system than by judicially created limitations on federal power."[51]

Whatever barriers *National League of Cities* may have erected against a federal preemptive law uniformly regulating labor relations between the states and their employees have thus been removed, but pursuit of that objective seems both unlikely and undesirable. There are at least four reasons for that conclusion.

First, at the level of practical politics, organized labor as a whole— its membership drastically reduced and declining—is in no position to lobby effectively for such a revolutionary change in the law. Although government employee bargaining organizations continue to grow, they still lack the power to accomplish such a formidable coup. In addition, any such change would prompt a firestorm of protest from the states.

Second, administrative agencies tend to reflect the ideology of the incumbent administration. The NLRB has thus become the target of official union outrage over the labor policies of the Reagan administration, and it is doubtful that there is any support in labor's ranks, at least

---

[46] 426 U.S. 833, 22 WH Cases 1064 (1976).
[47] Act of 8 April 1974, Pub. L. No. 93-259, 88 Stat. 55, 55-76.
[48] Specifically, the Court held that "insofar as the challenged amendments operate to directly displace the States' freedom to structure integral operations in areas of traditional government functions, they are not within the authority granted Congress by . . . [the Commerce Clause of the U.S. Constitution]." *Supra* note 46, 426 U.S. at 852.
[49] 469 U.S. 528, 27 WH Cases 65 (1985).
[50] *Id.*, 27 WH Cases at 72.
[51] *Id.*, at 74.

at the present time, either for expanding the Board's jurisdiction over state and local government employees or for creating a similar federal agency to deal with their labor relations problems.

Third, most states now have collective bargaining laws for government employees, and many administer them (from the unions' point of view) at least as favorably, and probably more favorably, than the NLRB administers the NLRA.

Finally, allowing the states to develop their own policies for dealing with labor relations with their employees has worked well. The number of state laws on this subject has steadily increased during the last two decades. Three of the four major states that had not passed government employee collective bargaining laws in 1974—California, Illinois, and Ohio—have now done so; only Texas remains outside the fold. Although there has been a certain amount of statutory inbreeding, the individual laws are for the most part tailored to meet the issues that are important to each state's citizens. Some statutory provisions, especially those dealing with the resolution of impasses, reveal considerable imagination. To be sure, there are a few states that have no statutes dealing with collective bargaining for any group of government employees,[52] but that hardly warrants imposing a Procrustean federal model, even in the extremely unlikely event that it is politically possible to do so.

The experience to date with statutory and judicial regulation of collective bargaining by government employees, especially in the area of unfair labor practices and strikes, suggests that further reference to the NLRA or the LMRA as models is unnecessary and undesirable. From now on, the federal government and the states will develop and modify collective bargaining laws applicable to their own employees on the basis of conditions and public attitudes within their respective spheres. Little, if anything, in the decisions of the current NLRB seems likely to have much relevance to collective bargaining in the public sector. To the extent that NLRB decisions may be relevant, they are not precedents that should be followed. It is not so much that strikes in government employment give rise to problems radically different from those associated with strikes in the private sector,[53] but labor-management relations in government employment in the various states have their own history, structure, and practices that should be taken into account by those who fashion the laws governing those relations. It may well be that certain labor relations practices in the private sector are relevant to collective bargaining in government em-

---

[52] See *supra* note 2.
[53] Compare John F. Burton, Jr. and Charles Krider, *The Role and Consequences of Strikes by Public Employees*, 79 Yale L.J. 418 (1970), 425-32 with Harry H. Wellington and Ralph K. Winter, Jr., *The Limits of Collective Bargaining in Public Employment*, 78 Yale L.J. 1107, 1117 (1969).

ployment, and that they will in time be adopted in the public sector. It is also possible that certain collective bargaining laws and practices in government employment will commend themselves to the private sector. Indeed, this latter possibility may be the more likely of the two.[54] If such changes come to pass, however, they will result primarily from voluntary decisions by the collective bargaining parties themselves, rather than from statutory mandates or judicial edicts. That is, at least, an outcome devoutly to be wished.

---

[54] See, e.g., Aaron, *supra* note 28.

Index